*The British Conservative Party
in the Age of Universal Suffrage*

The British Conservative Party in the Age of Universal Suffrage

Popular Conservatism, 1918–1929

NEAL R. McCRILLIS

Ohio State University Press
Columbus

Library of Congress Cataloging-in-Publication Data

McCrillis, Neal R. (Neal Robert), 1961–
    The British Conservative Party in the age of universal suffrage : popular conservatism,
1918–1928 / Neal R. McCrillis.
        p.   cm.
    Includes bibliographical references and index.
    ISBN: 978-0-8142-5339-7
    1. Conservative Party (Great Britain)—History.   I. Title.
JN1129.C7M38   1998
324.24104'09042—dc21   98-17141
                                                                                         CIP
Text design by Donna Hartwick.
Jacket design by Gary Gore.
Type set in Minion by Graphic Composition, Inc.

The paper used in this publication meets the minimum requirements of the American
National Standard for Information Sciences—Permanence of Paper for Printed Library
Materials. ANSI Z39.48-1992.

9   8   7   6   5   4   3   2   1

Contents

Preface   vii

Acknowledgments   ix

Introduction   1

1. The Representation of the People Act of 1918 and the
   General Election of 1918   9

2. The Women's Unionist Organisation and the Role of
   Women in the Conservative Party   46

3. The Junior Imperial League and the Young Britons   83

4. The Labour Committee, Trade Union Reform,
   and Conservative Wage Earners   110

5. Conservative Party Propaganda and Education   145

6. The Representation of the People Act of 1928 and the
   General Election of 1929   178

Conclusion   223

Appendix A   229

Appendix B   230

Appendix C   231

Appendix D   232

Appendix E   235

Notes   237

Bibliography   289

Index   309

Preface

At the time I write, only days after a victory by the Labour Party ended eighteen years of Conservative government, explanations for Conservative disaster run the gamut. The occasional journalistic references to comparable elections (1832 and 1906) have done little to examine the roots of this one. My research began in the 1980s, after Margaret Thatcher and the Conservative Party had scored their third, successive election victory, and now ends appropriately as that same party, after a fourth election victory under the leadership of John Major, heads into a very uncertain future as a rump party without representation from either Wales or Scotland. These events, and contemporary British politics in general, are rooted in the early twentieth-century response of the Conservative Party to universal suffrage and mass politics.

This work, as a study of popular Conservatism in the 1920s, depends on a range of disparate materials. Interested readers may consult the introduction and appendixes D and E for an analysis of the sources, local-studies methodology, and a descriptive chart of the constituencies sampled. The National Unionist Association was the representative body of the Conservative Party. At the end of 1924 its name was changed to the National Union of Conservative and Unionist Associations to reflect the decline of the Unionist issue. Likewise, the Unionist Party was the preferred name of that party before the First World War and remained common until the Irish Free State was formed late in 1921. Thereafter, as in the days of Benjamin Disraeli, the party was usually called the Conservative Party. After 1921 I have generally used Unionist to refer only to the Scottish

Conservatives, whose independent organization was called the Scottish Unionist Association. In addition, I have used "Diehard" to refer to Conservatives who opposed the Lloyd George Coalition, and "diehard" for those Conservatives who were merely on the right wing of the party.

Acknowledgments

I would like to thank those individuals and organizations who have helped me during the ten years I have worked on this project. Conservative agents in Wirral West, North Shropshire, and Skipton, who gave me access to records in their possession, and the staff at the Scottish Conservative Central Office in Edinburgh, particularly Ms. Ann Hay, were very gracious despite the inconveniences that I caused. Hugh Williams generously opened his home to me during a short visit to see his father's papers. Staff at the research facilities that I visited were also helpful, particularly those at the House of Lords Record Office, the Colindale Newspaper Library, the Bodleian Library, the Durham Record Office, the Shropshire Record Office, the National Library of Wales, and the Scottish Record Office. The former Conservative Party archivist, Dr. Sarah Street, made a great deal of material available to me—despite having to transport it in a pushcart through the streets of Oxford. I would also like to thank the archivists at the University of Birmingham and Liverpool City Libraries for allowing me to use the Chamberlain and Derby Papers, respectively. The interlibrary loan staff at the University of Illinois at Chicago and Methodist College made many research materials accessible.

During the earlier stages of this project, the University of Illinois at Chicago provided a graduate fellowship and Deans' Scholar Award Fellowship, without which I would not have been able to carry out the work. I would like to thank Professors Bentley B. Gilbert and James Sack of the University of Illinois at Chicago for their help and guidance. Copyeditor Nancy Woodington and the excellent staff at Ohio State University Press, particularly Beth Ina, provided corrections, suggestions, and guidance that improved my original typescript greatly. Together they corrected many errors in fact, interpretation, or style, although I am wholly responsible for the final product. I am grateful to my colleagues at Methodist College, particularly Peter Murray, who have provided unfailing support and collegiality. I would also like to thank my parents for their encouragement over the years, but most of all I owe a tremendous debt to my wife, Michele, who listened to expositions of many parts of this project and made many sacrifices during the years I worked on this project. In the last year she has done these things despite carrying our first child. That I finished this book is due in great measure to her encouragement and support. I dedicate this book to Margot, whose birth (and far swifter gestation) coincides with its completion.

Introduction

With the notable exception of biographies, historians of post-1914 Britain have not paid as much attention to the Conservative Party as they have to its rivals. The party has certainly received less attention from scholars than its counterparts on the Continent. Historians of Britain have largely dedicated themselves to understanding developments on the Left, particularly the rise and fall of the Labour and Liberal Parties. Yet the Conservative Party was victorious in thirteen of the twenty-one general elections between 1918 and 1992. Until 1979 it was probably most successful during the period between the two world wars when, alone or as the dominant partner in a coalition, it won five of the seven general elections and was in power for all but three years.

Yet during the two decades following World War I, conservatives faced some of the most difficult times and serious obstacles in their history. As the war was ending in 1918, the Labour intellectual Beatrice Webb reflected on the dangers that lay ahead. She was worried about bureaucracy, uncontrollable government spending, and especially Bolshevism. She was concerned that the Bolsheviks would prey on the tensions of "a working class seething with discontent, and a ruling class with all its traditions and standards topsy-turvy, with civil servants suspecting businessmen and businessmen conspiring to protect their profits, and all alike abusing the politician, no citizen knows what is going to happen to himself or his children, or to his own social circle, or to the state or the Empire. All that he does know is that the old order is seriously threatened with dissolution without any new order being in sight."[1] These signs of uneasiness and fear—expressed by a leading figure in the Labour Party—were endemic in the years immediately after World War I.

Four features of the political landscape are central to an understanding of the turmoil that characterized British politics after World War I and shaped the Conservative Party. First, the Unionist Party had demonstrated a dismal record of failure after 1905. Second, universal suffrage was established by the passage of the Representation of the People Acts of 1918 and 1928. The 1918 act increased the electorate far more than the 1832, 1867, or 1884 reform bills, and enfranchised millions of women. From the manageable Edwardian electorate of about eight million, the number of voters in Britain leaped to twenty-one million in 1918 and twenty-nine million by 1929. Third, the growth of an energized and expanding Labour Party enabled it to compete successfully against the two established parties and to offer radical solutions for the nation's ills. Fourth, the havoc caused by four years of both constitutional and Irish crises, followed by four years of a draining and difficult war effort, had disrupted older patterns of government and undermined or made irrelevant the traditional Unionist causes (preservation of the Union, preservation of the Church, and tariff reform).

These characteristics of the interwar political scene meant that, for the first time since the 1850s, the Conservative Party's existence was seriously threatened. Conservatives faced a decade of apparent political instability, with five general elections and four changes of government. Conservative leaders confronted a daunting combination of difficulties as they tried to escape from their wretched prewar experience; yet, in the end, bewilderment did not lead to impotence. One of the most remarkable features of politics in the 1920s was the Conservative Party's strong electoral performance and control of government. The historian and former Labour M. P. David Marquand commented on this conundrum in 1991: "Karl Marx had declared that, in Britain, universal suffrage would have as its 'inevitable result . . . the political supremacy of the working class.' After 1918, these predictions could be put to the test. Working men had votes; and the self-proclaimed party of the working class stood ready to receive them. . . . The outcome was two generations of Conservative hegemony." But as the bemused Ross McKibbin observes in a recent essay, the extraordinary achievement of the Conservative Party seems to be "something we almost take for granted."[2]

Most explanations for the Conservative Party's successful response to universal suffrage and other interwar factors are structural. Some historians point to remaining anomalies in the franchise and the redistribution of parliamentary divisions under the 1918 reform act. Conservatives were, for example, assisted by a remnant of plural voting, which decided the outcome of about twenty of the 615 constituencies.[3] They also gained as many as thirty seats as a result of the 1918 redistribution, which had recognized the growing suburban and middle-class population. Some historians also point out that the party profited from the disappearance of the perennially hostile Irish contingent as Sinn Fein first boycotted Parliament in 1919 and then left altogether when southern Ireland became independent in 1922—leaving behind, of course, the dependably right-wing Ulster Unionists.[4] Yet although the Conservative Party enjoyed certain structural advantages under the interwar system, they were considerably less than under the less equitable system before 1918. (Under that system, the Unionists lost three successive general elections between 1905 and 1910.)[5] There is as well always the argument that Conservative success, particularly in 1918 and 1924, was the consequence of those periodic swings that characterize democratic elections.

Historians whose primary interests are often Labour or Liberal history suggest that the emerging politics of the 1920s entailed a bipolar Labour-Conservative struggle in which the Conservatives played a passive role. The Conservative Party, in other words, remained powerful by reason of its continued existence, "naturally" filling the "necessary" role of protecting and representing the status quo. One such student of the period, for example, writes that the Conservatives "did not have to strive hard to win" in 1929 simply because they were "the defenders of the status quo."[6] Some political scientists and sociologists claim that a pervasive social deference in British society explains the support for the Conservative Party in this century, particularly from outside the middle and upper classes. The work of the most influential proponents of this approach is useful for understanding Tory wage earners, but it tends to ignore both the specific historical context of the 1920s and the Conservatives' active role.

In all these theories there is at least the inference that Conservative success was natural or inevitable, not a result of the party's actions. There is also often an element of incomprehension—or at least a sense that conservatism persists because of the public's ignorance (sometimes euphemistically described as its innate conservatism). The most obvious example contradicting these rather vague, comprehensive explanations for Conservative success is the party's unsatisfactory performance during the years immediately preceding and following the 1920s and 1930s. If voting Conservative was not "normal" in 1910 or 1945, why should it have been so in the interwar period?

Structural interpretations provide at best only a partial explanation of why the Conservative Party was so successful in the 1920s. As Frans Coetzee observes in his study of Edwardian Conservatism, sobriquets like "the stupid party" reinforce the erroneous notion that the party could as little be budged as its fortunes could be changed.[7] The Conservative Party had the largest number of members in every interwar Parliament except the one that sat from 1929 to 1931. Not until the era of Margaret Thatcher would the Tories regain the kind of dominance they had enjoyed in the 1920s and 1930s. Election results in the 1920s were not just chance; they arose from the Conservatives' triumph over two other parties. The Conservative Party won more than 40 percent of the popular vote in the five general elections between 1918 and 1929, and if a two-party preferred analysis is used (with votes for the declining Liberal Party redistributed among the other parties according to the pattern that was apparently emerging), the Conservatives were the preferred party of about 60 percent of voters.[8]

How could the Conservative Party secure a popular following despite the tumult caused by the disruption of the two-party system, the establishment of universal adult suffrage, and the rise of the Labour Party? This neglected question remains largely unanswered. In an address at a Conservative summer school in 1966, Lord Blake commented, "The whole question of how the Conservatives managed to acquire the hold over the middle ground of politics . . . in the twenties and thirties is one which would well repay further investigation by historians. I do not think anyone has quite explained why the Conservatives became, as it were, 'respectable' again to middle-of-the-road opinion in a way which . . . they had not been in the period immediately before the first world war. As I say, it would be worth investigation." More recently, in a caustic 1993 review of several works on early-twentieth-century politics, David Jarvis complains that the "Baldwinite hegemony remains insufficiently explained, and any combination [sic] to the field of postwar politics which touches upon this should be welcomed."[9]

No one has offered an adequate explanation for the rebirth of Conservatism in the 1920s. Cowling, in *The Impact of Labour* (1971), a detailed study of politics in the early 1920s, draws attention to the shift in the focus of politics from Unionism and the Church to Socialism. Cowling's study of the response of politicians, journalists, and other leading figures to Labour's arrival as the opposition party reveals how Conservative leaders tried to combat Labour, at first joining an anti-Labour coalition, then disassociating themselves from the Liberal Party and taking up the defense of the social order. Cowling concentrates on the world of high politics without attempting to study the Conservative Party's rank and file, its organizational and rhetorical response to Labour, or its electoral performance. Self's study of the Conservative Party between 1922 and 1932, *Tories and Tariffs* (1986), is also primarily an investigation of high politics. Self's belief that tariff reform provided the nexus for interwar Conservatism is, however, at odds with the results of my research. In fact, protection was a dangerous policy for the Conservatives to espouse, because it threatened to undermine their appeal to moderate, middle-class, and female voters.[10]

Standard accounts fail to explain that the Conservative Party triumphed in the 1920s by adapting to a new political landscape characterized most notably by universal suffrage and the Labour Party. Together the essays in Seldon and Ball's *Conservative Century* provide the best single-volume history of the Conservative Party. They ably summarize recent research into aspects of twentieth-century Conservatism and, in some cases, offer new insights. In *The Age of Balfour and Baldwin* (1978), Ramsden describes the operations, personnel, and policy making of the Conservative Party. Ramsden is also one of the first historians to study such neglected areas of party history as fund raising and local organization, but he largely ignores the phenomenon of popular Conservatism, and his emphasis on the period before the First World War slights crucial wartime developments. In his chapters on the post–World War I period, Ramsden does not explain what Pugh describes as "the Conservatives' capacity to adapt and maintain a popular constituency."[11]

In contrast, Pugh, McKibbin, Jarvis, and Williamson have tried to explain how the Conservative Party adopted popular political attitudes. In *The Tories and the People, 1885–1935* (1985), a groundbreaking study of the Primrose League, a group loosely connected to the Conservative Party, Pugh reveals how social relations and political ideas were mobilized among millions of citizens by the first popular political organization in Britain. Pugh's research, however, focuses on the late Victorian and Edwardian political system, not the interwar period. In 1990 McKibbin published "Class and Conventional Wisdom: The Conservative Party and the 'Public' in Inter-War Britain," one of the first attempts to address the issue of popular Conservatism in that period. McKibbin emphasizes the difficulties that faced interwar Conservatives and suggests that the party's success resulted in part from its ability to monopolize middle-class voters by focusing on a perceived socialist threat and, after 1920, committing to deflationary policies.[12]

In a more recent essay, Jarvis argues convincingly that the 1920s (rather than the Edwardian period or the war years) were "a fundamental disjuncture" in the history of popular Conservatism. In his analysis of Conservative propaganda, he shows that the party shifted from a Chamberlainite campaign aimed at a single working class to a more subtle and varied defense of property and other existing interests. This strategy appealed to different elements of the working classes, including women. Williamson advances a similar explanation in an insightful 1993 essay. Under Stanley Baldwin, he argues, the Conservatives created a positive ideology that dominated public life during the interwar period. In Williamson's view, Baldwin "created a 'spiritual glue' which evoked 'Englishness,' rural harmonies, Christian or ethical values, and the Elect Nation, and which called for the moralisation of industrial relations and bound all sides to their best constitutional behaviour." [13]

In this book I attempt to fulfill the demand for an explanation of the "Baldwinite hegemony" of interwar politics. My two primary goals are (1) to investigate the interwar origins of contemporary British politics and (2) to consider the role of the Conservative Party as it became a successful mass party during this period. At its heart this work is a reappraisal of the Conservative Party that successfully responded to universal suffrage and the rise of the Labour Party between 1918 and 1929. It also explains interwar politics as they were experienced by Conservative Party adherents and voters rather than by political theorists, politicians, and what have been termed the "articulate radical minorities." [14] I have sought to understand popular Conservatism between 1918 and 1929 by studying the Conservative Party's mass organizations, its propaganda and educational work, and its electioneering efforts. In contrast to David Jarvis, I devote considerable attention to organizational changes within the Conservative Party, for these played a very important role in the party's successful adaptation.

The records of the Conservative Party members' organization, the National Unionist Association, the Women's Unionist Organisation, the Junior Imperial League and other Conservative Party youth groups, and the Conservative wage earners' group, the Labour Committee, are vital sources for the party's interwar appeal. These mass organizations were designed to appeal to the new electorate. Consequently, I have focused on these popular organizations and activities of the Conservative Party. I have also relied heavily on the records of the regional associations of the Conservative Party, which served as liaisons between constituencies and London. In addition, various Conservative Party popular magazines, pamphlets, leaflets, and election addresses show what the world of rank-and-file politics was like. I have supplemented this research by consulting the personal papers of such leading Conservatives as Andrew Bonar Law, Austen Chamberlain, and Stanley Baldwin. The papers of Viscountess Bridgeman, the first chairwoman of the Women's Unionist Organisation, her husband, Cabinet minister Viscount Bridgeman, and J. C. C. Davidson, party chairman from 1926 to 1930, were rich sources of information about Conservative organizations and electioneering. Finally, I also used *The Times* and *The Observer* as additional sources for developments in the 1920s and for important contemporary appraisals of these events.

In contrast to some other political histories, particularly those dealing with Conservative affairs, I have also made use of constituency studies to locate popular trends in the Conservative Party. Searching through the available local records, I created a representative and manageable sample of twelve constituencies. The diverse constituencies reflect the most politically relevant variables of interwar Britain: geography, rusticity, class, religion, and party. For eleven of the constituencies, the minute books for at least the main association of each constituency have survived. In some cases there were also minute books for one or more of the auxiliary organizations and sub-branches. To supplement this research for each constituency, I consulted at least one local newspaper from among the collection at the British Library (Colindale). In a few cases I was able to find and study the personal papers of Conservative M.P.s and candidates.[15] Interested readers may consult appendixes D and E for an analysis of the local-studies methodology and a list of the constituencies, with their chief characteristics.

Conservatives were just beginning to adapt their party to the new political era when they were thrown into the first postwar general election in November and December 1918. The core of this book is a study of the sometimes massive organizational, propaganda, and educational activities of the party, and of its attempts to create popular mass organizations that would propagandize and educate voters. These innovations were highly successful. The new, socially conservative political organizations for women, young people, and wage earners gave the party a solid electoral base and a powerful body of volunteer organizers. In 1927 the historian and Conservative politician Sir John Marriott noted, "The rapid extension of the electorate [in 1918], necessitated the adoption of new methods of political persuasion."[16] The Conservative Party in fact adapted more successfully than either of its rivals. And in the process it became a broad-based party that represented moderate and conservative men and women, particularly those in the growing middle class.

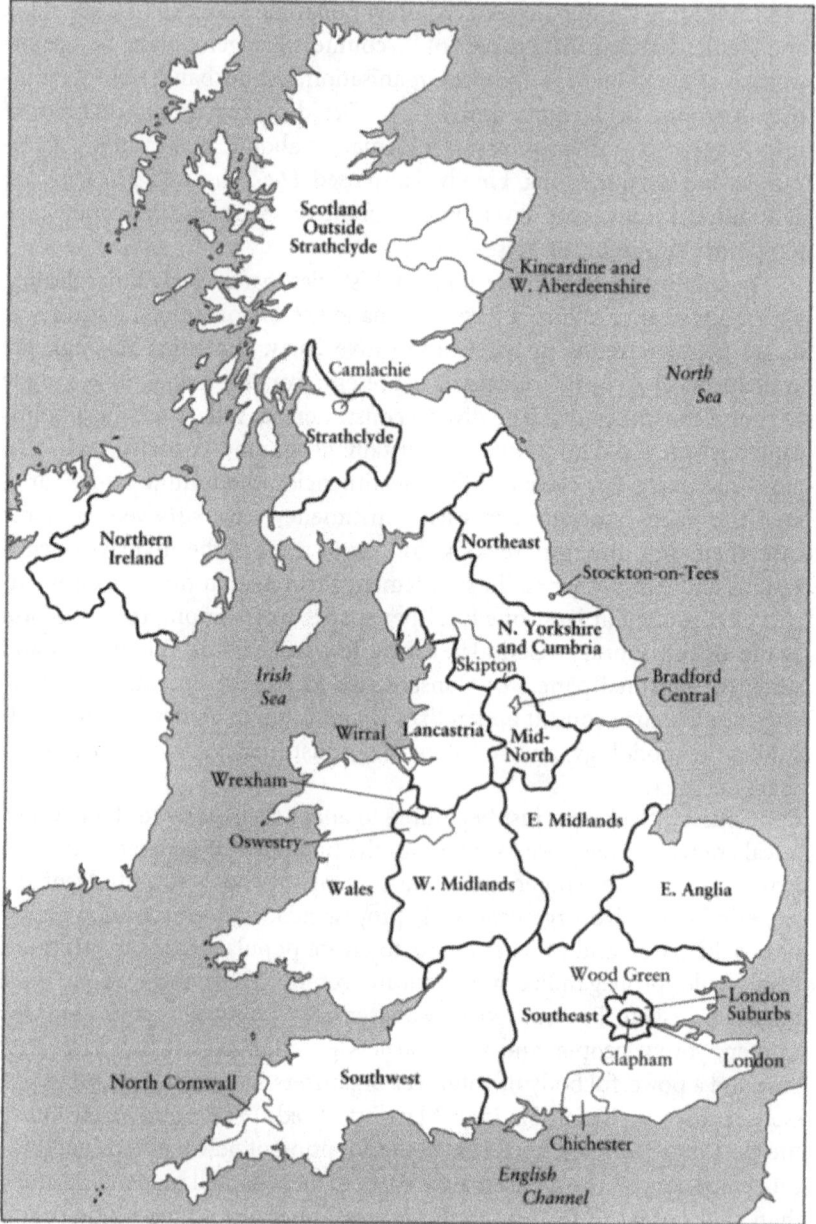

Scotland
Outside
Strathclyde

Kincardine and
W. Aberdeenshire

North
Sea

Camlachie

Strathclyde

Northern
Ireland

Northeast

Stockton-on-Tees

N. Yorkshire
and Cumbria

Skipton

Bradford
Central

Irish
Sea

Wirral   Lancastria

Mid-
North

Wrexham

Oswestry

E. Midlands

Wales   W. Midlands

E. Anglia

Wood Green

London
Suburbs

Southeast

Clapham

London

North Cornwall   Southwest

Chichester

English
Channel

1

The Representation of the People Act of 1918 and the General Election of 1918

The Representation of the People Act of 1918 was principally responsible for determining the organization and outlook of the Unionist or Conservative Party during the interwar era. The Unionist Party, precluded from public displays of partisan activity after all parties agreed to an election truce in August 1914, stagnated in the areas of organization, finance, and membership. The introduction of a parliamentary reform bill in 1917 revived Unionist activity. Although initially wary of the bill, Unionists interceded to shape the legislation once it was clear that they could not stop it. In February 1918 the Representation of the People Act was passed, enfranchising all men and a majority of women, and redistributing the parliamentary seats. Parliamentary democracy had arrived in Britain.

Party leaders responded to the passage of the reform act by altering party structure and organization to follow more popular lines. They changed the rules of their governing body, the National Unionist Association (NUA). They encouraged the development of popular organizations for wage earners and women. Most important, they set up the Women's Unionist Organisation (WUO) to bring women into the party. At the same time, they continued to support the coalition government headed by Lloyd George because they wanted a national government of energetic ministers determined to defeat the German menace. Yet Unionist support for the government was never absolute, and the coalition did not lead to a long-term electoral or policy agreement until the party was swept into a general election during the euphoria of victory in autumn 1918. In order to maintain the wartime spirit of nationalism and ensure the Labour Party's defeat, Unionist candidates fought the 1918 election—the so-called coupon election—as members of the Lloyd George coalition. The campaign, however, developed into an attack on the defeated German foe and a celebration of Conservative ideals. When the results became known on 29 December, the Unionists had won a great victory as the dominant partner in a coalition of national unity. Yet their position remained insecure because they lacked a broad-based party organization.

The Representation of the People Act of 1918

The truce among parties and the coalition subsumed prewar controversies in a mood of comradeship and a dedication to the overriding task of defending the nation. This nonpartisanship diminished all political parties, including the Unionist Party, which lost much of its cohesiveness and drive. During Asquith's coalition government, the Unionist Business and War Committees in the House of Commons preserved a tenuous party identity by expressing unified backbench opinion on certain policies, such as universal conscription. Meanwhile, outside Westminister, the Unionist Party's membership and organization dwindled. Rank-and-file members, activists, and M.P.s volunteered for military service in large numbers, and many never returned. More than 125 Unionist agents saw active military service. The Junior Imperial League (JIL), the Unionist organization for young men, experienced heavy membership losses during the war. By February 1915 the JIL claimed that 65 percent of its eligible members, including its president and secretary, were serving in the armed forces. What remained of the organization was dedicated to the Overseas Forces Reception Committee, which assisted 400,000 servicemen from the Dominions when they spent their leaves in Britain. The rest of the Unionist organization continued to function largely to recruit military volunteers on behalf of the Parliamentary Recruiting Committee. It also lent its aid to the National War Savings Committee, the National War Aims Committee, and the Red Cross. At a time when revenue was falling, these were activities it could scarcely afford.[1]

The Unionist constituency associations also became dormant during the war. A strong branch of the Chichester Unionist Association, for example, held only one meeting between 1914 and 1918. Skipton was typical of most constituency associations. The agent, Edward Whittaker, was given a leave of absence with full pay when he became a captain in the army. Local officers were unable to maintain the existing organization in Skipton without Whittaker, and by 1916 only a small management subcommittee was meeting. Monetary problems were not unusual. Expenses were generally low since there were few electoral contests, but subscriptions declined, and fund raising was nonexistent. Associations like the one in Camlachie, Glasgow, which had a budget surplus throughout the war, worried about their falling revenues in the event that the truce ended. Some constituency organizations maintained the semblance of fighting trim by redirecting their efforts toward charity and war work. In October 1914 Sir George Younger, then Unionist whip for Scotland, sent a circular to his constituency associations suggesting that they hold lectures in connection with the war effort and raise money for the Red Cross and other charities. Similarly, in the Palmers Green branch association in Wood Green, Middlesex, a Ladies Committee for the Entertainment of Wounded Soldiers gave concerts for soldiers and raised money for soldiers' medical needs.[2]

Meanwhile the mobilization of British citizens for the war effort changed Unionist attitudes toward the electoral system. The entry of respectable women into the workplace led some Tories to question prevailing notions about female suffrage. If women could serve the nation by making munitions and nursing the wounded, why could they not vote? Most Tories were, however, more concerned about the men who were serving their country, whom J. C. Williams described as "for all essential purposes this nation." But the increasingly outdated parliamentary register was effectively disfranchising many soldiers and sailors. By June 1916, William Jenkins of the Unionist central office estimated that only 60 percent of the men entitled to vote were actually on the register. An article in the April 1916 issue of the *Conservative Agents' Journal* signaled growing Unionist support for franchise reform. Problems with the servicemen's vote, the *Journal* stated, "are so far-reaching, and may have such unlooked-for results, that we can none of us give too much thought and care to the subject in all its bearings." In their meetings Unionist agents demanded that servicemen voters be given special attention, and during the summer the Unionist War Committee threatened to veto the extension of the Parliament unless a register was prepared to retain the vote for servicemen. Yet when such a bill was introduced by Walter Long, many Tory M.P.s demanded the vote for all enlisted men, even those ineligible under the existing property franchises. Long's bill had to be abandoned in mid-August. Concern for the servicemen, rather than, as John Turner suggests, for women or political tactics led rank-and-file Unionists to the question of franchise reform.[3]

The increasing possibility of a general election under the outdated register added pressure to the movement in favor of franchise reform. After his bill was rejected by the Commons in August, Long suggested that it might be necessary to call an interparty conference to deal with military voters. A few days later Lord Selborne, in a letter to Lord Salisbury, noted that a measure enacting a separate military franchise would almost inevitably lead to discussion about a broader male franchise, women's franchise, and, possibly, even universal suffrage. In hopes of creating a wartime consensus in favor of moderate reform, the Cabinet decided to call a conference of M.P.s and peers in which the speaker of the House of Commons, James Lowther, served as chairman. Thirteen Unionists, including Sir William Bull and Sir Harry Samuel, chairman of the NUA Council, served on the committee, which began meeting on 12 October 1916. The support of Walter Long, president of the Local Government Board and a respected, old-fashioned Tory who had opposed franchise reform before the war, was probably crucial in quelling Unionist worries about the conference.[4]

Other than the serviceman's question, what were Unionist attitudes toward electoral reform? Some Unionist leaders, like Long, belatedly came to support female enfranchisement. Long's hope was to remove a highly contentious issue from the postwar scene. In addition, as he explained in a letter to his brother, the war had changed his perception of women's political capabilities. "Women are engaged . . . in doing work of the most strenuous character," he wrote, "and I, at least, am satisfied that I was mistaken when I thought that they could not take their part in practically every form of government, save actually fighting in the ranks." A few Unionists, for example, Arthur Balfour, Andrew Bonar Law, and Lord Selborne, had long supported women's suffrage. Since 1917 Selborne's wife had been president of the Conservative and Unionist Women's Franchise Association. The personnel and the periodical of this organization exercised a considerable amount of influence. Lady Selborne, the eldest daughter of the third marquess of Salisbury, was intellectually impressive and solidly Conservative. Through studied moderation Lady Selborne and her organization sought to win "quiet domestic women" and conservative men over to the cause of suffrage. In the weeks before the First World War had broken out, there were indications that the Unionist Party chairman, Arthur Steel-Maitland, might support women's suffrage, probably out of fear that outright opposition would endanger the party's chances in the next general election.[5]

The typical Unionist, however, resisted any extension of the franchise. In 1912 Conservative Party headquarters had estimated that universal male suffrage would cost the party 103 seats in England and Wales. Most Unionists seemed to hold the political capabilities of eighteen million unenfranchised men and women in contempt. The suffrage campaign was also hampered by party concerns and widespread irritation with the suffragettes. Others felt, with the duchess of Atholl, that it was an inopportune time for change and that women needed more experience. Finally, the antisuffrage movement led by Lord Curzon, F. E. Smith, and other prominent Unionists was rooted in the gender ideology of separate spheres, the pervasive view that women embodied the emotional side of human nature. This, although it made them excellent mothers and nurturers, led them to be illogical and unstable, ill-suited for reasoned political analysis and voting. Antisuffragists also believed that women were physically incapable of ruling the empire, fighting wars, and maintaining order.[6] In their view, politicizing women would destroy their "womanliness" and undermine gender roles. As Tennyson wrote in 1847,

> Man for the field and woman for the hearth;
> Man for the sword, and for the needle she;
> Man with the head, and woman with the heart;
> Man to command, and woman to obey;
> All else confusion.[7]

Based upon this pervasive view of women, even some proponents of universal male suffrage, including the future prime minister, H. H. Asquith, felt no compunction in opposing the enfranchisement of "the gentler sex."[8] Antisuffragists believed that they were simply recognizing women's innate political inferiority. In 1916 most Unionists were in no hurry to expand an electorate of only eight million to include eighteen million more women and men. On 27 January 1917 the conference reported to the new coalition government headed by Lloyd George. Its proposals: a special register for servicemen, universal male suffrage based on a simple residency requirement, and redistribution of parliamentary seats in Britain (but not Ireland) to establish uniform constituencies of 50,000 to 70,000 inhabitants. The report also favored the enfranchisement of women older than twenty-nine years of age if they or their husbands possessed the local government vote. Three months later the government introduced its Representation of the People bill, which adhered closely to these proposals while providing a second vote under a business or university franchise. Instead of compiling a special military register, however, the bill proposed to shorten the residency requirement for servicemen from six months to one. Most Unionists approved of special treatment for servicemen but were shocked by the bill's other clauses. Some expressed their displeasure openly. Sir Arthur Steel-Maitland, recently rewarded for his work as party chairman with a mere (in his eyes) baronetcy and a post under Long, his perennial enemy, attacked the "mad" conference and drafted a highly critical memorandum to the NUA Executive Committee. According to him, "The interests of the Party have, wittingly or unwittingly, been gravely jeopardized [by its leaders]." The principal agent of the Unionist Party, Sir John Boraston, quietly supported the former chairman's attack.[9]

The NUA Executive Committee responded on 8 February 1917 by forming a subcommittee to consider the report of the Speaker's Conference. Initially Steel-Maitland served as its chairman, but he soon stepped down to allow the new party chairman, Sir George Younger, to head the investigation. In its report, presented on 13 March, the subcommittee denied that the present House of Commons, which it called unrepresentative, had the right to pursue such a radical measure.[10] The proposals in the Speaker's Report would enfranchise "the most unstable and emotional elements in the community, thereby increasing enormously the floating vote and the power of the demagogue." If the proposed changes had been in place, the subcommittee theorized, the Unionists would have won 105 fewer seats in the previous election. The subcommittee criticized the redistribution scheme for reducing rural seats and leaving Ireland overrepresented. Only if the House of Lords (or a new second chamber) was guaranteed full veto power, the subcommittee concluded, would it accept a broadening of the franchise.[11]

Other Unionists also voiced criticisms of the report. Sir Edward Carson circulated a petition against the Speaker's Report that more than a hundred Unionist M.P.s signed.[12] The *Conservative Agents' Journal* published hostile articles and letters, including a thorough analysis by the Wirral agent, Alfred Birkett, who argued that Unionists had won only the tentative promise of a servicemen's register in return for conceding to all the Liberal objectives. He did, however, accept the need for a measure of female enfranchisement. According to the *Conservative Agents' Journal,* ordinary Unionists believed that their party had been "diddled" and "hoodwinked" by Liberal trickery.[13] There is little evidence that provincial Unionists launched their own opposition to the bill, as party organization had decayed too much to make such action feasible. One of the few bodies to voice its irritation was the Yorkshire Provincial Council, which forwarded a very critical resolution to the central office and party leaders in late June 1917. Their unhappiness with the party hierarchy was presaged a few days earlier by a letter from the Chairman of the Bradford City Association to Sir John Boraston. Unionist leaders, he wrote, were "completely out of touch" with their members, who saw these "revolutionary proposals" as "a gross violation . . . of the Political Truce. . . . I have yet to meet a Bradford Unionist," he claimed, "who does not consider that the Party has been sold to the Radical and Labour Forces." The NUA Executive Committee had already surveyed constituency agents and officials about the Speaker's Report and found that respondents were overwhelmingly opposed to reform, at least during wartime, although they strongly supported female suffrage. The committee encouraged associations to accept the inevitable and to look after their own particular interests.[14] Active organizations took this advice and tried to deal with the impending redistribution. For instance, the Cornwall Provincial Division learned in the spring that the county would lose two M.P.s under the bill. Over the next year its chairman, J. C. Williams, sought to collaborate with the local Liberal and Labour parties to retain at least one of these seats but failed. In Skipton the Conservative association tried to exclude the industrial areas of Silsden and Cross Hills from its largely rural constituency.[15]

Whatever the sentiment of their rank and file, Unionist leaders eventually decided the issue by refusing to oppose the reform bill. Most party leaders were convinced that opposition to a measure that enfranchised valiant servicemen and patriotic civilians would undermine the Unionist claim to represent all Britons. In a letter written in late March, Long, now colonial secretary, emphasized to Sir George Younger that "it would be absolutely fatal to the future of our Party" to resist the reforms. The party chairman agreed, adding that central office would seek only to modify the proposals and strengthen the Lords. When the NUA Council met in April to consider both recent events and the executive committee's report of 13 March, it resolved that it was "strong[ly] in favour of an extension of the franchise[!]," if the Lords were reformed. By the time the Representation of the People bill went to committee on 6 June 1917, Unionists had shifted their focus from opposing to amending it.[16]

On 22 May 1917 the NUA Executive revived its earlier subcommittee, now with Sir Archibald Salvidge as chairman. Unionist agents were asked to inform and assist the subcommittee in its work. To ensure that Unionists were not pigeonholed as opponents of reform, the subcommittee informed the press, "The Unionist Party is not in any way hostile to an extension of the franchise or the general principles of the Bill, but are going to suggest some practical amendments." The twenty-seven-page subcommittee report, which recommended several changes, was approved by the NUA Executive and Council two days after the reform bill went to committee. It sought to reinforce plural voting and eliminate both proportional representation and alternative voting as detrimental to the Conservatives. All soldiers and sailors should be given a special franchise, and conscientious objectors should be disfranchised.[17] The chairman of the Yorkshire Provincial Division probably best expressed Unionist sentiment when, in November 1917, he attacked conscientious objectors as "anarchists . . . whose object was to destroy the whole National fabric."[18] In addition, the subcommittee argued that rural seats should be given special consideration by the boundary commissions for reasons of national security, and Ireland should be included in the redistribution scheme. Finally, the report favored reform and strengthening the Lords as a constitutional safeguard. A third of the subcommittee's proposed amendments were forwarded to Unionist M.P.s through Colonel John Gretton. Even after the subcommittee finished its work, a group of Unionist agents remained at work guiding Unionist M.P.s during the passage of the bill.

The report of the NUA subcommittee marks the beginning of the Unionists' more pragmatic and constructive approach toward the reform bill. Writing to the *Conservative Agents' Journal,* one Unionist M.P. admitted that his colleagues disliked the reform bill. But none of them would oppose it "for fear of arousing the hostility of the electorate . . . especially the women who are thirsting for the vote, while a good many are especially intent on giving sailors and soldiers the franchise." Their reluctance to reject the bill by no means signified wholehearted Unionist acceptance of democratic, majority rule. This is evidenced by Unionists' faith in the special role of rural areas and servicemen, and their support for strengthening the House of Lords. But some Unionists, most notably Walter Long, believed moderate reform during the war was essential for preventing unrest and revolution afterward. As one Unionist M.P. said during a debate on the bill, "The vote is granted nowadays on no kind of fitness, but as a substitute for riot, revolution and rifle." Writing in his diary at the end of 1917, the earl of Crawford, a former Unionist chief whip, described the bill as "the strongest if not the sole bulwark between this country and revolution."[19] This pragmatic outlook, the work of Unionist leaders who quelled outright opposition, and the nearly universal desire to reward patriotic servicemen and punish conscientious objectors served to deflate opposition to reform.

In most respects the Representation of the People Act, which became law on 6 February 1918, resembled the Speaker's Report, but Unionists in Westminster were able to obtain several important changes. First, they extended the military franchise to nineteen- and twenty-year-olds. Second, conscientious objectors who had not served in noncombat roles lost their vote for five years after the war's end. Chairman Younger himself introduced the conscientious objectors' clause on 22 November, and it passed with the support of some Liberals. Third, Unionists removed the alternative vote and limited proportional representation to a few university seats. Fourth, the home secretary, Sir George Cave, succeeded in retaining sixteen more rural seats than a strict redistribution justified. Taking into account the increase in suburban seats, the number of likely Unionist seats probably increased by about thirty despite the failure to extend redistribution to Ireland.[20]

Contemporaries regarded the Representation of the People Act as a milestone in British politics. On the basis of a six months' residency requirement, the act established universal suffrage for men over twenty years of age. It also gave the vote to all soldiers and sailors who were at least nineteen years of age. Men who had business property worth ten pounds per annum or were graduates of British universities could cast a second ballot outside their home constituency. After 1918 business voters were less than 1 percent of the electorate in England and Wales and played a significant role in approximately two dozen university and city center constituencies (2 percent of the total). Some historians argue that the simple residential franchise brought working-class men, particularly the urban poor, or "slummies," as some termed them, into politics. Yet the residency franchise also increased the number of young, often single, middle-class and working men who lacked any party allegiance, adding a large floating vote.[21]

Under the reform act of 1918 women thirty years of age and over who possessed the local government franchise (or whose husbands did) were also enfranchised. They were eligible for the same additional franchises as men but until 1928 could exercise only one of their votes in each election. In 1918 the enfranchisement of women was the most noteworthy effect of the reform act. Some contemporary commentators believed that the introduction of women into British politics would destroy its allegedly rational and patriotic character. Viscount Bryce claimed that, in Australia, the left benefited from female suffrage because women were "easy victims to any representation." The *Conservative Agents' Journal* predicted some of the undesirable results of Britain's reform act: "The introduction of such a large feminine element in the political arena must of necessity bring domestic legislation to the front to the exclusion of Imperial affairs. Prohibition campaigns, home welfare, equal opportunities for women in the labour market, sex equality, free meals for all children, permanent communal kitchens, free maternity nursing homes for mothers will all make their appearance."[22]

Except for the failure to establish full female suffrage, the Representation of the People Act created Britain's first system of universal suffrage, increasing the enfranchised portion of the population from 28 percent to 78 percent. Before the war, voters—exclusively men—numbered fewer than eight million. As a result of the reform act the number jumped to thirteen million men and nearly nine million women. The reform added more than twice the number of eligible voters than any other franchise reform. A comparison of the five reform acts shows that the electorate increased by approximately 50 percent in 1832, 84 percent in 1867, 88 percent in 1884, 177 percent in 1918, and 33 percent in 1928. It was not just hyperbole, then, when Long congratulated Cave on passing "the biggest Bill ... since 1832." Others made similar comments. In a 1927 political science text, the historian and Tory M.P. Sir J. A. R. Marriott stated that, compared to the 1918 act, previous reform acts "almost sink into insignificance."[23]

At a time of general uncertainty and revolutionary upheaval, the specter of a phalanx of volatile and untested male and female voters who might turn to the Liberals or the Labour Party caused considerable anxiety in the Unionist Party. Unionists' worst fears would have been confirmed by reading the diary of Beatrice Webb. In a June 1918 entry, Webb mused that the reform act would make the Labour Party a powerful force.[24] Unionist uneasiness was exacerbated by provisions in the act that shifted responsibility for the registration of voters from party agents to local government officials, like those who had long existed in Scotland. After 1918 agents were no longer able to manage the electorate, which previously had been relatively small and subject to complex, limited franchises.[25] In the 1920s Conservative politicians enjoyed neither the intimacy with voters characteristic of the Edwardian electorate nor the prognosticative and psephological tools of post-1945 politics. It is not surprising, therefore, that, in the wake of the reform act of 1918, there were many fears about the semieducated electorate, its discontent, and its malleability. The trepidation caused by the coming of mass society was not limited to Unionists, as D. L. LeMahieu shows, but it pervaded the party after the passage of the Representation of the People Act in early 1918.[26]

The Conservative Party's Response to the Reform Act

To avoid predictions like those of Beatrice Webb, most Unionists realized that they had to redirect their efforts to attract more voters. By early 1918 the Labour Party was already accelerating its planning for the next general election. It was especially active in integrating women into the party organization, hiring Dr. Marion Phillips as Woman Organiser in January 1918. Long and other Unionist proponents of the 1918 act may have saved Britain from turmoil by timely reform, but they left Unionists with the choice between a new kind of mass politics, decline, or even—possibly—a lingering death. At a special private NUA conference called on 30 November 1917 Bonar Law explained how the momentum of reform had produced an undesirably far-reaching bill. But, he cautioned, there was no turning back; the Unionist Party must see the reform act as an opportunity "to make our Party what Disraeli called it—and what, if it is to have any existence, it must be—a really national party."[27] 1918 marked the beginning of the ten-year process of remaking the Unionist and Conservative Party into a party suited to the new age of universal suffrage.

The most important means by which Unionists sought to popularize their party was by fostering organizations for women and wage earners and by involving more people in the party's operations. In an October 1917 report, Archibald Salvidge, longtime secretary of the Liverpool Constitutional Association, analyzed women's relationship to the party:

> They will form nearly two-fifths of the parliamentary electorate and the Unionist Party will, of necessity, be compelled to attract them. . . . Their importance in elections will be paramount and already the Labour Party are bent on a programme which will attract women. There seems no reason why women should not be welcomed into the Unionist organisation on equal terms with men.
>
> It is highly probable that Clubs and Branches will have to be formed for women or arrangements made for their

inclusion in present clubs or a separate meeting night assigned to them. Much opposition to such proposals may
be expected from men.... The bold course of "equal
rights" for males and females seems to be the best.

An alteration of the Rules of the Association will be
necessary and provision made for the inclusion of women.
It would perhaps be desirable to make some proviso that
the representation of women on divisional councils be limited so as to prevent them securing a predominance of
power in the direction of party affairs.[28]

Shortly afterward, Unionists in Yorkshire made the first attempt by party
members to form women's associations and to place women on party committees, but they were unable to decide on exact arrangements and awaited
developments in London.[29]

Delegates to the private NUA conference on 30 November 1917 devoted
considerable time to the question of a women's organization. Some expressed their distaste for female suffrage and their fears that women would
join in "an unholy alliance" with Labour. Most of the discussion, however,
concerned organizational methods. Herbert G. Williams expressed a widespread anxiety that a segregated association would cause internal division
and waste and would continue the suffragettes' "sex war." He also feared
that less experienced (and more irrational) women would be exploited by
"sentimental Socialist[s]." But the organizer of the JIL emphasized that the
party must accept all women: "You want an organisation that has now to
take in hand the element that is going to hold the balance of power in the
future elections in this country. You must take this matter so seriously that
not only must you be prepared ... to put these women upon your Ward
Committees, and your central electoral organization, but you must be prepared to welcome to your Councils, even to the [NUA] Council that is
meeting here to-day, the bolder and more active spirits amongst them."
The consensus was that the Unionist Party had to incorporate female supporters into the party with "the greatest possible co-partnership and cooperation" between the sexes.[30]

Sir George Younger informed the delegates that central office was considering an arrangement with the existing, autonomous Women's Unionist
and Tariff Reform Association (WUTRA). The WUTRA was an exclusively
women's group whose activities were overtly political. In many ways it
was a precursor of later organizations, but because it had relatively few

branches and was not formally connected either to central office or to the NUA at the constituency, regional, or national level, it was a poor candidate for a universal women's organization. Under its leaders, the countess of Ilchester and Mrs. Mary Maxse, the WUTRA maintained only very limited operations during the war. By mid-1917 it faced a dilemma. The prewar issues—particularly home rule and tariff reform—were no longer critical. But there was a promising future for a women's political organization if, as expected, women were given the vote. Lady Talbot was elated at the WUTRA's prospects. "We shall be an enormous power at every election . . . ," wrote Lady Talbot, "and . . . whichever party we support will have to rely on our votes and not only on our work as they have done hitherto." Such comments worried Unionists already concerned that the women's organization would put its interests before the party.[31]

But the only possible alternative to the WUTRA was the now declining Primrose League. Formed in 1883 in honor of Benjamin Disraeli, the league was the largest political organization in Britain, with nearly one and one-half million (mainly female) members in 1900. It supported the Unionist Party by mobilizing support for the established order of King, Empire, and Church. The league, almost like the Masons, had an arcane system of chivalric titles for its officers, and it offered a multitude of honors to members who contributed funds or worked on behalf of the organization. Aristocratic and other elite members added luster to local branches. Such members led pilgrimages to Disraeli's grave, held social events, canvassed, and registered voters. Women often served on executive committees and as officers. But the league's national Ladies Grand Council, formed in 1885, was largely powerless, and no women were chosen as officers for the regular national council. This shortcoming may in part explain why, during the Edwardian period, the league began to experience problems that worsened during the war. Although the leaders of the Primrose League were positioning their organization to take advantage of the reform bill in 1917 and 1918, many people believed that it was too old-fashioned, which proved to be the case. The league never became the women's movement of the Unionist Party, and it was increasingly seen as a ceremonial relic of Toryism.[32]

In January 1918 Younger devised a proposal for working with the WUTRA and forwarded to the NUA Executive two memoranda describing a possible Unionist Women's Organisation. The first memorandum, "Notes on Women's Organisation under the Representation of the People Bill," analyzed two possible methods of incorporating women into the local organization. Either women and men could join a single association as

equal members, or men and women could form separate district and constituency associations joined by a single executive committee and agent.
Whichever plan was adopted, Younger urged that women be given full representation. He intended to provide women with equitable representation
in the regional NUA organs and the party conference. In the second memorandum Younger used the model of the 1912 Liberal Unionist amalgam-
ation as a model for creating a women's department in central office from
the existing tariff group. He also tentatively suggested that a committee
monitored by the party chairman and principal agent be formed at Central
Office to oversee women's affairs and avoid gender conflict.[33]

These two memoranda became the basis for the Women's Unionist
Organisation (WUO), and although it initially existed only on paper and
was overlooked by many Unionists,[34] it was the only national organization
for women closely linked to the Unionist Party. Party leaders were hopeful.
Younger asked Caroline Bridgeman, a prominent member of the WUTRA
and the wife of a popular junior minister, to lead the WUO. Concerned
that the women would be dominated by the principal agent, Bridgeman
and other WUTRA leaders requested more power and autonomy for the
WUO than the proposed constitution allowed. This was necessary,
Bridgeman argued, in order to have cordial relations between men and
women; Unionist women worked best "where they have a dignified, recog-
nised position."[35] Younger agreed to give the WUO complete control over
personnel and all other matters except finance. WUO leaders would be
appointed by the party chairman in order to keep the group from becoming just another administrative department. Finally, Younger agreed to
form a NUA advisory committee to oversee women's affairs, although it
would have no official powers under NUA rules. The women succeeded in
obtaining their major demands, and by July 1918 the WUO was operating
in London, with Bridgeman serving as chairwoman and Miss Goring-
Thomas, formerly a WUTRA official, as secretary.[36]

Rank-and-file party members responded to the "Notes on Women's
Organization." Some seats already had women's branches. Before the First
World War, five of the twelve divisions in my sample had women's groups
of some kind. Before the war, the Oswestry Women's Constitutional Association (formed in 1904), whose chairwoman and secretary was Caroline
Bridgeman, had twenty-six branches and 2,868 members.[37] But most wom-
en's branches were much smaller and, like the men's associations, did not
meet regularly during the war. The situation quickly changed in 1918 as
women's organizations were established or reorganized in most English

and Welsh associations, and women were admitted to parent associations. In such constituencies as Oswestry, Bradford Central, Wood Green, and Clapham, women did not form their own associations until shortly after the war and the sudden November 1918 campaign.[38] Among the English and Welsh constituencies studied, only in Wrexham, where a women's branch was formed in 1923, was there any significant delay. And some Unionists, like those in North Cornwall and Wirral, opted for joint men and women's associations, although in both of these cases there were separate women's committees under the parent association.[39] In any case, the distinction between joint and separate organizations was often blurred. At the 1918 annual meeting of the Skipton association, the men demanded a single association, and the women agreed, provided they received sufficient representation on the executive committee; yet a women's branch continued at Skipton. Whatever the formal arrangement, WUO branches usually made their own rules, raised their own funds, and enjoyed general autonomy.

Compared to their achievements in the constituencies, however, women were at first unsuccessful at the regional level. Early in 1918, Yorkshire Unionists decided to organize women in the party, but they could not agree on a plan. Under the influence of Miss Goring-Thomas and Miss Thistlewaite, the secretary of the former regional women's group, officers from women's branches formed a separate organization. By the general election in November, the new women's federation had been incorporated into the WUO, and central office had hired Thistlewaite as its first female area agent. In Cornwall, WUTRA and Primrose League leaders met in June 1918 and decided not to form a regional WUO, but encouraged Cornish men and women the form joint Unionist associations. The early start in Yorkshire and Cornwall later contributed to the WUO's near monopoly over the women and the rapid decay of the Primrose League. In most parts of the country, however, regional women's organizations were not immediately established.[40]

In Scotland the independent Scottish Unionist Association (SUA) ordered an enquiry in November 1917 to find a means of responding to the Representation of the People bill. The SUA Executive called for equal treatment of men and women in local organizations. After studying a memorandum on reorganization from central office in London, the SUA council rejected separate female organizations. Instead it decided in February 1918 that "the fusion between Men's and Women's Associations should be absolute." It invited existing women's groups to cooperate in forming joint associations, while allowing associations to appoint women's committees to deal with any strictly female issues. Camlachie Unionists quickly adopted the SUA ruling, and merged the women's branch with the men's association. Later, after the SUA established a Women's Committee in 1920, Camlachie formed a separate women's committee.[41] In Kincardine, however, Unionists did not form women's groups, in part because the association had fallen into decay during the war and remained defunct until 1923.

After the passage of the reform act, women were also admitted into the previously male local Unionist associations. In 1917 none of the twelve divisional associations I have examined had female members, but by the end of 1918 all had brought women into their associations and committees. Suddenly women gained entry to the sanctum sanctorum of Unionism from which they had hitherto been barred. In February 1918 the SUA council sent a memorandum to its associations. Echoing an earlier directive, it declared, "Women should be admitted to all Associations on the same footing as men. . . . [and provided with] their proper share of representation [of offices and committees]."[42] The memorandum typified Unionists' new concern about women's participation.

Although specific local arrangements varied, associations followed a general pattern for incorporating women into the local associations. Usually women were given seats on a joint council or executive committee in proportion to their share of the electorate—usually one-third. Frequently these representatives were chosen by the women's executive committee. Some association offices, although not the highest post, might be reserved for women. In Stockton, for example, the women's branch was allocated four of the twelve seats on the executive committee and one vice-chairmanship. In Wirral, women composed half the polling district representatives on the executive committee, a third of the members of the general purposes committee, and one of the two vice-chairmen. In Skipton and North Cornwall, women were provided with separate facilities in a Conservative club that served as the local party headquarters. There were occasional conflicts between men and women. In Chichester, the development of a women's organization led to an attempt by the men to add the women to the existing men's association. This was held off and later repulsed by the women. Such fighting was, however, exceptional, as there were social and familial ties between the men and the women, and many of the women were already active in public life. When women first attended the Palmers Green branch in Wood Green, six of the seven were introduced by husbands who were already officers or members.[43]

Unionist efforts to bring women into the local associations were closely tied to attempts to make associations adapt their constitutions to the reform act. A February 1918 circular from the SUA summarizes Unionist hopes:

> The enlarged size of the constituencies, and even more than that, the spirit of the age, render absolutely necessary that *all classes and interests* in sympathy with Unionist principles should have a share in the direction of the affairs of the [Scottish Unionist] Association, and should be welcomed to its deliberations. To ensure this, committees should be large enough to enable representatives of all such classes and interests to be included, and should meet at such times and places as will suit the various members. This is the only way to keep in touch and in sympathy with the feelings and views of the community. Further, it is obvious that in order to ensure success constant and much more intensive work will be required than in the past. In view of the fact that all elections are to take place on the same day, each Association will require to rely [*sic*] more than ever upon the individual efforts of its members. Unless vigorous and persistent propaganda work is carried out *previous* to an election, it will be hopeless to attempt to make up the lee-way in the rush of an election.[44]

The circular indicates clearly the sense of urgency that characterized Unionist efforts to reorganize the party. That same month Younger asked Robert Sanders, unofficial party whip, to reorganize the local associations in England and Wales.[45]

Rank-and-file Unionists generally appreciated the need to update their organizations in response to franchise reform and redistribution. Developments in the newly formed Shropshire constituency of Oswestry were typical of associations which adapted quickly. At first there was a conflict over which Unionist M.P. would stand for the seat, but this was settled privately in favor of the junior minister, William Bridgeman. In August 1918 the Oswestry Unionist Association was formed. Membership was open to anyone who subscribed five shillings or joined a branch association. Branches elected the divisional council, and branch members were expected to canvass voters, collect subscriptions, maintain registration lists, and, under the supervision of the divisional association, prepare for elections. The annual meeting of the divisional council elected officers and the eight men and four women who served as an executive committee. In October the new executive hired an organizing agent. Women in Oswestry, however, did not have a WUO branch until early 1919. Eventually—in 1921—Oswestry Unionists, like a number of other associations, also created the position of chairman because the more ceremonial presidency was ill-suited to the demanding duties of the post-1918 electorate.[46]

These developments at the local level were accompanied by reform of the NUA structure and unsuccessful attempts to develop stronger ties with wage earners. Unionist leaders tried to bring the party's structure in line with the reform act by shifting responsibilities from self-elected groups of wealthy and titled men to adherents from all levels of the party. This, it was hoped, would create a disciplined but popular force. On 9 April 1918 the NUA Executive Committee adopted new rules based on the work of an investigative subcommittee. There were three major changes to the constitution. Before the war the council, the authority within the NUA that elected the managing executive committee, was an elite body of fewer than a hundred members. After 1918, provincial divisions—the regional party organs—elected more delegates to the council. Second, the larger boroughs (except London, which was its own provincial division) selected delegates to the council. Finally, women were allocated one-third of council and executive committee seats. The new rules created a larger council of 719 members, the majority chosen by the provincial divisions (519) and large boroughs (108). The rest were officials, agents, nominees of the party leader, and delegates from the conference or affiliated groups. Initially the WUTRA was asked to select five delegates to the executive committee, but after the NUA resumed peacetime operations in April 1919, men and women were elected jointly by the council, provided that women formed a third.[47]

The reform of the NUA in 1918 marked the beginning of a shift toward actual geographical and constituency representation in the NUA. Later, after the Conservative Party's defeat in the 1923 general election, the NUA Executive accepted an altered constitution proposed by Sir Herbert Blain, the new principal agent. Blain's aim was to make the body more representative of the rank and file by shifting the basis of organization from provincial divisions to constituency associations. The new rules provided associations with direct representation on both council and conference. The executive committee was still elected by the council, but delegates from each area (central office's administrative regions) would elect representatives according to the number of constituencies in their region. The three largest provincial cities were given direct representation on the executive committee, and constituency associations were allowed a third council delegate if he was a wage earner. The new Constitution and Rules were approved by the 1924 NUA conference and went into effect on 1 November. The bloated council—1,762 members—declined in influence, but the more representative NUA Executive was an effective administrative body.[48]

Unionists also hoped to capitalize on the spirit of wartime unity, which seemed to reveal the innate good sense and patriotism of British workers. Many Tories embraced the Disraelian vision of a Britain made better by economic cooperation and class harmony. The Unionist Party could assist in this goal if it brought workers—as well as women—into its organization. At the November 1917 NUA Conference, a delegate told Bonar Law that the party ought to create workingmen organizers to, as he clumsily put it, "pat the working man on the back . . . make him feel that he is something beyond a cog in the machinery of the party and . . . see if we cannot make him a crank-shaft." During late summer 1918, Long repeatedly pressed Younger to establish some kind of labor organization at central office. Although wage earners often agreed with Conservative aims, Long argued, some of their concerns and methods were different, so that they needed their own organization. Since there was not enough time to complete such a task before the next general election, Younger, the party chairman, refused. Only in 1919 did the Conservatives create a wage-earners' group, the NUA Labour Committee. For the time being, interested Unionists were forced to turn to an outside group, the British Workers' League (BWL), to attract the support of workers. Inspired and assisted by Lord Milner, a number of trade unionists and M.P.s had formed the BWL in 1916 to provide a patriotic and imperialist counterpart to the Independent Labour Party and Union for Democratic Control. But rank-and-file Unionists were wary of the independent group, especially after it became the National Democratic and Labour Party in May 1918.[49]

The changes outlined above were part of the Unionist Party's response to the disruption of war and the passage of the Representation of the People Act. Conservatives hoped to create a viable popular organization to provide the personnel, enthusiasm, and direction necessitated by near universal suffrage. Despite differing approaches to organization, the Unionist intention was to draw women, wage earners, and, as far as possible, all new voters into the Unionist Party. They were successful among women but not wage earners. Although some Unionist workingmen's clubs sent members to local associations, by the end of 1918 very few constituencies specifically provided for wage-earner representation, and Unionist efforts in this direction were stymied. Yet the organizational reforms undertaken during 1918 marked the beginning of the Unionist Party's evolution toward becoming a popular party capable of winning elections in the age of universal suffrage.

The Approaching General Election

Although significant in the future, alterations in the NUA constitution, the creation of the WUO, and (failed) attempts to form a workingmen's group were not considered sufficient to assure a Unionist majority in the next election. The new political system—defined by universal suffrage, wartime upheaval, and the rise of Labour—offered uncertainty and danger. Unionist leaders, as well as many rank-and-file members, believed that the party needed to collaborate with sympathetic elements in other parties to win the election and contain the Labour Party. They also felt that the continuation of the Lloyd George government reflected the desire of the British people for unity. Unionist leaders hoped to preserve the mood of national reconciliation by working with the prime minister and developing a reform program that would attract the newly volatile electorate. Beginning with a speech to trade unionists on 6 March 1917 Lloyd George assiduously publicized his aim of "doing big things." Unionists' postwar vision was in part a response to this. At a meeting of Yorkshire Unionists in November 1917, speaker after speaker applauded a resolution calling on the party to address "the legitimate demands of Labour." A Skipton delegate demanded that Unionists show wage earners that they were friends.[50]

To achieve far-reaching postwar reforms, Unionists felt that petty interests had to be submerged in a party of national unity. In early 1918 one M.P., J. C. Butcher, told Yorkshire Tories that he wanted "a rearrangement and regrouping of the old parties after the war . . . [consisting of those] who believed in the Empire and in the great future before us, so that all might join to repair the ravages of the war and set the country once more on the path of prosperity and greatness."[51] In October 1917 Archibald Salvidge asked Asquith if he would be willing to lead a "patriotic party after the war, made up of the best elements of the old parties? An appalling flood of unrest might sweep over Europe when hostilities ceased. Little was left of the pre-war questions for Tories and Liberals to fight about. Why not combine to build a better Britain for the men who had saved us?"[52] Asquith rejected Salvidge's offer, but many Conservatives and Liberals responded to claims that the alternative to unity, victory, and reform was revolution and chaos like that in Russia. Unionist propaganda even claimed that left-wingers and pacifists at home were pushing Britain in that direction.[53]

But some members of the Unionist rank and file were far from ecstatic about the Lloyd George coalition. The most notable manifestation of Tory dissatisfaction with the coalition was the formation of the National Party in August 1917. The ultraconservative M.P. and war veteran Henry Page Croft founded the party because he believed that the Unionist Party could not pursue a truly nationalist program of tariffs, cooperation with business, and eradication of foreign influences. Informed contemporaries judged the party a lot of "political mediocrities," and the party's historian agrees.[54] Although the journalist F. S. Oliver thought the party's popularity was the result of public anger with all politicians, Unionist leaders were worried.[55] Croft attracted disgruntled Unionists like Walter Morrison, a wealthy industrialist and former Skipton M.P.[56] Unionist leaders were particularly worried about the financial impact of losing men like Morrison, and in mid-September 1917, Bonar Law announced that National Party supporters would be opposed by Unionists at the next election. This threat and organizational problems soon stifled the young party, but many loyal rank-and-file Conservatives still felt that they were being ignored by their leaders. At a September 1917 meeting of the National Society of Conservative and Unionist Agents, an agent warned Unionist leaders that they might lose their most active followers. Even after the Unionist principal agent, William Jenkins, promised that a party conference would be called, the agents reiterated their demand that Unionist leaders "explain [themselves] to the Party as fully as possible." Similar statements were made at the October 1917 meeting of the Yorkshire Provincial Division.[57]

What caused Unionist discontent? It was partly inspired by personal antagonisms and the anger of job seekers who had been elbowed away from the trough by coalitionists. More significantly, the nonpartisanship of the coalition caused disenchantment among Tories who felt out of touch with their leaders and suspicious of both coalition ministers—particularly Liberals like Winston Churchill—and the government's compromise policies. In *Tory Democracy* (1918), Lord Henry Bentinck argued that Tory ideals of nationalism and paternalism were endangered by "cosmopolitanism" and selfish politicians.[58] Distaste for the coalition was most obvious in cases where Conservatives believed that government policies threatened national unity. A good example is the controversy over enemy aliens. The popular press soaked up antialien sentiment. The antialien movement peaked with a procession on 24 August 1918 in which marchers carried a petition signed by over a million persons to Downing Street. The petition demanded internment of all enemy aliens. The NUA Executive had already asked in July 1918 for "immediate action" against aliens, and the *Conservative Agents' Journal* carried articles condemning aliens. Some Unionist M.P.s even met with Bonar Law in the House of Commons to receive assurances about the removal of aliens.[59]

Party leaders finally responded to the growing discontent among Unionists at a private conference held at Kingsway Hall on 30 November 1917. The NUA Executive agreed a meeting was justified by the "need for a clearly defined policy [and] . . . a re-affirmation of Unionist Principles, leading up to a National Ideal." At the conference Bonar Law asked delegates to concentrate on party reorganization, not government policy. He told them to remember that Lloyd George was not only a minister of the crown, but also "the leader of the Government, and the leader of the nation, and to do . . . [his task] he must have the support of those who are working with him." As patriotic Britons all Unionists should support the prime minister. Despite these pleas, delegates criticized the reform bill, Irish policy, aliens, and other matters. When a delegate demanded to know what program would be adopted if there were a wartime election, Bonar Law stated only that the party would support the coalition. Under those circumstances, he argued, "There will only be two parties in the country—those who are determined to see the war through, and those who are not."[60]

The reform act and the possibility of an election shortly after the new register of voters was ready in October 1918 had already convinced most local Unionists that they had to regroup. With the assistance of Robert Sanders, local organizations began reorganizing. At the same time some Unionist associations collaborated with local Liberals against Labour. Particularly in urban areas like Bradford, for instance, the two parties simply expanded existing antisocialist pacts. When the Bradford central parliamentary seat became vacant during the war, the Unionist association was unprepared and reluctant to contest the seat. After the Liberal candidate, Sir James Hill, promised to vote for the Military Service bill and other war measures, the Unionist association supported him. Stockton Unionists similarly did not oppose a Liberal candidate in 1917 after he made clear his support for the coalition.[61]

Leaders and party officials may have hoped that reorganization would enable them to sidestep some of the difficult questions about the party's future role and policy, but such reform only begged those questions. J. W. Morkill, a leading figure in the Skipton association, told the Yorkshire Provincial Division Executive that, despite the new women's organization and other signs of progress, local associations were suffering anxiety and disaffection. He suggested that members press party leaders to develop a policy platform, or they would "be in the cart when an Election took place." The members agreed, but could do little more at the time than encourage wage earners to join the Unionist cause.[62]

Continued demands for a statement of postwar policy eventually led to the formation of a Unionist Policy Committee in March 1918. Meeting at the Colonial Office, Long, Younger, and the Scottish M.P. Lord Clyde quickly drafted a "Heads of Policy" program, which they sent to Bonar Law. The one-page document gave pride of place to victory over the enemy. In addition it sketched a program for national regeneration through government assistance to business, prohibition of foreign dumping, industrial conciliation, and agricultural improvement. It also proposed imperial preference and federation, revision of the financial clauses for disestablishing the Welsh Church, and reform of the House of Lords. Finally, the statement mentioned the need for improvement of health and housing and protection of women and children. In a letter to Bonar Law, Younger suggested that the terms of the program not be made public, at least until the term of the existing coalition government was fixed.[63]

This policy statement was temporarily forgotten when the Germans launched their spring offensive in 1918. Only after that crisis passed did a general election became a real possibility, particularly after the new electoral register was compiled in October. During the summer Lord Riddell, a newspaper owner and confidant of Lloyd George, noted in his diary the increasing talk about an election and future relations between government parties. The press was already requesting that the government give the new electorate a chance to exercise its voting rights, and the successful war effort created favorable electoral circumstances for the government. In anticipation of an election, the NUA Executive formed a publications subcommittee headed by Sir Laming Worthington-Evans. The subcommittee tried to secure an adequate supply of rationed paper and consulted central office about election literature. The subcommittee's report stressed two points. First, there was a crying need for leaflets "from the women's points of view." Second, the Unionist Party should fight the election as a patriotic opponent of socialism and pacifism. The subcommittee therefore recommended that Labour's proposals and literature be searched for Bolshevik and "pro-German" elements. But the subcommittee could do little until Malcolm Fraser, the head of Central Office Publications, finished his war work.[64]

During the summer and autumn of 1918, Unionist leaders began holding discussions with coalition Liberals to hammer out an agreement for the election campaign most felt was imminent.[65] In early August coalition Liberals presented Younger and Bonar Law with an election program. After comparing the Liberal program with the Unionist "Heads of Policy," Younger concluded that the Liberal proposals for nationalization of railways, secure land tenure, and national generation of electricity constituted unacceptable extensions of government power. He also argued against the Liberal proposal for women's legal equality, approving instead the Unionist program for protecting women and improving the health of mothers and children. Finally, Younger argued that Unionists must insist on tariff reform, protection for Irish Protestants, and amelioration of the financial consequences of disestablishing the Welsh Church. These issues formed major obstacles to an agreement between the two parties. Unionists were, moreover, wary of holding a wartime election, because it would strengthen Lloyd George's parliamentary position. Younger was "dead against an Election in Nov[ember]" because it would be "a huge gamble" while people were suffering from shortages and concentrating on the war. In any case, he thought that the Unionist organization would not be ready for some time. Bonar Law saw "great difficulties in any course" and had no plan for the future election.[66]

Lloyd George was more decisive, however, and Unionist leaders were finding it difficult to halt the slide toward an election. In early September Younger submitted a new draft for a coalition program, inserting the main points of the Unionist plan into the Liberal document. Lloyd George, Bonar Law, and Younger then discussed the draft, but tariffs remained a sticking point. Many Unionists were also suspicious of the prime minister and appalled at the prospect of petty electioneering while the nation was at war. Nonetheless, meeting with Lloyd George in late September, Bonar Law and Balfour tentatively approved an election for November.[67]

By the 8 October meeting of the NUA Executive Committee, the publications subcommittee was able to report that it had secured sufficient paper, composed a number of leaflets, and nearly completed the *Notes for Speakers* and a guide to the reform act. Yet the NUA Executive still knew nothing definite about a general election. A delegate asked about the possibility of a coalition election. Younger, unable to answer definitively, was subjected to a barrage of criticism. A majority of those at the meeting, Younger reported to Bonar Law, strongly opposed an immediate general election; only a quarter of them actually supported it. Many Unionists feared Lloyd George would sell them out to the Liberals. There were renewed demands for a statement of Unionist policy, because the absence of one retarded the development of the WUO and pushed Tories toward the National Party. To save Bonar Law from an embarrassing situation, Younger promised the NUA Executive that the party leader would announce plans very shortly. Younger ended his letter by warning Bonar Law of the increasing danger: "The atmosphere was distinctly electrical and whatever may be the prospects of an election it is clear that we must without any delay let these people understand exactly where we stand. It is not going to be possible to go on much longer in the indeterminate condition in which we find ourselves, and there could be no more fatal policy on our part than to permit any further unnecessary delay or we may precipitate a split amongst our supporters."[68]

Yet nothing succeeds like success: by mid-October, with Bulgaria out of the war and the German army in France beating a harried retreat, there was growing unanimity among Unionists that Lloyd George would be a valuable asset. In early September, Long had informed Bonar Law, "I really believe the P. M. could issue a manifesto which would bring the great masses of Electors to his support and give us a clean cut issue which would enable us to get rid of the rotters." It was commonly asserted that Lloyd George, because he was "one of the people," was uniquely suited to deal with the broadened electorate. And as Robert Sanders noted in a 13 October diary entry, interest in an election had increased, and Lloyd George, but not Unionist leaders, was gaining in popularity. Eventually the rising tide of support for Lloyd George swept along even Unionists like Steel-Maitland, who had opposed the coalition government.[69]

As the price for preserving the coalition, Lloyd George on 25 October agreed to Unionist demands for imperial preference, limited protection, freedom for Ulster, and financial revision of the Welsh Church Act. Eight days later the deal was outlined in a public letter from the prime minister to Bonar Law (who had actually drafted it). This document called for the election of candidates willing to support the government in securing the peace and carrying out reconstruction. Beyond this overriding task, the government pledged to "promot[e] the unity and development of the Empire" and to use anti-dumping tariffs and imperial preferences to restore the economy. The leaders accepted Irish home rule but rejected "the forcible exclusion of Ulster" from the United Kingdom. Finally, the Welsh Church Act was to be revised. In response to Bonar Law's request, Younger, Balfour, and Chamberlain all complained that tariff reform should receive more emphasis and reform of the House of Lords be mentioned, but they agreed that the letter presented an acceptable program. By this time a committee of Unionist and coalition Liberal M.P.s was already organizing publicity and propaganda for the election. In general, developments during 1918 reinforce Turner's argument in *British Politics and the Great War* (1992) that disagreements over the coalition program continued until a military victory suddenly seemed sure, at which point the Cabinet decided to continue the coalition and hurriedly assembled a program from existing proposals.[70]

The General Election of 1918

Three days after the armistice, the coalition government announced that it would hold an election a month hence. On 12 November, at the Connaught Rooms in London, Unionists, including the first women delegates to attend a party meeting, heard Bonar Law outline the coalition's election program. The introduction of women into public affairs, he began, would accentuate "two elements which are the basis of our Party: patriotism and stability." After pointing out the need for unity in dealing both with the enemy and with postwar problems, Bonar Law read the prime minister's letter. The rejection of "forcible coercion" against Ulster and the acceptance of preference and anti-dumping drew prolonged cheers from the audience. According to Long, the audience responded enthusiastically to Lloyd George's letter. Bonar Law finished his speech by reassuring Unionists that their party would remain a distinct organization within the coalition. The delegates wholeheartedly approved the resolution of support offered by Balfour and seconded by Long.[71]

Shortly after this, however, Unionists were disturbed to learn that, at the coalition Liberal meeting, Lloyd George had presented the same agreement as a Liberal document. Sanders pressed Lloyd George, who agreed to publish his letter to Bonar Law and hold a coalition rally at Central Hall. The prime minister led the 16 November meeting, inspiring the audience with his vision for postwar Britain. Bonar Law followed, presenting a lucid case for the coalition government. The difficulties ahead, he said, were as yet unfathomed, and they were approaching the future like "persons passing through a fog." Britain's problems needed to be approached with efficiency and pragmatism, not partisan rancor. This practical appraisal of the coalition became the basis for Unionist support of the postwar coalition government.[72]

After the coalition program was accepted, Unionist leaders resumed negotiations to avoid conflicts with coalition Liberal candidates. Unionist leaders had been asked by the coalition Liberal whip, Frederick Guest, not to contest the seats of 158 Lloyd George candidates, and this proposition was accepted in late October. Once a Coalition program was approved, it was decided that letters of support signed by Lloyd George and Bonar Law—"coupons"—would be distributed to coalition supporters. Most coupons went to M.P.s seeking reelection who had loyally supported the government regardless of their party affiliation. Nearly all sitting Unionists received a coupon. Within my sample, only in Bradford Central and Skipton did nonincumbent Conservatives receive coupons. The Liberal M.P. in Bradford Central was an Asquithian opponent of the coalition. In Skipton, where the Liberal M.P. was retiring, a Unionist received the coupon after his association made it clear that it would contest the seat. Allocation of the coupons caused some tension as polling day approached. Unionist and coalition Liberal leaders were mutually suspicious, and some local Unionists were appalled by central office's recommended Liberal candidates. In Wales, for example, Tories protested that coupons were provided for only two of their candidates, while Sir Alfred Mond, who was of German Jewish extraction, was a coalition Liberal candidate in Swansea.[73]

One particularly difficult issue for the Unionist Party was its relationship with the BWL. As part of the drive for national unity, party leaders had tried to bring workers to the Unionist Party by allocating seats to the BWL. In February 1917 the two groups reached a preliminary agreement giving the BWL free contests in ten seats, most of them in Yorkshire. But problems soon arose. The interventionist policies of the BWL worried some Unionists, and there were also concerns about the reliability of BWL leaders. Labour's condemnation of the BWL in early 1918 undermined the league's influence. Nevertheless, in March 1918, Sanders forwarded to Bonar Law a list of twenty-four seats—nearly all northern industrial divisions hopelessly beyond the reach of regular Unionists—that the BWL wished to contest. Unfortunately tensions between Unionists and the BWL continued, for although some associations were willing to use the BWL and its propaganda, few wanted an independent organization for wage earners. Suspicions increased when the BWL became an official party, the National

Democratic and Labour Party (NDP), in May 1918. Despite appeals from frustrated NDP leaders, Bonar Law was unable to improve relations, and Guest, who eagerly accepted all allies, became the NDP's patron. Guest provided coupons for twenty NDP candidates.[74]

In general the coalition arrangements worked reasonably well. One-third of the constituencies in my sample had coalition Liberal candidates. In these seats there were apparently no attempts to adopt Tory candidates, although this partly reflected the disorganized condition of the Unionist organizations and the unwillingness of many Unionists to return to partisan politics. John Bernard Watson, the recently elected coalition Liberal M.P. for Stockton-on-Tees, had, for example, already been accepted by the local Conservative association when the national agreement was reached. In North Cornwall some local Tories spoke on the platform of the coalition Liberal M.P., Sir Croydon Marks, and the North Cornwall association agreed not to oppose him. Often, as in Kincardine, Liberals were asked to give assurances that they would support the coalition government. Occasionally more than a simple assurance was required. In Wrexham, the coalition Liberal M.P., Sir Robert Thomas, told Unionists that he accepted limited tariffs and modification of the Welsh Church Act. During the campaign he received Unionist support, one Tory lady claiming that God had told her to vote for Lloyd George and Thomas! Since Thomas won 73 percent of the vote with a relatively high turnout, he probably drew many Tory votes.[75]

Most coalition Unionists were favorably received by Liberal voters, but there were exceptions. William Bridgeman recounted to his wife the troubles he faced trying to attract Liberals to his candidacy against the Labour candidate Tom Morris. After trying to bring prominent Liberals onto his platform but finding few takers, he concluded, "The sneaking Chapel Liberals will either abstain or vote for the Labour man." In early December, Bridgeman wrote a letter to the local Liberal newspaper inviting Liberals to attend his meetings—and putting them in the difficult position of rejecting an appeal for national unity. A number of Liberals began showing up at Bridgeman's meetings, and two of them even sponsored a favorable resolution. But many Liberals supported Morris, who was a moderate trade unionist and a Nonconformist. Similarly, the Unionist candidate in Wirral, Gershom Stewart, faced no Liberal opposition because he was a confirmed Free Trader, but the Liberal association refused to endorse him, and shortly after the election began denouncing Unionist dominance of the coalition.[76]

Contrary to some accounts of the election, the leaders of the Coalition Government did not set out to exploit the war victory with a jingoistic election in 1918. Until the last weeks before the election was announced, planners assumed that it would occur in wartime, and that it was justified by the reform act of 1918 and the need to strengthen the government in its task of defeating Germany. Even after an armistice was declared, Unionist leaders approached the election in a restrained mood and with a reasonably clear platform of wartime Conservatism. Early in the election the call for continued national unity dominated. The victorious prime minister, it was asserted, would lead Britain toward peace and prosperity. The coalition parties wanted, as Morgan writes, "a mandate for peace, reconstruction, and reform." Only as the campaign developed did it become a referendum on the victorious wartime coalition and the need to punish Germany.[77]

Initially the most noticeable feature of the campaign was a general unwillingness to abandon the euphoric unity of wartime for politics as usual. In Skipton the *Craven Herald* opposed any election leading to a revival of "Party" and "the old game of the 'Ins' and the 'Outs'—that sham fighting which rests not on any real divergence of principles and aims but in interests and ambitions." A journalist for the *Glasgow Herald* expressed similar views, but hoped that the coalition would be a means to avoid such pettiness by laying "the foundation-stone of a new political party in which will be incorporated the best elements of the three existing parties—sanely and moderately progressive in policy and steering a course between Bolshevism and extremism on the one hand and laissez faire and reaction on the other." Most observers noted the public's unconcern; Bridgeman feared that the election would be "fearfully dull."[78]

The Unionist campaign emphasized the nation's successful war effort under the leadership of Lloyd George. In a few cases Unionists proclaimed support for a coalition party and spoke of the need to be both Liberal and Conservative, but generally the person of the prime minister was central to the Unionist campaign. *Election Notes*, a campaign periodical published by central office, ascribed Unionist support for Lloyd George to the "utterly inadequate" Asquith government and their faith in Lloyd George's "boundless fire and energy, . . . rare imagination and fervour, and . . . powers of vivid and forcible expression." They pledged their "hearty and unswerving support" to the Welshman during the uncertain times ahead. Watching the electioneering, C. F. G. Masterman, a former Liberal colleague of Lloyd George, described "the lorries of the Tory candidates . . .

jogg[ing] sadly through the rain plastered with requests to vote for X [Unionist candidate] and Mr. Lloyd George; with a very small X and a very large Lloyd George. No appeal appeared for the other member of the Duumvirate: 'Vote for X and Mr. Bonar Law.'" Central office even provided Unionist candidates with posters like the one Masterman described. As they sought to win the votes of the huge number of unaligned and new voters, candidates emphasized their ties to Lloyd George. An advertisement for Sir Arthur Du Cros, a coalition Conservative candidate, in the *Clapham Observer* claimed, "Every Vote for Sir Arthur Du Cros is a Vote for Lloyd George." Bradford Unionists bought a whole page of the local newspaper to display "the[ir] Lloyd George candidates." Some Unionist candidates printed facsimiles of their coupons; most, like Colonel Richard Roundell, claimed to be "out-and-out supporter[s] of the Coalition Government." One journalist jokingly suggested that coalitionists should sue for copyright infringement anyone who incorrectly used the coalition coupon.[79]

Election literature, including the aptly entitled "7 War Winners," praised the achievements of the coalition government in war and at home. One series of leaflets credited the government for the nation's economic prosperity and high wages, the closer cooperation within the Empire, and the reform act of 1918. *Election Notes* elaborated coalition plans for agricultural and health reforms, soldiers' pensions, business and labor cooperation, and women's advancement. Unionist propaganda claimed that nation and Empire would be protected and promoted by the safeguarding of "key industries" and imperial trade preferences.[80]

Publications denigrating wartime enemies and noncoalition parties abounded. Numerous references to "Hun treachery, rapacity, and barbarism" evoked anti-German sentiments. One leaflet recalled Wilhelm II's 1908 statement that the British were "mad as March hares" not to trust Germany, and claimed that the former emperor was hoping for the defeat of the coalition government. Aliens were already a major concern—many believed that they threatened Britain's unity—and the National Party's campaign heightened antiforeign sentiment. Xenophobia unquestionably played a role in the Unionist campaign. In Clapham the war veteran Henry Hamilton Beamish campaigned to enthusiastic crowds as an independent Conservative and candidate of the National Federation of Discharged Sailors and Soldiers. His platform was a patriotic and xenophobic nationalism. Even against Unionist and Asquithian candidates, he polled 19 percent of the Clapham vote. Although extreme in his sentiments, Beamish was not the only Conservative to voice xenophobic sentiments. For instance, the

Bradford Central candidate, H. B. Ratcliffe, demanded an end to the "great bands of penniless alien immigrants who competed with the British worker for work."[81]

Conservative election literature also demonized the anti-coalition Labour Party as pacifist, pro-German, and Bolshevik. Voting for Labour, Unionist literature argued, would bring Bolshevism and attendant social and political chaos. For female voters, this meant the prospect of a "Bureau of Free Love." A prime target of Unionist attacks was Ramsay MacDonald, a former proponent of negotiated peace. In Chichester the Labour candidate F. E. Green was repeatedly forced to deny that he was a pacifist or a supporter of Ramsay Macdonald. Ratcliffe also tarred his Labour opponent with the MacDonald brush and contrasted such pacifists with men of action like Lloyd George. In Wood Green the Unionist candidate, Godfrey Locker-Lampson, suggested that electors vote for the coalition to maintain Britain's dominant position in the world and keep the country from Labour's "wrong and rotten policy." Yet among the twelve seats in my sample, only in Camlachie, Glasgow, was Bolshevism the overriding issue. Here the Unionist M.P., Halford Mackinder, opposed by the teacher and ILP candidate, Hugh Guthrie, told voters that the election was a contest between moderate Coalitionism and Bolshevism.[82]

Unionists used jingoism and scare tactics to win votes, although central office's recommended tactic was to appeal to voters to preserve national unity. The best means of achieving this goal was to elect a Commons that would aid Lloyd George and the coalition in securing peace and reform. Voters were in effect asked, as Sir Arthur Du Cros phrased it, to reward the government's victory with "a blank cheque." They "fought for liberty and justice," he said, "and now that the fighting has ceased, [they] must leave it to Mr. Lloyd George and a coalition Government to see us through the rest of the difficulty."[83]

Evidence from the constituencies shows that Unionists began their campaigns on this patriotic note. For those who had served in the armed forces, the approach was straightforward. As Sanders recorded in his diary, his supporters voiced their opposition to the Labour candidate very simply: "Sanders went to fight and Plummer did not." Whenever his war service was mentioned, Lord Edmund Talbot drew hearty cheers from the crowd. Other candidates dredged up their every contribution to the war effort. Part of Mackinder's election address dealt with his involvement in such war work as recruiting and the War Savings Scheme. He also claimed to have invented the concepts of "national manpower" and "key industries," expounding on them in his scholarly publications. Du Cros pointed to his efforts in raising troops, developing air defenses, and producing motorcycles for home defense. He also credited himself with encouraging his employees to join the armed forces, providing jobs for veterans, and paying for 150 military ambulances.[84]

Toward the end of November there was an upsurge in the xenophobic and retributory mood of the campaign. The return of British prisoners of war, in particular, brought the question of punishing the defeated enemy to the fore. The Unionist War Committee had been pressing the issue of German treatment of British POWs since July 1918, but only in mid-November did the POW story begin to emerge. At that time the first POWs stumbled across Allied lines in France in a state of "utter emaciation and feebleness" after walking from their camps in Germany. The first shipload of prisoners arrived in Hull on November 17. Stories of atrocities and barbarous treatment of Allied POWs quickly began to circulate. Initial astonishment was followed by outrage at the Germans. On seeing some freed American POWs, a newspaper correspondent in France wrote, "As I looked back on them, boys who had once been sturdy soldiers, I wondered how any decent man can ever look upon a German without the greatest loathing." At public meetings and in the press there were demands for the punishment of those responsible: the Kaiser, other German leaders, and the German people.[85]

As a result of the developing POW story and the growing demand for action, politicians were forced to deal with the fate of alleged war criminals and the possibility of making Germany pay indemnities. Neither Conservative nor coalition Liberal leaders were eager to open debate on a policy toward the defeated Germans, but it proved impossible for the government to remain mute. After the Cabinet considered the matter, Lloyd George finally addressed the question of punishment in a speech at Newcastle on 29 November. The Kaiser and Germany should be brought to justice, he said, for the damage they had caused and the crimes they had committed. He gave special attention to the plight of the POWs, but remained cautious, making no rash promises. A *Glasgow Herald* editorial praised the speech, noting that, for many voters, this issue "overshadows altogether the political issues of the General Election."[86]

By the time of the prime minister's speech, calls for punishing Germany and deporting aliens were increasingly common in the constituency campaigns. Speaking at the Clapham Constitutional Club on 25 November, Du Cros stressed the need to teach the Germans a lesson, even if it took twenty years and forced Britain to disregard the League of Nations. The next day Bridgeman noted the increasing number of questions about Germany and aliens. On 28 November he told his wife, "Vindicative action against Germany is the great cry—and huge indemnities etc." That same day Colonel Roundell told a crowd how angry the sight of returning POWs made him. It would be just, he said, to try the Kaiser and his associations. "He would not give them the honour of being shot," Roundell continued, "but would have them hung from the top of the highest tree as the dirty common felons they were (applause)." Later this anti-German sentiment seems to have led Roundell to advertise in the Skipton paper that he was for "The Outing of the Undesirable Aliens and no Further Innings For them in This Country." On 29 November, a Wood Green newspaper reported that Locker-Lampson, the Unionist candidate, was "strongly in favour of shutting out aliens and alien goods, and the punishment of cruel enemies, including the Kaiser." Yet the next day some voters pressed Locker-Lampson to take an even more aggressive stance. Ratcliffe's campaign in Bradford Central also took a decidedly anti-German tone at this time.[87]

By early December the campaign reports coming into Unionist headquarters showed that the question of German indemnity dominated public interest. The only other issues approaching it in intensity were related ones—the punishment of war criminals and the removal of aliens. Realizing the depth of anti-German sentiment, Sir William Bull, Unionist M.P. for Hammersmith, issued the following political poem on polling day:

> The German Fleet, as you all know,
> Is safely moored at Scapa Flow;
> The crafty Huns will have to pay
> And your friend BULL will show the way.
>
> Vote for BULL should be your cry
> As you'll discover bye and bye,
> He'll do his best to get the fruits
> Of Victory over German Brutes.[88]

Such "hang the Kaiser" rhetoric sometimes excluded other questions from discussion. According to a newspaper report, during a 29 November speech, Steel-Maitland questioned Macdonald's claim that Britain should seek friendship with Germany. Steel-Maitland then addressed the crowd: "'Can you imagine yourself going hand in hand with a gentle German?'

asked the speaker. (Voices: 'Yes, with a knife in the other hand.' 'Send them here we'll deal with them.') 'I am all for housing reform,' he continued, 'but I think the first thing we have got to do is to keep our own house to ourselves. We have got to make the Germans pay. The criminals who have been responsible for all this mischief have got to be brought to justice.' (Cheers, and a voice, 'Hang them first.')"[89]

Yet attacking the defeated enemy was certainly not an exclusively Unionist tactic, and most Conservative candidates did not completely forget their earlier platform statements. Steel-Maitland's audience also listened to Locker-Lampson speak on copartnership, care for veterans, and land reform. During early December Colonel Richard Roundell spoke to Skipton voters about Imperial preference, safeguarding, agricultural improvements, housing, and better wages. A full-page advertisement in a Bradford newspaper listed Lloyd George's achievements and asked "every right-thinking Elector" to support "the most Progressive and Energetic Statesman now serving Britain" by voting for "THE LLOYD GEORGE CANDIDATES." The city's Unionists held a "Coalition Rally" two days before polling day. In case there was any confusion, a full-page advertisement showed photos of the coalition candidates centered over copies of their coupon letters, with a message telling women that these were "Lloyd George's Bradford Men." Beside the newspaper's report of the coalition rally was a headline about two local Labour candidates: "Fritz's Candidates. Two Bradford Bolshevists. A Talk About Leach and Jowett. Kammerads in Arms." Unity and leadership remained potent elements of the Unionist election campaign.[90]

During the election coalition candidates faced only two difficult questions: the minimum wage for agricultural laborers and conscription. Some Unionists were criticized because they had voted to give agricultural laborers twenty-five instead of thirty shillings as a minimum wage. During the last days of his Oswestry campaign, Bridgeman was attacked on this issue. He believed that it cost him agricultural voters. Conscription was a problem because of Labour's claim that the government would continue it indefinitely. Unionist candidates vigorously denied this. Roundell's advertisements stated, "Colonel Roundell Is Strongly Opposed to Conscription. Pledged Against Conscription. Pledged Against the Germans. Pledged for the Sailor, Soldier and Worker of this Country." Both issues put Conservatives in the unusual position of having to defend themselves and the government's record and program.[91]

Because 1918 was the first parliamentary election in which women voted, they received special attention. They were certainly among the most eager campaigners and voters. Lloyd George used female speakers, including Christabel Pankhurst, and he held a special meeting for women at Queen's Hall. Many candidates held public meetings for women. One-fifth of Mackinder's meetings took place in the afternoon and were set aside for women. Central office distributed several leaflets for women during the election. One told them to cast their vote for the coalition, saying, "You Are A Trustee for the Silent," those foully treated, imprisoned, wounded, and killed by Germans. Other material contained civics lessons for these first-time voters. "To Women Voters" informed women it was their duty not to form a women's party. They should trust the Unionist Party and its program for Empire, religious education, housing, and better working conditions to look after the nation's best interests. A WUO leaflet claimed that that organization would give special attention to the interests of women at work and at home, to the health and welfare of children, and to equal pay for women. Similarly, in one of his leaflets Neville Chamberlain promised to provide child-care centers, assistance to women unable to support their children, and better homes, because "an attractive home means a contented husband."[92]

At the close of the campaign, Unionists were hopeful but very unsure of the outcome. In their reports to central office, Unionist area agents made generally optimistic forecasts but noted that the absence of a reliable canvass of the new electorate meant any prediction was guesswork.[93] Nevertheless, the party's forecast for the number of seats won by coalition candidates matched the outcome: 473. Included in this total were 332 conservatives. Fifty Conservatives who had not received coupons were elected. Excluding Sinn Feiners, who never attended Parliament, more than half of those newly elected M.P.s were Unionists. The Conservatives won 111 more seats than in the previous election of December 1910. In contrast, Asquithian Liberals and the Labour Party won only thirty-six and fifty-eight seats, respectively.

The party's success in 1918 led Unionists like Long to argue that the election was really more a Unionist than a Coalition victory, and some historians have echoed this interpretation. Kinnear claims that Tory gains were largely a result of the improved position of the party between 1910 and 1914, combined with the effects of the 1918 redistribution. There are, however, good reasons to question this thesis. In his analysis of election results, Turner argues that Unionist claims of a Conservative victory "by their own efforts were grossly exaggerated," pointing out that the coalition coupon and—to a much lesser degree—the program attracted support, especially from women and Liberals, and that the Unionist Party had little to do with its own success, which largely resulted from the existence of the coalition.[94] Although there is evidence to support most of Turner's statements, the 1918 election did tentatively establish the postwar electoral position of the Unionist Party.

Election results in the constituencies I have scrutinized show that a large number of votes went to the coalition parties, particularly the Unionists. The seven Conservative candidates (all recognized by the coalition) who faced opponents won a majority of the vote, polling on average 61 percent of the popular vote. Even in 1924, the best election for the Conservatives between 1918 and 1929, the party's candidates in these seven seats won less than 55 percent of the popular vote. In 1918 the Unionists even won the urban seats of Bradford Central and Camlachie, which by 1924 were safe Labour constituencies. In Skipton the Coalition Conservative candidate defeated a Liberal by 2,281 votes, winning 55 percent of the vote in a seat that had been strongly Liberal in the past. Since the four divisions where coalition Liberals were not opposed—North Cornwall, Wrexham, Stockton, and Kincardine—were considered safe Liberal seats in 1918, the Conservative Party sacrificed very little there. Only in Oswestry did the coalition Conservative not perform very well. Against a strong Labour candidate, Bridgeman won only 59 percent of the vote in a traditionally Tory seat.

The national pattern closely corresponds to my sample and reinforces the argument that the Conservative Party benefited materially from the coalition—to the particular disadvantage of Asquithian Liberals.[95] In two-way contests with Liberal opponents Conservatives averaged more than 72 percent of the vote, compared to less than 66 percent against Labour candidates. Over the whole country, Unionist candidates won an average of 58 percent of the popular vote in contested seats. Coalition Unionists, however, averaged nearly 60 percent of the popular vote, compared to less than 45 percent for Conservatives without coupons. The twenty-two Tory candidates who ran against coalition candidates won only 34 percent of the vote. Clearly coalition Conservative candidates won more votes than did unaligned Conservatives, especially those who faced coalition opponents. Although the type and location of sample constituencies may have influenced these comparisons, the wide variety of seats involved should make up for any such influence. Low voter turnout (57 percent)—due primarily to the servicemen's vote—may have affected the results, although there is no evidence that it did.

This analysis of the election results suggests that the Unionist victory was more the product of the coalition than of a swing from the Liberals to the Conservatives or the consequence of the 1918 redistribution. But Turner's statistical analysis seems to lead to an overemphasis on the electoral pact itself. True, most of the constituencies that Unionists did not contest in 1918 were barren ground throughout the interwar period, and the party did not waste resources on these probably hopeless seats. Yet a close study of the campaign indicates that the coalition's program of national unity and regeneration, as well as Unionist ideology and imagery, drew voters. This explains the extremely high proportion of the vote that went to Unionists, particularly coalition Unionists, who benefited from the prime minister's popularity and the war, which vindicated their vision of the nation. Without the coalition's war record and the electoral arrangements neither the Unionist Party nor the coalition Liberals could have performed as well as they did. The 1918 election was really an ephemeral success, and the Conservative Party's triumph a fragile one. The Conservatives had yet to establish a long-term response to the democratic age. As we know from the work of Morgan and Kinnear,[96] coalition leaders were unable to create a permanent anti-Labour party of Liberals and Conservatives, a failure that led to the collapse of the coalition government in October 1922. As a result the Conservative Party had to accelerate the development of popular organizations and political tools for the age of universal suffrage.

2

The Women's Unionist Organisation and the Role of Women in the Conservative Party

The enfranchisement of women under the Representation of the People Act of 1918 created considerable trepidation in the ranks of the Conservative Party. In 1923 the earl of Dartmouth penned a few lines for his friend Caroline Bridgeman, the chairwoman of the Women's Unionist Organisation (WUO). His poem reflected contemporary concerns about women's role:

> I've been thinking I've been thinking
> now that women have the vote
> That they should wear the breeches
> and the men the petticoat.
> For with these womens [*sic*] Institutes
> They'll run us off our legs
> And the men will do the cooking
> While the cocks will lay the eggs.[1]

Apprehension was not limited to Conservatives. Asquith commented on the female voters he encountered during his Paisley by-election in 1920: "They are for the most part hopelessly ignorant of politics, credulous to the last degree, and flickering with gusts of sentiment like a candle in the wind."[2]

Continuing neglect of the history of the WUO and of women in the Conservative Party reflects the mixture of discomfort and condescension about women in politics. In a recent work on female Conservative voters in the 1980s, Campbell noted, "The first thing to say about the Tory woman is that we think we know what she is, and yet she is a remarkably unstudied political animal. We take her for granted, and we don't take her seriously. . . . The right depend on her but don't take her seriously for sexist reasons, and the left can't stand her and don't take her seriously for equally sexist reasons."[3] Political partisans who tend to support the existing social and political system are not likely to attract progressive-minded feminists. Those who, like Campbell, are interested in right-wing movements often search for signs of "abnormal" development to explain why certain groups failed to support the "correct" cause.

During the period from 1918 to 1929, the leaders of the Conservative Party created a successful mass organization for women, the WUO. The WUO was the largest, most active political organization in interwar Britain, and Conservative politicians were aware of its benefits to their party. In April 1921, there were already 1,340 women's branches in England and Wales; within a year there were more than two thousand. Attendance at WUO conferences increased from approximately four hundred at the first in 1919 to 2,314 by 1924 (by which time there were 4,067 WUO branches in England and Wales). Membership figures either were not kept regularly or were lost, but just in the southeast area of England there were 104,681 members (16 percent of voting women) in 1926. Other areas apparently boasted higher percentages of women voters in their branches. By the late 1920s, central office claimed that there were approximately one million WUO members. By contrast, at its peak in 1926 the Women's National Liberal Federation had only 919 branches with 88,000 members. The Labour Party was more successful, but had at most 250,000 members in 1,867 women's sections.[4]

The high membership figures demonstrate the Conservative Party's ability to attract women. By the end of the decade there was no question about the WUO's value. Chamberlain's 1931 investigation of the party's organization concluded that the WUO was an overwhelming success.[5] It became the most important organization contributing to the party's success in the interwar years. The WUO developed a network of local, regional, and national bodies that the Women's Department in central office aided with its staff of female speakers, organizers, and area agents. WUO branches carried out a wide range of political and social activities that both attracted members and gave substantial assistance to the Conservative cause. The organization provided a pleasant atmosphere for its primarily middle-class members, most of whom were wives and mothers. In their activities, members were guided by an enlarged understanding of women's roles even as they rejected feminism for home and family.

Development of the Conservative Women's Organization

In the creation of a strong organization for Conservative women, three women played decisive roles: Caroline Bridgeman, viscountess Elveden, and Marjorie Maxse. Bridgeman, the first head of the WUO, was reserved, but generally respected for her sense of duty, party loyalty, and organizational and speaking abilities. The regard in which male colleagues held Bridgeman helped reinforce the WUO's position in its early years. Like her husband, William, Caroline Bridgeman came from an ecclesiastical family and possessed a strong commitment to public service. During the war she had helped provide hospital care for soldiers and worked for the Women's Land Service Corps. Despite a respite from February 1919 to April 1921 because of poor health, Bridgeman served the WUO as chairwoman from its inception in 1918 until 1924. In recognition of her many contributions, she was made a D.B.E. in 1924, and in 1926 was elected the first chairwoman of the Council of the National Union of Conservative and Unionist Associations (NUCUA). A woman who regarded herself as her husband's adjutant, she withdrew from politics after he retired in 1929.

Gwendolen Guinness, viscountess Elveden (countess of Iveagh from 1927), served as WUO chairwoman from 1924 until 1933. Elveden (1881–1966) came from a political family. Her father, the earl of Onslow, was president of the Board of Agriculture under Balfour, and her sister married Edward Wood, third viscount Halifax. Elveden campaigned extensively on behalf of her husband, Rupert Guinness, heir to the Guinness interests and the earldom of Iveagh. With her excellent memory and hardy but lively personality, she was a better public speaker and organizer than her husband. She worked on behalf of the National Prisoners of War Fund (for which she was recognized in 1920 with a C.B.E.) and was interested in the farming industry and the Empire. After her husband succeeded to the Iveagh title in 1927, the countess was elected to his former seat of Southend. This burden, in addition to her new responsibilities for the Elveden estate, caused some worry that she was not devoting enough attention to her WUO duties. This concern notwithstanding, she was a popular and effective chairwoman. In 1930 she was appointed one of two deputy party chairmen, and after her resignation in 1933 she was made a vice-chairwoman of the NUCUA council, with responsibility for the WUO.[6]

The fact that the WUO continued to flourish despite Iveagh's other duties was due in part to the head of the central office Women's Department, Marjorie Maxse (1891–1975), who expanded and professionalized the central organization. Maxse came from a family of public servants; she was the cousin of both Leo Maxse, editor of the *National Review,* and General Sir Ivor Maxse, the distinguished World War I commander. During part of the war she worked in a French military hospital. In 1921 she joined the central office Women's Department and became the first WUO Administrator two years later. Maxse used her position to develop the WUO and the Women's Department. As a consequence of the 1927 Reorganisation Committee headed by Lord Edward Stanley, she was appointed deputy principal agent in spring 1928. This ensured that the WUO would have a powerful and secure place in central office, free from the excessive interference of the principal agent. It was also a recognition of the WUO's importance to the Conservative Party. From 1931 until her retirement in 1939, Maxse also assumed the position of central office's Chief Organisation Officer. Sir Geoffrey Shakespeare, the former minister and Maxse's colleague in postwar charitable work, recalled Maxse's organizing skills, steadiness, and determination to further the interests of the Conservative Party.[7]

The progress of the Women's Department reflected the growing importance of the WUO after 1918. Before the war the only women central office employed were clerical workers, but a 1928 list of staff shows fourteen female area and visiting agents and a dozen salaried female speakers and organizers. At first these women had much lower salaries than their male counterparts. Then in 1923 Mrs. Costello, a professional speaker, complained that she and her colleagues had no hope of rising above an annual salary of £150, roughly what a female clerk made, even though she was college educated and well trained as a lecturer and speaker. By 1928 Costello and the other women speakers were given raises bringing them up to the men's level. The hiring of additional staff, in addition to these raises, increased the budget of the Women's Department to nearly £12,000 in 1928. The most important members of the expanding department were the female area agents. They worked in tandem with the male agents to stimulate and broaden women's political interests while improving the women's organization in England and Wales.[8]

The Women's Department was also in charge of the monthly *Home and Politics,* which began as a four-page magazine in September 1920. When a regular eight-page party magazine, *Popular View,* appeared in May 1921, *Home and Politics* became the women's edition of this magazine. In June 1923, however, a NUA Executive subcommittee decided that *Home and Politics* should be published separately by a female editor. The magazine's circulation increased rapidly, passing 100,000 by the January 1925 issue and 200,000 by June 1927. In 1928, the last year before the general election, its annual circulation was greater than 2.5 million, more than twice that of the men's monthly, *Man in the Street*. In part the improvement was due to the "localisation" of the magazine by associations. In Wirral, for instance, attaching a local cover and inserting local news boosted circulation from a thousand to sixteen hundred copies monthly.[9] In March 1924 the party gazette, *Gleanings and Memoranda*, also began carrying a women's column.

Although some articles in *Home and Politics* were the same or very similar to those in other party magazines, there were differences. Wives of M.P.s or members of the House of Lords, WUO leaders, and women prominent in public life were often featured, though it was always pointed out that the home duties of these women were more important than their public activities. For example, the March 1923 cover rather unsubtly showed Lady Sykes and her newly christened baby, the grandchild of Andrew Bonar Law. Princess Mary and her son were on the cover of the next issue. Although the family-and-home ethos dominated the magazine, entertainment and opportunities for women were not excluded. The October 1928 issue contained several such new features, including a serialization (of *The Thirty-Nine Steps*) and a "Careers for Women" column. Too lighthearted an approach, however, was unacceptable. A column on housekeeping tips and fashion was begun in June 1923. It was rationalized by the claim that "the housewife always likes to look her best and to have her house attractive," but was withdrawn after some readers complained that the material was superficial.[10]

As the WUO expanded across Britain after World War I, there were clear signs that it was the most successful and active of the Conservative organizations. In April 1919 a full slate of WUO delegates was admitted to the NUA Executive, and in June women were voted onto the important publications and speakers subcommittees. During 1919 a women's advisory committee was formed in order to keep the NUA Executive "in complete touch with the Womens [sic] side of the Organization." Originally the committee comprised female members of the NUA Executive plus women chosen by the party leader or co-opted by the advisory committee. After the WUO began developing a network of regional or area committees in 1920, these also sent delegates.[11]

The key contribution of the WUO to the Conservative Party was its local organization, which enjoyed continued growth throughout the 1920s. As the Lloyd George coalition first disintegrated and then collapsed in

October 1922, the WUO expanded significantly. The number of WUO branches rose 71 percent, from 2,100 to 3,600, during the year preceding the WUO conference of May 1923. Unfortunately, most branches seem not to have kept or published membership figures. The progress of the Stockton branch, however, is better documented than most. It began with eighty members in 1921 and slowly grew to two hundred eighty in 1923. After the Conservative candidate Harold Macmillan's surprisingly good performance in 1923 and success in 1924, membership passed one thousand. The number of members was sixteen hundred in 1926 and reached nearly three thousand after the equal suffrage act of 1928. Branch income rose from seven pounds in 1921 to thirty-seven in 1924 and more than eighty in 1926, despite the depressed local economy. The information available for other branches indicates that the Stockton organization was fairly typical. The Oswestry WUO, for instance, recorded steady growth from 2,549 members in 1924 to more than 4,000 in 1929.[12]

Rarely were detailed records kept of the polling district and ward branches of the divisional WUOs. Bradford Conservatives noted with pride in 1921 that every ward in their city had a "strong and virile [!]" WUO branch with a total membership of thirteen hundred in the city. After less than two years of existence, the Oswestry WUO claimed twenty-three branches. Yet particularly in the rural or suburban divisions, some wards or districts did not have WUO branches. Among the rural seats in my sample, only the Wirral WUO could claim to cover the whole constituency, and this only after a central women's committee was formed in 1923. The Wirral WUO was so successful that it contributed more money to its parent association than any other women's branch in Cheshire, Lancashire, or Westmorland. Sparsely populated rural areas, where it was difficult to maintain a political organization, tended to have a greater number of small branches. Unlike their opposite numbers in the Labour Party, however, at least some WUO members had automobiles, which made organizing considerably easier. Branches varied in number of members from a handful in a village to several hundred in a county town or city ward. In 1926, the Launceston polling district branch had 500 members, and the Skipton town WUO, after re-forming and establishing a monthly social night, recorded a membership of 570.[13]

Although separate WUO branches were the norm in organizing Conservative women, women were linked to the parent constituency associations by numerous means. In some cases—this was the prevailing model in Scotland—they simply joined the existing male branches and divisional associations. More commonly women created separate divisional branches and sub-branches that paralleled the existing male organization. Men and women then formed a joint divisional executive committee. In 1924, for instance, the Stockton WUO was "amalgamated" with the men's association to reduce expenses and duplication of work. In fact, this meant the creation of a joint executive, as the women retained their own officers. Most common were separate women's organizations that elected representatives to the executive committee of the male divisional associations, the de facto parent association. Arrangements at the district or ward level depended on local wishes and feasibility, particularly the number of potential members.[14]

As men gradually accepted the WUO branches, cooperation between men and women improved. In areas where women did not form separate branches, they usually established their own committees or councils, in some cases hiring women organizers. In North Cornwall, Conservative women, who had their own sub-branches, established a women's committee in 1925. With the assistance of the new M.P. and the men's association, the committee hired a woman organizer. Two years later the women formed a more formal women's council. Developments in Scotland also demonstrate the combination of autonomy and cooperation. Wary of prewar difficulties with women's groups, the Scottish Unionist Association (SUA) decided in 1918 to integrate women into the men's associations. Nevertheless, the next year the SUA Eastern Division hired a woman organizer, Jeanette Martin. There were worries that this would lead to "the old troublesome separation," and Martin was instructed to consult local officials at all times. The arrangement worked so well, however, that in December 1924 two assistant women organizers were hired. All were to be paid by the women's subcommittee established in 1923.[15]

In the Scottish constituencies women could already form their own committees, and in many cases the committees maintained separate financial accounts. During its reorganization in 1923, the Kincardine association authorized the formation of a women's canvassing subcommittee that gradually assumed responsibilities for most women's concerns. Camlachie Unionists went even further, deciding to reorganize the women's subcommittee as a "women's branch" in 1926. Some Unionists remained skeptical of such autonomy. This was a factor (money was another) both in the decision of the Kincardine Unionists not to appoint a woman organizer in 1928 and in the curtailment of the SUA women's organization. After Jeanette Martin resigned in 1929, the work of the women organizers was restricted, and the SUA Eastern Division women's subcommittee ceased to meet regularly. A woman adviser continued, however, to oversee speakers and maintain contact with local women's groups.[16]

WUO Activities

WUO branches carried out a wider range of political, educational, and social activities than their parent (or men's) associations. During one meeting of the Wrexham WUO, the executive discussed obtaining its own offices, ordering a thousand copies of *Home and Politics* to be sold by branches, organizing a trip to London, holding a fete at the home of the president and chairwoman, Mrs. Ethel FitzHugh, and planning a fundraising bazaar. As the 1928 SUA Annual Report pointed out, women's contributions were essential to the Conservative Party: "Women electors view their responsibilities seriously and show keen interest in general political questions, throwing themselves heartily into . . . organising, canvassing, speaking, and other political work, thus rendering good, efficient, and loyal service to the Party."[17]

The WUO did not, however, sponsor female candidates. There were few women candidates for the House of Commons. Their numbers grew during the 1920s, but amounted to only 4 percent of the total in 1929. Between 1918 and 1929 there were only forty female Conservative candidates; thirteen were elected. Although the Conservatives put forward the fewest women candidates, their rate of success was considerably higher than that of Liberal or Labour women candidates. The number of Conservative women M.P.s nearly equaled Labour's—and surpassed the Liberal Party's—but the paucity of female candidates was a concern within the party. Delegates to the 1921 NUA conference heartily recommended increasing the number of women candidates. In her speech supporting the resolution, Lady Astor, the first woman to enter the House of Commons, attacked the prejudices that kept women from contributing their talents to Parliament. Sir George Younger, the party chairman, pointed out that selection was the prerogative of constituency associations, which were reluctant to choose women. At the 1923 WUO conference the principal agent, Sir Reginald Hall, made the same point.[18]

Most of the reasons for the small number of women M.P.s are straightforward. Although less a problem in the Conservative Party than in Labour, the biggest obstacle to women was that they were often chosen for the most difficult seats. Women were less willing or able to spend years campaigning in hopeless seats before being selected for safer ones. And fewer women than men became candidates in part because fewer wanted political office or were able to devote enough attention to politics because of responsibilities at home. Some felt that women could not command the voters' respect. Finally, many women simply did not have the financial resources to pay election expenses and subsidize the local associations. For instance, Dame Helen Gwynne-Vaughan, a former commandant of the Women's Royal Air Force, was able to contest a Labour seat in Camberwell only because of the assistance of the Conservative London Municipal Society.[19]

Although not supporting great numbers of them in Parliament, the Conservative Party did depend on women to maintain its position in local government. At the 1923 NUA conference, two delegates emphasized that Conservatives were not among the "shrieking sisterhood" of irrational, emotional women. Women, they argued, could govern sanely and justly without resorting to "grandmotherly legislation." The expense of local elections was much lower and could be covered by the association's fund raising. In addition, local government seemed to suit the many women who were especially concerned with domestic issues. WUO members prized experience in local government, and such experience legitimized the role of women. Mrs. Annie Arnold, for instance, was probably chosen as the first chairwoman of the Bradford WUO because she was a city councillor. The role of Conservative women in local government has been an enduring one: Hills estimates that in the 1970s nearly one-quarter of Conservative local government candidates were women, compared to one in eight for Labour.[20]

The WUO's main political contribution was not providing candidates for office but carrying out the work of mass politics. Women routinely handled the thousands of polling cards, envelopes, and other materials that had to be circulated—often at short notice—in elections. The *Conservative Agents' Journal* admitted that such activities' success "stands or falls on . . . whether or not there is a good women's organisation in the constituency." If not for women, agents would have been forced to hire extra staff and rely upon more expensive bulk mailings. The most important work of WUO members, however, was canvassing and the distribution of literature. By the mid-1920s, members were experienced and systematic in their work. Female activists' method of canvassing was described in detail at the 1924 conference of the Primrose League. Younger, less experienced women went from house to house, distributing literature and noting voters' intentions on canvassing cards. Supporters were encouraged and supplied with literature. Seasoned workers then spoke to all voters marked as doubtful; if there was time, they attempted to win over opponents as well. Women distributed a great deal of party literature. During a municipal election in Glasgow, one women's branch handed out twenty thousand leaflets. Within hours after the North Cornwall association suddenly adopted a candidate during the 1923 election and scheduled a rally in Launceston, the local WUO branch had distributed fourteen hundred handbills around the town.[21]

The object of canvassing was as much to bring voters into contact with the Conservative Party and present a positive image of the party as to obtain information. Consequently, it was important, as Caroline Bridgeman emphasized at a meeting of the Oswestry WUO, to call on all voters and listen to their concerns. Keeping in touch with voters and addressing questions as they arose, Bridgeman told another meeting, depended on women using their talent for "talking to the voters sympathetically." Harold Macmillan noted in his autobiography that Lady Dorothy Cavendish became an expert canvasser in Stockton because she, though an aristocrat, had "the art of being natural, simple, and a little humble." Agents recognized that WUO branches were vital to canvassing because of their ability to tackle issues and get information from voters.[22]

In addition to propaganda and canvassing, Conservative women devoted much effort to educating fellow members and voters. WUO branches devoted so much attention to the education of members and others that the annual reports of the SUA dealt with education in a section entitled "Women's Work." WUO members seem to have liked educational work because they preferred to avoid public confrontation and rhetoric. Many Conservatives asserted, as the Wood Green agent said, that "if properly taught the principals [sic] of constitutionalism the large majority of woman [sic] would vote for constitutional government, [because] they were essentially patriotic and full of love for home life and the true welfare of the Country." In *Home and Politics* the WUO tried to teach Conservative ideals and warn readers of the dangers facing Britain. During the years immediately following women's enfranchisement, the WUO was especially active in distributing leaflets that propounded the Conservative or traditional point of view on the constitution and contemporary issues.[23]

Many WUO branches had educational facilities. In 1920 the GUA women's committee instituted Wednesday afternoon lectures so successful

that they continued throughout the decade. Over time the limited curriculum of economics, politics, and constitutional history was expanded to incorporate more contentious matters such as social reform and women's
issues. Lectures on housing proved especially popular. Typically a local notable or the women's area agent spoke to an audience of women about
current political issues, particularly social questions. In 1925 the Kincardine
women's committee arranged for Jeanette Martin to give talks across their
division. Martin followed her afternoon seminars on organization with political discussions and, in the evening, a public address. In North Cornwall
two hundred women (and their children) attended a meeting of the Launceston WUO in autumn 1925. There they met the M.P.'s wife and looked at
materials for an Empire food campaign. Then a speaker gave a talk about
socialism, the recent Widows and Orphans Pensions Act, and the need for
lower workers' wages to speed home construction. The meeting concluded
with a recipe for eggless Christmas pudding and a rendition of "God Save
the King." Two years later the branch organized a circle to study communism, education, trade unionism, and other current topics.[24]

Women went to Conservative conferences, "schools of study," and the
Conservative Party College (initially located near Northampton) to receive
a more thorough education. Women delegates often considered party conferences educational experiences. Almost half the delegates sent by constituency associations to NUA conferences were women; a majority of them
were not officers and attended only one conference.[25] Delegates had a sense
that they were involved in real political discussions as they shared information and experiences. One representative described the conference as "the
happiest time of her life." On their return home delegates shared their
knowledge, sometimes providing detailed reports of the meetings and
discussions.[26]

In late 1923 the SUA Eastern Division established schools of study in a
few locations. Women from the area around each school enrolled for two
to four days of intensive instruction. The inexpensive schools were popular,
helping to awaken interest and educate organizers. By the end of 1925, they
had spread across Scotland, and one advanced school in Edinburgh was
giving courses on foreign policy and international trade. Some WUO area
committees in England and Wales also organized schools, but many more
women attended courses at the Conservative College. By 1928 there were
nearly six hundred women attending the college.[27]

The WUO's large political role grew in part from its success in organizing the social activities that did so much to make the interwar Conservative Party a popular organization. At WUO branch meetings, women could socialize as they enjoyed inexpensive tea and snacks. This practice carried over into the parent (or men's) associations, which before the war had been limited to political activities—interspersed with smoking concerts and club activities. In the 1920s Conservative associations instituted "American teas" (rummage sales), whist drives, garden parties, dances, group outings, and other activities. Social functions drew new members and helped keep old ones because they were an enjoyable way to meet the M.P. or candidate and learn about Conservatism. A single beach outing organized by the Wrexham WUO in 1923 attracted nine hundred people. And although membership dues did produce revenue, social events were better at fund raising. In January 1929, for instance, the Bradford Central WUO made £37 from their raffle and annual dance.[28]

The epitome of branch activity in the 1920s was a whist drive and summer garden party at the home of a local notable. Both activities could be profitable. A branch in Wrexham, for instance, made nearly £17 from a whist drive. This card game was also popular because competitors could win prizes. And for a fee of only a shilling or two, women could enjoy several entertaining hours with friends or spouses. Mixed socials were used to attract members, and at least one women's association adopted evening whist tournaments so that men would come.[29] Both garden parties and whist drives were far more attractive to WUO members than the smoking concerts and clubs popular in the old Unionist Party.

A strong social life also provided opportunities for propagating Conservatism and strengthening the WUO. At a 1925 dance and whist drive in Bradford Central, for instance, Sir Anthony Gadie spoke about the government's successes in foreign policy, pension reform, and safeguarding. Because social gatherings also served to integrate people from different classes and backgrounds, many associations tried to keep admission fees low enough to attract members of the lower-middle and working classes. Association officers, M.P.s, and their spouses donated money and prizes or officiated at events. Allowing children to attend made it possible for more mothers to come, and this tactic undoubtedly brought more women into the Conservative Party. Once it became accepted practice to rely on women to organize Conservative socials, WUO branches profited financially and developed more esprit de corps. The *Conservative Agents' Journal* admitted in 1925 that women were essential for social events and suggested that

WUO branches receive their "fair share of the proceeds." Meanwhile, in their party work WUO members learned management and leadership, characteristics not usually encouraged in women.[30]

The WUO and the Party

Despite women's success, there was friction between the WUO and the rest of the Conservative Party. The most important causes of tension were Conservative clubs, female organizers, and the relationship of WUO branches to divisional associations. With few exceptions, members of the prewar clubs were men. The integration of women into local associations brought the clubs under female scrutiny since a great deal of party activity took place in clubs, the social center of local conservatism and often the headquarters of the organization. In 1922 the secretary of the Association of Conservative Clubs (ACC), Frank Solbe, argued strongly against women's admission into clubs. According to him, clubs would have to undertake expensive renovations and their camaraderie would be destroyed. He further asserted that separate women's clubs would be hard to sustain— women would not drink enough to make them profitable. Instead Solbe encouraged clubs to lease a room—maybe just for afternoons—in which women could meet separately.[31]

As a rule women, although they could use the facilities, were not welcome in clubs. There were exceptions, however. The Launceston Constitutional Club had already begun accepting women by 1922, and the local WUO had access to some rooms (it was unable to secure their exclusive use). When neighboring clubs expanded their facilities, WUO branches received rooms. An unusual situation obtained in the Cornish town of Camelford, where the club's rules were changed to admit women as full members, forbid gambling and drinking, and offer members tea, whist, and lectures.[32]

Men's reluctance to admit women into their clubs led some women to try to establish their own. The Chichester Social and Conservative Club for women was formed in 1924. Soon two hundred members were attending Friday gatherings featuring addresses, music, and the ubiquitous tea. In Edinburgh the SUA formed a luncheon club for young women; in Birmingham Mrs. Neville Chamberlain developed a strong women's club movement; so-called Fuchsia clubs were formed in some areas of London. Elsewhere—most notably in Wrexham—WUO branches were unable to form women's clubs. The club problems prompted the Bromley agent, Lieutenant Colonel Walter a Beckett, to propose at the 1925 NUA conference that separate women's clubs be formed. The resolution passed by only a small majority. Beckett later raised the matter in an article for the *Conservative Agents' Journal.* He argued that women could sustain clubs with fund raising and dues. After less than a year, the women's club in his division had hundreds of members, and he urged other agents to act before women joined other parties. In Beckett's view, clubs aided women's work and served as "a fitting, official recognition of their constant and untiring work for the cause."[33]

Another source of tension between the WUO and the rest of the party was the position of women organizers. Their number rose rapidly during the 1920s, striking terror into the hearts of some Conservative agents. In September 1923 the editor of the *Conservative Agents' Journal,* Elton Halliley, argued that the question of women organizers "affect[ed] the very foundations of all organisation," because by setting up an authority in the division separate from the agent and the main association, it raised the specter of an independent women's organization. Halliley's editorial generated considerable comment. One writer pointed out that an experienced and tactful agent could easily monitor inexperienced female secretaries. Other agents, however, demanded action, and the National Society of Conservative Agents expressed its concern to the WUO. The principal agent, Sir Reginald Hall, pointed out in a circular to the associations that first, both the agent and the female organizer were under the constituency association's supervision. Second, the WUO posed little threat of disunity, since the female central office agents, unlike their male counterparts, were almost exclusively concerned with organizational details. The Women's Department, Hall emphasized, "is not a woman's movement in any way, nor does it seek to obtain or divert funds for feminist purposes; neither has it ever been the idea of any Central Office Woman Agent to advocate the appointment of Women Agents."[34]

The question of women organizers again caused concern in 1926 and 1927, when a National Association of Conservative and Unionist Women Organisers attempted to form. The project was eventually shelved, in part because it again raised thorny questions about women's position in the Conservative Party. In 1926 the National Society of Conservative Agents recommended that its provincial unions admit full-time, paid women organizers as associate members. Several unions rejected the proposal, however, and women organizers attending the 1927 WUO conference decided to form separate bodies wherever the male provincial unions did not accept them. On the one hand, these problems show, as Sylvia Pankhurst argued, that party officials could be obstacles to women's progress. On the other, it demonstrates that the Conservative Party was gradually accepting professional women workers. A further indication of this change was the examination for women organizers given in January 1928. Half of the more than two dozen applicants passed the test to become the first female organizers certified by any party. Since then the number of female agents has increased, and today one-third of Conservative agents are women.[35]

The third major source of controversy concerning the WUO was whether its branches should be separate or combined with the men's organization. The columns of the *Conservative Agents' Journal* show that this issue worried many agents because their positions depended on the authority they exercised over the whole constituency organization. In 1918 central office recommended the formation of separate WUO branches linked to the parent or men's association by a joint executive committee. Addressing his colleagues in East Anglia, an agent presented the case in favor of such an arrangement: "Women require a different type of speaker, different arguments, different methods of propaganda. Separate Associations should produce a spirit of rivalry, and healthy rivalry generally proves a mutual stimulus, creates more interest, gives greater vitality, means better work, and secures more funds; and what people can be induced to pay for, they will generally work for. The Central [constituency] Association of which the Agent is Secretary must be the controlling power; the women must have full liberty in the internal management of their own Associations; but in ideals, and in policy, there must be no dividing line. In all essentials UNITY: in non essentials LIBERTY: and in all things CHARITY."[36] Rules could not create such a model organization, however, and differences continued.

In summer 1920 the central office chief organizing agent, Leigh Maclachlan, and the Northwest Area agent, Robert Topping, sparked a long-running debate in the *Conservative Agents' Journal* over the relationship between the WUO and the rest of the organization. Maclachlan argued that neither control nor unity of command was endangered by the WUO as long as it did not have a separate role in policy making or election management. By segregating men and women, however, the Conservative Party would get more members, more money, and more activity. Women needed their own groups, Maclachlan argued, in order to accommodate their routines and satisfy their distinct interests and attitudes. Failure to recognize this, he added, would alienate women, who might then join other parties or nonpartisan groups.[37]

Robert Topping quickly published a critique of Maclachlan's analysis. Topping accepted the establishment of women's sections in each association in order to make meetings convenient and encourage discussion, but he thought that an independent organization posed a grave danger to the unity of local parties. The reform act of 1918 had made men's and women's positions legislatively equal. Gender segregation would be counterproductive, would encourage feminist attitudes and give rise to conflicts over policy, candidate selection, and other matters in which unity was essential. Far from being healthy, Topping claimed the existence of an independent women's group spurred the "most dangerous of all rivalry—women versus men."[38]

The articles by Maclachlan and Topping did not go unnoticed. One agent agreed with Maclachlan, provided that each division had only one agent and that the men's chairman had exclusive control during elections. The overriding aim was to educate women voters, he wrote, and this could best be achieved if women were autonomous: "They want to learn much about politics; this we see and hear on all sides, but they want to learn in a simple, direct manner specially suited to their needs, their instincts, their own view of life, a method which would not appeal to many men's associations. Their enthusiasm too, so marked and so telling, differs widely from any enthusiasm shown by men, that 'sixth' sense which they possess—intuition—is also far better realised and utilised in a separate system, and above all—and this is an all-important point—they will be far readier to provide efficient workers ... than if there were but one Association." In contrast, another contributor pointed out that many areas that had had independent women's branches before 1918 were opting for joint associations. A woman organizer countered that the "eminently feminine trait which makes women take a special pride and interest in furthering the cause of something which they manage 'on their own'" would be crushed if there were joint associations.[39]

To guide participants toward a consensus, the editor of the *Conservative Agents' Journal* suggested as a model the typical household and its accepted gender roles:

> The husband and wife discuss their joint affairs, but he
> would be a foolish man indeed who would interfere with
> his wife's discretion or initiative, or meddle with those

> details of the home which a wife is perfectly capable of at-
> tending to on her own responsibility. . . . In the constitu-
> ency, as in the home, there should be for the well-being of
> the whole two separate working departments, the details
> of their individual management being entrusted to the care
> of those best fitted by temperament or training to deal with
> them. Interest a woman in the details of personal responsi-
> bility and management in her own home, and we all know
> how happy the result can be; interest women in the care of
> their own political home, and the trust will be repaid a
> thousandfold.[40]

In 1924 the WUO again came under scrutiny as a result of the disastrous tariff election of 1923 and the increasing number of women organizers. The newly appointed WUO Administrator, Marjorie Maxse, assured
London agents in April 1924 that the WUO wanted "to teach women to be
voters and Conservative voters, not to create a feminist movement within
the Conservative Party." In a short but cogent article that appeared a few
months later in the *Conservative Agents' Journal,* she claimed that fusion of
men and women's associations demoralized the women, reduced WUO
membership, and decreased the quality and quantity of the organization's
work. She ridiculed fears of disunity and conflict that resulted from "the
inability to realise that woman is a reasoning being just as anxious to serve
her party as a man, and with no desire to take but to give. And the reluctance to give women the responsibility of organising women, and of providing them with a legitimate sphere for their aspirations, has lost to the
Conservative Party large numbers of active workers whose influence might
have materially affected the issue. This attitude of distrust has done incal-
culable harm to our party, and has helped to swell the ranks of that legion
of non-party and feminist organisations where women feel they will make
their voice heard and their influence felt."[41]

Maxse's exposition was supported by Halliley, who recommended that
his fellow agents do everything possible to cultivate those women's
branches linked to men's organizations by joint executive committees. To
calm the agents Maxse also agreed to send them copies of all notices and
circulars issued to local WUO officers. The debate did not cease in 1924,
but women's invaluable and loyal work over the years and the success of
the party in the 1924 election allayed fears. Gradually agents realized that
autonomous women's branches enhanced the associations' revenue and

output. Agents and male officers accepted the WUO's independence, allowing Women's Department officials to encourage female volunteers to feel that they were vital to the party's progress. By the later 1920s most agents recognized that the WUO and the other party organizations did not undermine their authority so much as increase it by placing "an army corps of voluntary workers" in their hands. Agents signaled their acceptance of the WUO by allowing its branches to hire organizers, and by 1927 nine-tenths of WUO divisional associations had their own organizers.[42]

Although the WUO and the Women's Department strove to maintain autonomous responsibility over the women voters, for practical reasons there was a great deal of cooperation with other elements of the party. Many people continued to hold reactionary views on gender that shaped relations between the WUO and the rest of the party. Some Conservatives appraised women and their activities in ways indicating that they viewed women as flawed men. In the *Conservative Agents' Journal*, one agent wrote that women were so affected by their "senses" that they voted according to the physical attractiveness of candidates. Some central office officials, including Maclachlan, chief organizing agent and then principal agent from 1920 to 1928, did not fully appreciate women's contribution. Agents sometimes used WUO organizers for menial tasks and resented women's "too prominent part." This attitude was not appreciated by women, who considered their work of equal (and possibly greater) value than men's. Consequently, disagreements over the relationship between the WUO and the rest of the Conservative organization persisted.[43]

In Stockton, gender segregation sometimes made it difficult for the parent or men's association to find out women's views. For instance, during 1923 there were problems with the selection of a candidate and a dispute over some property in the association offices. After a joint executive committee was formed in 1924, the Stockton men seemed to accept greater cooperation—especially since the women did much of the work. Initially WUO members only lightly chided the men. As the next general election neared, however, they became less accommodating and resolved, "There should be more co-operation between the officers of the men's section and themselves than hitherto. It was felt that the men are leaving the greater part of the work to the women and that they are not doing as much as they should in the General Work of the Election." Similar problems arose in Chichester, where WUO branches did much of the work—and provided much of the association's funds. There women sometimes complained about male sloth, one WUO executive threatening to resign in 1922 because of it. When twin independent men and women's associations were replaced by autonomous branches in 1926, the new rules allowed any Conservative who paid a small subscription to join. Because there were more female than male members, some men complained that they would be "swamped" by the women.[44]

There was no easy solution to the tensions within the Conservative Party, because they grew from accepted gender roles. Antagonism gradually subsided during the 1920s, as the WUO strenuously avoided feminism and men accepted a greater role for women. The clearest indication of women's progress in the Conservative Party was their increased responsibility and power. They were, for example, given equality of representation. In 1926 seven men and women each were chosen for the executive committee of the Clapham association. Sometimes the practice was simplified by selecting married couples. Women were even admitted to the elite finance and management subcommittees that supervised day-to-day operations. Women began attending the finance and general purposes committees of the Kincardine association and the Yorkshire Provincial Division in the mid-1920s. From its incorporation in 1919, the Wrexham WUO held several places on the finance and management subcommittee of the main association, although women did not have equal representation. Occasionally there were setbacks. In 1924 the composition of the management subcommittee in Skipton was altered to include only the most prestigious and active leaders of the association, all of them men.[45]

At the district and ward levels, women's growing power was even clearer. Since branches were smaller, men and women often formed joint bodies. As women became more confident and more numerous, they also became more active. A good example of this development, although it falls outside the period discussed in this book, involves the Penycae branch in Wrexham. Within a year and a half of its formation in May 1929, the membership of the branch contained more women than men, and shortly thereafter Edmund Wright stepped down as chairman in favor of Mrs. Thomas, who assumed the title "Madam Chairman." Less obvious, but nonetheless notable, were the increasingly frequent contributions women made in mixed gatherings. By the mid-1920s, for instance, it was common for women members of the conservative council in Bradford to propose and second candidates for offices and to take part in discussions of policy or organization. In contrast to the prewar situation, men in the 1920s were learning to work with their female colleagues.[46]

Contrary to the view of some feminist historians that women's suffrage produced very disappointing results, Conservative appreciation of the WUO and of women meant that the party paid them special attention.[47] A common theme of Conservative campaigns throughout the 1920s—security, safety, and peace—was intended to appeal to women. Bonar Law's brief election address in 1922, which doubled as the party manifesto, stated the nation's "crying need [for] tranquillity and stability." Caroline Bridgeman echoed this in *Home and Politics*, promising voters peace abroad, goodwill at home, and a steady administration. By appealing to morality, order, prosperity, and peace, the Conservatives claimed to offer women an opportunity to reject "politics" and restore domestic bliss.[48]

This positive message was coupled with negative, antisocialist claims. In leaflets like "The Danger of the Class War" and "Call a Spade a Spade and the 'Labour' Party also by Its Proper Name—'Socialist,'" happy families were threatened by dirty, bearded, scowling bomb-throwers. In other words, a vote for Labour was a vote for revolution and class warfare. Such claims were routinely made. Even during the tariff election of 1923, many Conservative candidates pointed to the socialist bogey. Sir Henry Keith, the candidate for Camlachie, claimed, "Behind the [Labour] party the driving force is revolutionary propaganda and irreligious socialism. The[ir] aim . . . is to disintegrate society, to banish religion, and destroy the sanctity of family life." During the 1924 campaign, Conservative literature informed women that Bolsheviks would treat them and their children like cattle. They also claimed that divorce, abortion, prostitution, and child molestation were common in the Soviet Union.[49]

Except in 1923, when they offered tariffs rather than security, the Conservatives were usually able to appeal to women voters. Concerned about the potential effect of protectionism on women voters, Conservative literature tried to reassure them that there would be no new food duties. The Conservative manifesto of 1923 also promised lower sugar and tea duties. At the same time, central office leaflets like "Protection Means a Full Purse," and "Where's the Sunday Dinner?" denied that food would be expensive and emphasized that protection would lead to a stable home life by creating jobs for men. As the wife of one Conservative candidate argued in an amendment to her husband's election address, "Work is the first essential for the happiness of our family life." Finally central office developed a series of leaflets that some small newspapers also carried. "Over the Garden Wall" consisted of rather stilted conversations between a WUO

Table 1
Conservative Vote in Constituencies with (1) More and (2) Less than Average-Sized Female Electorates

Constituencies	Conservative Vote in Each Election (%)					
	1918	1922	1923	1924	1929	Average
1. More female voters	61.3	56.2	42.4	55.4	45.4	52.1
2. Fewer female voters	61.1	42.2	41.6	52.3	40.5	47.5

member, Mrs. Brown, and her neighbor, Mrs. Jones. The leaflets tried to persuade housewives and mothers to support tariffs that would create a more secure and prosperous home life.[50]

An analysis of election results from 1918 to 1929 shows that the "safety first" theme probably worked, but protectionism alienated many women. Table 1 divides the constituency sample into two groups of six, representing seats with higher (group 1) and lower (group 2) than average proportions of women voters. Group 1 constituencies averaged a Conservative vote more than 4 percent higher than did those in group 2. Group 1 seats also often had more middle-class or rural voters, who tended to vote Conservative in any case. Turner argues that both class and gender were important to constituency results; it is difficult to know which was more significant.[51]

Conservatives were apparently able to draw women voters in the original "safety first" campaign of 1922, but not in the tariff election of 1923. In 1922 the average Conservative poll in group 1 divisions was about 56 percent, compared to 42 percent for group 2 ones. This was the largest gap in the five elections between 1918 and 1929. In 1923 the Conservative vote in group 1 divisions fell dramatically to slightly more than 42 percent, though dropping only slightly in group 2 divisions. The different results can be attributed partly to the more frequent three-way contests in group 1 seats. But even group 1 seats with the same number of candidates in 1922 and 1923 (Clapham, Chichester, Skipton, and Bradford Central) showed pronounced decreases in support for the Conservatives. Group 1 constituencies also tended to be among suburban and middle-class divisions. Nationwide such divisions overwhelmingly rejected protectionism in 1923.

Although their role remains unclear, many Conservatives blamed women for the outcome of the 1923 election. Before the election, Austen Chamberlain warned his brother that protection was risky and might panic women, who tended to focus on household costs. After the election

Younger, the former party chairman, claimed, "It is the women who have done it. They have been frightened by the stories of dearer food, . . . and have swung right over." Other Conservatives challenged this interpretation. Caroline Bridgeman pointed out that protection was rejected before the war—when women did not have the vote. In any case, she stated, Conservative leaders should have recognized the party's dependence on women. Her colleague, Lady Frances Balfour, reiterated this point in a *Home and Politics* article: "It is not particularly useful to shout, 'We fell because the woman voted wrong.' That element of how women will vote is one of the things which must be taken into account in all future calculations. If that had been foreseen, other counsels might have prevailed. So much for the women who are in fault with the party who have lost in the gamble. Does anyone think of the seats lost, kept, or won by the women's vote—if people will still insist on separating the sheep from the goats?" Lady Astor and the editor of the *Conservative Agents' Journal* agreed wholeheartedly with Balfour.[52]

In the following year a high turnout among women may have helped the Conservatives win. Whether this is true or not, Conservative women were happy to credit their gender and the WUO for the party's triumph, repudiating earlier criticisms. After 1923, Conservative leaders did not repeat the mistake of offering tariffs to women voters. Protectionism was not mentioned, and imperialism took a back seat in Conservative literature, as central office limited its imperial appeal to exhorting women to buy products from the Empire. In 1926, for instance, the WUO published the *Empire Cookery Book*, which included more than seventy recipes using imperial products.[53]

In addition to the emphasis on safety first, the party also tried to lure women with promises of social reform. In 1922 Conservative candidates, recognizing popular discontent over overcrowding in many large cities, were very careful to mention social reforms, particularly housing, in their addresses. The 1922 *Campaign Guide* also detailed the party's views on housing and its claim to have inaugurated housing policy with the slum-clearance legislation of the late nineteenth century. The housing issue, however, became more prominent because in 1920, even as a serious shortage loomed, the government loosened rent controls and allowed rents to rise. Women suffered most from this change. In many areas, for example, Strathclyde in Scotland, they spearheaded agitation against rising rents. During the election Bonar Law even went to Glasgow and promised to investigate the matter.[54]

In later elections the Conservatives continued to use social reform to draw women's support. After the disastrous election of 1923, Conservative leaders carefully crafted the "Statement of Principles and Aims" in their program, *Looking Ahead* (1924), to appeal to women. The party offered a scheme of integrated pensions during the 1924 election that became the Widows, Orphans, and Old Age Pensions Act of 1925. The act expanded and integrated existing insurance schemes, creating compulsory or "all-in" and contributory insurance. Under the legislation, widows, dependent children, and orphans of individuals insured for health received pensions by right. Old-age pensions were bestowed on all men and their wives at age sixty-five instead of seventy. During the campaign, Conservatives also pointed to the success of Neville Chamberlain's Housing Act of 1923, which had led to the construction of 150,000 homes by private companies at half the cost to taxpayers as Labour's Housing Act (1924). Again appealing to women voters, the 1924 Conservative manifesto promised to create a royal commission to study rising food costs. A food council was in fact established by the Board of Trade. It promulgated guidelines for reasonable pricing, though it had no enforcement power.[55]

The Ethos of Conservative Women

The Conservative appeal to female voters and the growing cooperation between the sexes were largely due to the ethos of Conservative women, who avoided "sex antagonisms" and accepted a subordinate (although larger) role. By the late 1920s men had recognized, as Maxse pointed out in the *Conservative Agents' Journal,* that "there was no organisation of women today which is less 'feminist' than the Women's Unionist Organisation." The Conservative junior minister, the duchess of Atholl, told a WUO meeting in 1926 that they should take pride in their particular contribution: "They must not be ashamed of doing little things and doing them faithfully, when working on behalf of a great cause. They could not coerce men to attend to the little details of a great campaign, and it would be a dreary world if men were to do exactly the things which the women did. Let them continue working systematically and thoroughly, believing if they kept on steadily, and quietly, and effectively, they should ensure an ever-increasing measure of cooperation from the men." During the interwar period women of all parties suppressed feminist tendencies in favor of loyalty to their party. In *Women and the Labour Party* (1918), Henderson specifically attacked "feminist agitation . . . which tended to emphasise . . . sex-antagonisms." Like their Conservative counterparts, Labour women were expected to arrange meetings, prepare refreshments, and carry out other mundane tasks. In the Labour movement, the emphasis had long been on the home as men's haven from work.[56]

The position of women in the Conservative Party was based on the Victorian notion of separate gender spheres. At the core of this ideology was an emphasis on women's childbearing, nurturing, and civilizing tasks. As Frances Cobbe wrote, "So *immense* are the claims on a Mother, physical claims on her bodily and brain vigor, and moral claims on her heart and thoughts, that she cannot, I believe, meet them all, and find any large margin beyond for other cares and work. She serves the community in the very best and highest way it is possible to do, by giving birth to healthy children. . . . This is her *Function*. . . . No higher can found; and in my judgment it is a misfortune . . . when a woman . . . is lured by any generous ambition to add . . . any other systematic work; either as breadwinner to the family, or as philanthropist or politician." Before 1914, some Conservatives believed that women could be politically active, but only in a subordinate, "female" role. In an 1890 speech to the Ladies Grand Council of the Primrose League, one of the leading women in the organization, Lady Jersey, described the division of political labor that derived from innate gender differences: "We don't wish to govern the country. Our efforts tend towards two things. We want, so far as lies in our power, to assist in placing men in the Government who we think will lead our country in the paths of peace and prosperity—and we want to lead all who come within the sphere of our influence and to bring up our children in those principles of religion and devotion to their country and of patriotism which will make them good men, and therefore, good citizens."[57]

Most Victorian Unionists believed that any transgression of women's "natural" role would utterly destroy first femininity and then masculinity. In 1893 the Reverend Whitwell Elwin wrote to the teenage granddaughter of Bulwer-Lytton, "The gentleness, the tenderness, the refinement, the delicacy of a woman are her charm, and the traits to which she owes the chivalrous homage of the man. He is bound to treat with courteous deference the soft graces which demand his protection as well as his admiration. But when the woman apes the action of the man her claim upon his chivalry is gone. She has come down from her eminence, and has converted herself into an inferior and very trumpery sort of man. Nothing out of nature pleases. A masculine woman is a deformity." Women who accepted their femininity, with its limitations, would be admired and protected by men. Such views on gender remained intact in the early twentieth century. The antisuffrage poster "Always Make Room for a Lady," depicted hysterical, aggressive women and a petticoated man. After receiving a prosuffrage delegation in 1910, Asquith complained to his Cabinet colleagues that its only male delegate, Charles MacLaren, was effeminate. Sir Almoth Wright, a leading antisuffragist, pointed out that politicizing women would confuse gender roles and create "one vast cock-and-hen show."[58]

Most prewar suffragists and female activists accepted the notion of separate spheres and gender differences but wanted to enlarge woman's role because her special character and knowledge were needed to deal with Britain's social problems. In 1913, Mrs. Emmeline Pankhurst wrote that she wanted to give "a larger meaning to those duties which have been women's duties since the race began. . . . After all, home is a very, very big thing, indeed. . . . [It] is . . . everybody in the nation." Before 1914, women who participated in philanthropic or political work were ultimately most concerned with the family and the moral condition of society. In such prewar conservative groups as the Girls' Friendly Society, members were also motivated by the hope of maintaining social and political arrangements. Next to the Primrose League, the Girls' Friendly Society was the largest Conservative women's group, with about 250,000 members by 1913. Rather than bestow insurance benefits like their male trade unionist counterparts, the Girls' Friendly Society provided moral guidance and instruction to girls and young women. Members tried to integrate them into the existing system in part by presenting the British nation as a sort of extended family. This approach depended on a deference that was rapidly disappearing; the organization never engaged in partisan politics.[59]

The emphasis on family and the notion of separate spheres permeated the Conservative women's movement after the war. Normally these ideas were unarticulated, but occasionally they were expounded with some clarity. In 1922 Edythe Glanville, a member of the NUA Executive, wrote an article for *Home and Politics*, "Eve and the New Age." She asserted: "Men and women are the poles of society; they are opposite, but not opposed; different, but complementary. Neither has any interest permanently divergent from the other. . . . Eve, the maiden, may gain individuality by the approximation of her status to that of Adam, yet what if the result be to make it unduly difficult for a man to maintain a wife and family? If true happiness lies in alliance with one's true mate can anything which diminishes the chance of such a union be in fact a benefit?" Three elements underlie this sort of analysis. First, women are innately different from men. Second, these difference allow women to be, as Lady Glentanar phrased it, "keepers of the home, and . . . the future race. . . ." Third, men, the stronger sex, protect women who act in a properly feminine manner. In a separate article, members of one WUO branch described the female outlook: "Woman herself is never ruled by reasoned judgment, but is led more or less by conviction and belief in the ideal. Her nature is deeply rooted in the past; her character is moulded, the progress and prosperity of the race developed by the sympathy, service and devotion of man to her needs; her purpose and destiny exalted, her power extended, and her position and status improved by the spread of Christianity."[60]

Home, husband, and children dominated the WUO ethic, but this outlook broadened after 1918 to include social, economic, and even international questions. A January 1921 issue of *Home and Politics* argued for women's greater political involvement: "The State more and more concerns itself to-day with questions which are within the sphere of the 'Home,' such as health, education, welfare, housing and so on. Women, too, are intimately interested in the cost of living, prices, rates and taxes as keepers of the domestic purse. Wider questions have also a 'Home' aspect. War, with its dreadful toll of killed and maimed . . . may involve the loss of the bread-winner and increased responsibilities upon the women for education and up-bringing of the children. . . . Enough has been said to show the close connection between the 'Home' and 'Politics.'" In an August 1921 article on Lady Muriel Helmsley, a member of the WUO advisory committee, the magazine outlined the goals of Conservative women: "The home and the children have always been woman's sphere of interest. The vote has added to her duties. She now has the power of defending and advancing home life, which is the very basis of our civilisation. To do the Socialist justice he knows that his cause will advance but little unless he destroys the home, and orders our lives from birth to death." While they pursued political goals, Conservative women upheld traditional female roles. Even Lady Astor, who was sometimes criticized for brusqueness, was a supporter of traditional gender roles. During her successful campaign in 1919, she denied that she was "a sex candidate" or feminist, and emphasized that she was a mother who wanted to help the nation's women and children. Conservative women came to espouse a wider notion of separate spheres, altering the rhetoric of politics, removing some of the old gender barriers, and developing their own issues as they went.[61]

After World War I women became, as most suffragists had hoped, the matrons of society, crusading for greater morality and spirituality at home and in society. This did not mean an acceptance of feminism, but a recognition of the growing role of government and the need to guide the evolution of the family, on which rested the fate of the nation. The importance of the 1918 reform act, the 1922 Conservative *Campaign Guide* explained,

> is not that so many more electors are placed upon a register, but that the advice and opinion of the homemaker are being asked as complementary to those of the breadwinner. Such co-operation has, in fact, become urgently necessary, since legislation concerns itself increasingly with domestic life, and the child is viewed as an asset to the State. The problems of a changeful time need the co-operation of the woman, who sees them from the kitchen and nursery window, with the man, who looks through an office or workshop. Help and counsel, too, are due from that large body of women who do social service, paid or unpaid. . . . [They have] prepared the ground for our modern rapidly established organisation for betterment of conditions, and the care of the weak, the sick, and those who go astray.[62]

Their concern with the home led WUO members to propose moderate reforms that would improve conditions in Britain but preserve the governmental and economic system. They saw their particular contribution to Conservatism as eradicating the discontent on which Labour preyed and engendering national unity. Women, it was claimed, had more sympathy for the problems facing families and were in closer touch with people's spiritual and moral concerns. Mrs. Neville Chamberlain told a mass meeting of women at the 1920 NUA Conference, "If men had a fault—she did not say they had—(laughter)—she thought they were inclined too much to regard politics as entirely a matter of brains, and to leave out of it that human element and that personal touch which came so instinctively to women (applause). No matter to what class they belonged, they would enter into the lives of others, and in those lives they would always find the same troubles and sorrows, the same domestic affections, the same love of beauty, the same desire for greater knowledge of something higher and better that they found in themselves. That was the ground on which they should meet, and it was a ground on which Bolshevism could find no foothold." "Women," she reiterated, "were specially able to fill a gap that had not yet been filled by men—(applause)—and introduce into our political affairs ... sympathy and understanding." Mrs. Chamberlain herself cycled around Birmingham meeting her husband's constituents and visiting neighbors.[63]

WUO members were involved in social reform activities, including maternity and health care, housing, and local government, although this sometimes produced conflicts with other sections of the Conservative Party. At the 1923 NUA conference, Lady Selborne moved a resolution in favor of pensions for needy widows with children. She argued that the state must assist mothers of "the respectable working class" who lost their husbands. Many such women, she argued, had devoted themselves to raising a family before they received any job training—except possibly for domestic service. The meeting passed the resolution. The Stockton WUO branch was particularly proud of its Mrs. Mark, who spoke to the 1925 NUA conference about her work reducing maternal mortality. During 1928 a series of articles in *Home and Politics* discussed the invaluable role of women in local government and encouraged others to get involved.[64]

At times reform-minded WUO members contradicted accepted Conservative principles. During the 1923 NUA conference, Lady Astor moved raising the school-leaving age for unemployed youths from fifteen to sixteen, but another WUO member opposed the resolution because it would hurt industry and undermine proper work habits. The conference rejected the proposal, which they probably also considered too costly. At the 1925 SUA annual meeting, the duchess of Atholl and other women proposed that boys be prohibited from street trading. The resolution was defeated after F. A. Macquisten, a lawyer and proponent of laissez-faire economics, attacked the idea as an infringement on freedom and capitalism. In May 1928 the WUO conference supported the passage of a factory bill that opposition from businessmen had stalled. (The women's request was not addressed.) Middle- and upper-class members of the WUO occasionally expressed opinions that threatened working men and women. For example, the same WUO conference that supported factory reform was also in favor of longer shop hours. And to increase the supply of domestic servants, the Southeast Area women's committee proposed in 1925 that childless women be taken off the dole.[65]

Although the WUO was avowedly nonfeminist, it was not, a central office speaker told a group of Chichester women, averse to "making a fuss" in order to secure its objectives. The branch chairwoman agreed and pointed out that male legislators were naturally more interested in matters related to their own sex. The differences between male and female Conservatives centered on the different standards of conduct and morality for men and women. Although they were Conservatives first, WUO members, like many women activists, intended to extend the sphere of women's operations by restricting men's. Hollis describes women's point of view before the war: "Only when the streets were safe for respectable women, literally and metaphorically, could women come out of the home into the public domain. That meant not just repressing the outward and visible signs of brothels, gin palaces, and obscene windows. It also meant challenging assumptions about men and women's sexual and social nature.... They would if they could raise women to the public standing of men and men to the moral standards of women.... This meant inhibiting, as well as prohibiting, men's baser urges, in order to expand the public space available to women." For Conservatives like Sir Reginald Banks, such notions were irritating and intrusive: "Woman has rather rudimentary notions of abstract right and justice; she has a motherly, not to say, grandmotherly, attitude towards Man, and would be quite prepared to vote for compulsory woollen drawers, statutory hours for going to bed, and anything that will keep him safe at home. She is strong for the abolition of all temptations— except herself." This "motherliness" led women to an interest in temperance, sexual morality, and legal equality.[66]

After 1918 Conservative leaders recognized that they had to take into consideration women's views on temperance. Lady Astor was a leading prohibitionist, and she played a key role in the passage of the 1923 Intoxicating Liquors Act, which prohibited the consumption of alcohol by minors. That same year the WUO successfully pressed the government to pass the Dangerous Drugs Act to end drug use among children. Some WUO members favored the prohibition of alcohol as in the United States, or at least the local option to do so. Nearly all WUO members believed that wartime restrictions on pub and club hours had proven their worth and ought to be retained. There was a heated debate at the 1926 NUCUA conference when the delegate from a Tory club moved that these restrictions be lifted. Another (male) representative offered an amendment shelving the question. He noted, "The managers of their party organisation knew pretty well what was happening throughout ... the country, and they knew that the greater part of the active work carried on for the party was done by the women's organisations, and they should bear in mind the fact that if they antagonised one club member because the restrictions were not removed how many women were they going to annoy by removing them!

(Loud applause.)" Despite the plea of the ACC chairman, Sir Herbert Nield, the amendment passed. WUO members also called for the reform of public houses to make them respectable enough for women and children to patronize.[67]

The most important instance of WUO intervention on a sexual or legal issue was the Criminal Law Amendment Act of 1922, which mandated a prison term for statutory rape. Both Lady Astor and Caroline Bridgeman pressed the government to accept the measure as one that would advance "the moral standard of men." In July 1922 the WUO advisory committee asked the NUA Executive to inform party leaders, "the Unionist Women take a keen interest [in the bill] . . . and trust they will see that it passes." The Executive took action, and the measure was quickly adopted. Among less notable examples of WUO involvement, at least one WUO branch publicized the alleged "white slave traffic" in European women. At the 1924 SUA conference, women passed a resolution calling for an investigation of the sexual abuse of children. WUO members generally did not favor liberalizing divorce, but they did support the Matrimonial Causes Act of 1923, which gave women the same right as men to seek divorce on grounds of adultery. That same year the WUO also supported passage of the Bastardy Act, which increased the financial liabilities of fathers of illegitimate children. The WUO encouraged the second Baldwin government to pass a series of lesser measures requiring husbands to provide for abandoned or abused spouses and children, granting mothers equal rights of guardianship, and declaring that children born out of wedlock were legitimized by their parents' later marriage. In fact, all of the women's legislation passed during the 1920s was the work of the Conservatives or the predominantly Conservative coalition.[68]

Underlying the WUO's role was the belief that women had a special place in the existing social and political system and a unique ability to contribute to its preservation. To the WUO member, the family was both the basis of the social and political order and the key to women's security. In her 1931 text *Women and Politics,* the duchess of Atholl argued that Christian marriage raised women above the level of "child producing machines" by creating "a union of mind and character [and], best of all, a partnership in service." The responsibilities of marriage and family, she wrote, engendered "the finest elements in a man's character." During a parliamentary debate on divorce law reform in 1920, Lady Astor argued against divorce on demand: "In the Christian world it is the spiritual aspect of marriage that the law attempts to protect, . . . that makes marriages happy . . . [and] has elevated the Western woman." These statements would have been regarded as commonplace among WUO members who, accepting their role within an ordered and "civilized" society, expected to be harbored from predation and hardship.[69]

Considering the WUO's conservative ethos, Tory women's fear of Bolshevism and socialism was warranted and not, as Campbell suggests, the product of paranoia. The British press printed stories of "bestial orgies" and other atrocities during the early years of Soviet rule; Conservative publications carried those reports. There were stories that many Soviet women and children were abused, raped, and murdered by hoodlums or radicals, and of Red soldiers being barracked with schoolgirls. Revolutionaries were also credited with "nationalizing women" and using them like "breeding animal[s] on a stud farm." A commonly cited story concerned an early 1918 proclamation in the Caucasian town of Ekaterinodar. The so-called Ekaterinodar Mandate set up detailed regulations that abolished marriage and allowed men to use women as sanctioned by the authorities. The bizarre but true Ekaterinodar document became a Conservative leaflet in 1920.[70]

For Conservative women, who believed that marriage and other social institutions protected them, outrages in the Soviet Union and questioning of gender roles in the west made them cling more firmly to their traditional beliefs. In her 1921 work *World Revolution*, the protofascist and antimasonic crusader Nesta Webster claimed that "free love," supposedly advocated by radical thinkers, encouraged rape. She also argued that feminists were drawing themselves "into a plot of which they will be the chief victims. Women have obviously far more to lose than men by the destruction or even by a decrease of civilization." Webster was not associated with the WUO, but her views were not unlike those of WUO members. In 1921 a Conservative leaflet allegedly quoted a Russian as saying, "In our Russia there is no God, no religion, no Czar, no money, no property, no commerce, no happiness, and no safety." *Home and Politics* asserted that Bolshevism sanctioned quick divorces, in which the loyal wife was humiliated as she was exchanged for a younger "fluffy and attractive" woman or a purer comrade.[71]

Fears like these were linked to what some observers believed was an increasing lack of respect for femininity and motherhood. In the *Primrose League Gazette*, the wife of the Conservative activist H. G. Williams wrote that Labour supporters attacked her as she accompanied her husband during a campaign tour just before the 1924 election. She described her attack-ers as "insensate creatures" without concern for feminine frailty. The Conservatives warned women that feminist liberation would lead to their abuse and exploitation by a radical elite, as well as the destruction of the family by a "Ministry for Babies." Preposterous as they were, such statements reflected the Conservative reaction to the rise of the Left and the changing position of women.[72]

Conservatives associated traditional gender roles with social stability and security for women, leading them to describe radical threats to the established order in terms of their effect on established gender roles. Before the war, its opponents often conceived of female suffrage as a threat to masculinity and femininity and portrayed suffragists either as the domineering, masculine wife, or as the asexual, fanatical spinster. In 1871 *Punch* cast the belief that female activists were not feminine in an epigram:

> The Women who want Women's rights,
> Want mostly, Women's charms.[73]

After the war, Conservatives continued to believe that radicalism broke down gender roles. In *Democracy and Labour* (1924), a Tory historian warned against the revolutionary impact of what he called "anarchic individualism." The search for personal freedom leads to social chaos and, he claimed, "the leadership of the long-haired man" and "the short-haired woman."[74]

Conservatives used these gender stereotypes to attack their opponents. In one particularly mean-spirited attack, *Home and Politics* printed a very unattractive photo of Mrs. Asquith above the caption, "She has been told, she says, that she would always be young enough to make love and to inspire." A 1922 leaflet, "The Wallflower," was typical of the Conservative approach. The cover pictured a masculine and unattractive "Socialist woman" waiting for a dance partner. The leaflet warned readers, "Don't Have Her For Your Partner. Vote Unionist. Safety First!" Although designed to win votes, the leaflet also demonstrates Conservative concerns about gender roles.[75]

Some of the clearest evidence for the Conservative view of women is contained in a series of "Plays for Patriots" published between 1924 and 1926 and performed by party organizations. In the first of the three plays, *Look Before You Leap* (1924), Mrs. Climber marries a socialist schoolteacher named Mr. Hector and turns against her former employer, Mrs. Faithful. By the end of the story, Mrs. Climber, "dejectedly, plainly dressed with bobbed hair," according to the Labour dress code, has lost her savings to Mr. Hector, and her sons have become Socialist ruffians. *Roly-Poly Revolution* was written in 1925, as coal miners were poised to call a national strike. It portrays the effect on the home of labor agitation and "red revolution." In response to the selfish bravado of her husband, Bill Gunter, who has joined the miners' strike, Mary launches a domestic revolution. Bill is left floundering as he attempts to make his dinner and a roly-poly pudding. *Lady Monica Waffle's Debut* (1926) shows how a young lady of good background is treated by socialists. Lady Monica cooks waffles for a gathering of socialists only to be rewarded with contempt and rudeness. The obvious lesson of the three plays is that the existing order recognizes the special place and characteristics of women, while radicals and socialists reject them.[76]

Reiterating an old saying, the Wood Green agent told his WUO branch that "the hand that rocked the cradle, rules the world," and Conservative women considered their role as "mothers of the Empire" vital. Party literature and WUO records show the emphasis that women Conservatives placed on motherhood. An April 1924 contributor to *Home and Politics* argued that children should be given "a sound knowledge of Christian principles as the foundation of national character; . . . loyalty and patriotism should be instilled into them." To achieve these ends WUO members participated in both Conservative and non-party youth groups. They also demanded censorship of the press and of films to stop "the poisonous teachings" of the Left and the "immoral and unhealthy literature . . . which has as its object the perversion of the morals of the young." Conservatives were particularly worried by films, which were thought to be dangerously powerful propaganda. WUO members were concerned with allegedly anti-British and anti-imperial films from America, whose characters implicitly criticized the British social elite. Representative of their concern was a 1925 resolution from a women's area committee calling for more home-produced films "on the line of British ideas and morality and founded upon traditions of Imperial Unity." Such demands by WUO members helped to pass the Cinematograph Films Act of 1927, which set a minimum quota for the number of British films exhibited. The WUO was not, however, able to secure passage of bills to curb the Socialist Sunday School movement.[77]

Women's integration into politics in the 1920s did not free them from gender limitations and condescension. Asquith, for instance, blamed the Liberal defeat in the Spen Valley by-election of 1920 on gullible women who swallowed the promise of free sterilized milk, and Hugh Dalton suggested to his wife in 1919 that women's votes would be won if a candidate's oratory made them cry. Others thought that good looks drew women, while ugliness repelled them. Lord Esher actually made the ridiculous claim that Winston Churchill's defeat in the 1922 election was the result of his looking "so damned ugly" when angry.[78]

Despite progress, women's role remained circumscribed. Lady Astor's career as an M.P. gives some good examples of men's negative reactions to a woman in politics. As a consequence of what was considered Astor's aggressiveness and lack of party loyalty, her relations with other Conservatives were strained, and her determined pursuit of women's issues raised the specter of gender antagonism. When her projects met opposition, she attacked opponents as reactionaries and misogynists—hardly a womanly tactic! In 1922 she created the Consultative Committee of Women's Organizations to advance women's demands, and in 1929 she tried to gain the support of female Labour M.P.s for a women's party. Because her manner contradicted the definition of womanliness and angered some Conservatives, the fact that she was often well informed about the issues scarcely counted. Sibyl, Lady Stanley, wife of Lord Stanley, heir to the Derby estate, JIL chairman, and deputy party chairman, also alienated some Conservatives with her stridency.[79]

Yet despite their failure to capture many positions of leadership in the party and their outright rejection of feminism, Conservative women changed the character of politics and improved the position of women. Women's political involvement rearranged the hierarchy of issues and policies. To be successful, political parties had to offer policies acceptable to women. By 1929, Conservative leaders clearly recognized this. In making preparations for the election, they decided, for instance, that longer hours for Conservative clubs had to be sacrificed to female opinion. More important, the duchess of Atholl was placed on the Cabinet policy committee specifically to deal with "questions affecting the interests of women." Postwar politicians also had to be more concerned with their public and private morality, so as not to offend women, who were the custodians of religion and morality. Conservative women felt that the traditional male values and heroic stances associated, for example, with Lloyd George and Winston Churchill counted less than a sterling character. Lord Birkenhead's coarse behavior, for example, accelerated his decline in popularity after 1918. He even attended at least one session of a WUO conference while intoxicated, provoking disgust and anger. The M.P. for Wirral, John Grace, was forced to retire in 1931 because his marriage had ended in divorce. Meanwhile, politicians like Baldwin and Macmillan benefited by meeting women's moral expectations.[80]

The life and career of the duchess of Atholl (1874–1960) exemplifies the accepted role of Conservative women in the 1920s. Lady Astor once complained that the duchess did not "see straight about women," and it is true that she was neither a suffragist before 1914 nor a feminist after 1918. She was, however, active in public life before the war, and after it ended she won local office. When Lloyd George visited Blair Atholl in 1921, he suggested that she run for Parliament, and two years later she was elected from her home constituency of Kinross and West Perthshire. When she was appointed the parliamentary secretary to the Board of Education in 1924, she became the second woman—and first Conservative woman—to hold a government post. In contrast to Astor, Atholl was politically successful and respected by Conservative Party leaders and members in part because of her dedication and talent. The shy junior minister had problems, however, handling the overbearing and priggish president of the Board of Education, Lord Percy, and she disagreed with his cost-cutting measures.[81]

Like many other women, the duchess of Atholl refused to sacrifice private concerns for the sake of her public life. She believed that the primary duty of women was to nurture the "character and individuality" of others, and she avoided feminism and gender conflict. Lord Riddell approvingly noted that she dutifully accepted her husband's control over Blair Atholl. She believed in the "union of mind and character, . . . [and] partnership in service" that was the core of Christian marriage. The duchess of Atholl embodied a new ideal of Conservative womanliness: traditional female activities and attitudes combined with adventurousness and political savvy.[82]

During the 1920s the leaders and members of the WUO maintained the notion of separate gender spheres. They believed that it provided them with a role in public life and in their party while protecting them as women, wives, and mothers. The historian must be careful not to use present-day criteria in condemning these "Women in Hats" as staid and backward. Their participation in politics allowed Conservative women to redefine the legitimate concerns and activities of women. Could anyone have imagined Edwardian Primrose dames arguing the merits of birth control? Yet the majority of WUO members at their 1931 conference supported a resolution in favor of providing birth control information to married women at government welfare centers. During the mid-1920s several Labour women's conferences also passed resolutions in favor of dispensing birth control information, but they were ignored by Labour leaders. More-over, in 1930 the Labour Government decided to provide information only to women for whom pregnancy posed serious health hazards. And in 1936 Labour members on the Liverpool council opposed the distribution of birth control information by the local clinic. Not until 1967 did unmarried women gain access to birth control information at state clinics.[83]

Lisa Tickner's assessment of the prewar suffragists applies just as well to WUO members. These women "did not argue for the right to be unwo-manly," Tickner writes, "but rather the right to define its terms."[84] The WUO enabled Conservative women to engage in politics without trans-gressing accepted feminine roles. In so doing, they were able to avoid that greater vulnerability that they believed would result from challenging the social order.

Women's enfranchisement produced neither the catastrophe predicted by antisuffragists nor the utopia envisaged by suffragists. The Conservative Party attracted female voters and created a strong women's organization. The WUO ethos suited the mood and aspirations of many women in the interwar period. In 1923 Lady Lawson-Tancred, one of the first women magistrates, explained why in *Home and Politics*. She wrote, "The great majority of women are essentially home lovers, and few women are utterly devoid of the instincts of motherhood. They will not neglect or forsake their domestic occupations for the public platform and the police court. What they are doing is to extend their knowledge and experience into a wider field." From 1918 the Conservative Party supported assistance to mothers and children, not sexual equality. Beatrice Campbell, a Marx-ist and a feminist, has labeled the WUO ethos a "celebration of . . . subordination."[85]

Most Conservative women in the interwar period had no interest in escaping from what they regarded as their natural function. They perceived feminism and radicalism as threats to their persons and to their roles as wives and mothers, and they embraced motherhood, domesticity, and womanliness. After World War I, the Conservative Party mobilized women by supporting an enhanced version of their traditional gender roles and by offering stability, protection, and assistance to women and their families. With this approach, the party attracted more female volunteers and voters than any other. Today it continues to have both the greatest number and highest percentage of women members. Public opinion polls since World War II show that more women than men vote Conservative. Only in the two mid-1980s elections did this pro-Conservative tendency among women voters disappear, but it reappeared in the 1992 general election.[86] The Conservatives' long-lived success with women dates from the 1920s, when the party successfully developed the Women's Unionist Organisation, offered limited but real opportunities to its members, and carefully appealed to the conservative values and traditional gender expectations of women.

3

The Junior Imperial League
and the Young Britons

Next to the WUO, the most important organizations of the post-war Conservative Party were its youth groups, the Junior Imperial and Constitutional League (JIL) and the Young Britons, neither of which has so far been the object of a historical inquiry. (Ramsden's history of the Conservative Party during this period mentions the JIL only in passing.) The JIL and the Young Britons were not the largest youth groups in interwar Britain, being outnumbered by the nonpartisan Boy Scouts and Girl Guides, with their more than half a million members. But the JIL was the largest political organization for young people, and it was considerably more popular than other parties' counterparts. By 1929 there were about 2,000 branches and 200,000 to 300,000 Imps, as JIL members were known, compared to fewer than two hundred youth sections in the Labour Party. For younger children the Conservatives in 1925 created the Young Britons, which grew to 470 branches and 49,000 members by 1929.[1]

Although founded before the First World War, the JIL blossomed after 1918, gaining popularity and attention during the 1920s. By adding more appealing social activities to the JIL's other functions, Conservative leaders were able to attract youths and use their enthusiasm for the often mundane tasks of organizing, canvassing, distributing literature, speaking, and office work. The JIL also provided a forum in which young people could learn about politics, carry on political discussions, and develop their political talents. Conservatives saw the JIL as an important body for propagating their views, especially among Britain's youth, and securing votes for their party. The SUA Eastern Division noted in 1929, "The future existence of all the political parties depends on the youth of the nation, and it is imperative that no effort of ours should be spared in making an attractive appeal to them to join the Unionist Party."[2]

The North Cornwall constituency offers an excellent demonstration of the JIL's character and appeal. A JIL branch was formed in the town of Stratton in 1926. During the inaugural meeting, the president of the Stratton Conservative and Unionist Association emphasized that the JIL would "train the young to fight Communism and . . . instil them with noble ideals so as to enable them to deal with their enemies in an honourable way."[3] The constituency agent then spoke on the JIL's role in developing support for the Empire. After the speeches came a dance, with music provided by the Launceston Imps Orchestra. The evening ended with forty-six youths enrolling in the new Stratton branch. Such social and educational activities brought young voters into the Conservative Party and mobilized them for political work.

Development of the Junior Imperial League

The JIL was established during the Edwardian age, but it did not become a successful mass organization until passage of the reform act of 1918. Members of Britain's Conservative male elite met in July 1906 and created the JIL to promote imperialism and tariff reform and to encourage young men's interest in politics. The JIL was an ad hoc organization administered by members of the Junior Constitutional Club and dominated by wealthy London contributors. In 1907 Henry M. Imbert-Terry (1854–1938), a historian, former Unionist candidate, and past chairman of the NUA council, became chairman of the JIL, a position he occupied until 1927. During his long tenure, Imbert-Terry devoted himself to the JIL, using his connections in the Conservative Party to ensure the continuing importance of the JIL. In 1908 the JIL began adding branches in the provinces. Three years later its leaders decided to make the JIL an official Conservative organization in order to ease its financial problems and quell conflicts with the regular Conservative organization. Central Office provided funds to hire Henry Hardman Cannell (1864–1926) as a full-time JIL organizer. In return the JIL accepted central office's authority and added the Conservative treasurer, chief whip, and party chairman to its council and executive. When war erupted in 1914, the JIL had about 70,000 members in 300 branches. In

Scotland some associations formed junior branches, and the SUA Western Division formed the Junior Imperialist Union (JIU) in 1910, but the number of youth branches was small.[4]

After four years of decline, JIL leaders in 1918 faced the task of reviving and adapting their organization to combat socialism. Conservatives worried about youth because of the interest Marxists and socialists took in education and propaganda. In 1901 a Russian police official had claimed to notice that Marxists were transforming young people into "a special type of semi-literate *intelligent*, who feels obligated to spurn family and religion, to disregard the law, and to deny and scoff at constituted authority." After the war, British Conservatives were similarly quick to allege, "Seditious teaching ... is spreading and inculcating thoughts and educating the young in a way subversive of law and order, and against King and Country." Conservatives were genuinely shocked by what they considered pervasive socialist and anti-imperial subversion. The WUO was particularly disturbed by a popular culture which "pervert[ed] ... the morals of the young." The problem became worse, Conservatives thought, when nonpartisan youth groups like the Scouts turned away from their original imperialist, patriotic, and warrior ethos.[5]

Conservatives saw evidence of subversive and immoral activities in many areas of British life. They campaigned against foreign films, which often, they believed, had a bad influence on children. A 1924 article in *Home and Politics* described the "active propaganda" of these films, which degraded human beings, portrayed the upper class as cruel and extravagant, and undermined values dear to Conservatives. During the second half of the 1920s the NUCUA repeatedly demanded action against "subversive" and "anti-British" films, and the Baldwin government eventually passed the Cinematograph Films Act of 1927, which set limits on the exhibition of foreign films.[6]

To Conservatives the most offensive forms of subversion were the Socialist Sunday Schools, the Communist Sunday Schools, and the Young Comrades' League of the Communist Party. Of the three, the largest was the Socialist Sunday Schools, which was founded in 1891 in Glasgow and had 140 branches by 1925. Both the Proletarian Sunday Schools and the Communist Sunday Schools were postwar creations that were less popular—but even more hostile to the existing economic and political system—than the Socialist Sunday Schools. Conservatives tended to view these schools as part of a plan to win power by corrupting the young. In 1926

Lord Birkenhead, then a Cabinet minister, told a JIL meeting that the groups were part of a Soviet conspiracy to deceive youth "with pernicious and poisonous doctrines." The schools, though few in number, were disproportionately disturbing to Conservatives, who were already concerned about unpatriotic and immoral currents in British life. As their numbers increased after 1918, Conservatives became even more worried. By early 1921 the *Primrose League Gazette* was warning of the "insidious propaganda" of these schools, which denounced all authority except the revolutionary party. If these schools and youth groups were not stopped, the magazine claimed, children would never become "hard-working, decent and law-abiding men and women, fit to take their place among the citizens of Britain." By 1927 *Home and Politics* even claimed that these subversive groups were creating "a race of hooligans, neurotics and drug maniacs." Central to Conservatives' worries was their fear, articulated by one WUO leader in *Popular View,* that seditious, blasphemous, and immoral groups would undermine "the Christian home . . . the foundation of a patriotic, right-thinking community."[7]

During the 1920s, Conservatives proposed a number of ways to deal with allegedly subversive activities affecting British children. Quite a few Tories wanted to ban some materials used by local educational authorities. There were also largely unsuccessful attempts to organize Conservative teachers. Other proposals included patriotic courses in schools and endowed chairs of patriotism in the universities. Such outlandish notions were ineffective, however, because relatively few professional teachers were responsible for spreading socialist ideas. Some Conservatives also demanded the legal suppression of groups like the Socialist Sunday Schools. In 1924 Conservative backbenchers and peers introduced a Seditious and Blasphemous Teaching to Children bill that would have established a procedure to root out such schools, but party leaders did not support the bill.[8]

After the First World War most Conservatives regarded their own party as a valuable tool for fighting leftists. They realized the need to draw young people into the Conservative Party. In particular they regarded the JIL as the best tool to promote "patriotism, love of country, interest in historical episodes, with their attendant morals; fundamental Constitutional principles, [and] interest in the Empire and all that it stands for." The JIL could provide youths with a thorough grounding in Conservative values and ideas—the best method of protecting young people from socialism and securing Britain's future. Central office decided that adolescents and young adults who were in the "danger zone" between fourteen and twenty-five should be recruited vigorously for the JIL, whose task was to instill Conservative and patriotic values, provide a knowledge of politics and economics, and train its members to work on behalf of the Conservative Party. By this method, not only would JIL members be made immune to the "attractive promises and . . . appearance of profound knowledge" characteristic of socialism; they also would be empowered to fight it.[9]

JIL leaders were eager to accept their antisocialist mission. In an October 1919 circular asking branches to re-form, JIL leaders emphasized the constant effort needed to uphold "the principles of domestic justice and liberty which are now menaced by the actions of self-seeking and seditious demagogues." JIL leaders began distributing antisocialist literature from central office and other party organizations. By 1920 the JIL's primary aims were to protect private property and liberty, prevent class warfare, and combat left-wing parties. Because of its new emphasis on antisocialism, the JIL was soon recognized by Conservatives as a key component of the party organization.[10]

The first postwar meeting of the JIL council in December 1919 found a weak organization with only fifty active branches. JIL leaders decided that they needed to admit girls and young women because "there was a great future for the League if we can bring to bear on the Women electors the same influences as we had, in the past, on the male element." Branches were firmly encouraged to admit female members, although they could maintain separate sections for the two sexes. Shortly thereafter the JIL admitted women representatives to its council and executive committee. Gradually women were appointed to the important publications and finance committees and were chosen as delegates to the NUA. To avoid problems between young men and women, and to ensure the cooperation of the WUO, the JIL Executive formed a subcommittee to handle women's issues. By 1922 the meritorious conduct of women was already being noted: "The inclusion of women in . . . the League has proved of the greatest value both in increase of members—many Branches having more than doubled their membership—and in efficiency, the ladies having taken part readily in political as well as in the social activities of the League. In no case has any difficulty arisen through the inclusion of female members." The addition of women to the JIL was a boon, and it later enabled the organization to take responsibility for the younger women enfranchised by the reform act of 1928.[11]

The vast majority of local branches readily accepted young women and formed joint branches. In this respect the JIL differed from most of the senior associations and from some foreign youth organizations. For instance, the Italian Fascist Party segregated girls, gave them very little training, and allowed them to engage in only those activities that prepared them for motherhood. In the JIL, however, young women were integrated into the organization and its activities. Typically they formed at least one-third of the local executive committee, although they were not generally selected as chairwomen. In part the success of the integration reflected young men's willingness to hand over to young women the "female work" of organizing socials, sewing for fund-raising efforts, working with children in the Young Britons, and generally using their "woman's influence for good."[12]

In contrast to the members of the WUO, the young women of the JIL joined the men in activities, including all sports except football. As a male member noted in a letter to the JIL magazine, "the modern girl with her fair outlook on general affairs, and her interest in matters of welfare, housing, etc., is a great asset." He added that some of the success of JIL activities was due to the attraction between the sexes. Yet the JIL offered young women more than a dating service. It provided them, one young woman noted, with "Work for their Country, for the greatest Empire that the world has ever seen, work for the welfare of their fellow beings, and work for our future children."[13]

Some JIL branches created separate male and female sections that held joint social events. The Oswestry WUO formed female branches of the JIL closely tied to the WUO. But this arrangement seems to have left male JIL members floundering, either unwilling or unable to operate separately. Originally there were separate branches in Stockton, but they were consolidated into a joint branch in 1923. The most notable exception to the joint-branch format was in Lancashire and Cheshire, where the existing federation of youth organizations affiliated with the JIL in 1920 but retained considerable autonomy. The Lancashire and Cheshire federation refused to admit girls and women, despite repeated requests. Its leaders warned against interfering with WUO branches and undermining political activism by allowing the sexes to socialize. Only after the 1924 election did the Lancashire and Cheshire federation recognize that its style of operation was a serious obstacle to progress. At that time, despite opposition from older members, the younger generation of men and women who were taking control of the federation encouraged female membership in the joint branches.[14]

Because of the JIL's potential as a popular youth group, Conservative leaders and organizers were eager to develop it and integrate it with the regular party. Under the NUA rules of 1920, the JIL was allowed to elect two delegates to the NUA council. When Sir Malcolm Fraser became principal agent the following year, he cultivated the JIL by attending its meetings and praising its work. He named Cannell, the JIL organizer, to the post of central office agent for junior organizations, improving Cannell's and the JIL's position while gaining more influence over them. In spring 1920 the JIL finally started a magazine, the *Junior Imperial League Gazette*. It gave branches an opportunity both to learn about the work of other branches and to make money by selling magazines, but it unfortunately provided little of interest to young readers. Because of the low circulation figures and the financial drain, in mid-1921 JIL leaders agreed to make the *Gazette* an edition of the new Conservative magazine, *Popular View*. Toward the end of 1921, Fraser also appointed a canvassing agent for the JIL and encouraged the NUA conference at Liverpool to double the JIL's representation on the NUA council. Despite these gains, the uncertainty and infighting characteristic of the coalition period hampered the JIL's revitalization. At the JIL dinner in April 1922, for instance, the Diehard leader Lord Salisbury spoke on the need for "a pure Conservative Government" even though the party, of which the JIL was a component, supported the coalition government.[15]

After the fall of the coalition, Conservative leaders redoubled their efforts to develop the JIL. At the 1922 NUA conference, H. G. Williams attributed the electorate's ignorance largely to young voters. Concerned about "insidious and incessant Socialist propaganda" among the young, delegates supported "a wide extension of the operations of the Junior Imperial League as an effective method of counteracting the pernicious work of extremists among the younger members of the community." The JIL did enjoy an immediate revival after 1922, and Cannell, the organizing secretary, reported in June 1923 that interest in his organization was greater than at any other time in its history.[16]

In early 1923 Fraser and the party chairman, Sir George Younger, increased the JIL subsidy from central office from £500 to £800 per annum and agreed to hire a clerk for the youth organization and to put more party officials on its governing bodies. Among the more important officials were Philip G. Cambray and A. T. Rivers, heads respectively of the publications and finance departments. The JIL gained further recognition when its chairman was made a permanent member of the NUA Executive, and, in 1924, JIL representation on the NUA council was again increased, from four to six. By 1924, JIL leaders were certain that their organization "has now succeeded in impressing on the authorities, both at the Central Office of the Party, as well as in the various constituencies, the absolute necessity of the League, and the indispensable assistance which such an organisation can give in promulgating the political principles upon which good government depends." With the party's recognition and assistance, the JIL grew rapidly. It added thirty-nine new branches—including Bradford and Oswestry—in the first three months after the December 1923 election. During August, September, and October 1924, the JIL distributed more than 100,000 copies each of "The Objects of the League" and the JIL membership form.[17]

In the years after the 1924 election, the JIL underwent significant changes in its leadership, duties, and organization. A younger, postwar generation took control. After a prolonged illness, Cannell died in August 1926. Although saddened by the loss of their respected organizer, the JIL Executive quickly filled the vacancy with Captain A. G. Mitchell, a former Conservative agent at Burton-on-Trent. Mitchell had been Cannell's assistant for a year and also enjoyed the confidence of the party chairman, F. S. Jackson. Less than a year later Imbert-Terry retired as JIL chairman. He was replaced by Edward Montague Cavendish, Lord Stanley (1894–1938), who served until 1933. Imbert-Terry had become something of a liability, alienating some Conservative leaders by his egotistical behavior. Stanley, a decorated war veteran, was a different sort of leader. He and his beautiful wife, Sibyl, embodied the Imp ideal of youthful vigor. As heir to the powerful earl of Derby, respected Lancashire M.P., Conservative junior whip, and a rising star in the party, Stanley was also a more important political figure than Imbert-Terry. The selection of Stanley in 1927 was an indication of the changes affecting the JIL and a sign of the rising influence of a new generation of Conservatives.[18] These younger leaders of the JIL successfully responded to the passage of the Representation of the People Act of 1928.

As an equal-suffrage bill was being prepared in 1927, Conservative leaders gave the JIL responsibility for recruiting young women who would be enfranchised. At a March 1928 rally celebrating equal suffrage, thousands of Imps gathered at the Albert Hall and its overflow meeting in snowy Hyde Park. The JIL president, Lord Plymouth, told Imps that they must "educate the young people . . . [and] spread amongst them the principles of patriotism and loyal citizenship and constitutionalism." Anticipating this challenge, the May 1927 conference of the JIL had raised the age limit for members from twenty-five to thirty, a change that helped the JIL establish its authority over younger voters. Branches could also more easily keep older members to serve as officers.[19]

Recognizing the increased importance of the JIL, the new party chairman, J. C. C. Davidson, again increased central office's financial support in 1927. He paid the JIL's outstanding debts and increased its budget by 50 percent. Central office also took over production and distribution of JIL literature and provided regional organizers. Between 1921 and 1927, central office's financial assistance to the JIL increased from £500 to £1,200 per annum, exclusive of salaries for the organiser and his assistants. By 1930, budget and salaries for the JIL were almost £1800, triple the 1924 figure. In part this reflected the organization's more ambitious propaganda efforts, particularly its magazine. In May 1925 the inadequate *Junior Imperial League Gazette* was replaced by *Imp*. *Imp* was a true JIL magazine with articles specifically for members and contributions from Imps across the country. Monthly circulation jumped from 7,000 first to 14,000, then to almost 30,000 after central office halved the magazine's price in October 1927.[20]

Another major development in the postwar JIL was its system of regional and constituency bodies. Area federations were originally authorized in 1911, and after the war JIL headquarters promoted their formation and provided affiliated federations with representation on the council and executive. The affiliation fee was also lowered. Federations served several purposes. First, they promoted ties between branches, especially within the area. Second, central office could assign a professional organizer to each federation. Third, through NUA's provincial divisions, JIL federations were able to cooperate more readily with the rest of the Conservative organization. In 1925 there were six affiliated federations; by 1929 every area in England and Wales had a federation.[21]

In addition to developing regional federations, JIL leaders decided to estabiish divisional councils and to incorporate the JIL into the local Conservative organization. (Initially most JIL branches were only loosely tied to their senior association.)[22] Despite concerns about overbearing constituency agents, the 1926 JIL conference decided that branches should adapt to the Conservative Party's divisional organization. Under the JIL rules adopted in 1928, divisional councils became the focus of activity. By the end of 1929 all but forty-four of the parliamentary divisions (excluding

Lancashire and Cheshire) had councils. North Cornwall was typical. In December 1928 local Conservatives formed a JIL divisional council composed of two delegates from each of the thirteen branches and the officers of the regular Conservative association. In addition, JIL delegates were added to the governing bodies of the senior association.[23]

The JIL was a significant presence in each of the ten English and Welsh seats in my sample. Clapham was particularly fortunate in having the JIL organizer and proponent J. H. Bottomley as divisional agent. He ensured that a JIL branch offering a range of social activities and political support was in operation by 1921. The example of Clapham showed the importance of local Conservative agents, officers, and candidates or M.P.s to the success of JIL branches. In Stockton a thriving JIL branch was formed with the assistance of the agent, a member of a prominent Conservative family, and the chairman of the local labour committee. The existence of a Bradford Central branch was in large measure the work of the Bradford agent. In North Cornwall, Conservative leaders, including the young M.P. A. M. Williams, worked hard between 1925 and 1929 to form JIL branches in the rural division. Across Britain local Conservatives valued the JIL, as Cuthbert Headlam once noted, particularly for its ability to rejuvenate associations with "younger and fresher blood."[24]

In Scotland the youth organizations were separate from the JIL, and the two regions of the SUA—western and eastern—had their own groups. There was a JIU in the west; in the east, Junior Unionist branches were joined in 1930 to form a Junior Unionist League. Despite the assistance of the prewar Unionist Workers' League, there were relatively few junior branches in Scotland, although the number did increase during the 1920s. The youth organization developed more quickly in the west, where the JIU had eighty-two branches in 1925, although by 1929 the eastern SUA was catching up, with ninety junior branches and a youth magazine. In that same year there were 219 junior branches and 20,000 members in all of Scotland. A particularly successful group of juniors was the Camlachie JIU branch, revived in 1921. The branch held regular lecture series and musical entertainments, and demonstrated an aptitude for political work. It membership grew continuously, reaching more than 250 in 1929, even though the senior association was experiencing problems. The Unionist association in rural Kincardine and West Aberdeenshire established its first junior branch in 1925; as more branches formed, the juniors took on such new responsibilities as fund raising. The senior association also included juniors on their committees. Scottish Unionists tended to press junior branches to become part of senior associations.[25]

Although it gained new responsibilities and a degree of independence during the 1920s, the JIL remained subordinate to the Conservative Party, particularly at the local level. In a speech to the JIL council before the war, Steel-Maitland, the party chairman, had emphasized branches' duty "to place their services at the disposal of the Unionist Agent for their own Constituency and . . . the party." This dependent relationship continued after the war, and the JIL did not take independent policy positions. But both Imbert-Terry and Sir Alan Sykes, chairman of the Lancashire and Cheshire Federation of Junior Conservative and Unionist Associations, strongly opposed the Lloyd George coalition. In a January 1922 letter to Austen Chamberlain, Imbert-Terry claimed that he was voicing a general opposition to the government within the party and the JIL: "Day by day it is forced upon me that unless some definite announcement is made most speedily as to the attitude our Party will assume at the coming Election with regard to the Coalition, we shall meet with widespread disaster. Agents and workers come into my Office every day declaring that they cannot keep their Organizations together; some large and energetic branches of the [Junior Imperial] League have completely withered away. . . . Others have separated from the Senior Associations which support the Coalition." Other sources do not corroborate Imbert-Terry's claims, and the JIL never took a stand on the issue. As early as 1919, however, the JIL Executive had claimed that the absence of "a clear statement of present Party policy" was retarding growth.[26]

The growth of the JIL occasionally created tensions with the rest of the party, especially the WUO. Some associations dominated their JIL branches. Oswestry WUO leaders, including the WUO chairwoman, Caroline Bridgeman, created a JIL branch for girls. WUO leaders attended JIL meetings, and JIL officers were included on WUO governing bodies. Under this arrangement, the JIL branch was expected to contribute money to the WUO. Although nominally self-governing, the JIL branch was obviously dominated by the WUO.[27] But most JIL branches were able to avoid such domination. They could, for example, deny admission or charge punitive fees for older Conservatives who refused to transfer to senior associations. Experienced and diplomatic Conservative agents were essential to prevent open conflict and maintain friendly ties between the JIL and senior associations. Lord Stanley's appointment as deputy chairman of the Conservative Party in 1927 also eased tensions. Although Davidson, the party chairman, worried about greater tensions between the JIL and the WUO, Stanley protected the JIL's interests without openly challenging those of any other party organization.[28]

JIL branches depended heavily on older Conservatives, especially WUO members. Developments in North Cornwall were, as usual, typical. The members of one WUO branch, for instance, played a decisive role in the formation of a JIL branch by gathering names of potential JIL members and serving as officers pro tem for the juniors. Another nearby JIL branch was organized with the aid of a WUO leader. An important reason that JIL branches did not seek too much independence was their financial dependence. Relatively few JIL branches had meeting places of their own. The West Kirby Imps raised enough money to open a club and headquarters in 1927, but they were an unusually successful branch in a wealthy middle-class area. Oswestry Imps obtained a hut only because Lady Harlech, the local WUO president, provided both the land and the money. Senior associations also often provided subsidies for JIL branches' operations and educational activities. In 1928 and 1929, the Chichester association granted five pounds to a JIL branch and paid for a JIL member to attend the Conservative College. Wrexham seniors assisted their youth branch by obtaining office space and literature. They also paid for a delegate to attend a JIL conference. The Bradford Central JIL, in an ill-fated bid for independence, nearly went bankrupt after moving into its own facility. It was eventually forced to return to the local party offices.[29]

Despite financial problems, the JIL was a popular, primarily middle-class, youth organization. In some areas its growth was inhibited by the existence of other youth groups, but by 1929, there were nearly two thousand youth branches. Evidence about the number or type of person who joined the JIL is unfortunately scanty. In part this reflects the transient nature of any youth organization. From the information that is available, however, at any moment in the later 1920s there were probably about 250,000 members in the JIL and many others who participated without joining.[30]

Like the Conservative Party in general, the JIL asserted that its membership and outlook were universal, not class-based. Although most Imps came from the middle class, the organization claimed to include many working-class members. One branch even reported that its three hundred members were the children solely of Durham miners! Formal restrictions on members were few. They had to swear an oath to maintain the Constitution and the Empire, uphold liberty and national unity, and improve the condition of the people. Branches were advised to demand a one-shilling annual subscription. Branch events and meetings were usually scheduled for the evenings, when most young people might be free from school, work, and other responsibilities.[31]

The cost and time required for full participation in the JIL, however, would have strained the resources of the average worker, who was making less than two pounds per week. One model winter program outlined in *Imp* included dancing lessons costing five shillings, several dances costing at least one shilling each, a two-shilling entrance fee for carnivals and whist drives, and an annual ball and dinner, each of which cost four and a half shillings. Members were also often expected to contribute refreshments and other items. And some activities, for example, mock debates and parliaments, required an education beyond that of many wage earners. The quintessentially elitist activity of the JIL was the annual dinner at the Connaught Rooms in London. Although they did not have to wear evening dress, those who attended did have to pay seven shillings for the meal—plus transportation and accommodation. Because of these practical obstacles, the JIL, like the rest of the Conservative Party in the interwar period, had a predominantly middle- and upper-class membership, which may have caused southern England to be overrepresented.[32]

JIL Activities

Because of its popularity, Conservative leaders recognized that the JIL was "a real and live force in the affairs of the nation" and an important tool in combating the Labour Party and socialism.[33] They gave the group three tasks: (1) to bring young people into the Conservative Party, (2) to teach them Conservative principles, and (3) to use them for political work on behalf of the Conservative Party. With its mixture of social, political, and educational activities, the JIL attracted young people and encouraged them to develop a Conservative outlook. Once recruited, JIL members provided a considerable amount of the volunteer labor needed for propagandizing and electioneering. As they became adults, Imps transferred to the regular party organization, which benefited from the infusion of experienced, energetic, and enthusiastic workers.

The primary function of the JIL was the political education of British youth. With the assistance of such older supporters as H. G. Williams, the JIL organized classes in London soon after the war to teach public speaking to young Conservatives. Classes were begun in other parts of Britain as well. In Glasgow eighty juniors participated in a single course on public speaking during the winter of 1921–22. JIL branches also sponsored lectures and study circles on economic and political topics. The syllabus of one Glasgow branch included lectures on labor, trade unionism, housing, political economy, direct action or syndicalism, socialism, and Conservative Party policy and organization. Students were warned strongly that direct action was dangerous to unions, the state, and liberty. The JIL magazine offered suggestions for courses. One issue gave course outlines that taught students to recognize the merits of British rule in India and the threat posed by a Labour scheme to abolish the monarchy. During 1927 alone there were one hundred study circles and classes for Imps. Lantern lectures and, later, films were often used to teach about the Empire, the Constitution, Bolshevism, and politics. Although political subjects were the most common, Imps also heard lectures about such topics as the beauty of nature, local history, and the modern woman.[34]

The JIL's educational task was frequently aided by lively debating. During the winter of 1923–24, the Stockton branch had classes on capitalism, "the Bolshevik Labour Party," and public speaking. Spirited debates on the merits of Capitalism and Socialism followed, with the lecturer adopting "the Bolshevik position" as Imps challenged him. This format was later repeated as certain Imps represented "the Clyde Brigade" of ILP M.P.s or "the Bolsheviks." The adventurous Bradford Central branch actually debated real socialists. "Hat night" was an amusing and popular form of debating in which each Imp delivered an impromptu speech on one of a wide range of serious or humorous topics drawn from a hat. Members of one branch, for example, spent an evening debating prohibition, hairstyles, the age of sexual discretion, women councillors, equal suffrage at twenty-one, Sunday boxing, test matches, reparations, and the navy. There were also opportunities to consider contemporary political and social concerns, among them the position of young people and men's and women's proper roles.[35]

The mock election or parliament was another educational activity. North Cornwall Imps held an election in which three male and three female candidates presented election addresses dealing with local issues like housing and public works. The Stockton JIL organized a mock parliament that lasted for several weeks. Various members portrayed the speaker of the

House of Commons, Stockton's M.P. Harold Macmillan, and such Labour figures as the passionate M.P. for Middlesbrough, "Red Ellen" Wilkinson. During the sessions Imps introduced and debated bills on safeguarding, housing, and the trade union political levy. These exercises increased knowledge and respect for the Constitution, "English virtues," and modern Conservatism while also training JIL members to assist the party.[36]

For the most active members, the premier reward was the Conservative Party College, where students received a thorough grounding in Conservative principles and policies. During the college's second session, in the summer of 1924, fifty JIL branches sent students; the next year sixty branches sent Imps. At the college, students heard distinguished lecturers and discussed political economy, constitutional history, public speaking, and party operations. They also had opportunities for recreation and social activity that promoted camaraderie. Recognizing the merits of the institution, the JIL Executive asked the college to design special Imp courses in 1927. JIL leaders also arranged for central office to pay for at least seventy JIL students to attend. Of the 370 Imps at the college in 1927, more than a third received scholarships. Many Imps were inspired by their two weeks' training and recreation. *Imp* noted in 1928 that graduates understood that "the work of the world is done by the enthusiastic. . . . who blaze the trail and break down obstacles and carry the lethargic crowd along with them." Students often returned to their branch with a new sense of purpose.[37]

Although JIL conferences and rallies had other purposes, they also developed Imps' political knowledge and enthusiasm. Branches could send delegates to the organization's annual dinners and conferences. For youthful Conservatives these events were memorable occasions where they might at least glimpse the Conservative leaders. Imps could move and second resolutions at the JIL conference—an unusual privilege for young adults in a party largely dominated by elderly gentlemen. Observers sometimes lampooned young and inept speakers, but the party benefited from the image of youthfulness and enthusiasm they contributed. Meanwhile JIL members had an opportunity to learn the rules of conduct that were the rudiments of good government. Such exercises were practical lessons in responsible democratic politics or, as *Imp* phrased it in May 1925, "government from the Imps, by the Imps, for the Imps."[38]

One of the greatest thrills for Imps was to hear Stanley Baldwin, who spoke regularly at JIL gatherings. On these occasions Baldwin, who was committed to educating voters, often expounded his favorite themes of citizenship and service. In particular, he tried to create trust in the British system of government by emphasizing those traditional "John Bull" values of which he was the exemplar. Baldwin's speeches, many of which were printed in popular collections, often dealt with public morality. In a December 1924 speech at the Albert Hall, he appealed to "a widespread instinct in the British people," urging them to take a "stand on public right and a law of nations . . . rather than with Machiavelli . . . to moralise our public intercourse." Baldwin especially deplored manipulative rhetoric. In March 1924 he told members of the Cambridge Union that he had a "positive horror" of rhetorical flourishes. He claimed that rhetoric poses a grave danger to democracy because it "stirs the emotions of the ignorant mob and sets it moving." Baldwin's speeches seem to have had the effect he hoped for. Even a critic like Charles Masterman, the Liberal M.P. and writer, was attracted to what he considered a "public-school schoolboy" and his "public-school traditions."[39]

One of the most memorable of Baldwin's addresses to the JIL was delivered at the Albert Hall Rally in March 1928. Enthusiastic Imps greeted Baldwin with a powerful "Imp Whisper," their name for their deafening roar of enthusiasm. The prime minister spoke of public service as its own reward. The progress of Britain and the world, he claimed, depended on British democracy, and the Imps could help create the necessary individual character, national unity, and imperial purpose. He exhorted them to "take up the torch from the hand of the generation that drops it. Make it give a brighter light than we have been able to; carry it further with stronger step, so that we may feel, when our time comes to hand it on, that you will do your duty, and pass it on to the generation instructed by you which will do yet better, so that in time long distant, and after our puny lights have been extinguished, the kingdoms of the world may be flooded with a light which we only see to-day in our dreams." Response to what at least one old Conservative regarded as "the best political meeting that had ever been held" was appropriately enthusiastic. Leaflet, phonograph, and film versions of the speech were later used for recruitment and campaigning.[40]

Imps aided the Conservative Party directly by working at the mundane and time-consuming tasks of mass politics. Initially their political activity was confined to distributing materials at NUA conferences. In 1921, however, newly revived JIL branches distributed literature, spoke, and provided manual labor to contribute to the victory of Conservatives in London's local election. Thereafter the JIL remained very active in the metropolis and even campaigned for JIL candidates in later local elections. Outside London, JIL leaders carefully developed the Imps' knowledge and nurtured their enthusiasm for canvassing, speaking, and such unexciting tasks as addressing envelopes. Imps served as stewards, singers, and other highly visible personnel at meetings, where they gave the party a youthful and progressive image. They were also encouraged to reconnoiter and harass the opposition.[41] During the tariff election of 1923, Imps used their own campaign song, set to the tune of "Yes, We Have No Bananas":

> Yes! we've got no employment,
> We've got no employment to-day.
> We've dumping, tub-thumping,
> And business all slumping,
> In spite of what Free Traders say.
> We've got the old "open door" system,
> It ain't 'arf given us a twistin'.
> O, yes we've got no employment,
> But Protection is coming hurray.[42]

There is no way to measure how much political work the JIL did, but one branch in West Ham, for instance, claimed that it performed three-quarters of the work for the 1922 and 1923 campaigns of Captain David Margesson, later a chief whip.[43]

Less important to the JIL's political role were its direct financial and membership contributions to senior associations. Most JIL branches were financially dependent, but they sometimes raised funds for the party. After the election defeat in 1929, the North Cornwall JIL raised enough to pay a substantial part of the senior association's debts, but this was far from typical. Instead of money, JIL branches sent many of their best members on to the senior associations. As Lady Dorothy Macmillan told the Stockton WUO in 1926, the JIL educated youths in "a sense of duty and loyalty to the country, so that when they arrived at the age of men and women they could join the Senior Organisation." Some JIL members also chose careers in the Conservative Party. This respectable profession, the March 1928 *Imp* stated, "offer[ed] a very varied and interesting life and sufficient remuneration to ensure personal independence."[44]

The Imps' political importance must be kept in perspective. The JIL was never so independent as to put forward its own candidates for public office. Only senior associations could adopt official candidates although some Imps contested elections. Some Imps felt that this was too restricting. One JIL member wrote to *Imp*, "Every young Conservative should be made to feel and know that here is a systematic means of providing an outlet for his or her abilities, and that in the Conservative Party there is nothing tangible or intangible, that is prejudicial to their reaching any position, even the highest, within the Party. If there be such an intangible obstacle, purge it. . . . If tangible, e.g., older people whose minds are unable to move forward beyond 1900, relegate them to their true sphere of Bumbledom!" Such hostility toward older Conservatives was not typical, but Imps did not want to be the stooges of the regular party, and they sometimes chafed at their limited role as an educational organization for young people, which was more circumscribed even than the WUO's.[45]

Another more common criticism of the JIL was its members' limited political commitment. One contributor to *Imp* complained that political activity was infrequent or even nonexistent—unless followed by a dance or social. Imps, he insisted, must answer the call for "Service, not self" by spending less time on trivialities and more on social and political issues. In the late 1920s there were several unsuccessful attempts to remove the name "Imp" from use because it "implied playing at politics" and belied the organization's serious work for the Conservative Party. Many JIL leaders and members were aware of the long-standing problems and tried to ensure that socializing did not overwhelm other activities. Imps were strongly warned against admitting non-Conservative youths and allowing their branch to become "a weekly free social club."[46]

The JIL also encouraged branches' political work. The *JIL Handbook* claimed, "The most virile Branches, even in the matter of social and sports, are those which make political service their first and foremost aim." Some branches used incentives to encourage and maintain political work. The Stockton JIL, for instance, held Monday night dances at the Maison de Danse; Imps who attended the previous JIL meeting were admitted for half price. To ensure that no one wholly escaped the politics, all dancers had to take a ten-minute intermission to hear a political address. But Conservatives in Stockton (and elsewhere) did not make too many demands, because they wanted converts, and popular organizations like the JIL could not be too restrictive. JIL leaders also tried to encourage political activity by bestowing awards. The JIL branch whose report best integrated politics with other activities won a set of the Westminster Library of political texts. Every year each branch could award Special Service Bars to its most active members, whose names were added to the JIL Roll of Honour. Beginning in 1924, the two most effective branches also received special awards (Simner Shield and Gould Cup) at the annual meeting.[47]

As the JIL grew, its leaders recognized that social activities were crucial. "Leavening political propaganda with social entertainments" were effective in attracting and keeping members who might otherwise have found politics too dull. Social activities also raised money while encouraging comradeship. For these reasons successful branches frequently held dances, offered community singing, and gave theatrical performances in wintertime. Some of these entertainments, for example, the Empire tableaux, were exercises in propaganda and education. In good weather there were outdoor activities. Some Imps went on excursions, on cruises, or to summer camps, but these activities were too expensive for many branches. Instead, members took part in sports during the warmer months. Branches often competed against each other. Beginning in 1930, the JIL held a National Sports Gathering at the Crystal Palace. Sports created an esprit de corps and served a didactic purpose. "The admiration of skill, of close cooperation, of sacrifice of self . . . and [doing] one's best for the side one represents," Lord Harris argued, "all these are good moral lessons, quite as worthy of study as any literary treatise." The tenets of good sportsmanship even reinforced the Conservative ideology of obedience, hierarchy, imperialism, and heroism.[48]

Although the JIL was much more than a social organization, the social component suited the mood of the postwar young. Young men and women could have a good time without interference from stodgy seniors—even if an activity were outlandish or bizarre (for example, fund-raisers in which Imps dressed as Ku Klux Klansmen and performed "Hollywood-style hold-ups"). The Imps' enthusiasm and energy were demonstrated by their "Whisper" and by jazz bands with names like the "Syncopated Imps" or the "Imp-possibles." And, of course, they enjoyed meeting JIL members of the opposite sex. Remembering her one summer as an Imp, a woman recalled in 1960 that she joined "because I was 15 and the girl I was friends with was a sophisticated 16 and she said it was the best social club in the district and . . . all the best looking boys belonged." JIL leaders understood the importance of a successful social event. According to the *JILG*, gatherings with "large attendance, a splendidly-decorated room (with our beloved flag everywhere), good music, the latest dances, and hosts of pretty girls" were the keystone of the JIL's popularity. Imbert-Terry told the

NUCUA conference in 1927, "It was his experience that where the boy was there would the girl be also—("Hear, hear," and laughter)—and even in the present day a shingled head and ornamented pyjamas did not make a boy. (Loud laughter.)"[49]

The social, educational, and political activities of the JIL that attracted members, created camaraderie, and awakened a social sense or service ethos also brought the energy of youth to the Conservative cause. JIL socializing helped re-create the unity and purity of purpose associated with the "pals battalions" of the Great War, and the organization sought "to keep alive that flame of service and sacrifice for the common good." Some Imps claimed that the JIL fulfilled their desire for unity, idealism, and activism. At their best, JIL branches integrated entertainment with educational and political activities. The model winter program of the Preston branch included a full schedule of political addresses, debates, mock parliaments, and speaking classes. At the same time, however, members could attend dancing classes, dances, concerts, whist drives, carnivals, plays, and other entertainments. Some social events raised funds for political work or for students attending the Conservative College. Other money was given to senior associations or to charities. By providing young people with meaningful activity in an autonomous organization, the JIL led them into Conservatism and made them feel that the party was open to their ideas and aspirations.[50]

The Young Britons

The Young Britons was founded to include children younger than fourteen, the minimum age for membership in the JIL. After World War I most Conservatives believed that a Conservative training could scarcely begin too early, but in the absence of action by the WUO or the JIL, the only national Conservative organization for children was the Primrose League's Junior Branch. The Primrose Juniors (or Buds, as they were sometimes called) was formed before the war but lost most of its members and funds after 1914. In the 1920s the Primrose League revived the group, with Mrs. Austen Chamberlain as president and the former Bradford M.P. Sir Ernest Flower as chairman. In early 1926 the Primrose League began publishing a monthly magazine, the *Primrose Bud*, for the organization.[51]

The development of the Buds was supposed to counter socialism by teaching morals, discipline, and patriotism to middle-class children. They "should be taught," the *Primrose League Gazette* stated, "that social service does not consist only of working for the benefit of the poor. They should be taught to think for others in everything, boys . . . to give up their seats in tramway cars and trains to women and old people. Children should be taught . . . not to ask for the help of servants. . . . They should be trained too, in the spending of their pocket money, and reminded that when they go abroad each one of them is responsible for the fair name of England." History—which supposedly showed how Britain's virtuous political leaders and explorers had upheld individual liberty, protected the state, and built the Empire—was the primary educational tool. The Buds also had a full sports program, culminating in a meet at the Crystal Palace that thousands of participants and spectators attended. The Primrose Juniors proved to be one of the Primrose League's few successful postwar innovations.[52]

After the 1924 election, Conservative leaders realized that they had to develop their own children's group to complement the JIL and combat "the pernicious teachings of the Socialist and Communist Organisations." The Conservatives wanted an organization like the Buds, or even the Boy Scouts and the Girl Guides, that would attract all children and turn them into upstanding, patriotic, and imperialistic youths. Of course, they also hoped that the children would gravitate toward the JIL and the Conservative Party as they grew older. Though not intended to be an overtly Conservative organization, the Young Britons would serve as "the first link in the chain" leading to Conservative Party membership.[53]

Aided by JIL and WUO leaders, the Conservative principal agent, Sir Herbert Blain, founded the Young Britons in mid-1925. Any child between the ages of six and fourteen could, with parental permission, join the new group. Publicly Conservatives were careful to present the Young Britons as a nonpartisan educational and recreational group that taught citizenship. In fact, however, it was avowedly Conservative and antisocialist. According to the group's 1931 handbook, members were usually children of Conservative parents, and only older youths and adults who were members of local Conservative associations could act as officers or helpers. Furthermore, the aim of the Young Britons was to "instill . . . into the minds of children love of their country, pride in our traditions and ideals, and a simple realisation of Conservative principles" to combat allegedly unpatriotic, left-wing elements in Britain. Within a year the Young Britons had become an established part of the Conservative organization, with 24,346 members in 259 branches, and its own magazine, the *Young Briton*. In 1927 central office appointed Allan Hand, a former agent and the successful organizer of Durham County Conservatives, as Young Britons organizer. The organization continued to grow, and by 1929 there were 471 branches and nearly 50,000 members.[54]

Although the Young Britons officially administered their own branches, the organization depended wholly on the JIL and especially the WUO. It was natural for WUO members, many of whom were mothers, to take an interest in the children's organization. The WUO vice-chairman, Lady Muriel Newton, and WUO Administrator, Marjorie Maxse, were named national officers of the Young Britons, and each provincial WUO advisory committee had considerable authority over the Young Britons. Conservative women were essential to the formation of Young Britons branches, and they provided much of the needed direction and assistance. The first branch of the Young Britons in Cornwall was formed by the Launceston WUO early in 1926. WUO officers ran the Young Britons branch with some assistance from the JIL. Women in Kincardine and Stockton were also instrumental in creating and managing their local branches of the Young Britons. The men's associations, on the other hand, were notoriously negligent.[55]

WUO branches were strongly advised not to monopolize the Young Britons or exclude the JIL. The JIL was active in the Young Britons because it hoped to enroll Young Britons members as they grew up. In 1927, Lord Stanley and his sister-in-law Maureen, Lady Stanley, became officers of the Young Britons. Later the JIL and the Young Britons exchanged representatives to encourage greater cooperation. Unfortunately, however, the JIL did not provide as much support as leaders of the Young Britons had hoped. Imps cooperated on some activities, such as Empire Day, and guided children who were moving up to the JIL. But compared to the WUO, JIL leaders treated the Young Britons casually.[56]

During the 1920s, Scottish Unionists developed their own organization for children. Initially the SUA had taken no action except to approve patriotic and imperialistic—but ad hoc and nonpartisan—"Children's Circles." Shortly before London formed the Young Britons, Glasgow Unionists established Young or Junior Unionist associations for eight- to sixteen-year-olds. By giving entertainments and simple lessons, Young Unionists aimed "to help boys and girls become good citizens, with love for their country and a wish to serve it." The 1924 SUA conference encouraged local associations to form Young Unionist branches in order to counter socialist activity, especially the Socialist Sunday Schools. Within a year there were twenty-five Young Unionist branches, some of which had hundreds of members. Both Kincardine and Camlachie had children's branches. In rural Kincardine several towns had branches, while in urban Camlachie there was only one, very active, branch. The success of the Young Unionist movement was demonstrated toward the end of the 1929 election when one thousand members celebrated Empire Day with a parade and ceremony at Glasgow's Cenotaph in George Square.[57]

The most notable feature of the Young Britons was its role in teaching patriotic and imperial values in order to combat what were considered corrupting Socialist and "foreign" influences in postwar British culture. The magazine *Young Briton*, the "Who Knows" leaflets, and other material were carefully designed to counter the teachings of groups that were "attempting to instil class hatred into young minds, [and] carry on teaching subversive to morals and good conduct."[58] Without the Young Britons, its proponents claimed, Britain was headed for moral anarchy, dissolution of the family, and the destruction of the Constitution and the Empire. The tone of the Young Britons was didactic, and it pervaded the group's literature and activities.

Young Briton was the children's organizations' most important educational weapon. In early 1925 *Home and Politics*, the WUO magazine, began offering historical lessons and stories for children. For instance, the May 1925 issue contained the play *Under One Flag*, written by Una Norris, a central office staff member. Several characters representing England and various dominions recited vapid dialogue showing the friendship among the nations of the Empire under the mother figure Britannia, while the strong-willed Ramana, representing India, gets lost after refusing Britannia's lead.[59] In October 1925 the children's column was moved from the women's magazine to *Young Briton*. The new magazine skirted obviously partisan issues in favor of material about Britain's history, heroes, Constitution, and Empire. *Young Briton* tried to demonstrate that Britain had progressed because of its tradition of liberty and Conservative government. It occasionally presented a simple analysis of a political issue, such as the Locarno Treaties, that it deemed a national question. The magazine contained suggestions for didactic recreations like a British Empire Stores toy that allowed children to buy goods made in the Empire and learn about the benefits of Empire.[60] The "Betty and Billy" cartoon in each issue showed readers a part of the Empire.

Young Britons branches also used patriotic leaflets and pamphlets from central office. A typical example was the pamphlet *Union Jack*. According to the pamphlet, the crosses and colors of the flag represented praiseworthy qualities and the kingdom's unity. "Our flag," it stated, "calls on all the members of the British Empire to stand *united* . . . for freedom, truth, justice, righteousness, and brotherhood, all members of one family living happily together, loving one another." The "Who Knows?" leaflets were also popular. Each leaflet gave insight into some symbol of British authority—one such was the "bobby"—in order to re-inforce its legitimacy.[61]

In their activities, Young Britons branches attempted to make patriotic lessons enjoyable, but they were sometimes very heavy going. Every meeting began with community singing and a short lesson sent from headquarters. Afterward there were games and crafts, followed by a carefully scripted rendition of the national anthem, including salutes. All the elements of a branch meeting were intended to provide recreation for the children while inculcating patriotic and moral values. In 1926, at the first event of the Launceston branch of the Young Britons, A. M. Williams, the Conservative M.P., told the children that "they could not really be happy unless they did work, and if they could learn to enjoy their work, then they were sure of a happy life." The children, however, seemed to enjoy more the tale of St. George and the dragon. They were told that the dragon represented sin, which was destroyed by the honorable and good St. George. St. George was the model for all children who wished to make something of their lives.[62]

Young Britons leaders emphasized imperial themes because they saw imperialism as ideal for neutralizing socialism and class warfare. The high-light of the Young Britons year was the celebration of Empire Day with parades, rallies, and pageants. Because Empire Day was 24 May (and also Queen Victoria's birthday), it was used to contrast Conservative values with the alleged Red celebrations on 1 May. Branches held military drills designed, as one historian notes, to teach children "the duties and respon-sibilities attached to the high privileges of being subjects of the mightiest Empire the world has ever known." Another popular activity was the Em-pire Tableau, in which Young Britons wore costumes representing colonies, dominions, the armed forces, and supposed British qualities. On the stage, characters arranged themselves around the central figures of Britannia and John Bull as the narrator described the glories of the united Empire. Young Britons also performed plays like *Flag of the Free*, in which Britannia tells the history of the Union Jack as children appear dressed to represent parts of the Empire (e.g., sheaves of wheat for Canada, a sailor's uniform for England).[63] With the Empire gathered before her, Britannia recites,

> Go take this flag. In honour raise it high.
> Wherever it does float, justice shall reign,
> And peace and unity. Men shall be free.
> Beneath the glorious standard of our realm.[64]

The imperial message was pervasive. When, for instance, children saluted the flag at the close of a branch meeting, they were grouped in "dominions." All these activities emphasized imperial unity and showed children that "the British Empire was really something to be proud of."[65]

Despite some success, the Young Britons faced several serious problems. First, many Conservatives were wary of undermining or duplicating the work of other patriotic organizations like the Primrose Juniors and the Scouts. In places—Wood Green and Skipton, for example—the Conservative association preferred cooperation with the Primrose Juniors to forming Young Britons branches. Other Conservatives sometimes failed to see the rationale for a nonpartisan Conservative youth organization when groups like the Scouts served that purpose.

Second, the Young Britons depended on the other Conservatives' aid. Was it necessary to give children a separate organization, or could they be incorporated into the WUO or JIL? Considering that most members were probably children of Conservative parents, how effective was the Young Britons? Did the Conservative Party need a group to educate children from already Conservative households?

Third, there was an underlying conflict in the Young Britons' aims. On the one hand, the organization was supposed to teach British values to all children, regardless of their parents' political affiliation or social class. Participation in the Young Britons did not constitute membership in or direct aid to the Conservative Party. The small subscription fee, halfpenny magazine, and inexpensive activities allowed children from all social classes to participate. But on the other hand, the Young Britons was designed to teach Conservative principles and funnel children into the Conservative Party. The hope was that the group would win over children of non-Conservative parents, even though this contradicted the emphasis on traditional authority. Although children were supposed to obtain their parents' consent before joining the Young Britons, the 1928 conference decided not to require written consent because they "would probably lose an opportunity of winning non-Conservative children for the movement."[66] For all of these reasons, the Young Britons sometimes seemed an unnecessary drain on associations and central office. As a result, the Young Britons lost some funding and its magazine after the party reorganization of 1931.[67]

Despite its shortcomings, the Young Britons continued to operate until World War II. In a 1927 *Home and Politics* article, an Imp correspondent explained the importance of the Young Britons. The Conservatives, she wrote, had a mission

> to rescue the children from the darkness of Communism and bring them into the Young Britons' movement. Take them out into the countryside and show them the wonder and beauty of her lanes, her woods and her fields; take them out on the sports fields, and let them feel the thrill . . . when smiting the cricket ball. . . ; teach them her songs of the sea, of love and of home, hymns and her songs of praise, and tell them of the men and women who gave their lives that they might enjoy these things.
>
> Once the children learn to love Britain the disease of Bolshevism will be powerless to affect their healthy bodies and souls and they will grow up proud to be called British men and women.[68]

The Young Britons met the Conservatives' desire for an organization to instill patriotism, morality, and discipline among children in order to fight Socialism and subversion.

For Imps and Young Britons, membership in a Conservative youth organization satisfied several needs. It provided social activities and friendships, learning experiences, and political opportunities. Despite their limited impact on the Conservative Party's programs and policies, these organizations gave youths an identity as members of a Conservative British community. With its typical interwar imagery, the Imp anthem, written by Imbert-Terry to the tune of "The Old Brigade," is an accurate expression of the ethos of the young Conservatives:

> We are the hope of the coming age,
> The light of the rising morn,
> Gaily we welcome the battle gage
> Aglow with our might newborn.

No chill of the years our soul [*sic*] dismay
    All wide the horizon gleans,
Illuming our hearts with its lustrous rays,
    The sun of our Empire beams.
Then join in our triumph of glory,
    As won by our Fathers of old;
Washed by the sea, this realm of the free
    We Imps mean to guard and hold.

Spread o'er the world in the bloodstained fields
    We gave of our brightest and best,
Each corner of victory mutely shields
    The bones of a brother at rest.
Shall we make naught of their warrior sleep,
    Make dust of each glorious grave?
By the vastness of Empire we vow to keep
    The Freedom they died to save!
Then join in their triumph of glory,
    May their fame through the ages be told.
Won by the free, the World's liberty,
    We Imps swear to guard and to hold.[69]

Conservative youth groups were undoubtedly less influential and smaller than the WUO, but they were the largest political organizations for young people in interwar Britain. During World War II, the JIL and Young Britons disappeared as their patriotic, imperialistic ethos collapsed. But before 1939 these youth groups helped preserve among some Britons an underlying faith in their nation's imperial mission and illustrious historical development, both allegedly threatened by left-wing extremists.

The JIL did not consider itself a policy-making body, and the rest of the Conservative Party felt no compunction about the group's lack of direct influence at Westminster. Nevertheless, the JIL contributed to the party's success in attracting the support of an electorate created by universal suffrage. Youth groups formed the base of the mass organization that the interwar Conservative Party comprised. With these popular organizations for younger and future voters of Britain, the Conservative Party projected its influence into the lives of ordinary electors. The party also successfully used the Young Britons, the JIL, and the WUO to attract hundreds of thousands of children, young adults, and women, giving Conservatives a solid organization for the modern political system and guaranteeing it a larger share of the vote.

4

The Labour Committee, Trade Union Reform, and Conservative Wage Earners

Between the two World Wars the Conservatives attempted to develop a popular organization for wage earners, the NUA Labour Committee. Although sociologists and political scientists have studied the larger phenomenon of working-class Conservatism, only one chapter in a dissertation has looked at the working-class organization of the Conservative Party. The NUA Labour Committee was an important part of the Conservative response to the full enfranchisement of wage earners and the increased power of the working class after 1918.[1]

The NUA Labour Committee, responding to the growth in size and influence of trade unions—and their closer links to the Labour Party—tried to attract wage earners by offering them a different political identity. Compared to other interwar Conservative organizations, however, the Labour Committee was relatively unsuccessful. Although large numbers of wage earners voted for Conservative candidates then (and continue to do so now), the Labour Committee was never able to attract a significant number of wage earners into the Conservative organization. Local labour committees existed in only a third of the seats in England and Wales, and these often had fewer than twenty members. The Labour Party was far more successful in mobilizing wage earners and their resources through the trade unions.

The problems confronting the NUA Labour Committee were due less to policy differences with the regular Conservative Party than to administrative conflicts and social divisions. First, because the committee maintained a network of branches that were quasi-independent from local associations, it was not fully accepted either by rank-and-file Conservatives or by organizers. Second, class and gender divisions were a nearly insurmountable obstacle for the Labour Committee. The Conservative Party of the period relied on its largely middle-class, heavily female, organization. These rank-and-file Conservatives came to dominate the Conservative Party, particularly at the local level. They were reluctant to welcome an alien group, male wage earners, particularly if it was to be admitted as a distinct, autonomous organization. They were also not very interested in working-class candidates. And workingmen were often less attracted to the local associations than to traditional Conservative clubs, which at least provided tangible benefits for working-class members.

The shortcomings of the Labour Committee did not destroy working-class support for the Conservative Party, which depended more on conservative social and political values than on workers' role in the party. Working-class Conservatism was based on deference and the desire for national unity.

In addition, some workingmen and women supported the Labour Committee and the Conservative Party because they wanted to alter some of the privileges the prewar Liberal government had granted to trade unions. In fact this issue, the legal status and privileges of trade unions, was the primary concern of the Labour Committee and its members during the 1920s. The Labour Committee particularly objected to what it considered the politicization of trade unions. Its members helped to maintain the pressure for trade union reform and ensured that the Trade Disputes and Trade Unions Act of 1927 dealt with trade union contributions to the Labour Party. On this issue the Labour Committee played a crucial role, one that forces us to question the traditional interpretation of the 1927 legislation as a punitive response to the General Strike.[2]

Development and Structure of the Labour Committee

Since the mid-nineteenth century there had been Tory workingmen's groups, most notably the Conservative clubs, which had about two million members by the early twentieth century. Many clubs were affiliated with the Association of Conservative Clubs (established 1894), which encouraged them to offer educational and political activities for members. The political value of these clubs, however, was limited: the typical older married man who joined a club was more interested in games, music, conversation, and cheap beer than political activity. The result, observers often noted, was that clubs created good card and billiards players—not Conservative volunteers. After the war some Conservative associations tried to mobilize clubs in their area, but to little effect. Even in Wrexham, where clubs were components of the party organization, and Lancashire and Cheshire, where Tory workingmen's groups were very active before the war, clubs contributed little to the Conservative Party. Only Sir Archibald Salvidge in Liverpool, where anti-Catholicism remained a powerful force, was able to rely on a strong network of political clubs. By 1931, because the clubs were not doing their part, central office had cut all subsidies to them.[3]

Before the war the only other major organization for Conservative workingmen was the National Conservative League (NCL). The NCL was founded in 1884 as a loose federation of workingmen's lodges and was completely independent of the NUA. Lodges followed Masonic practices, with secret initiation rites and titles, and they served as a sort of friendly society, operating limited insurance schemes. As political organizations they had the same failings as the clubs. Most lodges were dissolved during the war, including the national Grand Lodge, nominally headed by the Duke of Somerset. In northern parts of England, however, they were revived after the war and were at least loosely connected to the local associations. During the mid-1920s Allan Hand, who later became the Young Britons organizer, formed many lodges in Durham County, and by 1925 there were seventy branches and several thousand members in northern England. Hand claimed that the friendly society and Masonic elements attracted workingmen. Other Conservatives, however, were less enthusiastic. The M.P. for Barnard Castle, Sir Cuthbert Headlam, thought that his local lodges were politically inactive and contained too many dreary old Tories. In general the lodges were ill-suited to the age.[4]

During World War I the establishment of universal male suffrage and the rise of trade unions and the Labour Party convinced many Conservatives that they had to establish a new, avowedly political organization for wage earners. Conservatives were worried, as the *Conservative Agents' Journal* pointed out, that "nearly all workmen are now joining Unions of one kind or another and . . . unless some steps are taken to enlist their interest in the Unionist or Constitutional Labour programme there is great danger of their being swept bodily into the political bag of the Independent Labour Party." Many Conservatives believed that they had to incorporate Britain's presumedly patriotic wage earners into the party. In February 1918, the Lancashire Provincial Division's council revived its trade union organization, the Conservative Labour Committee. Working with constituency agents, the Lancashire labor organizer used subscriptions and donations to establish antisocialist committees in unions and clubs. Because the committees were linked to divisional associations, and the whole organization was supervised by the Lancashire Provincial Division, the labour committee managed to avoid the institutional and class segregation characteristic of earlier wage-earner groups. A number of Conservatives in other regions expressed interest in setting up such a group, but to no effect.[5]

At a 20 May 1919 meeting of the NUA council, the chairman of the Lancashire labour committee, John Whittaker, suggested that his organization be adopted throughout Britain. In a memorandum presented to the NUA, Whittaker argued that the Conservative Party needed a group to mobilize trade unionists against "the tide of Socialism and . . . revolutionary doctrines." The group could also be used to encourage Conservative workingmen just as the Labour Party encouraged its members. An investigative subcommittee of the NUA Executive agreed that a committee should be formed to educate wage earners, gather working-class opinion, bring Conservative wage earners into the party, encourage them to take action in their unions or cooperatives, and field working-class political candidates. The NUA Executive asked local associations to form such committees. It also appointed the members of the subcommittee to the new NUA Labour Committee, which elected Whittaker chairman. They hired the Scotsman Robert Mathams, a war veteran and former central office agent for Lancashire, as labour committee organiser. The president of the Federation of British Industries, Sir Vincent Caillard, and central office made funds available for the Labour Committee.[6]

In its first years the Labour Committee was most concerned about discouraging revolution and socialism and politicizing trade unions. The NUA council recommended training more working-class speakers to attack Labour Party policies, particularly nationalization. The Labour Committee organized a national conference of wage earners and put forward resolutions condemning nationalization of mines and railways, deploring municipal socialism and syndicalism, and supporting retrenchment and tariffs. Because of a railway strike the conference was canceled, but nine hundred men and women from seven northern counties attended a March 1920 meeting where delegates passed resolutions against nationalization, direct action, and excessive government spending. They praised unions "as an instrument for the well-being of . . . wage earners" and claimed that Conservatism was compatible with "genuine, loyal, and life-long support for trade unionism." Trade union and cooperative members were told it was their duty (1) to stop Labour supporters from using those organizations for political purposes and (2) to work against radicals, who were causing domestic instability and destroying the British way of life.[7]

In the five years following its creation, the Labour Committee made slow progress. In part this was because its role in and relationship to the Conservative Party remained unclear. The local and regional organization was linked to the national Labour Committee, in practice remaining largely separate from the regular Conservative organization. During the coalition years this was sometimes useful, as antisocialist wage earners could work on the committee without having to join the Conservative Party. In 1920 the editor of the *Conservative Agents' Journal* described the Labour Committee as "a hybrid organisation . . . informing when it desires to do so the existing Unionist Organisation of the considered views of working men . . . exercising a watchful eye on the operations of the local Trades Union branches, while elastic enough to welcome into its ranks men who would not dream at present of enrolling . . . [in] the Unionist Party Organisation." The editor added that agents should be able to control committees by pulling strings and handling finances. Agents were less confident of their power, and in some constituencies associations asserted control over their labour committee by designating its members. Labour committees also irritated some Conservative women because they generally excluded women and often operated like workingmen's clubs.[8]

Another perennial concern was real wage earners' lack of influence. In the early years very few served on the Labour Committee. After the fall of the coalition government in October 1922, the NUA conference, expressing grave concern about the Labour Party and its "insidious and incessant Socialist propaganda," urged greater efforts to bring wage earners into all levels of the Conservative Party. Similar views were expressed at all levels of the party. The NUA Executive soon tried to encourage provincial divisions to elect more working-class delegates to the NUA council so that there would be a larger pool of wage earners for the Labour Committee.[9]

Complaints resurfaced in later years. In October 1923, the 1923 NUA conference heard that the upper echelons of the Conservative Party were inaccessible to wage earners. A few months later, after their defeat in the election, Conservative leaders returned to the problem. In a *Home and Politics* article Caroline Bridgeman, WUO chairwoman and wife of a former Cabinet minister, emphasized the importance of making the party "thoroughly democratic . . . bringing into it representatives of all ranks of life . . . ensuring that the working man and working woman shall be in a position to take an active part in its management." But Conservative activists and central office officials largely ran the Labour Committee. Neither Mathams nor Whittaker was a wage earner. The Conservative Party's chairman, deputy chairman, principal agent, chief organizing agent, and the NUA secretary were also key members of the Labour Committee.[10]

The Labour Committee also failed to promote working-class candidates. In 1923 one agent argued in the *Conservative Agents' Journal* that although the adoption of workingmen in appropriate constituencies should "follow as a matter of course the formation of . . . Labour Committees," he could see no "vigorous and sustained" efforts to elect Conservative workingmen. A year later the NUA conference at Cardiff devoted much time to discussing this matter. In a long speech, a member of the NUA Executive moved a resolution demanding more wage earners as candidates. She implored the delegates to rid themselves of the biases that kept them from selecting wage earners, claiming that the absence of workers from the Conservative delegation to Parliament was a major reason that working people identified with the Socialist Party. After the 1924 election, the NUA Executive made a similar request, but associations refused to change their practices. A final problem facing the Labour Committee in its early years was the lack of its own publication. Instead it had to beg space from other Conservative magazines for Labour Committee news. Beginning in August 1921, *Popular View* included a column, "Workshop Talks," which was gradually given over to the Labour Committee. In late 1922 the Labour Committee gained access to the *Democrat,* the weekly magazine of the "nonpolitical" General Federation of Trade Unions.[11]

The absence of a periodical became one of the less serious of the Labour Committee's problems when Sir Herbert Blain became principal agent in March 1924. After the unexpected death of Mathams in April 1924, Blain appointed G. E. M. Walker, Matham's assistant, as the new organizer. Blain then launched an investigation of the Labour Committee, presenting his findings to the NUA Executive in July 1924. In his report, Blain argued that the Labour Committee had failed and would never succeed without major reforms. He found that there were only eighty-eight labour committees in England and Wales, some of them not even affiliated with the NUA Labour Committee. Except in Durham, Northumberland, Lancashire, and Glamorgan, many committees were paper organizations with an "almost negligible" and "quite unrepresentative" membership. Local Conservative associations and agents were often indifferent or hostile to the committees, which they considered threats to their organization, while Tory workingmen held the committees in contempt. The Conservative Party would never attract wage earners, Blain claimed, unless it showed an ability to cooperate and a willingness to accept working-class members at every level of the party, "right up to the Executive Committee and . . . Parliament." Blain suggested a number of reforms. First, labour committees should be made more representative by electing members from the sub-branches of Conservative associations. Second, committees should become advisory organs of the association's executive committee. In return, associations were expected to offer workers opportunities in the party and select them as candidates for political office. Finally, Blain suggested that the NUA Labour Committee take an advisory role and co-opt more wage earners.[12]

The NUA and central office supported Blain's proposals, but they met with only moderate success. The former coal miner, Gwilym Rowlands, became Labour Committee chairman when Whittaker stepped down in 1925. The new NUA rules adopted in mid-1924 allowed divisional associations to send a third delegate to the NUA council if he was a wage earner. Baldwin gave his blessing to the reforms in his speech at the 1924 NUA conference. He hoped that the changes would provide workers with "a ladder by which a man, whatever his means or his origin, may hope, by the exercise of his own natural ability, to render service to his country into whatsoever office he may be called." And *Home and Politics* acclaimed the "magnificent conference" as proving that "One of the chief and abiding appeals of our Party is that it can truly claim to be desirous of the welfare of each and every class; and it is hoping in a short time to claim, even more truly than before, that it is also 'representative' of all classes." Yet at an early 1925 meeting of the NUCUA Executive, the party chairman, F. Stanley Jackson, complained that many associations had still not established labour committees. Blain again circularized the divisions. He declared the results satisfactory; by mid-1927 the number of divisions with committees had doubled. But this number still included only a third of the seats in England and Wales, and the labour committee in London still had few wage earners.[13]

Under Blain's direction the Labour Committee also encouraged the development of provincial committees, but without a great deal of success. As a result of reforms in 1925, the Lancashire and Cheshire labour committee (the two provincial divisions were consolidated in 1925), which remained strong throughout the 1920s, elected a working-class chairman and women members. It also began meeting on Saturdays for the convenience of its wage-earner members. Outside Lancashire and Cheshire—and other regions where labour committees were already established—progress was limited. The Yorkshire provincial division recognized the need for more working-class men and women members, and it formed a (weak) provincial labour committee. Few rural regions had such committees because there were few unions and little industry.[14]

In Scotland, an independent Workers' League had existed since 1910. It was headed by a former apprentice wood turner from Glasgow, William Templeton, who served as M.P. for Banff from 1924 to 1929. The league was particularly interested in tariff reform and, like the NCL, was organized as a network of lodges. After the war it became the Unionist Workers' League (UWL) and was loosely tied to the SUA. In return for financial assistance and accommodation at Unionist headquarters in Edinburgh, the UWL conformed to the policy laid down by the Scottish whip and the SUA. At the time of the 1924 general election, Unionist leaders decided that the UWL should concentrate solely on party propaganda and education, and its magazine, *Common Sense,* was discontinued. In effect the UWL became a subcommittee of the SUA Executive. Its lodges were closed and its activities limited to propaganda work requested by local associations. It continued to decline, rejecting merger with the Scottish juniors in 1925, and finally disappearing in 1928.[15]

Both the UWL and the Labour Committee were considerably less important than the women's and youth organizations. Labour committees were fairly common in working-class seats, particularly if, as was commonly the case, the seat was dominated by the Labour Party. Yet by the end of the 1920s, less than half of the constituencies in my sample had active labour committees. Clapham had one, possibly as a result of the activities of its energetic agent, J. H. Bottomley, but virtually no other London association did. In North Cornwall the Conservatives formed a labour committee only in 1925. The advisory committee was composed of a workingman chosen from each of the constituency's five districts. Three were quarrymen from the Labour stronghold of Delabole, one was a railway worker, and the last was a gardener.[16]

In the industrial and mining seats of Wales and England, labour committees were reasonably common. Greenwood estimates that in 1939, after a difficult decade for the Labour Committee, more than a quarter of the divisions in northern and northwestern England, Yorkshire, and Wales had labour committees; in central office's Northern Area, almost two-fifths of constituencies had committees. Wrexham Tories provided representation to wage earners in 1921, and in the following year the executive elected delegates to form a "Unionist Labour Wing," which served in an advisory role. The two industrial seats of Bradford Central and Stockton had active labour committees. The Bradford Central committee, formed in 1920, included several branches and workingmen's clubs, and was part of a city-wide labor organization that had hundreds of members. The committee taught constitutional principles and encouraged the advancement of wage earners in the Conservative Party. The Stockton organization, revived and reorganized after the war, sent delegates to the first Labour Committee conference in 1920 and formed its own committee in 1925. The committee benefited from the strength of the NCL, which had three lodges in the city and strong support in the rest of the county. During the 1920s, the Stockton committee had about forty regular members; membership increased in the early 1930s.[17]

Even associations without labour committees made some efforts to attract wage-earner support and participation. Until the North Cornwall labour committee was formed, the association rules mandated the election of wage-earner representatives to the executive and allowed the waiver of subscription fees in hardship cases. In response to suggestions from central office, the Chichester association claimed that a labour committee was unnecessary, because branches were required to elect wage earners to the executive committee. The Skipton association's rule also reserved places on the executive committee for workers. Oswestry Tories, however, twice refused to form a labour committee, alleging that it would foment class divisions.[18]

To encourage wage-earner participation in Conservative activities, working-class representatives were sometimes paid or reimbursed for their expenses. The Skipton and Oswestry associations altered their rules to pay for needy delegates to attend local, regional, or national meetings. In return, delegates were expected to work on propaganda and other activities. Under the rules adopted by the Chichester association in 1924, the expenses of a wage-earner delegate to the NUCUA council were paid. The same practice was followed in North Cornwall, but other local and regional organizations either did not help or did so on an ad hoc basis. Yorkshire Tories decided in 1924 to bring working-class members onto the provincial executive and send them to the NUA council. After estimating that the annual cost would be about thirty pounds per delegate, they instead opted to select "a good working man" only if another member would pay.[19]

Another practical issue that hampered Conservative efforts to increase wage-earner representation was meeting times. Workers who depended on an hourly wage could not leave work to attend party meetings, but the middle-class members of most associations preferred to meet on weekday afternoons. Conservative women especially liked this arrangement because they often had to be home early to cook dinner. Saturday was impractical because it was shopping day. The dilemma was insoluble. The Yorkshire provincial division changed the time of general meetings from weekday afternoons to Saturdays, but the powerful committees continued to meet as before. When the Chichester association tried to hold meetings in the evening, so many members protested that the association returned to afternoon meetings. In late 1924 the NUCUA Executive decided that action on this issue was useless, but it did ask local associations to pay wage-earner delegates who attended national party meetings. Because they were being asked, in effect, to select more costly delegates, local Conservatives sent few wage-earner delegates to the NUCUA.[20]

The Labour Committee and its local branches were involved in different Conservative Party activities with varying degrees of success. Labour committees contributed to the general efforts of the local associations by distributing propaganda and holding public meetings. In 1929 labour committee members handed out almost 1.3 million leaflets in factories and clubs across the country.[21] Most labour committees, however, did not have enough members to do the same sorts of tasks as the women's and youth groups performed.

More important, Labour Committee leaders realized their organization's success depended in large measure on providing equality of opportunity for wage earners to advance in the Conservative Party. To achieve this goal, the Labour Committee sponsored educational programs and encouraged wage earners to run for local office. The Labour Committee used education to rouse wage earners from political apathy and turn them against socialism. Members could study a variety of subjects for their own pleasure or to equip themselves as Conservative workers. The Stockton committee learned about the economics of coal mining and the possibilities of reviving the local shipbuilding industry, as well as the dangers of socialism and the glories of the Empire. Some members also volunteered to work with the JIL. Beginning in 1920, the NUA Labour Committee organized summer schools at which Conservative workingmen and -women attended courses on politics and economics. They were taught by scholars like the M.P. and historian J. A. R. Marriott; the editor of the *Edinburgh Review*, Harold Cox; and the economist Sir William Ashley. The Labour

Committee also played a crucial role in establishing the Conservative College. Such schools gave wage earners the chance to take part in political work and, possibly, become candidates for local or national office.[22]

Unfortunately, the Labour Committee had few successful wage-earner candidates. In Lancashire and Northumberland, a number of labour committee candidates were elected to local councils and boards. The Bradford committee sponsored its chairman, Jonas Pearson, as a successful candidate in a board of guardians election and as an unsuccessful Conservative candidate in the 1923 general election. In 1922 the Wrexham association considered a workingman candidate but decided instead to continue supporting its coalition Liberal M.P. To encourage the adoption of wage-earner candidates, central office offered subsidies to divisional associations who picked from a list of working-class candidates. The poor response led Younger to create a fund for wage-earner candidates. This also failed to have much effect, however, and the next party chairman promised only to try to convince associations that they should adopt wage earners.[23]

As proponents of workingman candidates grew frustrated, they increased pressure and encountered greater resistance. In 1928 Gwilym Rowlands, a candidate in four hopeless contests, attacked hypocritical Conservatives who "cheer working men on that [Conference] platform when there were safe seats going [to others]. They took jolly good care they did not invite them [wage earners] to fight. He was satisfied that they had in their party working men quite equal to the best Labour men in the House of Commons. (Applause.) We want to follow them in trade union and Labour matters in the House of Commons and tell people what we know from experience. Give us that right and privilege to fight where we can do more work than we are doing from outside." The resolution passed easily, but probably quite a few of the delegates agreed with another speaker who thought that politically ambitious workingmen should make their own way rather than "expecting Lord Somebody or Lady Somebody to be constantly nursing and carrying ... [them] about." The efforts of NUCUA and central office were largely unsuccessful. In the 1929 election there were only three Conservative workingmen's candidates, and none was elected. Except for William Templeton, no Conservative wage earners were elected until Rowlands finally won Flintshire in 1935.[24]

The reasons for the failure to adopt working-class candidates were both financial and social. Most associations lacked the money to pay candidates' expenses. Candidates were expected to pay these expenses themselves; if possible, they should also contribute to the association and other local activities. In addition, most Conservatives were insensitive to the workingman's view. In 1921, for instance, the Labour Committee was shocked to find Conservative M.P.s opposing subsidized fares for M.P.s. Conservatives did not want working-class candidates. Between 1922 and 1924 there was enough money for associations to adopt such candidates, but only ten workingmen were selected in three general elections. And all of the candidates except one (in Walsall, Birmingham) were adopted in hopeless seats. There is good reason to blame, as one observer put it, "the rocklike snobbery of Conservative constituency associations, which have almost invariably tended to confuse aspirants from the unions with delinquent ex-butlers looking for a reference." The Labour Committee removed selection of wage earner candidates from its list of official aims in the 1930s.[25]

Despite its failures, the Labour Committee made sure that Conservative leaders understood its position on several issues, particularly trade union reform. In common with other Conservative workingmen, labour committee members generally objected to restrictions on "sinful" activities, especially those on alcohol consumption imposed during the war. Newport Conservatives claimed that the restoration of "pre-war liberties" would actually reduce the number of socialist open-air meetings. At least one labour committee asked the chancellor of the exchequer, Winston Churchill, to liberalize gambling rather than restrict or tax it. For both issues, however, public opinion, particularly among women, dictated that nothing be done.[26]

A more serious concern was unemployment compensation and other forms of state assistance. The chairman of the Bradford labour committee tried to have the Yorkshire provincial division pass a resolution in favor of allowing those on part-time unemployment benefits to receive their money with their usual paycheck. His intent was to lessen "the moral degeneration and great inconvenience" of the existing method of distribution. But the provincial division did not take any public action. Under the guidance of Allan Hand, labour committees in Durham advised Conservative workingmen before they went to the sometimes hostile bodies that dispensed unemployment benefits. With the assistance of their M.P., the Stockton labour committee dealt with unemployed persons who had lost some or all of their benefits. They also suggested to the government and Lord Blanesburgh's 1925 Unemployment Insurance Committee a number of practical changes in the insurance system. For example, the committee requested special consideration for necessitous areas and the exclusion of servicemen's pensions from all means calculations.[27]

Trade Union Reform

By far the most important issue for the Labour Committee in the 1920s was trade union reform, particularly the political levy collected by unions. Scholars have not generally studied popular attitudes toward the trade unions even though they have been a key institution during the twentieth century. What little work has been done tends to look at this issue from the perspective of trade union and Labour Party leaders. Because of its importance for the Labour Committee and popular Conservatism after the First World War, trade union reform needs to be fully explained and analyzed. Moreover, the persistent demands of some Conservatives for legislative action undermines the traditional interpretation of the Trade Disputes and Trade Unions Act as a punitive response to the General Strike.[28]

Two pieces of prewar Liberal legislation were central to the debate over trade union reform in the 1920s. The first, the Trade Disputes Act of 1906, provided wide-ranging civil immunity for unions and facilitated the greater use of picketing. A few years later the courts decided in favor of a trade unionist and railway worker, W. V. Osborne, who refused to pay his union's compulsory political levy. The Liberals then passed the Trade Unions Act of 1913, which prohibited unauthorized compulsory political levies, but allowed unions to engage in politics and to collect levies if a majority of members approved. The law also allowed an individual trade unionist to exempt himself from a levy, but it left the matter in the hands of union officials who, perhaps inevitably, tended to prevent such "contracting out" even if they had to resort to intimidation or harassment. (In fact, Osborne was ejected from his union.)[29] Nevertheless, before the war the union problem did not appear to be very serious.

The situation changed as the power of the unions increased dramatically during and after World War I, and unions took a more aggressive political stance. By 1929, trade unions' contributions to political causes were twenty-four times their 1913 level. In part this was due to the rising union membership, but a more important factor was the Labour Party's decision to triple affiliation fees for unions between 1917 and 1920. In addition, during the unsettled early postwar period, strikes were common and often had a political slant. As a result public opinion, particularly Conservative opinion, increasingly subscribed to the belief that unions had too many privileges and too much power with which to threaten the freedom of the individual and the safety of the community. Workers who were members of the Labour Committee were especially interested in trade union reform. They felt that they suffered unfairly because of their political convictions and wanted to stop what the Stockton committee termed "the Socialist element in Trade Unions" who were "using the [union] Branches for political purposes." Trade union reform remained a major issue throughout the 1920s.[30]

The Lloyd George government gained a measure of safety from the general strike under the Emergency Powers Act of 1920, but there were demands for further measures. The Cabinet considered—and rejected—legislation to outlaw strikes and establish compulsory strike ballots. A coalition government whose ministers included former radical reformers like the prime minister was unlikely to restrict the unions. Lloyd George and most of his ministers wanted to appease labor in order to ease tensions and undermine the demand for nationalization. The government indicated its unwillingness to pursue trade union reform when it denied time on the legislative agenda of the Commons to the Trade Union Ballot bill of 1921.

Outside the Cabinet, some Conservatives suggested compulsory arbitration, prohibition of sympathetic strikes, limits on picketing, and other reforms aimed at protecting the community from "abuses" of union privileges. Proponents of such measures argued, as Eden Philpotts stated in 1921, that the existing laws allowed "a handful of men—many declared revolutionists—to suspend the industrial life and squander the means of a nation." Lawyers, who filled the back benches of the Conservative Party, regarded legal privileges for any corporation (except the legal profession) as "unEnglish." In the early 1920s Conservative M.P.s, particularly diehards like Sir Frederick Banbury, introduced a half dozen private members' bills aimed at restricting the Trade Disputes Act. They failed, however, to attract the support of Conservative leaders, who feared that such bills would turn wage earners against the party. As a contributor to the *Conservative Agents' Journal* warned in 1923, "drastic legislation, or undue interference, would easily upset the labouring population, who are very sensitive about what they regard as their rights and privileges." Instead, moderates should be encouraged to take control of the unions.[31]

After 1921 the number of strikes and the syndicalist threat diminished, and the Labour Party gained votes, turning Conservative attention from strikes to the electoral threat of Labour and its union backers. Many Conservatives, including those in the NUA Labour Committee, began to demand that unions separate their industrial and political operations. This suited Conservative workingmen, who regarded the right to strike as sacrosanct but were disenchanted with their unions' support of the Labour Party. Among the skilled trades in particular there was a large minority of what one Conservative leader called "respectable old boys" who opposed such political activity. About 15 percent of the members of the National Union of Railwaymen, Amalgamated Society of Woodworkers, and Amalgamated Engineering Union received exemptions from the political levy. In contrast, only 0.1 percent of the unskilled laborers who were members of the National Union of Agricultural Workers, the National Union of General Workers, and the Transport and General Workers Union received exemptions. George Barnes, a former secretary of the Amalgamated Society of Engineers and a former Labour leader, expressed a typically conservative craft union mentality in his 1924 memoirs. "Labour representation," he wrote, "means practical participation in the life of the nation and not a sounding of abstract theories on the one hand or the furtherance of sectional Trade Union views on the other." Barnes claimed that extremists had "intimidated and over-ridden the common sense, and made havoc with the interests of the . . . rank and file . . . [and] enabled the woolly-headed and the truculent to foment trouble."[32]

Initially the Labour Committee and the NUA, in hopes of wresting control of the unions (and cooperatives) from the Labour Party, did not take a decisive stance on legal reform. The 1920 NUA conference tabled the question of union political levies, while the Labour Committee printed booklets of exemption forms that were distributed to local labour committees and wage earners. Once it recognized the Labour Party's strength in the postwar unions, the NUA Labour Committee moved to try to protect antisocialist wage earners and reduce union political activity by challenging the political levy procedure. Instead of contracting out, the Labour Committee wanted union members to contract in. Union members would no longer be expected to contribute to a political fund unless they signed an agreement so stating. Besides aiding Conservative trade unionists, reform of the political levy would cut out some Labour Party revenue. But most Conservative wage earners—Greenwood's assertions notwithstanding—were more interested in assuring individual (i.e., their own) liberty and depoliticizing the unions than in weakening them or the Labour Party. In a 1923 lecture to a primarily trade unionist audience at the Conservative

College, F. J. C. Hearnshaw gave voice to Conservative workingmen's disgust: "What is quite intolerable, wholly tyrannical, and utterly incompatible with the elementary principles of democratic freedom, is that a person should at once and the same time (1) be compelled, on pain of economic ruin and physical violence, to join and remain in an association, and (2) be compelled without any redress to subscribe to and support whatever political action it may choose to take." Reform of the political levy enjoyed widespread support among Conservatives, including trade unionists.[33]

In February 1921 the Labour Committee finally took action by supporting the Milnerite Conservative M.P., Henry Wilson-Fox, who introduced a private member's bill for contracting in. The government opposed the bill, which was then dropped. But the NUA Executive pursued the issue, and both NUA and SUA conferences approved contracting in and secret balloting for trade union political funds. On 10 February 1922 Colonel Ernest Meysey-Thompson introduced a private member's bill for trade union reform that received an enthusiastic response from Conservatives. Under his bill a union would have been required to obtain at least a 60 percent approval rate (from a minimum of half its members) in a secret ballot before it could pursue political objectives. The bill also would have compelled unions to create separate political funds and to collect political contributions only from members who contracted in each year. During the bill's second reading on 19 May, the former Conservative junior minister Sir James Hope argued that the bill was no more than an attempt to disengage the legitimate interests of all trade unionists from politics. In a vivid attack on "Prussianism," Balfour attacked procedures that imperiled freedom and forced a union member "to contract into his liberty." Despite Labour's claim that the bill was an attack on unions, it passed the second reading.[34]

During the late spring and summer of 1922, Conservative organizations voiced their support for the Meysey-Thompson bill. The NUA council asked the government to provide facilities to enable the bill to be passed before the summer recess. In a *Democrat* article reprinted in the *Conservative Agents' Journal*, Mathams, the Labour Committee organizer, urged every Conservative M.P. to support "the cause of free men" by voting for the bill. Only by protecting individual liberty, he wrote, could "the headlong impetus of majority impulse" be contained. Conservatives around the country gave the bill their strong support.[35]

When the session ended in August without the bill's passage, Conservatives blamed socialist union officials, but they also expressed irritation with the government. Trade union reform was becoming a test of the merits of coalitionism. Central office and many Conservative groups pressed for change even as senior Conservatives expressed fears that the issue would prove a divisive one at the NUA conference scheduled for November 1922. Lord Derby, among others, warned Austen Chamberlain that failure to pass the bill would have very serious consequences. The chief whip, Leslie Wilson, also supported the bill and noted that William Appleton, a former lacemaker and the secretary of the General Federation of Trade Unions, thought the bill had the support of many trade unionists. Widespread Conservative interest in this issue was made clear only days before the coalition's fall. On 10 October, a coalition supporter, Sir William Bull, joined with an anticoalitionist, Sir Arthur Steel-Maitland, to push a strong resolution for reform through the NUA Executive.[36]

If any doubts remained about the level of Conservative support for trade union reform after the fall of the coalition, these were quickly removed at the NUA conference in December 1922. Delegates welcomed a resolution demanding action to relieve trade unionists who were being forced to support "Labour-Socialist principles." In a letter to Bonar Law, the new prime minister, Younger stated that ending the levy was a "very strong desire amongst thousands of Trade Unionists." The introduction in February 1923 of a private member's bill by Lieutenant Colonel Martin Archer-Shee raised hopes, but Baldwin, the chancellor of the exchequer, took no immediate action. During the summer the NUA council again demanded action. The party's principal agent, Sir Reginald Hall, suggested to Baldwin, now prime minister, that he collaborate with the Labour Committee on the issue. Although the NUA conference welcomed another reform resolution in October 1923, the country was soon thrown into a tariff campaign during which the political levy issue virtually disappeared.[37]

Conservative demands for trade union reform recurred after the 1923 election. Charles Ainsworth, a Lancashire cotton manufacturer, introduced a moderate private member's bill addressing only contracting in and the separation of political funds, but it was defeated by Liberal and Labour M.P.s during its second reading. In spring 1924, proponents of union reform were very concerned with the outcome of the Conservative leaders' conference, or shadow cabinet, which was setting future party policy. The NUA Labour Committee sent material and offered advice to the conference that made it clear that both branches and regular associations wholeheartedly supported reform. A central office memorandum, probably prepared by Mathams, warned party leaders that failure to change the levy would cause "a breaking away from the Party . . . of a large body of Conservative workingmen." Finally, after the Labour Committee sent another memorandum detailing union officials' many alleged abuses of the law, and the NUA Executive and party chairman added pressure, the shadow cabinet finally adopted trade union reform. In *Looking Ahead*, Conservative leaders stated that a trade unionist must "be free to exercise his own unfettered discretion as to whether or not he should contribute to any political levy through his union." The party was endorsing contracting in.[38]

After seeing their party win a tremendous victory in the 1924 election, Conservatives expected trade union reform, but the government neither spoke nor acted on the issue. A number of Conservative organizations then demanded that the pledge made in *Looking Ahead* be honored. The Labour Committee gathered experts to draft its own bill. In February 1925, Baldwin formed a Cabinet committee to study reform. Birkenhead was chairman, and Baldwin and the chief whip, among others, were members. Before the Cabinet committee could make much progress, however, the Scottish barrister F. A. Macquisten introduced a private member's bill requiring annual contracting in and protecting union funds from political misuse. Conservatives across the country, the NUCUA council, and 1922 Committee of Conservative M.P.s expressed support for the bill.[39]

But Conservative opposition to Macquisten's bill was not wholly lacking. The Unionist association in agricultural Kincardine, on the advice of the local M.P., was one of a few to oppose the bill. More significant objections came from influential Conservatives who, like the editor of *The Times*, Geoffrey Dawson, and Duff Cooper, a member of the young, moderate "YMCA" (or do-gooder) faction of the party, considered the bill unnecessary, inopportune, and provocatively partisan. Although limited in numbers, these were supported by Baldwin and such key ministers as Birkenhead and Neville Chamberlain. On 25 February the progressive M.P. Noel Skelton led a deputation of twenty Conservative M.P.s to inform the prime minister of their opposition. The structure of the Conservative Party ensured that senior ministers would decide the bill's fate, and Macquisten, not wishing to challenge his leaders, met with Neville Chamberlain to devise the government amendment for the second reading.[40]

The compromise amendment that Baldwin later introduced recognized the merits of reform but refused to sanction a private member's bill on such an important issue. Macquisten considered this only a temporary delay, but Baldwin wanted to put off the question indefinitely in order to foster a more reconciliatory spirit at home. The prime minister set the stage for the bill's second reading with a speech at Birmingham on 5 March. Returning to an old theme, Baldwin decried suspicions between employers and workers, and urged them to seek "a truce ... that we may compose our differences, that we may join all our strengths together to see if we cannot pull the country into a better and happier condition."[41]

The second reading of the Macquisten bill was accompanied by a number of notable speeches, including Baldwin's eloquent and emotive appeal, and half a dozen maiden efforts. In moving the second reading, Macquisten appealed to British fair play, which was violated by "political conscription," a "festering sore in the side of trade unionism." After the bill was seconded, Baldwin moved the government amendment. In this often quoted speech, he focused on the wider issues involved and on his hopes for Britain. He effectively stilled the urges of his party by tapping into "Englishness." Baldwin recalled the idyllic conditions at his family's business—before the arrival of corporations, unions, and strikes. The future, he claimed, would be decided by a new partnership of employers and unions, whose recent progress in that direction the bill threatened to undermine. Baldwin asked his party to drop the bill as "a gesture" toward "the removal of suspicion in the country." Some Tories considered the speech curious, but, according to *The Times,* this "very typical Englishman" made a "profound impression" and swayed opinion in favor of conciliation.[42]

Because Baldwin's intervention virtually ensured that the bill would be shelved, the remainder of the debate was anticlimactic. In his maiden speech, William Templeton criticized the bill's sponsors for redressing minor problems while allowing union leaders to continue their political activities. In another maiden speech, the Tory M.P. Cuthbert Headlam accepted the amendment but warned Labour not to ignore this opportunity: "If we can do things without legislation which will lead to better relations between employers and employed, we should do our best in that direction. If it is found to be impossible to do what we wish without a change in the law, then we must have the courage to bring forward a Bill which will revise the whole question of the position of trade unionists under the law. This is not a subject for a Private Member's Bill, and I hope it may become the duty of the Government to bring forward a Bill dealing with the whole subject." During the debate, M.P.s who had introduced the bill and members of the 1922 Committee of Conservative M.P.s announced their acceptance of the amendment, which passed in a straight party vote.[43]

Many Conservatives were nonetheless unhappy with this outcome, particularly as labor relations worsened. Sir Philip Stott, a leading figure in the Labour Committee, expressed great disappointment and, unable to turn the party against Baldwin, temporarily withdrew from the NUCUA Labour Committee and Executive. Others regarded the setback as temporary and waited for a more opportune moment that would allow the government to introduce its own bill. The Labour Committee made it clear that it would not abandon the political levy and that it expected the government to fulfill the party's pledge. And during the months after the bill's defeat, Conservative interest in trade union reform increased because of developments in the coal industry. After weeks of rising tensions and a threatened general strike, the government appeared to surrender to coal miners' demands by agreeing on 31 July to pay a nine-month wage subsidy. A Trade Unions Congress (TUC) conference in September 1925 aggravated Conservative anger over the episode. The outbursts of some delegates, which later appeared in Conservative literature, proved to many Conservatives that extremists were abusing union privileges in order to "attain Socialist and Communist ends."[44]

As a consequence, proponents of reform acquired added support, and they began to extend their demands to include the prohibition of sympathetic strikes and closed shops as well. The more aggressive mood was evident at all levels of the party. Delegates at the NUCUA conference in October 1925 advocated a change in the political levy. They erupted into "loud and prolonged applause" when a representative demanded that the government, elected by antisocialist voters, end the extremists' stranglehold. Baldwin's conciliatory tactics had failed, Macquisten told delegates, and further offerings would weaken the party and destroy the Empire. In response the party chairman vowed to take up the issue rather than "sacrifice justice on the altar of political expediency."[45]

The conference's positive response led Macquisten publicly to accuse Baldwin of using weak "Christian Scientist methods" and abandoning his promises. Macquisten vowed to introduce another political levy bill. His new bill, introduced on 20 November, was quickly dispatched, but in February 1926 the NUCUA council reiterated its support for contracting in and reducing "the political activity of Trade Unions." Several Cabinet members also expressed displeasure at recent events and began to consider the need for secret strike ballots, penalties for sympathetic strikes, and restricted picketing. Birkenhead stated in October 1925 that the government might have to give "complete reconsideration of the exceptional legal status conceded to trade unions [which] seem[s] to me, under the influence of extremist elements, to have been grossly abused." In a speech made on 4 November he warned, "We, and we alone, not the trade unions, not the Communists, not the employers, are the trustees of the community as a whole, and if and when the threats of industrial anarchy imperil that cause, there is no responsibility of intervention from which we shall shrink and there will be found little which we have not thought out and prepared beforehand." In other words, even the present conciliatory government would have to act if there was a general strike.[46]

Support for reform increased dramatically after the General Strike (4–12 May 1926). Shortly after the failure of the Meysey-Thompson bill, Barnes had predicted that no union bill would ever succeed, "providing that the Labour Party confines itself to constitutional methods and takes steps to clear itself of revolutionary verbiage." The General Strike, by appearing to demonstrate the unconstitutional and revolutionary views of union and Labour Party leaders, pushed trade union reform into the limelight. During the crisis, central office distributed more than three million pieces of antistrike literature. Conservative leaders were careful to portray their cause as a struggle for the Constitution. In a BBC speech Baldwin asked listeners, "Can there be a more direct attack upon the community than that a body, not elected by the voters of the country, without consulting the people, without consulting even the Trade Unionists, and in order to impose conditions never yet defined, should dislocate the life of the nation and try to starve us into submission?" Baldwin's handling of the crisis was widely approved, and he received hundreds of supportive letters. Bradford Conservatives, for instance, expressed "admiration and pride" and agreed with the government's rejection of the "organised assault upon the rights, liberties and freedom of the citizens." An NCL lodge in Stockton claimed that reform was now necessary "to make further attacks on our liberties, our King and our Constitution for ever impossible."[47]

Shortly after the General Strike ended, the Cabinet formed a committee under the chairmanship of Lord Chancellor Cave to consider trade union reform. Leading moderates within the party, for example, Harold Macmillan, Lord Swinton, and Neville Chamberlain, advocated measures that would include arbitration procedures and generally promote cooperation between workers and owners. In October 1926 the NUCUA conference demonstrated, however, that rank-and-file Conservatives were more interested in legal restrictions. One delegate introduced a motion in favor of conciliation and arbitration, but it was easily defeated. The collapse of the General Strike had reassured Conservatives that their way of life would not be "destroyed by a Socialist Junta sitting at Eccleston Square," but it also made them even more eager to purge unions of extremists and foreign ideologies. For six weeks after the General Strike, *The Times* and other newspapers printed countless letters demanding action against levies and illegal strikes. At their annual meeting, Wirral Conservatives claimed that dangerous revolutionaries "secure the key positions in the industrial Trade Union organisations, and are filling many important posts in the organisations of the Socialist party itself. When the Trade Union machine, largely immune from the legal consequences of its actions, is used by Extremists to threaten paralysis and stoppage of vital public services . . . [it] involves the public welfare, [and] it calls for the attention of the present Government." Typically Conservatives demanded contracting in, strike ballots, restricted picketing, more legal liabilities on unions, and the end of "foreign propaganda."[48]

By early summer Conservatives had made it clear that they expected reform. The government responded with reassurances. At its 22 June 1926 meeting the NUCUA council gave much attention to union reform and agreed on several immediate changes in the law. First, they demanded the right to work and the balloting of workers before they went on strike. Second, they requested that all unions provide audited financial accounts. Third, despite the resistance of Sir Robert Sanders, a former minister and party organizer who did not want to embarrass the government, the Labour Committee asked for the repeal of the 1906 and 1913 acts. The council was reassured by what one observer described as a "rather indiscreet but much approved speech" by Birkenhead, who broadly hinted that the Cabinet was planning a reform measure. Meanwhile Lord Cave asked the Labour Committee to poll members in order to present their views to the Cabinet committee. In the House of Lords, Cave shelved Lord Banbury's new reform bill on 20 July, but he held out the promise of a more constructive government bill.[49]

But many Conservatives remained wary of the government's attitude, and their concerns surfaced at Conservative meetings in the autumn. At the NUCUA conference in October 1926, delegates repeated their demands and asked for immediate action. On behalf of wage earners, Stockton's James Gardner warned, "If the Government let us down this time I am seriously thinking of what my future political views shall be, and there are thousands more like me." Another delegate simply instructed the leaders to "Get on with it or get out." A particularly hostile motion criticizing the government's lassitude was withdrawn only after the party chairman promised action. Six weeks later the SUA conference passed its own list of union reforms, including secret strike ballots, restricted picketing, and separate political funds. The Primrose League and the National Citizens' Union (which had gathered forty thousand signatures on a proreform petition) made similar statements. Even after the chief whip stated on 11 November that the government intended to present a bill in the next session, Conservatives remained uneasy; four days later the Labour Committee again demanded legislation to make unions "purely Industrial Organisations."[50]

Working methodically to devise an acceptable bill, the Cabinet considered almost every issue. All the ministers wanted to outlaw general strikes, restrict picketing, and prevent intimidation, but they differed on several issues, particularly compulsory strike ballots and contracting in. Eventually the Cabinet dropped strike balloting as an unworkable and needless interference in union activities. Based on their knowledge of rank-and-file opinion, central office informed the Cabinet that contracting in and the separation of political funds were essential. These changes would reduce unions' political activism and protect individual unionists' rights. A few Conservatives opposed these changes, but the Cabinet decided to adopt contracting in.[51]

The government finally introduced the Trade Disputes and Trade Unions bill on 4 April 1927. The first of its five main clauses declared illegal any nonindustrial strike designed to coerce the state or community; the second protected trade unionists who refused to join illegal strikes and was retroactive to the General Strike; the third prohibited picketing individuals or property in an attempt at intimidation; the fourth required trade unions to create separate political funds and adopt contracting in; and the fifth prohibited civil servants from joining trade unions affiliated with outside bodies (e.g., the TUC) or espousing political objectives. In its analysis of the bill, *The Times*, hitherto hostile to reform, emphasized the bill's reasonableness and fairness, and applauded the Cabinet's moderate, conservative approach. It would be a "perversion of language," *The Times* stated, to consider the bill "an 'attack' on trade unionism."[52] Furthermore, it argued, even contracting in was not repressive: if it did not reduce the number of trade unionists contributing, then it was irrelevant, while if it had a demonstrable effect, then contracting out was unjust.

Parliamentary debate on the bill was long, legalistic, and often heated. In moving the second reading on 2 May, Attorney General Sir Douglas Hogg was constantly interrupted by Labour M.P.s, particularly union leaders who resented what they considered an attack on their authority. One particularly keen heckler, John Jones, the general organizer of the National Union of General and Municipal Workers, had to be removed from the chamber for calling Hogg a liar. Baldwin made a largely ineffective speech during which he, too, was treated discourteously. Labour M.P.s like John Clynes claimed that the bill was an attempt to cripple unions and the Labour Party, and repeated their earlier vows to repeal it as soon as possible. Among the moderates who supported the bill, Macmillan and Leslie Scott suggested that it should be part of a progressive program of reform and conciliation. George Spencer, a Labour M.P. and leader of a breakaway union of moderate Nottingham miners, gave a moving account of his own victimization and attacked the machinations of union leaders who used their organizations for selfish, non-union, and political objectives. Conservatives applauded Spencer and claimed that the bill would satisfy the many wage earners who considered it "a charter of freedom and liberty ... [which would] release them from the tyranny under which they are suffering."[53]

The committee and report stages in the Commons and the proceedings in the Lords produced only one significant change in the bill. As soon as the bill was introduced, the Labour Committee and some Conservative M.P.s declared that employers' lockouts should be subject to the same restrictions as strikes. The idea generated widespread support, and the government decided to make the change itself in committee. In the House of Lords, opposition parties fought the bill by linking it to recent proposals for second-chamber reform. Lord Arnold claimed that the bill was part of the Conservative Party's "double attack" on the Labour Party's financial and electoral base. Most peers, however, greeted the bill favorably. They joined the bishop of Durham in praising the bill as a safety measure against unions that had established "a ubiquitous, cruel and continuing tyranny, degrading to the character of their members and very perilous to the State." On 25 July, after eight days of debate and discussion, the Lords passed the bill. Its minor amendments protecting dependents from intimidation and loosening prohibitions against civil servants in unions were adopted by the Commons, and on 29 July 1927 the Trade Disputes and Trade Unions bill became law.[54]

No one was certain how the public would react to Labour's outcry against the legislation, but Conservatives were reasonably confident. In February 1927 *Man in the Street* had noted that Labour was preparing "its big guns" and claimed that they would "make a terrific noise but their destructive effect is likely to be very small." During the debates most Conservatives agreed with Sir Robert Sanders, the new chairman of the NUCUA council, who thought that the measure would be received "with enthusiasm." One Tory peer claimed to see the telltale signs of Labour's failure to generate any support on the melancholy faces of opposition peers who returned from public tours. Even the normally cautious Baldwin told Thomas Jones that he thought most workmen would welcome the measure.[55]

Meanwhile, Labour was trying to mobilize working-class opinion. At least one Tory union member criticized the bill, and others were concerned that it marked the start of a drive to cripple unions and repress wage earners. After the bill was introduced, Conservatives began their own campaign to win wage-earner opinion. They aimed to ridicule Labour's protests and tap the widespread desire for security and stability. Central office distributed material like the cartoon "A Perfect Scream," which depicted the unions as a dirty and choleric boy trying to avoid Mother Baldwin's cleansing bath. Conservatives also appealed to trade unionists by portraying their leaders as, in Macquisten's words, a "priesthood" trying to evade "the law of the land." In a May 1927 article in the *Conservative Agents' Journal*, G. E. M. Walker suggested that Conservatives present the bill as protection against insecurity and the abuse of strikes and political funds, and he urged agents to use workers and Labour Committee members for the campaign.[56]

Central office produced informative and analytical booklets, but it was chiefly concerned with popular leaflets and pamphlets, of which nearly nine million were distributed by the end of May. One North Cornwall branch association handed out a thousand leaflets during a month of campaigning. A single leaflet explaining the bill to trade unionists accounted for almost one-fifth of those distributed nationwide. Central office also organized a movie van tour, with a "talkie" of Hogg explaining the bill. They distributed Spencer's speech at the second reading and other broadsheets and posters. Much of the material went to special campaigns in a hundred marginal seats. Some regions also organized activities. In both southern Wales and the eastern Midlands, hundreds of trade unionists gathered to convey their support for reform by listening to leading Conservatives explain the bill. The SUA carried out a campaign blanketing Scotland with hundreds of thousands of pieces of literature.[57]

The actual effect of the Trade Disputes and Trade Unions Act was limited. Only the provisions regarding civil servants and the political levy were ever implemented, and the civil servant clause was relatively unimportant. Contracting in reduced the portion of the union membership paying political levies from three-quarters to one-half. Eventually, however, trade unions compensated for the drop in funds by drawing on reserves and increasing the levy paid by union members who contracted in. The views of interwar Labour leaders and some historians notwithstanding, the figures indicate that quite a few trade unionists were forced to contribute to unwanted political activities before 1927, and a significant portion of Britain's wage earners favored reform.[58]

The views of Labour leaders like Ernest Bevin and the Bradford ILP activist Frederick Jowett have skewed our assessment of the Trade Disputes and Trade Unions Act. Before the bill was introduced, Labour assumed a heroic posture—some of its M.P.s even pledged to abstain from alcohol and tobacco for six months if the bill was passed! They continued to claim, in Jowett's words, that the act was part of "a planned capitalist offensive against the working class." Bevin, the founder and head of the largest trade union in Britain, attacked the measure "as an act of petty vindictiveness inspired by class and party spite." As foreign secretary under Clement Attlee, Bevin took great pleasure in pressing for its repeal in 1946. His biographer largely accepts Bevin's version of the reform, asserting that the "savage piece of legislation" was popular only with reactionaries and big business. Some historians argue that the act was responsible for the Conservative defeat in 1929. In fact, only in regions like southern Wales, where a large part of the population was already suffering from long-term hardship and economic dislocation, was the act seen as vindictive. The posturing of Labour leaders created a heroic myth that triumphed after 1939, but it did not reflect popular opinion in the 1920s. The TUC and Labour were unable to mobilize majority opinion against the measure. Somewhat to his surprise, the Conservative Party chairman, J. C. C. Davidson, found that the populace generally approved the act, which may even have revived the government's waning popularity.[59]

The leaders and members of the Labour Committee should receive some credit for the trade union legislation. They persistently advocated reform, particularly contracting in, through public resolutions and private advice to Conservative leaders. The Labour Committee's work ensured that the issue was not displaced either by moderate pragmatists, who preferred to abandon it altogether, or by reactionaries, who were eager to hamstring Britain's trade unions. That a significant number of wage earners were able to express support for reform through the network of labour committees undermined trade unionists' claims that Conservative policy was directed against the working class.

After the passage of the Trade Disputes and Trade Unions Act, the Labour Committee supervised the implementation of the new laws. For instance, it publicized attempts by the National Union of General and Municipal Workers to maintain its political fund by raising other fees. One of the Labour Committee's few new missions was a vain attempt to halt the politicization of cooperative societies. Since the formation of the Cooperative Party in 1917, cooperatives affiliated with Labour had been a perennial problem for Conservatives. In 1922 the Cooperative Party agreed to an electoral arrangement with the Labour Party, and the Cheltenham Cooperative Conference in mid-1927 approved the affiliation of the Cooperative Party with the Labour Party. Some Conservatives saw the Cooperative Union as a "half-way house to Socialism," but most simply objected to political activity by cooperatives. In contrast to the trade union question, however, few practical remedies—and no legislative solution—were available.[60]

Conservative Wage Earners

Many members of the interwar working class identified with Conservative policies and attitudes, as both support for trade union reform and election results indicate. Although Labour's popular vote included many non–trade unionist men and women, it averaged only slightly more than four million votes in the four elections between 1918 and 1924. Union membership, however, ranged from a peak of more than eight million in 1920 to nearly five million in the late 1920s. Only after equal suffrage was enacted in 1928 did Labour's vote reach or exceed the number of trade unionists, but even then it was only about half the estimated fifteen million adults in Britain who were wage earners. A large proportion of the working class clearly did not vote Labour in the 1920s, and the Conservative Party was just as clearly drawing votes from beyond its middle- and upper-class core constituency. In 1929 it polled eight and a half million votes, more than Britain's entire middle- and upper-class population.[61]

Thanks to the work of Nordlinger, McKenzie, and Silver in the late 1960s, we know something about the nature of working-class Conservatism. Despite the jibes of left-wing critics, Tory wage earners were not ignorant or somehow historically immature. The historian and former Labour M.P. David Marquand criticizes the reigning interpretation, developed by labor historians, that the working-class Tory was "somehow an aberration or an anachronism: a pale and ghostly figure sliding inexorably toward the margin of history, not a robust, red-blooded creature, with as much sociological staying power as his Labour-voting, dues-paying neighbours."[62] Conservative wage earners were attracted by three major social and ideological elements of Conservatism: nonpolitical trade unionism, deference, and patriotism or a desire for national unity.

First, as the trade union reform controversy revealed, a substantial portion of workers objected to the increasingly politicized postwar unions and felt that the original nonpartisan aims of unions and cooperatives were being subverted. This explains William Appleton's views on trade unionism. In common with many other skilled craftsmen, Appleton admired the "sane or business trade union," which ignored politics. He regarded the American Federation of Labor as the model of this kind of trade union. Appleton took pride in his organization's ability to serve trade unions while avoiding "grandiloquent, but non–trade union and financially unsound enterprises." He supported copartnership, profit sharing, and worker participation, and contemptuously rejected "yellow unions." The former Labour leader George Barnes, who was involved in the highly skilled and exclusive engineering trade, held similar views.[63]

In a recent essay, Jarvis seems to indicate that this respectable, self-sufficient, and non-party trade unionism was largely a creation of imaginative propagandists working within the Conservative Party, but the trade union issue and the agitation for reform suggests otherwise. Conservatives successfully marshaled wage-earner support for their cause by identifying their party as the defender of the English workingman and his traditions. In many public statements echoing his famous March 1925 speech in the House of Commons, Baldwin praised the English people as "born and bred into the qualities of individuality, initiative, enterprise, thrift, common sense, moderation, calmness, kindliness, brotherliness, honesty, respect for the law, and love of freedom and justice." In so doing the prime minister attempted to retain the traditional hierarchy while merging with it a new democratic emphasis on individual responsibility. It is true, however, that workingmen's support for the Conservative Party was regularly undermined by the party's sometimes conflicting appeals to women and middle-class voters. Sometimes Baldwin could get support from all the new constituencies, but holding together several distinct versions of Conservatism was a very difficult task.[64]

A second reason behind working-class support for the Conservative Party was social deference. Deference toward one's betters was based both on regard for the superior training, education, and socialization of this group and on faith in the benefits of cooperation in an organically conceived society. Sociological studies of working-class attitudes show that the allegiance of Conservative wage earners, in contrast to Labour supporters, is based in part on their regard for the Conservative Party's ability to harmonize divergent social and economic interests. The Conservative belief in mutual dependence and deference reveals itself in the loyalty of rank-and-file members to party leaders and in the emphasis on consensus decision making. Deference, which remains an important component of the working-class outlook, was not a sign of political immaturity, for it permeated all parties. For instance, Arthur Ponsonby claimed that he was selected as a Labour candidate in Sheffield precisely because of his self-described middle-class upbringing. The Conservative Party between the wars benefited from what Nordlinger describes as wage earners' "normative satisfaction with a . . . perceived lack of influence," even though it often did not bring them working-class members or volunteers.[65]

A final, key source of Conservatism among wage earners was patriotism and the desire for national cohesion. Tories rejected what they considered a "self-interested calculus" and assessed policies by what they claimed were the nation's interests. In 1913 F. E. Smith succinctly defined the Conservative view: "The conception of unity is at the bottom of the Tory attitude of mind. It is nothing but the instinct of patriotism, the sense that the nation is a single unit, and not a haphazard collection of individuals, and that the unit must at any cost be strengthened and preserved." After the Great War, Conservative Party propaganda cultivated the notion that only its leaders had the ability and the experience to lead the nation and protect its interests. The Labour Committee and the Conservative Party declared that true progress was "possible only by the good will of all sections of the community, and not at the expense of any one section, be it rich, or be it poor." Baldwin was an especially powerful advocate of stability and harmony based on English traditions and Christian values. As he told one audience, "The country represents the eternal values and the eternal traditions from which we must never allow ourselves to be separated."[66]

Conservatives alleged that the Labour Party was dominated by self-seeking leaders, abnormal individuals, and leftist foreign interests. Tories claimed that Labour was not a national party, but a class party. They exploited any disreputable incident involving Labour, such as the gifts Ramsay MacDonald received from the owner of McVitie's biscuits in 1924, to accuse the Labour Party and union leaders of using their positions for personal benefit. Conservatives also marginalized Labour supporters by calling them maladjusted. In the late 1940s, the Conservative M.P. and minister Nigel Birch described the Labour supporter as someone who "is continually sweating and whining about his condition, [and] has an exceptionally good face for a grievance." The Labour Party, the argument went, was a bogus title for a group of incompetents, socialists, and revolutionaries who sought class conflict, nationalization of property, and the destruction of the British way of life.[67]

Conservative leaders consistently claimed that the capital levy—a one-time progressive tax on all capital—proposed by the Labour Party immediately after World War I, would hurt workers who had worked hard to save money or buy homes. Conservatives in Bradford even arranged for Ben Tillett, the Labour M.P. and leader of the Dockers' Union, to speak against the levy during the 1922 election. At the start of the 1923 election, Younger, the former party chairman, urged Conservative candidates to exploit the capital levy issue "for all it is worth." In September 1923, the NUA published *The Capital Levy: Its Real Purpose*, written by the laissez-faire Liberal Harold Cox. Cox tried to demonstrate that a levy would be unjust, would penalize patriots who had bought war bonds, and would destroy capitalism and leave the way clear for socialism. Like other Conservative candidates, Locker-Lampson told voters in Wood Green that the levy was "crazy" and proved that Labour was "bankrupt in ideas, and utterly unfitted to govern a great civilised community."[68]

Conservatives also believed that revolutionaries and foreign ideas and individuals controlled Labour, never hesitating to use such claims during elections. The *Campaign Guide* for the 1922 election claimed that pro-Germans, pacifists, and revolutionaries dominated Labour and were engaged in unconstitutional activities to undermine the state. Labour's pledge to lighten the demands of the Versailles Treaty was construed as recklessly pro-German. Conservatives attempted to tap antiforeign sentiment among working-class voters. In 1925 the Stockton labour committee chairman, James Gardner, suggested a "Britain for the British" campaign to develop imperial trade and shipbuilding and to deal with the alleged problem of "3000 aliens in receipt of the dole." Conservative literature of the mid-1920s claimed that the more radical trade union leaders were controlled by Moscow and were trying to use strikes to destroy the British nation. Such allegations may have attracted some wage earners. Although a longtime member of the ILP, Barnes criticized "foreign" theory and rhetoric. In his memoirs he described going to a prewar meeting of socialists where he was "belaboured with words about exploitation, proletariat, bourgeois and others of learned length and thundering sound just then imported from Germany."[69]

Along with their nationalist rhetoric, Conservatives tried to appeal to wage earners with imperialism. The party's propaganda argued that trade within the Empire improved the economy at home, relieving unemployment and increasing wages. The 1922 *Campaign Guide* claimed that Britain exported more than eight times the value of goods for every inhabitant of Australia, New Zealand, South Africa, and Canada as the country exported to the United States, Germany, and the Soviet Union. Many leaflets and a regular column, "An Empire Note-Book," in the party magazine, *Man in the Street,* stressed the Empire's economic importance.[70]

The view of the Empire that Conservatives offered wage earners was an idealistic one. In his memoirs John Buchan, the M.P. for the Scottish Universities and chairman of the Conservative and Unionist Educational Institute, reflected on his interwar ideal of imperialism: "I dreamed of a world-wide brotherhood with the background of a common race and creed, consecrated to the service of peace; Britain enriching the rest out of her culture and traditions, and the spirit of the Dominions like a strong wind freshening the stuffiness of the old lands. I saw in the Empire a means of giving the congested masses at home open country instead of a blind alley." Other Conservatives expressed similar feelings. Baldwin's colonial secretary, L. S. Amery, argued that the British Empire was a force for international cooperation more promising than the relatively untried League of Nations. In a May 1927 essay, he claimed that the "British League of Nations," rooted as it was in history, was stronger than its counterpart in Geneva. He also argued that the Empire could have a more positive effect because of its "ideals and principles . . . of ordered freedom, of the supremacy of law over arbitrary power, of fair play and toleration, [and] of trusteeship for the weak."[71]

Conservatives hoped that imperialism would encourage patriotism and undermine the appeal of socialism. For Conservatives like the prospective candidate for Camlachie, P. D. Ridge-Beedle, imperialism acted as a moral tonic against the prevailing "weak-kneed, slouching, vacillating, undecided attitude." All Britons, Ridge-Beedle claimed, could rest in the knowledge that they deserved to rule the inferior peoples of the Empire. As one historian of the British Empire, John MacKenzie, explains in his work on popular imperialism, many Conservatives saw imperialist rhetoric as a unifying force that drew the classes together under Conservative leadership. Yet after the First World War imperialism was less powerful than it had been, and the failure of protectionism in 1923 meant that the imperial message was almost exclusively rhetorical.[72]

The difficulty of the 1923 general election demanded that Conservatives use every rhetorical element they could think of to mobilize working-class support. First, they claimed to have a solution for Britain's social ills. During a stop at Bradford, Baldwin expressed concern for the effects of unemployment. The uncertain economy was undermining society, consuming workers' savings, "destroy[ing] the very springs of thrift in the people themselves," and generally breeding despair. Under these conditions, Baldwin said, "extremists" would be able to "sow their poisonous seeds" of hatred and class warfare. The solution was protectionism. Conservatives provided specific examples of the results of free trade versus tariffs. One leaflet detailed free trade's destructive effect on twelve industries. But, Conservatives said proudly, the protection of domestic motor vehicle manufacturing under the Safeguarding of Industries Act (1921) had led to large increases in production. Wage earners were told that the high standard of living enjoyed by American workers was due to protection. Candidates invariably mentioned any local industry that might benefit from protection. Jonas Pearson, trade unionist, chairman of the Bradford labour committee, and candidate for Bradford Central, relentlessly attacked the importation of French gabardines, which was hurting worsted producers in his city. In Wrexham, Edmund Bushby printed a letter from the manager of a steel works warning of layoffs if steel producers were not protected.[73]

Second, Conservative propaganda appealed to working-class patriotism. Central office rewrote the wartime song "Keep the Home Fires Burning" to a tariff theme:

> Keep the Home Fires Burning
> Keep for British earning,
> Wages that the Foreigner would steal away.
> Stand for Home and Neighbour.
> Spurn all foreign labour,
> Baldwin's way's the British way, and it's bound to pay.[74]

The leaflet "It's Your Money They Want, But It's Work British Labour Wants" stated that importers and foreign manufacturers benefited from free trade at the expense of British workmen. Conservatives even accused foreigners and importers of financing the Liberal campaign. In Skipton the Conservative candidate, Colonel Roundell, said that he wanted to protect workers from "the Foreign Black-Leg who robs you of your Wages and destroys your industry." In his election address the Clapham candidate, Sir John Leigh, reproduced a NUA leaflet alleging that Labour was controlled by the suspicious-sounding, "foreign" Socialistische Arbeiter-International, i.e., the Second International.[75]

Going by their defeat in the 1923 general election, the Conservatives failed to win working-class voters to a tariff program. Nationally the poll for Conservative candidates in contested seats declined from 49.6 percent to 43.6 percent, and the number of Conservative M.P.s fell dramatically from 345 to 258. In some working-class divisions, however, results were better than in 1922. The Stockton Conservatives claimed a moral victory when their first postwar candidate, Harold Macmillan, missed victory by only seventy-three votes.[76] And although there were fewer Conservative M.P.s from predominantly industrial regions, their numbers declined less there than in such areas as the southwest and the heavily middle-class southeast. The decrease in Conservative support in the mostly working-class and Conservative West Midlands was relatively small even though the number of M.P.s fell from thirty-six to thirty. In other working-class areas such as Lancastria, the Mid-North, the Northeast, and Strathclyde the relatively stable position of the Conservatives was largely due to the party's earlier problems in those regions.

The protectionist campaign attracted relatively few Labour voters, but it alienated many middle-class male voters and women from all classes. For instance, in the fifteen predominantly working-class seats with straight Conservative-Labour contests in 1922, 1923, and 1924, the Conservative vote dropped from 46 percent to 41 percent between 1922 and 1923. In the 1924 election, after the Conservatives had abandoned tariffs, they won 44 percent of the vote in these seats. For every working-class voter the Conservatives gained with the tariff program, they lost more than one middle-class or female voter. In the 167 predominantly middle-class southeastern and London seats, Conservative M.P.s fell from 132 to 97. In the London metropolitan area the drop was particularly notable. Conservatives had held 68 of the 96 metropolitan seats before the election; after it, they held 46. The 1923 election demonstrated that any appeal to wage earners must not threaten the Conservative Party's core of middle-class and women voters. After dropping protectionism, the Conservative Party was able to retain the primary elements of its appeal to workers—trade union reform, deference, and nationalism—throughout the 1920s.

After 1927, however, the NUCUA Labour Committee gradually lost its importance. Initially this did not affect local labour committees, but later, during the 1930s, the number of constituencies with committees fell from more than one-third to less than one-quarter. The Conservative Party's greater strength and the stability of the government, both of which made a wage-earner organization less vital, were partly responsible for this trend. The Labour Committee's decline changed its relationship with the party. After the trade union issue was settled, the national committee was demoted to a largely administrative role, and in 1929 local committees became strictly advisory bodies of the Conservative associations. Without a national issue to motivate members, the Labour Committee also lost its direction, and some members abandoned the movement. As a result of Chamberlain's party reorganization in 1931, the Labour Committee became no more than a subcommittee of the NUCUA Executive, wholly elected by and as dependent on it as any administrative subcommittee. Central office downgraded the Labour Department as well by incorporating it into the Publicity Department.[77]

These changes meant that the NUCUA Labour Committee had to abandon its goal of becoming a popular organization for Conservative wage earners. Henceforth, it was largely a skeleton body handling literature for the working class. By most criteria the Labour Committee failed to attain its goals. It sponsored few wage-earner candidates, and it was unable to establish a broad base of support. These failures resulted mainly from two factors. First, the Labour Party was identified as the working-class and trade union party, forcing the Conservative Party on the defensive. Second, Conservative attempts to organize wage earners were inevitably undermined by the party's dominant character and outlook. To mobilize and organize middle-class and women voters after the war, the Conservative Party had to adopt their views and prejudices. This meant facilitating their domination of constituency parties, selecting them as candidates, arranging Conservative activities according to their sensibilities, and rejecting policies that undermined their electoral support.

Despite its courtship of the middle-class and female vote, however, the interwar Conservative Party, like its post–World War II descendant, continued to draw a significant portion of the working-class vote. During the 1920s the activities of the Labour Committee at least demonstrated that working-class voters could be Conservatives. As a Unionist magazine inelegantly noted, "genuine, loyal, and life-long support for trade unionism is not incompatible with political opinions which are not those of the 'Labour' Party."[78] The debate on trade union reform validated this assertion. Many wage earners were attracted to the Tory ideology of respectable and nonpolitical trade unionism and national unity, and they responded to Conservative claims that the Labour Party could not provide capable or stable leadership.

The similarities between the 1920s and the era of Margaret Thatcher are obvious. In both cases union power was curtailed dramatically by legal reforms, widespread unemployment, and the decline of unionized industry. In his survey of recent British history, Morgan notes the analogous public response to "irresponsible" union activism and the parallels between the coal miners' strike of 1984–85 and the General Strike of 1926. In both cases, "The old legend of . . . workers' solidarity and union power . . . [was] exploded . . . [after] a long, and indeed largely popular campaign . . . to undercut union monopoly in the labour market, and to exorcize memories" of union domination. In both periods Conservative attempts to develop working-class groups (a Conservative Trade Unionist Organisation was formed in 1978) were only partially successful.[79] In spite of its limited membership and achievements, the Labour Committee assisted in the Conservative Party's adaptation to the age of universal suffrage in a way that suited the ethos of the interwar Conservative Party.

5

Conservative Party Propaganda and Education

Propaganda and education were two of the most important political tools for the Conservative Party in dealing with voters after the First World War. Party publicity was not a completely new development. For some years the Conservatives had used traveling agents to address public meetings and had published pamphlets and leaflets for election campaigns. Shortly before the war the veteran journalist Malcolm Fraser was hired to organize the party's publicity. These efforts were minor, however, compared to postwar propaganda and educational work. In 1927—not an election year—the NUCUA published nearly twenty million pamphlets and leaflets and more than six million copies of the various Conservative magazines. At about the same time the Yorkshire provincial division spent nearly seven hundred pounds, more than a third of its ordinary budget, and North Cornwall Conservatives one hundred pounds from their meager resources, on propaganda.[1]

After 1918 the Conservative Party's educational efforts were as impressive as its propaganda. Before 1914 the party made no concerted effort to educate the electorate, which was relatively small and highly politicized. After 1918 the Conservatives were challenged by an influx of voters and an influential socialist message. Many working-class educational institutions, for example, were becoming Labour's preserve, providing a socialist, or at least leftist, education to tens of thousands of students every year. Conservatives needed to counteract this trend and recognized that their party was becoming more dependent on its rank and file, which had to be trained for modern political operations. Education was therefore crucial to the success of the interwar Conservative Party. The Conservatives created a network of lecture courses, study circles, and schools to educate voters in politics and ideology, and train volunteers. At the pinnacle of the educational system was the Conservative College. The party also printed a wide array of educational materials. Year in and year out during the 1920s—and the interwar period generally—Conservatives devoted their resources to education in an unprecedented manner.

Although historians have largely ignored the focus on education, the importance of propaganda has not gone unnoticed. The manipulative nature of propaganda makes it an attractive explanation for the Conservative Party's dominance in interwar politics.[2] Certainly Labour Party leaders saw Conservative mass persuasion as an attempt by the monied elite to delude "the uneducated" and undermine democracy.[3] Conservatives, or at least their leaders and organizers, appreciated the power of propaganda when appropriately used, but they also recognized the utility of education for increasing party members' and voters' political knowledge and for training volunteers.

Propaganda

There were several reasons for the increased interest in propaganda and education after 1918. Even before the war, an influential political scientist at the London School of Economics, Graham Wallas, had argued in *Human Nature in Politics* (1908) that accident, sentiment, and habit were decisive factors in politics, particularly in democracies. During World War I, the impressive effects of propaganda on a mass audience vividly demonstrated the validity of Wallas's ideas. In 1923 a contributor to *Nineteenth Century and After* noted that practices like Lloyd George's prewar use of publicity stunts were becoming common because of the war and the advent of film. Educated Britons had a high regard for propaganda partly because the Germans were willing to attribute their defeat to Allied propaganda. The "stab in the back" theory developed by General Ludendorff in 1919 and later popularized by Adolf Hitler blamed Germany's defeat on domestic unrest inspired by British propaganda. Sir Campbell Stuart's *Secrets of Crewe House* (1920), Arthur Ponsonby's *Falsehood in War-Time* (1926), and the American Harold Lasswell's groundbreaking *Propaganda Technique in the World War* (1927) emphasized the power—for good and evil—of propaganda. Philip G. Cambray, head of central office publications from 1921 to 1927 and briefly deputy director of publicity, grounded his book *The Game of Politics: A Study of Principles of British Political Strategy* (1932) on an understanding of propaganda as warfare. If anything, Britain's leaders tended to overemphasize propaganda's effectiveness.[4]

Modern psychology added a new luster to propaganda. After the debate over shell-shocked soldiers, popular interest in Freud, Havelock Ellis, and other pioneers of psychology grew rapidly among the educated public. For many politically active Britons, psychology offered a view of humanity that was deeply disturbing even as it buoyed their interest in propaganda. In 1923 Wreford attacked propaganda for its denial of human qualities: "Propaganda is a great and never-ceasing force operating . . . upon the malleable minds of men. . . . Evil propaganda is that which being interested, strives to appear disinterested; which influences, pretending merely to inform; which stultifies, claiming to educate; which is overt, but accomplishes fell work secretly as a thief. And indeed it is a thief, for it steals away our judgment and so confounds our conscience. And if we are conscienceless, who then are we? We are of no account, for conscience is the soul." For conservative-minded members of the cultural and political elite, the specter of propaganda was worrying because, as Wyatt noted, it facilitated "appeal[s] to the animal in man, wrapped up in a mantle of democratic phrases." They also feared its power to incite revolution and chaos.[5]

Psychology's apparent view of humans as irrational was in keeping with postwar fears about the mass electorate. Conservatives were made uneasy by the confusion resulting from the passage of the Representation of the People Act, the increased number of unaligned voters, the rise of Labour, and the chaotic party situation. They faced an unknown and seemingly unknowable electorate which, under the provisions of the reform act, had to be polled in a single day. At the same time they saw a growing Labour Party with allegedly superior propaganda capabilities. Labour leaders recognized the need for propaganda and engaged in continuous propaganda efforts, particularly the highly visible public meeting, but their efforts were more imposing in appearance than in fact. Conservatives worried that the Labour Party was winning the battle for voters' minds. In 1924 Noel Skelton, a leading moderate Conservative M.P., wrote that the 1918 act had given power to a "sensitive, receptive, [and] plastic" electorate who threatened to destroy both of the older parties. Inexperienced voters were drawn to Labour only because, he argued, they craved "mental nourishment." Even an experienced advertiser and propagandist like the Conservative M.P. Charles Higham referred to the "shrewd and almost ceaseless activity" of Labour's propaganda machine, which flooded the country with "socialistic literature."[6]

Conservative leaders perceived propaganda as both a significant threat and a potential tool. In *Looking Forward* (1920), Higham proposed a "State Publicity Department" that would "harmonize" British politics by aligning the unwieldy electorate with the state. "Public opinion is the cement that holds the State together," he wrote. "Democracy left to judge complicated matters without guidance, or the latest data, or the most trustworthy information, *given in tabloid form,* is like a great ship without steering-gear on the high seas.... At present we are simply drifting. We have a democratic theory of government ... and a thoroughly autocratic neglect of the judgment of those people whose will we contend is all powerful." Higham's faith in publicity and education reflected the trend among Conservatives. As an early 1930s *Morning Post* editorial stated, "History suggests that of all weapons the idea is the most potent for good or for evil. Sound conceptions of life have made nations great; false conceptions of life have brought them to destruction.... A nation acts as one when it is inspired by the unity of a great tradition of duty and of patriotism; it may tear itself to pieces under the influence of a subversive philosophy.... If, however, there is danger in false ideas, there is safety in true ideas ... and in this way ... the intelligent may defeat the intelligentsia with their own weapons." Pronay notes that in the 1920s all political leaders accepted propaganda "as one of the many new, disagreeable but unavoidable facts of postwar political life, alongside others such as an 'immature' mass-electorate and incipient class war fuelled by 'Bolshevik agitation.'"[7]

After the fall of the coalition and the defeat of the Conservatives in the 1923 general election, Conservative leaders struggled to develop a more effective system of propaganda and education. They increased their lead over Labour's leaflet and pamphlet production, distributing more than twice Labour's output in the 1929 general election. But not until 1929 did the Conservative literature distributed exceed the level of either of the 1910 elections. Election propaganda was, the editor of the *Pall Mall Gazette* noted in a 1923 memorandum to Baldwin, one of the "methods of the Victorian age." Launching a blitz of literature during a hectic election campaign, he argued, was largely ineffective, especially with an unreliable mass electorate. The Conservatives needed a coordinated effort employing a continuous and widespread approach.[8]

More than anyone else, the party chairman from 1926 to 1930, J. C. C. Davidson, spurred the development of an innovative program of Conservative propaganda and education. Under him the publicity budget more than doubled, from £22,000 in 1926 to almost £50,000 in both 1928 and

1929. Davidson was also able to create a large fund for antisocialist propaganda by appealing to City businessmen. In addition, he reorganized central office by creating an autonomous publicity department in 1927. By early 1928 the department had sixty staff members. It was headed by Sir Joseph Ball, a former barrister and veteran operative of MI5. Sir Patrick Gower was hired in February 1928 as its deputy director. Gower replaced Cambray, who had been caught scheming against party leaders. In contrast to Cambray, a librarian, Gower was a respected civil servant who had served as private secretary to several prime ministers. He also had connections in the advertising and publicity industry. In February 1928 Davidson named the energetic area agent Robert Topping as principal agent. Davidson complained that Topping's predecessor, the aged Leigh Maclachlan, was "ignorant . . . of new forms of propaganda" and "opposed to education altogether in any shape or form."[9]

The new regime in central office recognized the need for extensive and continuous propaganda and education. In an early 1927 memorandum to Davidson, Ball emphasized the dangers presented by Labour's influence in the unions and cooperatives and by subversive, left-wing elements. He also noted the public's dislike of some government policies. Ball argued that the Conservative Party must pursue "an intensive propaganda campaign, carefully planned and co-ordinated on the most modern lines." He outlined a program to use newspapers, leaflets, posters, canvassers, cinema vans, outdoor speakers, and other tools to reach voters at home and at work, at every time of day and day of the week. Such systematic propaganda, he said, depended on using hundreds of thousands of party workers who would be educated in day classes, by correspondence courses, and in schools.[10]

During this period the SUA also revamped and expanded its propaganda organization, and propaganda grew faster than any other item in the SUA budget. While the organization spent less than £3,000 on propaganda in 1923–24, in 1925–26 it spent more than £5,000, and by 1928–29 the figure approached £9,000. For most educational and propaganda efforts, the SUA depended on London, but it did develop a major training program, for the simple fact that, after 1918, the Unionists needed thousands of trained party volunteers to combat Labour. Typically the 1925 annual report for the SUA Eastern Division urged members in all constituencies to "spare no effort . . . in face of the persistent and widespread propaganda which is being untiringly carried on by the Socialist Party." In 1925 Unionists formed the Scottish 1924 Club "for the express purpose of training speakers, and also of providing through a very complete reference library, the means of acquiring knowledge of all the political and social questions of the day." Two years later the SUA Eastern Division also hired someone to coordinate its propaganda and education.[11]

Conservatives used all the propaganda tools available: professional and amateur speakers, pamphlets and leaflets, posters, the press, magazines, performance propaganda, lantern slides, and films. In the mid-1920s central office claimed that its speakers addressed almost six million people. Because of its high costs and low impact, the party let the Speakers Department atrophy during the 1920s, and by 1928 its staff had dwindled from a prewar high of 160 to 39. Increasingly the Conservatives relied on amateur speakers trained locally or at Conservative schools, although in 1928 central office still had to budget a minimum of £9,000 per annum for speakers' salaries.[12]

In the 1920s the Conservative Party increased its lead over Labour in the production of election literature. Distribution of NUA election leaflets mushroomed from eighteen million in 1922 to twenty-six million in 1923, thirty-six million in 1924, and more than ninety-three million in 1929. In this last election the SUA also distributed millions of leaflets on its own. By comparison, Labour's distribution of literature during this period increased only from fifteen to forty-three million. Not until 1929, however, did the Conservatives establish a national format for candidates' election addresses, although Labour adopted one in 1922. The Conservatives also only belatedly responded to Labour practices by deciding in 1927 to provide literature for municipal elections. Within a few months, 426,040 pamphlets and leaflets were used for local elections. Conservative experts had long questioned the utility of small posters, and following the advice of professional advertisers, central office in 1929 switched to the much larger and more expensive hoardings posters, which consumed a quarter of the publicity budget for the election.[13]

More significant than the increase in election material was the growing use of Conservative literature between elections. The NUA spurred leaflet purchases with subsidies and inexpensive bulk rates for leaflet series. In 1920, for instance, they offered a series of twelve leaflets on nationalization; more than four million such leaflets were circulated. During the second half of the 1920s, production of pamphlets and leaflets averaged more than ten million items annually. Pamphlets and leaflets were relatively inexpensive and could be distributed through constituency associations, the WUO, the JIL, and the Labour Committee. On the negative side, as Philip Cambray wryly noted in 1932, mass production of literature sometimes seemed to benefit the wastepaper dealers more than the party. Obviously, high production levels did not guarantee an avid readership, but careful distribution by skilled volunteers reduced waste.[14]

In contrast to pamphlets and leaflets, the more expensive posters were rarely used. In 1925 central office began a poster subscription service that lowered the cost of each poster. More effective designs helped, too; posters began to enjoy a modest success, and more than fifteen thousand were distributed in 1928 alone. The Conservative Party was not, however, able to follow the standard but expensive commercial practice of displaying posters continuously. Except for elections and notices of meetings, posters made up only a small part of party propaganda.[15]

A central feature of Conservative propaganda after the Great War was a wide array of periodicals. These provided a steady stream of information and propaganda for supporters and unaligned voters alike. In 1919 central office resumed publication of its gazette, *Gleanings and Memoranda*, which carried a mass of political information. Similar was the *Conservative Agents' Journal*, which was made available to non-agents in 1926. Both were specialist publications with a circulation of only one or two thousand copies per month. The popular Conservative magazines that started up after 1918 were far more significant. As Adams Gowans Whyte, the head of central office magazine propaganda, noted in the *Conservative Agents' Journal*, "The real productive work of propaganda, as of organisation, must be done in the intervening quiet periods" between elections. The popular party magazines were designed "to meet th[is] need for steady educative work." The magazines were sold in bulk to associations at the rate of less than half a penny per copy. With price markups or the addition of local copy and advertising, associations found that the magazines were an inexpensive but effective propaganda tool.[16]

The first official Conservative magazine, founded in 1919 and driven out of business within a few years by three magazines created by central office, was the SUA's *People's Politics*. The first magazine to follow was a women's magazine, *Home and Politics* (1920). It reached a monthly circulation of 100,000 in 1925 and (after it was given a separate female staff) 200,000 in 1927. *Popular View* (1921) and its youth edition, the *Junior Imperial League Gazette* (1921), followed. In June 1924 *Home and Politics* passed *Popular View* to become the Conservative magazine with the largest circulation, and central office soon replaced *Popular View* with two new magazines, *Man in the Street* (1924) and *The Elector* (1924). *Man in the Street* was an improved version of *Popular View*, with better graphics and cartoons and lighthearted features on gardening, sports, and even political notes penned by a football player, "Centre Forward." Yet the magazine did not attract many male readers, and monthly circulation remained about 100,000.[17]

The Elector, however, gained a large readership. From the perspective of central office, *The Elector* had the benefit of being financially self-sustaining, unlike both *Home and Politics* and *Man in the Street*. Local associations liked *The Elector* because it was an inexpensive, leaflet-style magazine useful for general propaganda. Its circulation increased rapidly, reaching an average of about 180,000 copies per month in 1926. The SUA decided in 1924 to distribute *The Elector* because it was inexpensive. In May 1925 the *Junior Imperial League Gazette* was replaced by the aptly named *Imp*, an upbeat magazine that proved somewhat more popular with youthful readers.[18]

Increasingly associations "localized" party magazines by adding a cover and local material to the regular magazine. The practice was particularly prevalent among strong WUO branches like those in Wirral and Oswestry, and it led to substantial increases in circulation. Adding local advertisements paid for the magazine as well as for local production work. The JIL also encouraged its regional and constituency groups to localize *Imp*, although relatively few did. When localizing first became popular in 1926, there were 62 local editions of Conservative magazines; by early 1929 there were 180. A few associations even attempted to operate their own magazine, but these were usually too heavy a drain on resources. Despite disappointments, however, it was a golden age for Conservative monthlies. Party magazines enjoyed a combined monthly circulation of more than three-quarters of a million by the late 1920s. After 1929 the magazines decreased in both numbers and circulation, and today there is one magazine, whose circulation is only 80,000.[19]

The Conservatives also exploited national and local newspapers. Their many complaints notwithstanding, after 1918 Conservatives generally benefited more from the press than the other parties. They could depend on the support of the *Morning Post*, *Daily Telegraph*, and, usually, *The Times* and *The Observer*. In the 1920s these four newspapers had a combined average daily circulation of one million. Frequently the Conservatives were also supported by independent Conservative newspapers—the *Daily Mail*, the *Daily Express*, the *Weekly Dispatch*, the *Evening News*, and, until it was sold in 1925, *People*. Together these papers had a daily circulation of at least six million. The newspapers backing the Liberal and Labour Parties had circulations of less than two million and one million, respectively.[20] But because daily newspapers depended on brisk sales—inspired by sensational reporting—they were more effective in promoting stunt campaigns than in developing lasting support for any party. The Conservatives also had the support of a majority of the provincial newspapers, such as the respected *Yorkshire Post, Western Mail,* and *Glasgow Herald.*

In some cases the Conservative Party's influence on the British press rested on financial investment, but more commonly it depended on support from individual owners and editors. Reliable and wealthy Conservatives continued to purchase and operate local or regional newspapers in the interest of the party, and Conservative leaders often used their personal connections to newspapers. For instance, Lords Kelmsley and Camrose (the Berry brothers) owned the largest newspaper combine in Britain, and they worked closely with Conservative leaders during the 1920s. Local associations and newspapers also often worked together. In Skipton the agent managed the *Craven Herald.* In other cases local Conservative newspapers provided space for regular articles from or about the local association. Local Conservatives paid the press for advertising, on which newspapers depended. If their relationship became strained, as it did in Kincardine and West Aberdeenshire, there could be difficulties for both. Access to reliable national and local newspapers gave the Conservative Party an advantage in leading (not directing) public discussion and undermining the opposition.[21]

In addition to its informal contacts, the Conservative Party had an effective press department in central office. This quiet operation was begun by Malcolm Fraser shortly before the war in order to supply confidential material and advance copies of speeches to newspapers. Subscribing newspapers also received articles that many provincial editors published. By 1927, about 250 newspapers in Britain subscribed to the service. Beginning in 1924 central office used Industrial Publicity Service Ltd. to funnel material into the more independent or non-Conservative newspapers. Some of the material, such as the column "Our Member," was carried by dozens of local newspapers. In addition, central office retained a staff of correspondents who wrote letters to provincial newspapers. In 1924 E. J. Moyle, the head of the press department, commented that these activities were intended only to help journalists who otherwise would be "compelled to write their own personal opinions . . . [causing] mischief . . . which is difficult, and often impossible to counteract." As the Conservative junior minister Philip Lloyd-Greame noted in 1921, "the art of propaganda" depended on concealment, and the work of the press department was a particularly artful means of influencing public opinion.[22]

Conservative propaganda was not limited to the print media; the party also used newer techniques, including radio, performance propaganda, lantern slides, and, most important, films. The Conservatives benefited from the noncommercial BBC. Although both Lloyd George and MacDonald were renowned public speakers, they were ill-suited for radio, and, at least in the case of MacDonald, generally indifferent to its potential. In contrast, Baldwin told J. C. W. Reith in 1925 that radio was uniquely able to mobilize the public. For both Reith and Baldwin, radio was an educational tool, an "integrator for democracy." Baldwin's carefully refined speaking style was particularly well suited to radio.[23]

The Conservatives largely failed to develop gramophones and public address systems for propaganda use during the 1920s. They made only two gramophone records during this period. The first was a recording of the 1928 JIL rally; the second was the "Stanley Boy" record used during the 1929 election campaign. They also failed to tap the potential of public address systems to amplify radio broadcasts, records, or speeches. The technology enabled a large number of people to hear a speech—and it had the added virtue of drowning out distractions and hecklers. One agent who used a "propaganda car" with a public address system during the 1924 election proposed the construction of a fleet of such vehicles. According to his estimate, each fully equipped car would cost about £350, with running costs about £200 per year. Except for one van, however, the Conservatives did not develop mobile public address systems until the 1930s.[24]

On a different tack, central office promoted the use of propaganda that entertained while conveying a political message. At public meetings and fetes, one local association displayed life-sized wax figures vilifying the opposition and glorifying Conservative leaders. Performance propaganda was more common. During the 1920s central office issued staging instructions for plays and pageants to local associations. The "Plays for Patriots" series was reputed to be especially popular among youths. These one-act plays were simple to stage but entertaining. They were, wrote one Conservative magazine, "good Conservative and patriotic propaganda ... [under] a thick layer of jam."[25]

Conservative community singing also combined entertainment and propaganda. In 1927 female members of the Conservative London Municipal Society created a Conservative Musical Union. Mrs. Baldwin was appointed president, and Davidson chairman. The Musical Union organized the first annual "Festival of Song" in May 1927, and the women made a great effort to include Conservative youths and wage earners. Using the model of the eisteddfod, the event involved competitions of soloists and choirs who sang traditional British songs and recited British ballads. Organizers claimed that the event did more than promote musical talent. It also tapped "a deep and genuine patriotism" and "the unity and harmony for which Conservatism stood." Central office decided to expand the group, making it a national organization, and distributed song sheets with both traditional and new songs, such as "Motherland of the Free" which was actually set to the music of "The Red Flag." Community singing became very popular in some local associations. In Oswestry it was an integral part of the local organization, which even sponsored some participants.[26]

An even more common propaganda practice was lantern shows, which combined lantern slides with lectures. The magic lantern had long been a source of entertainment and education; the Conservatives adapted it for propaganda. In 1919 central office offered slides with lectures detailing the government's achievements and the dangers of Bolshevism. These slides, which could be obtained free of charge, were immediately booked for 120 showings in local associations. The Primrose League soon produced lantern lectures for children on its history, the Union Jack, St. George, and the Navy. Later central office created lantern lectures entitled "The British Empire," "Parliament," "Progress under Capitalism," "A Day in the Life of a Member of Parliament," "The Air Force and Its Duties," and "Agriculture—A Year on the Land." In the mid-1920s the Primrose League also offered lantern lectures on South Africa, Canada, and even birds.[27]

Lantern lectures were an effective and popular propaganda tool. Between December 1924 and April 1925, central office's lectures were booked more than 400 times. The same period in 1925–26 witnessed more than a thousand bookings. During a two-month period in 1925, the JIL recorded fifty bookings for its own lantern lectures. Local associations frequently booked imperial lantern lectures, and according to *Home and Politics*, these shows demonstrated "the might of the Empire, the size and wealth of it, its value to us at home, what it can produce and grow for us, Imperial Preference . . . the need for Imperial Defense, and last, but not least, Emigration and Overseas Settlement Schemes." In addition to their educational value, lantern lectures were entertaining. This was particularly true in rural areas with few other sources of entertainment. Some associations even purchased their own magic lantern.[28]

One of the most important and innovative developments in Conservative propaganda was the production and distribution of motion pictures. Film was ideally suited to publicity and propaganda because it provided what Higham called the "arresting image" that "epitomizes, dramatizes, and simplifies." Because the Conservatives were in government for most of the interwar period, they were in a position to influence the British Board of Film Censors, whose secretary had formerly worked on wartime film propaganda and was continuing to serve on the Committee of Imperial Defence (CID) subcommittee on censorship. The Conservative Party had other links to major film manufacturers and exhibitors. Newsreel companies eagerly filmed Conservative personalities like Baldwin because they were popular. Several leading newsreel producers were even on close terms with Conservative leaders.[29]

But Conservatives were not able to use the commercial cinema for direct propaganda. Producers and exhibitors were businessmen who did not want to lose customers by bringing overt partisanship into their entertainment industry. In 1928, for example, the JIL found that only nineteen cinemas in the country would show their trailer. Almost by default, therefore, the Conservative Party was forced to create its own film production and distribution system. They responded to the lack of venues by developing portable units to show films in public halls or outdoors. In this they may have been inspired by the "cinemotor" tours organized by the National War Aims Committee in 1918. Using a van and portable equipment, the committee showed films in industrial centers to 160,000 people per week at a weekly cost of only £14. By war's end the committee had twenty vans touring the country.[30]

The Conservative Party began using cinema vans relatively early. Just before the 1924 election, a central office van toured East Anglia and southwest England. At the rear of the heavy pantechnicon was a screen on which films were projected from within the vehicle. Because the screen was hooded, it could be used for daylight screenings. After a film was shown, a speaker delivered an address and answered questions. Two years later the Junior Carlton Club provided central office with a second van that had a portable projector for indoor screenings as well as a fixed platform for speakers and a display of Empire products. Generally the films shown were on imperial or military subjects; the Navy League's *Grand Fleet at Sea* and Pathe's *Empire's Sure Shield* are two examples.[31]

The early cinema van tours evoked an enthusiastic response, particularly in rural areas. Among a village population of six hundred, four hundred might attend a screening. Two or three meetings could be held each day, one of them in the afternoon for women and children. Because the van was mobile, films could be shown to many people over a large area. Finally, outdoor screenings drew larger crowds and included fewer confirmed Conservatives than did indoor meetings. Many associations were eager to host a cinema van, even paying the substantial fee required. In Oswestry, for instance, the Junior Carlton Club van was booked for three and a half weeks in 1927. The association declared the results so "eminently satisfactory" that they brought the van back the next year. Considering the effectiveness of a van, the cost (£30 to £40 per week), shared by host associations and central office, was low. Conservative leaders became convinced that cinema vans should be fully exploited for propaganda.[32]

The Primrose League seems to have experimented with filmmaking immediately after the war, but central office's film department, created in 1926, was the first systematic attempt by any party to produce films. Early films showed Cabinet ministers at work and demonstrated government successes, particularly in housing. Although Austen Chamberlain, among others, complained about the unseemliness of being shown on screen like a Bovril advertisement, these "intimate peeps" on film introduced the public to ministers. Central office also made a series of cartoons ridiculing opposition leaders, and an animated film, *Red Tape Farm* (1926), attacking Lloyd George's plan for land reform. Central office was fortunate to sign an exclusive deal with one of the few British animators of the period.[33]

When Davidson took control of central office in 1926, he accelerated the development of film propaganda. His most important contribution to filmmaking was the purchase of the rights to an early sound system, phonofilm, which recorded a synchronized audio track onto standard film stock. Before the end of 1927, he had a phonofilm van built and sent it on a national tour. It screened films of party leaders' speeches, including Sir William Joynson-Hicks (on the General Strike) and Sir Douglas Hogg (on the trade union reform bill). In 1927 central office made phonofilms of Baldwin, Earl Beatty (on disarmament), and Neville Chamberlain (on housing and pensions). Sir Laming Worthington-Evans and Leo Amery were also phonofilmed, and the JIL made and screened a phonofilm of its 1928 Albert Hall rally.[34]

By 1928 Davidson regarded the cinema vans as "the most powerful agency at the disposal of the Party . . . one which neither the Liberal nor the Socialist Party possesses." With the assistance of a wealthy contributor, Davidson purchased and staffed nine more phonofilm vans and a dozen vans similar to the Junior Carlton Club's. By the May 1929 election, central office had a fleet of twenty-three cinema vans. One phonofilm van operator toured nine northern cities and towns in eighteen days, drawing an average audience of five hundred people at each screening—and more on Sundays and in the last days of the campaign. R. A. Butler, standing as a candidate for the first time in 1929, found that in his constituency films generated more interest and a more varied crowd than public meetings.[35]

When the films department was placed under the direct control of the director of publicity in 1928, it had only one full-time staff member. Most of the work went out to private firms, which took advantage of central office's inexperience by overcharging it. When central office was reorganized in 1930–31, it was found that the films department and its vans had lost more than £10,000 just in the first nine months of 1930. The newly named director of publicity, Patrick Gower, established the autonomous Conservative and Unionist Films Association in autumn 1930. Under the close supervision of Sir Albert Clavering, a former war propagandist and leading cinema owner, the unit controlled film production and exhibition but was funded by central office.[36]

Educational Efforts

The Conservative Party's educational efforts were associated with but distinct from propaganda. Much of the party's activity—particularly among women and young people—included educational elements. Here, however, I discuss only Conservative efforts to teach economics, politics, and history, and to train volunteers for modern political activity. Conservatives' interest in education was spurred by many of the same concerns as their interest in propaganda. In an early 1919 memorandum to the Primrose League ruling body, Sir Alan Sykes warned that they could no longer depend on old methods. "There is undoubtedly," he wrote, "a demand for the instructional side in addition, and such things as speaking classes and lectures and discussions on the current topics of the day need organising." Universal suffrage necessitated more educational work. As a Conservative magazine noted in 1927, "Every man and woman is a joint governor, for good or bad, in the greater Empire that has grown out of it [Britain]. If that power is in the hands of unthinking and ignorant men and women, the decline and fall of the British Empire and of British civilisation will be the next chapter in the world's history."[37]

There were two further reasons for Conservatives to consider the need for education. First, educational institutions attended by wage earners were increasingly under Labour's control. Every year during the 1920s the Workers' Educational Association, Ruskin College and other labor colleges, and the Fabian and ILP summer or weekend schools gave thousands a socialist education. These institutions sometimes received government funding, but they had close ties to trade unions and the Labour Party, both of which supplied students and money. As a Conservative magazine pessimistically noted, "The Socialist schools . . . grow like mushrooms in the night under the manure of Trade Union funds." It was clear to Conservatives that they had to counter leftist influences in many educational organizations. Second, the Conservative Party was increasingly dependent on volunteers who served as organizers and conduits of information. These rank-and-file members had to be trained for modern politics at Conservative classes and schools. As a consequence, education was, as the SUA said in 1926, "probably the most important and essential part of modern political organisation." It was certainly as important as propaganda to the party's success.[38]

Conservative educational efforts were of two types. General courses not directly intended to train volunteers made up the first type. Conservatives wanted to create educated, "reasonable," and antisocialist citizens. To carry out this objective, Conservatives across Britain organized lectures and discussions on a range of topics. Both party members and new or unaligned voters were encouraged to attend lectures and study groups where they learned about the Constitution, economics, and current affairs. This enabled the party to educate hundreds of thousands of citizens who were eager to transcend their provincial horizons.

The first attempts to organize classes took place in Scotland. In early 1919 the GUA began offering regular lectures. These proved so popular, particularly among women, that the GUA created a series of weekly afternoon or evening lectures. By the mid-1920s the weekly lecture was a fixture of the local political scene. Sometimes each lecture was on a separate subject. Councillor Mary Snodgrass gave a "Housing" talk in 1926 that drew almost 150 students. In other cases the GUA held a series of lectures on a single topic. In autumn 1924, for instance, there was a ten-week course on the history and prospects of the Constitution, and a six-lecture sequence on "Economics and Politics." In England there were also attempts to develop courses. The Primrose League began organizing fortnightly anti-Bolshevik classes in late 1919. In 1921 the WUO asked the writer and pamphleteer H. G. Williams to give morning lectures to London women.

Williams lectured about industrialization, trade unionism, Marxism, Capitalism, and democracy in industry, among other topics.[39]

Many constituency associations organized their own educational activities. One Scottish association held a week-long series of lectures entitled "The Class War," claiming to demonstrate that "Socialism was a policy of [the] work-shy" and that cooperative societies were better. Other associations opted for weekly meetings on general topics. Debating societies sometimes served educational purposes. In 1921, for instance, the Clapham agent organized a popular group that debated the Empire, tariff reform, trade unions, profiteering, socialism, Bolshevism, Ireland, and the political role of young people. Chichester Conservatives also held debates during which, in addition to the usual topics, members discussed national health insurance and medicine, the excess-profits tax, the Ruhr crisis, roads, and capital punishment. In many seats, however, education was ad hoc and dependent on members who volunteered to give lectures.[40]

To ensure that general education courses were available to all Conservatives, central office and the SUA encouraged constituencies to form study or reading circles that discussed a variety of historical and contemporary issues. Nonpartisan study circles were already proving popular, particularly among young people and women. The SUA took the lead in 1920 by devising a syllabus of twelve sessions. The success of the program, particularly among women in rural areas, encouraged the SUA to form more study circles. Such groups, SUA leaders hoped, would "prove of interest in places where there was little chance of amusement in the winter evenings, and afford opportunity for mutual self-education in the fundamental principles of Politics." The SUA also began collecting materials for a lending library for study circles.[41]

The NUA and central office also recognized the merit of study circles and encouraged their formation after the fall of the Lloyd George coalition. During 1923 the NUA Executive began considering a national system of study circles, an idea that the 1923 NUA conference greeted with enthusiasm. Delegates urged study circles to teach constitutional principles to citizens and to establish a broader base of support. *Home and Politics* carried an article with the suggestions of a local WUO chairwoman who had organized what she called "cottage meetings." By changing the meeting's location and setting, facilitating the attendance of mothers with small children, and making sure that there were refreshments, she found, the meetings attracted many women. The group read *The Times,* "Communist newspapers," and the local press. Members would then "chat of home affairs, the price of food, the housing shortage, religious education for the children, unemployment, trade unions, the Socialist menace and Communism, the danger of apathy, National Credit and how we are meeting our liabilities—in fact, everything that people who have the privilege of voting ought to know." The meetings helped to educate and, at the same time, make each woman "feel, with a sense of pride and responsibility, that, in spite of a humble position, her country is looking to her to maintain the highest ideals of citizenship, for the sake of those who have died for her in the past and for the happy future of those to come."[42]

Conservative interest in educational work increased after the party's defeat in 1923. In Yorkshire, for instance, the annual budget for lectures jumped from £13 in 1923 to £201 in 1924. Part of the upsurge in education came from the launch of a national plan for study circles. According to the NUA leaflet outlining the scheme, the object of the fortnightly circles was to enable an individual member to analyze and "ferret out for oneself answers to difficulties." According to the leaflet, reliance on other members of the circle rather than outsiders made for a less costly but more enriching educational experience. The leaflet provided a list of possible topics (with suggested readings) that included economics, government, Conservatism, socialism, capitalism, the Empire, and tariff reform.[43]

Initially the readings assigned for study circles were either Unionist Workers' Handbooks or propaganda pamphlets, but in 1924 Conservative leaders established the Westminster Library, a series of books published by Philip Allan in cooperation with an NUA committee composed of Leo Amery, John Buchan, Ronald McNeill, the author Edythe Glanville, and Philip Cambray. The Conservative Party was given the right to sell inexpensive editions of the books. The first nine works published were all by Conservative M.P.s or academics. The more prominent authors included the duchess of Atholl, Amery, the minister of agriculture, Edward Wood, and the former Labour Party minister, G. H. Roberts. Over the next few years a dozen more volumes were added to the series. Westminster Library works were available for purchase by individuals and study circles or by loan from the central office library.[44]

Thousands of copies of "The Study Circle" leaflet were soon distributed by central office. In associations like Wood Green and Oswestry, circles were quickly organized, despite complaints about the reading matter and the lack of interest on the part of some male party members. Many associations failed to respond initially, and in December 1925 central office began to broaden its system of adult education. It first created an education department, under publicity, headed by Colonel H. Williams. The education department urged agents and associations to set up regular courses on constitutional history and politics, and gave them syllabi and books. Williams told them that educated party members would be a great resource, as ordinary men and women were the "most effective missionaries on our behalf in season and out of season, daily and almost hourly."[45]

The new study circles were popular. During the first four months of 1926, three hundred were established in half as many constituencies. By the end of the year Williams was able to report that the number had doubled. Led by volunteers, some of them graduates of the party college, the study circles numbered from a handful to several dozen students who met weekly or fortnightly for six to twelve sessions. They discussed a variety of historical and contemporary political questions, but the most common were socialism, industrialization, the Empire, economics, and constitutional history. To supplement the study circle scheme, central office also began offering correspondence courses. Adult education prospered in the later 1920s in part because the work of the education department was transferred to the Conservative Educational Institute. John Buchan led this quasi-independent organization, which was able to pursue its goals singlemindedly. During peak educational season, autumn and winter, in 1926–27, there were six hundred study circles with twelve thousand students. The next year there were over eight hundred groups and eighteen thousand students. The SUA developed a similar system with the assistance of the Scottish 1924 Club, and by 1927 there were over three hundred study circles in Scotland.[46]

But general education was only one side of Conservative education; the other component was training the rank and file for direct use by the party. In part this task involved disseminating information to activists. Central office had long been a source of information for Conservative candidates and workers, and, after the war, Cambray reorganized and expanded the Information and Research Department. He encouraged volunteer speakers, local officers, M.P.s, and candidates to seek information. They could obtain material on policy, the opposition parties, propaganda, and organizing. Headquarters published *Gleanings and Memoranda*, *Hints for Speakers*, Unionist Workers' Handbooks, informational pamphlets, and regular articles in the party magazines to guide its workers. This, however, was not sufficient for the hundreds of thousands of volunteers needed to

canvass, distribute literature, and electioneer among the postwar electorate, so the Conservatives initiated a multitude of training courses and
schools.

A primary concern of Conservative leaders was training a sufficient
number of political speakers. To meet the continuing need for speakers,
Conservatives increasingly relied on trained volunteers. In 1920 central
office began cooperating with various Conservative and business groups
to operate evening classes on public speaking in London; in 1926 it began
offering its own classes for women on public speaking; and later it added
classes for men and advanced speakers. The Primrose League carried out
its own training efforts by launching courses for speakers and workers and
instituting a regular column, "Notes for Speakers and Workers," in its magazine. In Scotland the GUA began offering regular courses for speakers
in 1922.[47]

One of the most successful educational innovations of the interwar
period was the Conservative College. Once again the initiative came from
Scotland. Jeanette Martin, the women's organizer, suggested, and the SUA
Eastern Division agreed, to hold a two-week "Summer School of Political
Study." They planned an August 1920 course that would so thoroughly
ground wage earners and other students in economic and constitutional
theory that the graduates would be impervious to socialism. It was hoped
that the residential school would also create social solidarity "between
widely different grades of society." Martin rented St. Ninian's School in
Moffat, Dumfries, and agreed to serve as the school's warden. The Conservative whips in London urged the Tory M.P. and historian J. A. R. Marriott
to give the lectures on constitutional history. Harold Cox, editor of the
Edinburgh Review, agreed to lecture on economic and social topics. Once
it heard of the plan, the NUA Labour Committee immediately decided
to send forty students. They obtained financial assistance from Chairman
Whittaker and Sir Philip Stott, a successful Lancashire architect and cotton
manufacturer who was interested in working-class education and Conservative politics. Nearly all of the one hundred students who attended Moffat
were trade unionists.[48]

The Labour Committee organizer, R. M. Mathams, attended the
school and afterward wrote about the exchange of views that took place in
classes and elsewhere. It was, he believed, a vivid demonstration of the
union of classes and races that would allow Britain and the Empire to re-
cover from the war. The success of Moffat encouraged the SUA and the

Labour Committee to collaborate on another school. This time they used St. Andrew's during July and August 1921. The Labour Committee's new educational subcommittee and the SUA agreed to organize two fortnightly courses open to one hundred students each. Following the example of Moffat, the cost of the course and accommodations was about £6. Mathams, who was a co-organizer of the school, asked for the party's support. He argued that the school would win adherents, combat the "poisoned knowledge from the Labour 'Colleges of Unreason,'" and fulfill the Conservative ideal of "Democratic self-expression and freedom."[49]

Again following the Moffat precedent, the predominantly working-class students in each course at St. Andrew's were lectured on constitutional history and economics by pairs of eminent scholars: F. J. C. Hearnshaw and A. W. Kirkcaldy, and Sir William Ashley and Dudley J. Medley. The school also held mock elections and parliaments, which were a popular means of teaching constitutional issues and current politics. The contest between Unionist-Labour and Anti-Waste candidates, and the second reading of a bill to establish contracting in for trade unionists were, said the *Conservative Agents' Journal*, particularly exciting. The participation of students in all activities demonstrated, as one newspaper noted, Hearnshaw's argument that democracy rests on the community's "corporate existence and spirit." Neither Moffat nor St. Andrew's taught "readymade answers." Instead they tried to teach students "sound economics and . . . the lessons of history." In this way, it was thought, Conservative supporters learned to think for themselves so that they would "be enabled to come to a right conclusion, not only on the questions of the moment, but on any future questions which may arise."[50]

The success of Moffat and St. Andrew's encouraged Conservative leaders to broaden their efforts. After the tumult of 1922 passed, Conservatives turned to creating more schools of study and to developing a Conservative College. In 1924 the SUA women's committee organized a school of study in Edinburgh. Students heard lectures on economics and socialism and were trained in public speaking. Later that year there was another school in the west at Dollar, East Renfrewshire.[51] Scottish Unionist leaders appreciated the practical training these schools offered. They also believed that they could attract more students, especially from rural areas, by changing the location and avoiding the cost of a permanent facility. The SUA accordingly held schools of study in various parts of the country, preparing students to combat socialism.

The SUA organized other party schools as well. In 1925 they held a three-day course at Stirling in which students learned about women's issues, economics, housing, trade unionism, Conservatism, and imperial and defense policy. In the same year there were seven such schools just in the SUA Eastern Division. Typically these schools were attended by ten or twenty of the most interested members—particularly women—from nearby local associations, who devoted themselves to studying contemporary political issues, although more than two hundred students participated in a 1927 school at Stirling, studying constitutional history, Conservatism, and women in politics. They were also able to hear addresses by the duchess of Atholl and Arthur Shadwell. In Kincardine the association had enough funds to collaborate in a school for women held at Stonehaven in autumn 1926. The women learned about the "poisonous doctrines" of "envy, hatred, malice, and uncharitableness" that Bolshevik Sunday Schools allegedly spread, and they heard a lecturer from the Unionist Workers' League explain how tariff reform would lead to higher production, higher wages, and imperial unity. Students also met with local political notables, including their M.P.[52]

In contrast to the Scottish Unionists, Conservatives in England and Wales tended to rely less on schools and more on the Conservative College and the party's expanding system of adult education. Still, Conservative organizations held a number of schools. Regular classes at Leeds were run by the Yorkshire provincial division and central office area agent. In 1924 the WUO organized a weekend school in North Wales. After holding a six-day course of lectures and public speaking classes at Torquay in 1928, the WUO decided to establish schools in each area. The JIL sponsored schools in Ilkley and Torquay in 1928, and it also began collaborating with the Conservative Educational Institute to offer regional weekend schools. Like the Scottish Unionists, the JIL organizers were trying to offer an experience more intensive than study circles and more practical and accessible than a college. Even the Primrose League had schools, the first being a two-week course at Torquay in 1925. Primrose League schools differed from party schools in their emphasis on recreational activities. They were generally in the south (where the Primrose League was strongest) and were inaccessible to many potential students.[53]

As important as schools of study were, the creation of the Conservative College was the pinnacle of the party's educational effort. Stott was instrumental in creating the college. Having demonstrated his support for wage-earners' education by visiting the summer schools at Moffat and St. Andrew's and making substantial contributions to both, Stott decided to create a permanent college. In 1922 he purchased the late Lord Overstone's home, built in 1862 and located near Northampton. For a nominal rent he gave the Labour Committee use of the house and grounds for half of every year. While the Labour Committee created a fund for the college's operations, Younger, the party chairman, provided assistance from central office, the WUO, and the JIL. By spring 1923 the newly named Philip Stott College, which Marriott described as a "roomy, solid, ugly Victorian structure," was ready.[54]

For the first session ten fortnightly courses were planned in hopes that each would draw one hundred students paying £7 for course, room, and board. Before arriving, students were asked to read the works on a syllabus to ensure efficient use of their time at Stott. In the mornings Stott students attended two lectures followed by questions and discussion. As lecturers the college hired seven eminent scholars, five of whom had taught at the summer schools. These included the economists Cox and Kirkcaldy and the historians Hearnshaw, Marriott, and Dudley J. Medley. The new instructors, academics Arthur Radford and J. L. Morison, taught economics and imperial history, respectively. In the afternoons students could enjoy cricket, tennis, bowls, golf, boating, billiards, music, and dancing, or they could take classes on speaking or policy matters. And, for the first time, students had access to resident tutors and a small library. In addition, there were sometimes field trips to sites of historical or economic importance. Although none of their work at Stott was graded, students were expected to apply themselves.[55]

At first Stott College continued along the path established at Moffat. Its founders' primary objective was to encourage Conservatives to study under "the greatest minds of our day" in order to become better citizens. Students were mainly wage earners. The college was, *The Times* noted in March 1923, "primarily intended to benefit working men and women of the party who have not access to facilities for post-school education which Socialists obtain at the various Labour colleges." A Labour Committee member, Sir Francis Watson, told Conservatives in Bradford that they were attempting to fill the gaps in the education of working-class Conservatives to prevent Labour and trade union colleges from doing so. In addition, Conservative organizers believed that wage earners who attended Stott would spread a "gospel of goodwill" among their colleagues and neighbors. Some Conservatives considered this the chief benefit of Stott. But the student body was not completely homogeneous: forty Imps, many of whom were given scholarships, attended, as did a few agents and organizers.[56]

Despite its promise, Stott College faced difficulties, particularly a shortage of students. In 1923 one of the courses had only two dozen students, and there were only about five hundred students enrolled during the 1923 session. Fortunately, the college received the endorsement of leading Conservatives, including Baldwin. On 27 September 1923 the National Society of Conservative Agents held its annual meeting at Stott with Baldwin in attendance. The prime minister toured the establishment accompanied by various Conservative leaders, including Davidson, Amery, who was a lecturer at the college, and F. S. Jackson, who was taking a course at Stott. The younger students responded enthusiastically to Baldwin, seeking his autograph and even "chairing" their placid leader. In a short address Baldwin praised the college as part of Britain's tradition of voluntary and pragmatic education. Stott's superior education, he stated, rejected materialism and "the east wind of German Socialism and Russian Communism and French Syndicalism." Instead, he added, the next generation was being taught to rely on native common sense and insight, which would enable them "to save democracy, to preserve it and to inspire it."[57]

In the next few years changes were made to improve the situation at Stott College. First, organizers engaged leading Conservatives to address the students even as the capable staff of lecturers was expanded. Second, to improve the administration, the overburdened and ailing Mathams was displaced by a Philip Stott College subcommittee under the NUA Executive. The subcommittee included Amery, Stott, Whittaker, Dr. W. George Black, and Sir Geoffrey Butler. F. S. Jackson, who knew Marriott from the Oxford University Extension scheme, appointed the historian to head the subcommittee. Third, central office and other Conservative organizations gave the college publicity and general assistance. Before the 1926 session began, for instance, over nine thousand copies of the college prospectus was distributed to candidates, M.P.s, local officials, WUO and JIL branches, and clubs. Central office also provided more scholarships for students attending Stott.[58]

Response to the changes was an immediate increase in enrollments. In 1924 there were more than nine hundred students, and, during the seventh course of the 1925 session, a milestone was passed when the college reached its maximum enrollment for the first time. In its first three years of operation, 2,500 students attended Stott. After 1923 the college also expanded its student body by drawing more non-wage earners. JIL headquarters sent and paid for more than fifty students in 1924, and the following year more than two hundred JIL students attended. Sixty of those were awarded scholarships from headquarters. Special rates for Imps further increased the number of JIL students at Stott to 270 in 1926 and 370 in 1927. At the same time the number of women in attendance increased substantially. In 1923 many women did not apply because of a mistaken belief that the college offered only dormitory accommodations. Thereafter Stott organizers made great efforts to attract women, making sure that curtained cubicles were available for all women and providing a ladies' drawing room. The party chairman was largely unable to obtain female lecturers or tutors, but he added Dame Helen Gwynne-Vaughan and Miss Flora Fardell, the founder of the Young Conservatives (a Primrose League youth group) to the governing committee in order to give women and youth more say in running Stott. By 1927 nearly six hundred of Stott's students, more than half, were women.[59]

Following the model of the early summer schools, Stott's curriculum continued to be dominated by constitutional history and economics. This enabled the college to emphasize progressive Conservatism while avoiding some of the more contentious issues and violent partisanship. Lectures on constitutional history and economics inculcated students with the desirability of continuity and unity. Commenting on the first session at Stott, the JIL magazine praised the lecturers for conveying the lessons of history and "the truths of economic laws which have resulted in human progress and national development." The assumption was that history and economics enabled students to appreciate reality and made them insusceptible to radicalism. "To understand how well the principle of evolution has served England," *The Times* claimed, "is to be armed with a thousand arguments against revolution." One Stott lecturer told his students that Britain's constitutional history demonstrated how "'liberty' was always asserting itself" and how the constitution, which grew from "an acorn of mere custom" into a mighty oak, was endangered by "the axe of Communism." In the preface to Arthur Bryant's textbook for students, *The Spirit of Conservatism* (1929), John Buchan argued that Conservative beliefs were rooted in a regard for "historic continuity" and the nation's "essential unity." A Conservative, he elaborated, "believes that the State is an organic and not a mechanical thing, and that there should be no violent disruption in growth." Instead Conservatism should uphold individual opportunity and liberty and careful institutional reform while strenuously opposing bureaucracy.[60]

The other subjects in the Stott curriculum were imperialism and religion. During 1923 Amery delivered a lecture on nationalism and imperialism, expressing his concern that Conservatives were "drifting into a mere acceptance of the old *laissez-faire* individualism as an alternative to Socialism." He was careful to dissociate Conservatism from both Liberalism and socialism. While Conservatism was based on a "historical, national, and Imperial conception," Liberalism and socialism were merely "a series of abstractions." Amery lectured as well on aspects of imperial economics and defense. Another tariff reformer, W. A. S. Hewins, frequently lectured on the Empire and imperial preference. He tried to inspire students with "the pomp and majesty" and "the Divine purpose underlying and influencing the rise and fall of Empires." Marriott and the Maharajah of Burdwan also taught courses.[61]

The only other topic of importance at Stott was religion or morality. Each day's activities began with religious services, and on Sundays students attended the chapel in Overstone Park. Some lecturers, like Marriott, dealt with moral issues. His talks on personal ethics were the basis of *Economics and Ethics* (1923). Marriott claimed that his book showed students how "to order their daily lives, in the home, the shop, in the factory or on the farm, in conformity with the highest ethical standards, or in more familiar words in accordance with the will of God." In a 1926 lecture entitled "Christianity and Socialism," Marriott voiced the common Conservative cry that socialist tenets ran counter to Christianity.[62]

Organizers repeatedly claimed that students found a sense of national community at Stott by fraternizing with a variety of students. Many reports emphasized the integrative function of the college and offered picturesque illustrations of the camaraderie. One contributor to *Imp* noted that, at his first dinner, he was seated between a Durham miner and a Surrey clerk. Later he played doubles with a lawyer, a weaver, and a parliamentary candidate. Such encounters were common at Stott, he wrote, and they revealed "the spirit of true democracy." In another party magazine, a graduate claimed that the college was "the most democratic institution in the world" because aristocrats "answered to their surnames in the same way as the miners, engineers, machinists, operatives, railwaymen, clerks, housewives, and the others." Such comments purported to demonstrate the claims of classlessness made by the college and the Conservative Party.[63]

Conservative leaders were eager to develop this camaraderie. They encouraged Conservative M.P.s and ministers to visit the college and cultivated ties among alumni. In addition to Amery, who was a regular lecturer, Eustace Percy, Walter Elliot, Sir William Bull, Sir Leslie Scott, Henry Page Croft, Austin Hopkinson, Sir Herbert Nield, Robert Gee, Thomas Oakley, and Oliver Locker-Lampson visited Stott in 1925. The next year Marriott brought Stott, Lord Cave, and Neville Chamberlain to the school. These visits created camaraderie within the party and encouraged rank-and-file members to identify with their leaders. In 1925 central office also began making more systematic use of Stott alumni by sending area agents lists of graduates in their region. With the assistance of the St. Stephen's Club, central office also developed Overstonian Clubs. These clubs' purpose was to help students maintain the enthusiasm of the Stott experience, provide them with libraries and expert organizers, and encourage them to carry out party work. By 1925 several clubs had been formed in Scotland, Yorkshire, and Lancashire.[64]

There was a noticeable shift in emphasis in the fourth year of the college's existence when it was designated the training school for party workers. Critics declared that the curriculum was too impractical for a party college and that Stott was not training enough professional and volunteer workers. Discourses on economics or constitutional history, they complained, would not produce the personnel the party needed to fight socialists. To a considerable degree, changes in Stott after 1926 were Davidson's work. Some years before, he had made it plain that he considered education the key to creating a Conservative elite. For him education was a religion, and he made it a major concern of central office. Davidson led Stott College toward a firmer recognition of its role as a party training school as he shifted more responsibility for general education to study circles and schools of study. By 1928 only two of the fourteen courses at Stott were devoted to general education.[65]

At Stott the most visible sign of these changes was the introduction of new classes and special courses for particular groups within the Conservative Party. To open the 1926 session, a one-week Easter course was arranged for members of the Young Conservative Union. Four other one-week courses followed, designed particularly for those who wanted more training in policy and organizing and were unable to devote two weeks to the endeavor. The National Society of Conservative Agents and the *Conservative Agents' Journal* urged that this practice be expanded. They wanted their own course on election law, advertising, propaganda, fund-raising, and organizing. The new approach proved so successful that in 1927 there were separate courses for the JIL, the Young Conservative Union, trade unionists and members of cooperatives, and WUO branch officers. In 1928 the college organized a two-week course for Imps, plus a one-week course for Imp officers. With the election approaching, JIL members received instruction about key election issues—trade union reform, local government, derating (relief of businesses' local property taxes), and agriculture. They were also trained extensively in propaganda, speaking, and registration and election law.[66]

Another change in Conservative educational work was administrative restructuring. In early 1927 responsibility for Stott was completely removed from the Labour Committee and placed under a central office committee, although Marriott remained chairman, and less than a year later, Davidson moved central office's educational operations to the Conservative and Unionist Educational Institute. This organization was nominally headed by Baldwin and Davidson, but Buchan was chairman. His assistant, the director, Hugh Williams, controlled day-to-day operations. The institute expanded the system of general education, increasing the number of study circles and local courses. It also took over Stott College, hiring professional staff for the school. Major General Sir Reginald Hoskins became the college's first principal.[67]

Buchan, a former wartime director of information, planned a full-scale educational and research effort to stop socialism. Within days of assuming control, Buchan sent Baldwin a pamphlet, "Political Research and Adult Education," outlining his plan for the organization. Like the prime minister, Buchan was a scholar-statesman who believed that it was necessary to attract young people of intelligence, energy, and idealism to the Conservative Party. In his view the political future would be determined by the party's ability to create a graduated educational system including study circles, temporary schools, and a residential college to train the party cadre. He also believed that the Conservative Party needed a research organization comparable to Labour's research department and the Liberal Party's industrial inquiry. Buchan wanted the institute to assume this role and "co-ordinate the efforts of the industrialists . . . give expression to scientific interpretations of economic laws," and "inquire as to means by which a party may remain in power." He failed, however, to create such a research organization. Joseph Ball argued strenuously against the proposal, which would have seriously undermined his position as director of publicity. Only at the end of 1929, after the general election, was a Conservative research department created, with Ball in charge.[68]

Buchan brought new vigor to Conservative educational activities. In the April 1928 issue of the *Conservative Agents' Journal*, he argued that the future of the Conservative Party depended on challenging the domination that Labour and its allies exercised over adult education. Thousands of students "working directly or indirectly under the Socialist aegis" would become Labour supporters unless provided with an alternative. Buchan tried to counter Labour's perceived strength by increasing the number of classes, study circles, and schools of study, and by making Stott College the apex of a Conservative educational system. Some Conservatives, particularly Stott and other Labour Committee activists, were angered by Buchan's changes because they had intended the college to educate trade unionists. In May 1928 Stott publicly criticized the college for failing to attract students and abandoning its mission of educating wage earners. Both Davidson and Marriott denied the charges, noting that only the spring courses were not full and that more than four thousand students had already matriculated.[69]

The achievements of Stott College were consolidated by Andrew Bonar Law Memorial College, which replaced it in 1929. Davidson had long hoped to develop a year-round facility where a greater number and variety of courses could be offered. In mid-1928 the party chairman learned that Ashridge in Hertfordshire was available. Ashridge, an early nineteenth century Gothic house with beautiful grounds, was larger and more conveniently located than Overstone. Shortly before his death the successful engineer and railwayman Urban Broughton had bought the building and one hundred acres and donated it to an Andrew Bonar Law Memorial Trust for use as a party college. Other wealthy Conservatives established a handsome endowment for the school. The college opened in July 1929, and it quickly proved a success. After the first few years enrollments rose and remained steady at 2,500 students per year, more than twice the number at Stott. Andrew Bonar Law Memorial College, or Ashridge as it was popularly known, offered both political training and general education courses. It ran a special eight-week course on citizenship for younger students, as well as courses for university students, peers, M.P.s and candidates, wives of M.P.s, and constituency officers. Ashridge courses retained the nonpartisan but antisocialist flavor of Stott College.[70]

Local associations' activities also show the importance Conservatives attached to education and political training in the 1920s. Many associations held canvassing and speaking courses. Oswestry was among the first to organize such classes in 1923, but others soon followed. In 1924 the North Cornwall association began holding regular public speaking classes, and a small sub-branch operated classes in both the afternoon and the evening. Similarly, in early 1926 the Chichester association contributed funds and students to a countywide educational scheme, and two years later they were running their own canvassing class in preparation for the next election. Some associations also operated lending libraries and hired professional advisers. Beginning in late 1925, local workers could use central office's new reading room, which had recent books, magazines, and propaganda from all three political parties.[71]

Local Conservatives also recognized the potential benefits of the Conservative College. The Stockton labour committee sent several students, including the committee chairman, James Gardner. The cost of attending Stott was an obstacle for others, however, although some associations tried to assist them. Prominent local Conservatives often gave scholarships to needy students. Associations like Bradford Central regularly offered scholarships but had difficulty locating worthy candidates, especially wage earners. Provincial divisions, too, often helped to pay for students. As Stott developed into a complete Conservative college, local associations responded with greater enthusiasm. A leading member of the North Cornwall association, for instance, argued that the college would train excellent speakers. Oswestry Conservatives were eager to send their Imps and funded scholarships for that purpose. Several Conservatives in Stockton were sent to Stott in 1926 with the assistance of Macmillan and their WUO branch. On their return, two students spoke about their experiences, particularly the camaraderie and invigorating nature of the college. The WUO member mentioned proudly that she had successfully chaired her first meeting. The wage-earner student described how he had portrayed a communist agitator in a debate. His performance was so well received that Sir Philip Stott had invited him to tea afterward.[72]

The emphasis on education in the decade after 1918 marks the beginning of a long-lasting change in the Conservatives' approach to politics. In the 1920s some Tories were unwilling to accept these innovations, which they considered useless or even degrading. When he was asked in 1924 to help central office with its educational work, Sir Cuthbert Headlam was unenthusiastic. In his diary he commented that one "cannot teach people to be politicians. . . . These fellows seem to imagine that they can be spoon fed into Parliament and taught the requisite amount of history, economics and political claptrap by means of lectures and text books." Such views were still being advanced by the former Conservative official Sir John Green in the 1930s. Green described Ashridge as "a pretentious extension of the principles of political education" that demonstrated "the extent to which the Conservative Party is the slave of democratic values."[73]

Headlam and Green, however, were not representative of the interwar

Conservative Party. During the 1920s Conservative interest in education reflected wider contemporary trends in party (and other) education. Because they could rely on the ILP, the Fabian Society, and the Workers' Educational Association, Labour leaders never bothered to develop their own educational system, while the Liberal Party relied on the research-oriented summer schools it had instituted in 1921. The Conservative Party created the most extensive network of party education in Britain. It included hundreds of thousands of students working in local classes, correspondence courses, study circles, schools of study, and the Conservative College, the first permanent party college in Britain.

Propaganda's utility and effect is more difficult to assess than education's. What effect did the extensive use of propaganda have in the 1920s? By its nature propaganda attempts to shape politics by influencing the opinions and, therefore, the behavior of citizens. There is no sure way of measuring or verifying how well it worked, but we can say that propaganda was useful in conveying Conservative aims and attitudes to millions of voters. Different types of propaganda varied in their effectiveness. In part propaganda, particularly in its more traditional forms, was best suited to maintaining enthusiasm and explaining policies to supporters.[74] Speakers revitalized supporters and communicated information to party adherents, who transmitted it to the wider public. Pamphlets and, to a lesser extent, leaflets also helped Conservative voters' support remain strong.

Other types of propaganda, such as lantern lectures, films, and newspapers, were most effective at reaching the wider public. A study of one seat during the 1951 election found that only 10 percent of voters attended public meetings; 50 percent read party literature; and 80 percent read newspapers, listened to radio, or watched television broadcasts. As Higham recognized in 1920, "The best way of imparting . . . information is not to tell the people how to get it, but to force it upon their notice, gratis; to eliminate, as far as possible, all need for initiative." Lantern lectures, films, and newspapers were most effective because they provided information in a seemingly objective or entertaining way.[75]

In its propagandizing, the Conservative Party contributed to a long-term shift in the character of British politics. Propaganda is most effective among new or unaligned voters when it encapsulates and conveys information through readily accessible, nonrational means. During Britain's first years of universal suffrage, Conservatives found that propaganda enabled them to create favorable images for themselves and negative ones for their opposition. A significant portion of the electorate based its votes on these fragmented and transitory political impressions. For some members of the political elite such a development was deeply disturbing, even if it was inevitable and helped to maintain Conservative dominance. In a thoughtful passage in his diary, Headlam claimed that politics was better and "good taste and good manners" reigned when "no one troubled about the lower classes." And in 1918 Baldwin had told the Commons how he deplored the clandestine nature of propaganda. This may have been just the grumblings of two aging Victorians. Yet, at a deeper level, as LeMahieu argues in *A Culture for Democracy,* interwar propaganda, and the media generally, developed new types of literacy. Politics was shaped by the public's familiarity with the new, nonrational techniques, just as voters today are affected by their extended exposure to television.[76]

This development also explains in part why politics in the 1920s was characterized by personalities at the expense of complex issues and logical analysis. Amery once noted after a speech that his audience responded to him as the "ploughing, climbing, [and] bathing . . . film star" of the phonofilm more than as colonial secretary. One who most benefited from the emphasis on personality was Baldwin, who came to personify the assorted elements of postwar Conservatism just as Ramsay MacDonald seemed to embody Labour. As one journalist noted in 1932, film was especially effective in promoting this sort of appreciation. "To me," she wrote, "Mr. Ramsay MacDonald, Mr. Baldwin and others have only become real personalities since I met them on the screen." Of course there were critics. One Conservative attacked the cult of personality, which was based upon a false view of Baldwin as "a sort of yeoman farmer who had been pitchforked . . . into the onerous role of Premier." Baldwin's pipe and mannerisms, the writer complained, were "props, like Charlie Chaplin's little cane," and his actions were the rituals of a cult of mediocrity. Ironically, a large part of Baldwin's attraction rested on what one Conservative propagandist termed Baldwin's "deep repugnance towards the spectacular side of politics." In his speeches, especially those to nonpartisan organizations, the Conservative leader successfully associated himself and his party with English values threatened by "the smooth and clever tongues" of unscrupulous or radical politicians.[77]

There remains, however, the question of cause and effect: did propaganda create public opinion or only reflect it? In their wholehearted acceptance of the new techniques, professional party workers usually overestimated the power of propaganda. For instance, in the early 1929 issues of the *Conservative Agents' Journal,* an advertisement for a duplicator machine reads, "Your member goes to Parliament on Propaganda." Such simplistic views permeated politics in the 1920s. A more careful assessment of propaganda must first recognize that in part effectiveness depended on the circumstances of the exercise and the information being imparted. Conservative propaganda's potential was obviously limited by Conservative principles and aims. In contrast to commercial publicity, which promoted sales—a tangible result—propaganda worked more obliquely. On occasion this had a debilitating effect. One SUA meeting was unable to decide on propaganda material and could agree only to distribute it more effectively.[78]

Political operatives in the 1920s tended to accept a too simple Pavlovian model for the voting public. As one agent noted in 1927, publicity stunts are often ineffective precisely because the public refuses to believe them. In addition, propaganda is predicated on common determinates rather than on responses which, of course, differ with individual and circumstances. One person might respond as desired and vote Conservative, but another might not. Under a different set of circumstances, neither or both might respond as desired. "Safety First," for example, was an effective slogan in 1922 and 1924, but a failure in 1929. The lesson was that propaganda was only effective insofar as it tapped existing opinions and moods. As Milne and MacKenzie noted in 1954, "Propaganda may provide a stimulus to some latent impulse, but the key to the problem of behaviour still lies in the social and mental background of the elector." Propaganda cannot, in other words, create opinion and bring about a specific action unless it correctly appeals to existing conditions; it must be absolutely relevant. In the years immediately after World War I, "Safety First" was appropriate, but by 1929 it was much less so.[79]

The Conservative Party propaganda and education system developed after 1918 is one indication of how "the party of the status quo" successfully adapted to the postwar era. Propaganda and publicity were a key factor in the party's performance, as by these means Conservative leaders were able to compete successfully against the opposition parties and reach out to the vastly increased—and seemingly unknowable—electorate. No single factor was decisive in creating the Conservative Party's domination of interwar politics. The party's educational efforts enabled it to win adherents, but just as important, it trained a growing number of members to work for their beliefs on behalf of the Conservative Party. Such trained personnel were crucial in spreading Conservatism among the populace, as propaganda was most effective when its dispersal was carefully monitored and controlled by trained party members. In large part both education and propaganda depended on the WUO, the JIL, and the Labour Committee. The popular organizations and the propaganda and educational tools of the Conservative Party were put to the test in the 1929 general election, the last election of the 1920s, after the passage of the equal suffrage act in 1928.

6

The Representation of the People
Act of 1928 and the General
Election of 1929

By the late 1920s the Conservative Party had largely adapted to mass politics. It had successful mass organizations, extensive propaganda capabilities, and a system of party education. Yet as the Conservatives approached a mandated general election in 1929, they faced a new challenge: the Representation of the People Act of 1928. The property and age requirements of the 1918 reform act had restricted women's vote to three-fifths of adult females, but the 1928 act established equal suffrage, confirming that the franchise was a right of all adult citizens. The history of the 1928 reform act and the Conservative Party's response to it has been largely ignored by historians. The standard history simply states that nearly all Conservatives, including the party's professional staff, considered equal suffrage at twenty-one anathema.[1]

Many Conservatives greeted the changes engendered by the reform act of 1918 with what David Close describes as "reluctant, and somewhat cynical, resignation."[2] Although many never considered the measure beneficial, they accepted it as inevitable and, with Baldwin, realized that the role of the party for the foreseeable future was not to obstruct this development, but to win elections while educating the new electors and maintaining political stability. In effect, Conservatives, or at least an increasing number of them, accepted the principle of universal adult suffrage even if they disagreed on when to equalize the franchise. The different female and male franchises of 1918 were an expedient but illogical halfway measure. By late 1924 all three parties were pledged to full women's suffrage. Baldwin's government was expected to introduce an equal suffrage bill, and it did. The resulting Representation of the People Act of 1928 established universal suffrage in Great Britain.

In May 1929, as soon as the new voter registers were ready, Baldwin's government called a general election. During the campaign the Conservatives mobilized all their organizational capabilities but failed to present a program that appealed to the mass electorate. Their most innovative proposal was the partial derating of industrial and agricultural property to increase British competitiveness. Derating, however, inspired as much hostility as enthusiasm, and Baldwin and the party were thrown back on their record of small but steady achievements and their ability to provide safe government. The 1929 campaign was closely associated with the Conservative Party leader and his opposition rivals. In contrast to the 1918 election, in which Lloyd George's appeal helped the coalition to a major victory, Baldwin's personal appeal, as great as it was, was not enough. A decade of economic trouble and unemployment, the decline of internal and foreign threats, and five years of safe but unremarkable government had sapped voters' patience. When presented with a Conservative campaign dominated by Baldwin and a "Why Change?" slogan, many electors seem to have had a ready answer. They voted for Labour and Liberal candidates in unprecedented numbers, and the Conservative Party lost its parliamentary majority.

The Representation of the People Act of 1928

Before the Representation of the People Act of 1928, there were attempts to enfranchise adult women who lacked the vote in 1918, 1919, 1920, 1922, 1923, and 1924, but each collapsed in the face of Conservative opposition. The Labour government of 1924 introduced the most important of these failed bills. The 1924 bill provided universal adult suffrage but abolished the business vote and removed the property qualification for the local government franchise. Conservative agents led the attack on the bill, pressing the NUA into action and creating a subcommittee akin to the one that had altered provisions of the 1918 reform bill. Together Conservative agents and M.P.s shelved the bill.[3]

Although Close defines all Conservative opposition as a rejection of the principle of equal suffrage, most Conservatives attacked the bill by criticizing it as premature, unnecessary, and a threat to the business and local government franchises. Yet the debate revealed tensions among Conservatives on the question of universal suffrage. Some were pledged to equal suffrage at twenty-one, while others opposed equal suffrage or demanded a higher minimum age. Opponents of equal suffrage used many of the same arguments that had dominated the suffrage debate before 1918. They claimed that an equal suffrage bill would enable women to dominate the three-fourths of the parliamentary divisions where they outnumbered the men. Conservative opponents were also worried that enfranchising young women, particularly factory workers who might be trade unionists, would give Labour an insurmountable electoral advantage. Many opponents claimed that there was no public demand for reform or that the 1918 act had been passed on the understanding that it would remain in effect for at least ten years. (According to Butler, this claim was unfounded, but it might have been based on an unrecorded agreement.) And some Conservative opponents just could not accept votes for all citizens. They still believed, with the Tory historian Hearnshaw, that voting was a responsibility limited to "worthier" citizens. In other words, they were hostile to democracy.[4]

Quite a few Conservatives accepted equal female suffrage but thought that the minimum voting age for all citizens should be raised to twenty-five. This proposal received nonpartisan support from educational elitists like the Labour peer Viscount Haldane and the Liberal M.P. Sir John Simon. Some Conservative women also supported the idea, and the 1926 WUO conference passed a resolution in favor of it. Such a measure might satisfy the demand for equality while excluding ignorant young people, particularly factory girls. Conservative backers of this proposal deplored the frivolity of the younger generation. To them, people under twenty-five (of whatever sex) were too immature to exercise their franchise properly.[5]

Other Conservatives, particularly women, supported universal suffrage at twenty-one. Nancy Astor and Dame Helen Gwynne-Vaughan publicly supported the Labour bill during a debate on equal suffrage at the 1924 WUO conference. Most proponents of universal suffrage believed that (1) political elitism was dead, (2) the state could not exclude adults from voting because they happened to be women, and (3) the Conservatives might as well concentrate on educating voters and bringing them into the party. As John Buchan had said in 1910, if "duty to the State" was the criterion for the franchise, then intelligent and politically active women and hardworking mothers of Britain ought to have it. There was no way to distinguish these women from the rest. Once voting became a right for all men in 1918, whole groups of women could not be excluded indefinitely, and many thought that it would better to pass a conservative reform measure and earn the credit from doing it than to leave the question to left-wing parties.[6]

The new Baldwin government, particularly the prime minister, was pledged to equal suffrage. Since 1918, both Bonar Law and Baldwin had publicly supported equal suffrage. During the 1924 campaign Baldwin vowed to call an all-party conference to devise an equal franchise measure. Baldwin did not detail specific franchise qualifications, but most believed he would allow women to qualify for the existing male residential franchise. In response, one speaker at a WUO branch in North Cornwall agreed that the government should "level up" the franchise. Moreover, some Conservatives argued, if they raised the voting age to twenty-five, they might alienate a large number of voters to whom another government would grant the franchise.[7]

Conservatives divided over the suffrage question again when Labour introduced a franchise bill in 1925. One of the chief Conservative complaints was that the bill would nullify dual voting. Others accepted the argument of one M.P. that the electorate already included too many "unenlightened people" and immature women who were "apt to be attracted by those glittering prophecies" of Labour "like a moth attracted by a candle." During the debate, however, the home secretary, Sir William Joynson-Hicks, rejected the bill but vowed to pass an equal franchise bill "within the lifetime of the present Parliament."[8]

A number of Conservatives were already impatient with the government. Astor pointed to the party's election pledge. She also attacked the "antiquated and out-of-date" M.P.s from ultrasafe Conservative seats. She urged Conservatives "to take a leap in the light towards trusting women." Astor's remarks indicated the growing support for equal female suffrage among Conservatives, especially women. In early 1927 the *Conservative Agents' Journal* urged the government to establish universal suffrage at twenty-one. It was inevitable, the magazine argued, and the Conservatives might benefit by passing such a measure. But the king's speech in February 1927 did not include equal suffrage. Several women on the NUCUA council responded by criticizing the government's lethargy. Astor again voiced her dissatisfaction in the Commons and led a nonpartisan deputation demanding equal suffrage. Outside Westminster the issue was becoming something of a concern. Conservatives in Bradford, for instance, passed a resolution "emphatically in favour of the granting of the Parliamentary Franchise to both Men and Women . . . on attaining the age of 21 years."[9]

In March 1927 the Cabinet finally formed a committee to investigate the franchise question. One of the committee members was the chancellor of the exchequer, Winston Churchill. With the assistance of the secretary of state for India, Lord Birkenhead, Churchill vehemently opposed equal female suffrage, but it was too late to stop universal suffrage at twenty-one. Even Cabinet ministers like Neville Chamberlain and Leo Amery, who wanted equal suffrage at twenty-five, admitted that it was not a feasible option. Davidson, the party chairman, polled central office agents and found that the older minimum age was considered impractical. Agents thought it would disfranchise large numbers of men and irritate proponents of suffrage reform. In any case, Davidson and many other Conservatives did not believe that universal suffrage would have a detrimental effect on the Conservative Party. On 14 April the Cabinet announced that it would introduce legislation to give women the same residential franchise as men. Birkenhead later complained that the Cabinet had been forced to make this decision by Joynson-Hicks's 1925 promise, but this is not true. Despite their wariness ministers were not forced to provide equal suffrage at twenty-one as a consequence of Joynson-Hicks's statement, which, after all, simply reiterated earlier Conservative pledges.[10]

During the months that followed the Cabinet decision there was considerable debate within the party over the merits of a twenty-one or twenty-five year voting age. Proponents of equal suffrage at twenty-one, for example, the duchess of Atholl, stated that many women who would be given the vote were not flappers, but mature wives and mothers. The franchise, she argued, would encourage "a dawning sense of a wider life and comradeship." On the other side of this controversy, the newspaper magnate Lord Rothermere began attacking equal suffrage with a series of articles, "Stop the Flapper Folly," in April 1927. Rothermere cultivated the image of the flapper as asocial and ignorant. He tapped contemporary worries that changing gender roles and falling birthrates were a sign of racial and cultural decay. The *Daily Mail*'s flapper agitation was a mishmash of contradictory worries about deviant youths, uncontrollable females, and social disorder.[11]

Conservative leaders notified the party organizations of the government's intentions and tried to relieve their anxieties. In a 27 May 1927 speech at the Albert Hall, Baldwin castigated Conservatives who wanted to set the voting age at twenty-five. He pointed out that equal suffrage at twenty-one was neither revolutionary nor unexpected. Bonar Law had accepted it in principle in 1922, and Baldwin had all but promised it in 1924. Most English-speaking nations already had universal suffrage at twenty-one. Besides, he added, it would be electorally disastrous to take away the voting rights of some men by raising the age requirement. The *Conservative Agents' Journal* explained the government's proposal, emphasizing that less than 30 percent of the women who would be enfranchised would be under twenty-six, and more than a third would be over thirty. Many of these potential women voters would be college women, public servants, wives, and mothers, who wanted security and stability like other Conservatives. One agent canvassed his constituency, Plymouth, and reported that 59 percent of the potential new voters were Conservatives.[12]

Conservative organizations demonstrated a mixed reaction to the prospect of universal suffrage. Of the messages received by the NUCUA Executive, a majority advocated equal suffrage at twenty-five. Both the Chichester and the Skipton associations supported the vote at twenty-five, and the GUA Executive warned party leaders that equal suffrage at twenty-one would be disastrous in industrial seats. At a SUA women's conference, Sir Robert Horne drew prolonged applause when he spoke in favor of equal suffrage at twenty-five. Some groups were unable to agree on the issue. JIL leaders pressed for the franchise at twenty-one, but delegates at the 1927 conference were divided and left the matter unresolved. The Oswestry association also decided not to take a position. Yet other Conservatives supported the government's plan. The young Conservative M.P.s for North Cornwall and Wirral, A. M. Williams and John Grace, both welcomed the proposal as an extension of the 1918 act. Williams especially attacked the notion of young women as flappers incapable of mature political decisions.[13]

The ongoing debate within the Conservative Party made the 1927 NUCUA conference held in Cardiff particularly significant. On the eve of the meeting the *Conservative Agents' Journal* again tried to calm worried party members by reminding them that there was no longer any reason to discriminate against women, who had proven to be as mature as men (and possibly more so) and who did not use their vote for feminist purposes. On the first day of the conference, a member of the NUCUA council made a motion in favor of extending the residential suffrage to all citizens above twenty years of age. A delegate proposed an amendment that only women above twenty-four years of age be given the vote. He was supported by the diehard A. Maconachie, who protested that the party did not wish to give women control of the political system. He added tactlessly that there were "too many unintelligent and hopeless electors on registers already." In reply, Captain Ian Fraser, a blind war veteran and an M.P., delivered a pragmatic defense of government policy that drew loud cheers and destroyed the doubts planted by Maconachie. Fraser emphasized that the Conservatives had to fulfill their pledge by establishing universal suffrage at twenty-one. To do otherwise would be both impractical and dangerous. There was no reason to fear women, because they would never use their vote to "promote the domination of their own sex." The amendment garnered only a handful of votes, and the original motion passed.[14]

At a mass meeting following the debate, Baldwin claimed that he wanted to complete the work begun in 1918. Conservatives had to accept full democracy and recognize that it meant adopting "a national policy which will bring to our support the armies of those who owe no particular allegiance, and . . . who prefer a stable Government." Refusal to accept universal suffrage at twenty-one, he said, would demonstrate a lack of faith in women and "would be an unwarrantable slur on the efficiency and enthusiasm of [the women in] the party organisation."[15] Using a tactic to which he later resorted frequently, the prime minister called on loyal Tories to support the proposal and lambasted opponents as tools of Rothermere, who was supporting Lloyd George and the Liberal Party.

The Cardiff conference boosted the government's efforts to pass an equal franchise measure, and the momentum increased when, less than a month later, the SUA conference debated the issue and passed a resolution of support. Forwarding a motion passed by a women's conference, Lady Findlay, the first female president of the SUA, moved that the government establish universal suffrage at age twenty-one. She attacked the flapper imagery of the antisuffragists and argued that equal suffrage was the natural consequence of the 1918 act. After further discussion on the merits of universal suffrage at twenty-one as opposed to twenty-five, Davidson implored the delegates "to face facts and be practical." They must accept women and demonstrate their faith in Conservatism by accepting universal suffrage at twenty-one. The delegates passed the equal suffrage motion by an overwhelming majority.[16]

With the introduction of an equal suffrage bill now approved by the party, opponents generally bowed to the inevitable. They were continually assured that most prospective female voters were neither trade unionists nor Labour supporters. Furthermore, as Harold Macmillan told his Stockton constituents, if Conservatives really believed in their fellow Britons, they had to give voting rights to all citizens. The Conservative M.P. for Skipton, E. R. Bird, and his wife admitted that they still felt that twenty-five was the best minimum voting age, but they rejected the flapper agitation and acknowledged that equality at whatever age was crucial. The former party chairman, Lord Younger, was offended by the lack of "a reasonable pause" before establishing universal suffrage, but he accepted it, praising the contributions of Conservative women. The 1922 Committee of Conservative M.P.s also accepted twenty-one as the minimum. At a late 1927 meeting of Yorkshire Conservatives, a motion against equal suffrage at twenty-one was defeated by a large majority.[17]

On 12 March 1928 Joynson-Hicks introduced the Representation of the People (Equal Franchise) bill. The editor of *The Times* noted that the bill's success was a "conclusion foregone," and, facing only sporadic opposition, the bill quickly became law in early July. Both opposition parties accepted the measure, although in committee Labour M.P.s tried halfheartedly to abolish the business franchise. The government proposed to make the spouses of those who occupied business premises eligible for the business vote, and, for the first time, to allow women to cast votes under both residential and business franchises. Despite their dislike of the business franchise, Labour M.P.s supported the equal suffrage bill, but a small band of ultraconservatives opposed the bill on principle. During the second reading these M.P.s again rehearsed the arguments that reform was unwarranted and dangerous because, as one M.P. stated, it would give the Labour Party "absolute supremacy at the polls." Opponents also claimed that women were too concerned with their families to seek the public good and that they would use their votes to take away men's freedoms, recklessly increase government spending, and ignore the Empire. In an especially histrionic speech, the historian and diehard M.P. for Oxford, Sir Charles Oman, even claimed that the party would be destroyed.[18]

Sir Robert Sanders, a former chairman of the NUCUA council, dismissed Labour criticisms, denounced claims that the Conservative Party was being harmed by its leaders, and reminded his audience of Conservative support for equal suffrage, which the NUCUA conference exemplified. Establishing equal suffrage at twenty-one, he went on, was more practical and responsible than disfranchising young men by raising the minimum voting age. Astor and the WUO chairman, Lady Iveagh, ridiculed arguments that the bill would cause conflict between the sexes and create instability. Rather than enfranchising a sex, she said, the bill simply recognized that women were equal citizens who had something special to contribute to public life. The prime minister ended the debate by reiterating his pledge to equalize the franchise and outlining a progressive vision of the effects of franchise reform: "To-night marks the final stage in the union of men and women working together for the regeneration of the world. It may well be that by their common work together, each doing that for which they are the better fitted, they may provide such an environment that each immortal soul as it is born on this earth may have a fairer chance, a fairer home than has ever been vouchsafed to the generations that have passed." Opposition to the bill, the former suffragette Frederick Pethick-Lawrence derisively noted, was "but the twitterings of sparrows, that can no more delay the progress of events than Mrs. Partington with her mop could sweep back the ocean." The bill easily passed its second reading with only ten M.P.s, all Conservatives, voting against it.[19]

During the committee stage of the bill, the elderly Scotsman Sir Alexander Sprot moved an amendment to establish a universal residential franchise for citizens at twenty-five. The home secretary quickly attacked the motion, arguing that the party was committed to twenty-one and that a higher minimum age would be a terrible electoral liability. Sprot's amendment won the support of a few diehards who were angry that the government had failed to reform the House of Lords, but it was easily defeated, 16 to 359. The committee did agree, however, to alter the maximum election expenses for candidates in county seats, a question the government had left open for discussion.[20]

In the Lords there was rather more opposition to the reform bill than in the other house. A diehard and virulent opponent of female suffrage, Sir Frederick Banbury, now Lord Banbury of Southam, moved to reject the bill. The right-wing duke of Northumberland seconded the motion, noting that women should never have been given the vote and that democracy was destroying the country. Viscount Sumner argued that it would be impossible to reform the Lords once this "gigantic, amorphous, unmanageable electorate" was created. Lord Balfour of Burleigh, a proponent of the bill, appealed to the peers' practical sense. There is no argument against a measure, he stated, that springs directly from the universal education system, the reform act of 1918, and the party's pledges. In a suitably cynical speech, the antisuffragist Lord Birkenhead closed the debate by recounting "the slippery slope" of events that had led to the equal suffrage bill. "The moment that you had settled the principle that women were to have votes at all," he declared, "it became a lost cause to argue that there should be differentiation between people of the same ages." There was no choice but to accept the measure with "resolute resignation." The bill passed 114 to 35. After a futile attempt in committee to set a minimum voting age of twenty-five, the House of Lords passed the Representation of the People bill on 18 June, and it became law on 1 July 1928.[21]

The Representation of the People Act contained three significant elements. First, women became eligible for the same residential franchise as men. Second, about 150,000 women gained a second vote because of their husband's business premises, and some men also received a second vote through their wives' businesses. (The increase in the business vote was negligible, from about 1 percent to 1.5 percent of the electorate, and it remained unimportant.) Third, after 1928 women were allowed to exercise either a business or university franchise in addition to their residential franchise. In all, the act increased the number of women voters by more than five million. Women accounted for approximately 53 percent of all voters. In 70 percent of parliamentary divisions, female voters outnumbered male voters. Through the reform acts of 1918 and 1928 (and the 5.5 percent increase in population between 1914 and 1929), the British electorate increased from less than eight million in 1914 to nearly twenty-nine million in 1928.[22]

Preparations for the General Election

Conservatives responded to the creation of universal suffrage with a mixture of confidence and uneasiness. A contributor to one party magazine argued that the 1928 act demonstrated the Conservatives' faith in democracy, while, the writer claimed, Labour "stands to-day for class privileges." In the same issue the Conservative scholar Arthur Shadwell congratulated Britons for their good sense. They had accepted universal suffrage "step by step by force of circumstance" and thereby avoided both revolution and chaos. The vice-chairman of the WUO, Lady Newton, confidently argued that women were inherently moderate and would thus be attracted to Conservatism. Women, she told the 1928 party conference, "were out for peace and quiet and the safety and advancement of their children. They stood for the happiness of their husbands, and the peace and security of their homes. They did not believe in a noisy minority, and were determined to uphold the grand old constitution of this country. (Applause.)"[23]

But other Conservatives were uneasy about the large electorate. In the 1930s Sir Gervais Rentoul, the first chairman of the 1922 Committee, described universal suffrage as "the greatest political experiment ever undertaken by any democracy.... We have now reached the stage when every man and woman possesses a direct vote in the government of the country—not by reason of any property or educational qualifications, but simply because they happen to have been born British citizens and have reached the mature age of twenty-one. The majority of them have no fixed political ideas. . . . The existence of this large unattached floating vote without any definite political principles obviously possesses dangers against which we need, as a nation, to be constantly on our guard." The act reawakened Conservative concerns about an unmanageable electorate that might be attracted to opposition parties. Like many others, the Conservative agent in North Cornwall was "stunned" by the huge increase in voters. The Conservative Party had to redouble its efforts to reach out to the millions of voters, many of whom had no political allegiance, if it was, as Baldwin had said, "to make democracy safe for the world."[24]

To reach those enfranchised by the 1928 act, the Conservative Party used all its propaganda and organizational techniques. Under Davidson's leadership, central office continued to enlarge its operations. Shortly after Davidson had taken over as party chairman in late 1926, Lord Irwin suggested to him the need for "broad-based propaganda." Davidson accordingly expanded party propaganda. From October to December 1928, central office distributed more than a million leaflets and pamphlets, and in the four months before the 1929 election, they circulated sixteen million pieces of literature.[25]

Conservative literature appealed to women, playing on their gratitude by reminding them that the government had trusted their common sense. Such a claim was made in "Mademoiselle of 1928," set to the tune of "Mademoiselle from Armentieres" and published by the National Conservative Musical Union. Its lyrics ran:

> Mr. Baldwin thought it time
> Parley vous,
> To bring the ladies into line
> Parley vous,
> Along with the men, an equal vote
> If only to stop the Socialist dope,
> Inky, pinky, parley vous.
>
> Join our ranks and show your worth
> Parley vous,
> Accompany us in work and mirth
> Parley vous,

If social ills you wish to cure,
Vote for Baldwin then you're sure,
Inky, pinky, parley vous.[26]

Central office described the Conservative record of helping women in the leaflet "What the Conservatives Have Done." They distributed millions of copies of "The Woman of To-day and Tomorrow," a leaflet outlining the party's concern for women's issues. In autumn 1928 the WUO magazine, *Home and Politics*, introduced new features, including the "Mrs. Maggs and Betty" column, in which the older, sensible charlady, Mrs. Maggs, guides a young and formerly apathetic maid named Betty through the perils of politics. Mrs. Maggs accomplishes this feat with frequently memorable commentary, calling the Liberals, for example, as fickle as the weather on washday.[27]

The real work of maintaining and expanding Conservative influence among women was given to the WUO, by now an invaluable part of the party machinery. Shortly after the equal suffrage bill was passed, the NUCUA rules were changed to increase representation of women on the NUCUA Executive from one-third to one-half. The women's advisory committee of the NUCUA Executive was given a more powerful and secure position, in effect becoming the oversight body for the WUO and its expanding network of area committees and area agents. The advisory committee was assigned the role of channeling women's views to the NUCUA Executive, and it proved so successful in promoting understanding between men and women's groups that in 1930 the quota of female constituency delegates at the NUCUA conference and council was allowed to lapse.[28]

The women's advisory committee was accepted as an official, representative organ, partly because of the rapid development of WUO area committees. Outside Yorkshire the first regional WUO organization was established in the Southeastern Area in 1920. Wives of Conservative M.P.s from Southeast England and women from the county associations formed the Women's Parliamentary Committee. Members raised their own funds and hired a missionary, who cycled through the area organizing women voters. This and other area committees varied in their composition and activities, but most tended to operate more like select women's clubs than popular organizations. In 1927 central office began urging area committees to re-form as committees of their provincial divisions. The Southeastern

Committee had recently adopted this plan, becoming the Southeastern Area Women's Advisory Council. Other areas soon followed. Each association selected one of its female delegates at the provincial level to serve on the women's area committees, which acted as subcommittees of the provincial divisions. Female area agents served as secretaries. Area committees raised funds and monitored women's opinions.[29]

At the local level, Conservative associations responded to universal suffrage and an expected election by hiring women organizers. They were faced with an average of eight thousand newly enfranchised women in each constituency. One of the first decisions of the North Cornwall women's committee, created in 1925, was to hire an organizer. Other WUO associations also hired woman organizers in hopes of bringing new female voters into the party. Inspired by their central office area agent, the officers of the Wrexham women's branches met in late 1926 to discuss hiring an organizer. They appointed Mrs. Palin, the chairwoman of a ward branch, as unpaid secretary for a six-month trial period. The area agent continued to press the women to hire an organizer, but they were able to pay Palin only as a part-time worker. Kincardine Unionists did nothing about a woman organizer until their defeat in the 1929 election.[30]

The JIL also grew significantly in the late 1920s as it assumed responsibility for younger new voters. Baldwin emphasized the JIL's heightened importance in an address at a March 1928 rally of young Conservatives. JIL members used leaflet, phonograph, and film versions of the speech for recruiting and campaigning during the next year. Central office also encouraged the development of JIL divisional councils that could work more closely with the senior associations. In addition, Lady Myra Fox and Marjorie Maxse were added to the JIL's governing bodies, and Fox became the first female vice-chairman of the JIL. Davidson increased financial support for the JIL, took responsibility for its literature, provided it with organizers, and trained its members in special courses at the Conservative College.[31]

The JIL and the WUO launched major recruiting and canvassing drives during the months before the May 1929 election. Maxse suggested that WUO and JIL branches cooperate in canvassing new voters by dividing electors between the two organizations according to age. She proposed that branches of both organizations invite new voters to special social events, during which the women would be told about current politics, Conservatism, and the benefits of belonging to the JIL or the WUO. Maxse thought that many women would join one of the groups for the social activities and the sense of solidarity. With the assistance of central office

agents, many youth and women's organizations adopted Maxse's suggestions. JIL recruiting drives in November 1928 and March 1929 gave rise to
hundreds of new youth branches by April 1929. JIL activities, organized by
a horde of JIL recruiters known as the "Baldwin Brigade," attracted press
coverage and encouraged many associations to prepare for the election.
During recruiting drives, JIL headquarters distributed more than 183,000
"Voluntary Service Forms" to JIL secretaries and constituency agents to
sign up volunteer workers for the election, and JIL headquarters sold
nearly 14,000 copies of its *Hints for Canvassing* handbook.[32]

The WUO held a more subdued recruiting drive in February 1929. A
special issue of *Home and Politics* offered suggestions for publicity, meetings, entertainments, and speeches designed to appeal to women's desire
"to be made to feel they are wanted." Mrs. Baldwin and the WUO chairwoman, Lady Iveagh, asked readers to have confidence in a prime minister
who understood women's interests. The WUO also organized a special
campaign among nurses, whose work brought them into contact with
many women. Sixty thousand registered nurses received a letter from the
chairwoman and the administrator of the WUO, information on the government's work for women and children and equal suffrage, and an invita-
tion to join the WUO. Women's branches were then given the names of
nurses in their area so that they could follow up. With speakers provided
by the SUA women's department, Unionist women in Scotland canvassed
and held more than a thousand meetings for female voters.[33]

The months prior to the 1929 election saw considerable organizing
in the divisions. During autumn 1928, for example, Kincardine and West
Aberdeenshire Unionists overhauled their organization. They expanded
the parish and district committees and purchased a car for the agent, who
had to crisscross the large division in the course of his work. In addition,
the association planned propaganda, checked the new voter register, and
arranged for the transportation of voters on polling day. A Chichester
branch organized an extensive program that included a visit by a Conservative cinema van. In Wrexham and North Cornwall, WUO branches recruited members with meetings during New Voters' Week in February
1929. The North Cornwall and Stockton WUO branches also sent women a
letter from their M.P. appealing for their vote. Local associations, especially
WUO branches, worked hard to canvass and distribute the appropriate
material to each household.[34]

Despite notable improvements in the party's organization, quite a few
Conservative leaders were unsure about the upcoming general election.

Support for the Conservative Party was expected to decline from the spectacular levels of the previous election, and some sections of the party were suffering a kind of malaise. Grumbling over second chamber reform and equal suffrage was part of the problem, but some Conservatives were also unhappy at the government's failure to lower taxes and cut spending. Publicans, shopkeepers, and Conservative club members, all important Conservative supporters, complained about restrictions on public houses and shops. For these Tory critics the government's failings were more noteworthy than such successes as the Pensions Act (1925). The first lord of the admiralty, William Bridgeman, had already, in 1927, lectured Conservative critics "in the Club" who were distracting attention from the opposition's faults but acknowledged that the euphoria of 1924 was gone. Davidson made a similar assessment in September 1928.[35]

The Conservative government had scored some midterm successes; its deft handling of the General Strike, the Trade Disputes and Trade Union Act, and the Chinese Crisis of 1927, provoked by clashes between British troops and Cantonese, certainly increased its popularity. During the last eighteen months before the election, however, the government seemed unwilling to act decisively on serious issues, and it lost popularity. In summarizing the achievements of the session ending in August 1928, *Man in the Street* was forced back on the trivial Protection of Lapwings and the Post Office (Sites) Acts. Such inactivity encouraged apathy among supporters. Even in relatively safe seats like Wirral and Wood Green party morale seemed to be declining; in Labour or Liberal preserves like Glasgow the effect was much stronger.[36]

Although they worried about their own supporters, Conservative leaders were more concerned about nonaligned voters who might think that the government was unresponsive to international and economic troubles. The government's inability to bring about lasting international peace was a potent issue for the opposition. The Conservative government refused to accept the Geneva Protocol establishing compulsory arbitration for League of Nations members, and in 1927 the Geneva Naval Conference failed mainly because of Anglo-American disagreements on parity. After signing the Locarno Treaties in 1927, the ailing foreign secretary, Austen Chamberlain, had become increasingly out of touch. The president of the board of education, Lord Percy, later recalled how the public believed that the government was missing opportunities to cooperate with its former allies. Instead, according to the M.P. Sir Reginald Mitchell Banks, ministers were being labeled incompetent.[37]

Even more damaging to Conservative election chances than the peace issue were the high level of unemployment and continuing economic depression. After a brief drop in 1927, the percentage of insured workers who were unemployed returned to double digits; in the year preceding the election, unemployment averaged more than 11 percent. Even in the Midlands, the north of England, and Scotland, where unemployment levels were stable, the Conservatives were in trouble. Except for the General Strike, the winter of 1928–29 was the worst period of unemployment since 1923. Between 1924 and 1929 unemployment in strongly Labour areas, especially the mining and heavy industry regions of northeastern England and Wales, increased. There was ample opportunity for the revived Labour Party to exploit the economic issue. Labour's new program, *Labour and the Nation*, used R. H. Tawney's lofty moral language to attack the government for protecting the interests of the rich and propertied, while ignoring the economic and social problems of ordinary Britons. Labour leaders pushed trade unionism, the General Strike, and nationalization into the background to present what Jones calls "a pose of studious moderation."[38]

Another problem facing the government was the continuing agricultural depression, which allowed the Liberals to gain support in rural Britain and jeopardized Conservative chances of winning the next election. Between 1924 and 1929 the amount of land devoted to wheat, barley, and oat cultivation declined by 773,764 acres. After 1926 wheat and barley prices fell steadily, and during the twelve months before the election wheat prices dropped to their lowest level since 1923. The government was also blamed for higher costs, particularly the petrol tax, food quality injunctions, and higher benefit and wage costs for laborers. As a result, rural regions were easy game for Lloyd George, who launched a land campaign in 1925. With a radical plan to empower county committees to expropriate land and lease it to farmers, Lloyd George and the Liberals scored several by-election victories. North Cornwall was representative of the rural seats where Conservatives faced growing Liberal support. Once local Liberals had restructured their organization and selected a strong candidate, Sir Donald Maclean, their vigorous campaigning against "arrogant, swanking Toryism" generated considerable support.[39]

Since most Conservative leaders had rejected food subsidies in 1921 and tariffs in 1924, the ministry of agriculture was hard-put to come up with something for farmers. Edward Wood, minister of agriculture in 1924 and 1925, later wrote that he found the job one of "almost complete futility and frustration." The government, however, pointed to its record of building roads, spurring sugar beet farming, and requiring imported foods to be labeled. As a 1926 white paper lectured farmers on the need for "realism," the government rejected requests from central office, the NU-CUA council, and the Conservative M.P.s agricultural committee to enact barley duties and wheat price guarantees, preferring to try to undermine Liberal support. The Liberal Party, Davidson told a Bradford audience in 1927, was "try[ing] to breach that [Conservative] dam, the only result of which will be that the waters of Socialism will pour over the land and destroy it." Davidson's claim was reinforced by the defection of the former coalition Liberals Hilton Young and Sir Alfred Mond to the Conservative Party. The Conservatives also claimed that the Liberal Party was a rump controlled by a Welsh mountebank, Lloyd George, using "tainted money," a reference to the sale of honors by the coalition government. Finally, the Conservative propaganda attack, spearheaded by Sir John Green, central office's agricultural expert and the author of *Political Pills for Farming Ills* (1926), tried to raise fears about Lloyd George's land plan. Green argued that subsidies would lead to inflation, higher taxes, and more bureaucracy. Conservative propagandists even claimed that the Liberal model was Soviet collectivization. The Conservatives nevertheless continued to lose support in rural areas. The National Farmers Union was so disgruntled that it considered adopting its own slate of candidates in 1929.[40]

As the mandated 1929 election drew nearer, the Cabinet considered a variety of programs and tactics to revive Conservative support. Shortly after he had become party chairman in late 1926, Davidson urged the prime minister to form a Cabinet policy committee. Baldwin agreed, and the committee was created in September 1927, but Davidson had difficulty arousing interest in the work. Under Worthington-Evans the policy committee met sporadically until mid-1928. The thirty-four Cabinet and junior ministers who worked on the committee were asked to study future Conservative policy, particularly with regard to agriculture, industry and trade, social reform, and the Empire. In anticipation of an equal suffrage bill, the duchess of Atholl was placed on the social reform subcommittee specifically to handle women's issues. But the committee's vague report in July 1928 was no basis for a clear and substantive program.[41]

Some Conservatives felt that the party's platform should still be tariff reform. Virtually all Conservatives had accepted the safeguarding policy that the government established in 1925. The Safeguarding of Industries Act empowered nonfood trades to petition for a committee of inquiry, which considered unfair trade conditions, the efficiency of domestic producers, and the effect of safeguarding on prices and employment. If the board of trade and the treasury approved, the government could introduce a bill to protect the industry. Conservatives claimed that safeguarding provided jobs and higher wages for some British workers while keeping prices low by encouraging economies of scale among home producers. A few industries were protected by safeguarding, but, except for the automobile and motorcycle industry, larger concerns were excluded.[42]

Conservative tariff reformers, however, believed that the party had to move beyond safeguarding to full protection. Among the most important tariff proponents were the Cabinet ministers Amery, Joynson-Hicks, and, to a lesser extent, Neville Chamberlain. Each was active in the Empire Industries Association, an important tariff organization founded in 1925 and headed by Sir Henry Page Croft, a leading protectionist in the NUCUA. Amery, the colonial secretary, pressed protection on the prime minister, claiming that only it would free Britain from the high unemployment and high taxes that "breed Communism at the lower end of [the social] scale, and apathy at the upper." Tariff reformers could not, however, win the policy committee's approval for tariffs or even extensive safeguarding.[43]

After the policy committee's failure, leading tariff reformers attempted unsuccessfully to steer the party toward a protectionist platform. Joynson-Hicks made a statement in July 1928 in favor of more tariffs, particularly for the iron and steel industry. The ensuing controversy was an embarrassing show of ministerial squabbling on a divisive issue. In a leading article, the editor of *The Observer*, J. L. Garvin, a longtime tariff reformer, argued that safeguarding iron and steel necessitated agricultural protection, which would destroy the party's election chances. *The Times* also warned that the Cabinet's plans would "disappear in a faction fight over tariffs." In early August Baldwin denounced protection and food taxes in a public letter to the Conservative chief whip.[44]

But tariff reformers did not admit defeat, in part because many Conservatives were still searching for an election program. In a letter to the prime minister, Bridgeman offered some thoughts on the coming struggle. Although his wife, Caroline, the former WUO chairwoman, thought that the government should campaign on its social reform record, Bridgeman believed that the Conservatives had to offer something else. According to him the government should promise to expand safeguarding, possibly to include the iron and steel trade. At the NUCUA conference in September 1928, Page Croft moved a resolution critical of the government's "slow progress" and urged "the widest possible extension" of safeguarding. The conference rejected a moderating amendment in favor of an amendment that specifically asked for protection of iron and steel. At the mass meeting that evening, Baldwin expressed his support for safeguarding but rejected protectionism, warning, "It is not wise in a democracy to go too far in front of public opinion." Shortly before the 1929 election the issue resurfaced when a board of trade committee proposed safeguarding lightweight woollens. Ignoring the demands of the NUCUA council and Amery, Baldwin decided to quash the report in order to avoid a tariff campaign.[45]

Winston Churchill, the chancellor of the exchequer and the most important Conservative to oppose protectionism, proposed an alternative program. Like Lord Derby, the party organizers, and many other ordinary Conservatives, Churchill remembered vividly the debacles of 1906 and 1923. He believed that he had found a less risky means of aiding domestic production by lowering local rates. Agricultural land had already been partially derated, and progressive Tories, like the young M.P.s who wrote *Industry and the State* (1927), proposed that it be applied to industry. In his April 1928 budget, Churchill announced a plan to reduce three-quarters of the burden of local rates on industrial properties and railways and to remove all rates from agricultural land. Much of the shortfall in local revenues would be compensated for by a national petrol tax. Such a measure would fill the need, foreseen by Churchill in 1927, for a "large new constructive measure which, by its importance and scope, by its antagonisms as well as by its appeal, will lift us above the ruck of current affairs." Such a policy would sidetrack protectionists and avoid the electoral risks of tariffs. In a letter to his mentor Churchill, Macmillan predicted that derating would unite and revive the Conservatives: "If it goes right, it will put new life into the Party. It will provide a constructive policy other than Protection. It will rally the waverers. It will consolidate the moderate vote. It will put fresh hope and enthusiasm into the hearts of all those who have supported the Conservative Party because they honestly believed it to be a Party capable of constructive thought and progressive effort."[46]

The derating scheme seemed like a natural campaign issue, and Conservatives tried to convey its merits to the public. Speaking in Stockton in mid-1928, Macmillan claimed that derating demonstrated the "democratic and progressive" character of the new Conservative Party, which was willing to risk an appeal to voters on this complex program. In *Man in the Street,* Macmillan claimed that, with derating, "the Conservative Party . . . definitely turns its back on the policy of negative, and enters the lists with a clear and definitely constructive plan, audacious and comprehensive. . . .

After a long period of comparative inaction, the bugle is sounded for a general advance." Despite Macmillan's claim, derating was not an immediately successful rallying cry, though less from opposition than from lack of enthusiasm. At a 1928 meeting of the NUCUA council, Churchill's derating presentation evoked no response, and at the SUA conference a prospective candidate criticized the plan as incomplete. Derating proved difficult for both Conservative workers and voters to understand and appreciate; many linked it with Neville Chamberlain's complicated administrative reform, the Local Government Act of 1929. Even the party magazines admitted that the public did not understand these measures. The records of the library and information department at central office show that Tories in the constituencies were less interested in derating and local government reform than in such issues as Lloyd George, international peace, socialism, unions, farming, pensions, and tariffs. During 1928 and 1929, of more than seventy-five queries from my sample constituencies, only three concerned derating or local government.[47]

With no popular program, the government was increasingly forced to rely on its record and on its claim to be the only party able to provide stable government. In his address to a women's meeting at the 1928 NUCUA conference, the Conservative M.P. Major Sir Archibald Boyd-Carpenter tried to turn Lloyd George's land plan and the absence of a Conservative alternative to the benefit of the government:

> What was Mr. Lloyd George's solution? You were to be inspected and directed to the prosperity of agriculture; to have people sit above you who did not know a turnip from a potato, telling you what crops to grow upon your land; hordes of officials coming down. (Laughter.) Just fancy one coming down who mistakes a pheasant for a peasant. (Laughter.) . . . It would be absurd if it were not so wicked to try and delude people into the belief that there was help and comfort in that way. Mr. Lloyd George believed that by waving the magician's wand he could produce prosperity. . . . Mr. Baldwin, one of the honestest and straightest men in England to-day, told the people of this country that he would not promise them sugar when he could not even promise them bread. He told them what he could do and that it could only be done by patience, striving, struggle, faith, and hope. (Applause.)[48]

Boyd-Carpenter's theme of safe and steady government guided the Conservative Party as the election approached. In October 1928 Baldwin accepted the advice of central office that it was best to call an election as soon as the new registers were ready in May 1929. The Conservatives, whose party organization was unrivaled, should have an advantage in a short campaign.[49]

The slow pace leading to the 1929 election ended abruptly when Lloyd George announced a startling plan for economic recovery. After he became leader of the Liberals, he authorized an investigation by politicians and economists, among them John Maynard Keynes. They developed an innovative program based on deficit spending and government planning. The research had already led to the publication of the Liberal "Yellow Book," *Britain's Industrial Future,* in February 1928. On 1 March 1929 Lloyd George delivered an astonishing address to Liberal M.P.s and candidates in which he pledged to reduce unemployment to normal levels within a year of taking office. Less than two weeks later he published the "Orange Book," *We Can Conquer Unemployment,* an electioneering pamphlet that set forth a program for rebuilding Britain's infrastructure and lowering unemployment to 5 percent. The central feature of the plan was a massive road-building and home construction scheme. He energetically publicized the plan, beginning with a question-and-answer luncheon for reporters in Westminster the day before the pamphlet was released. He followed this with a rally at the Albert Hall that was broadcast to fourteen sites across the country. He then threw himself into a countrywide campaign, beginning in southwestern England.[50]

Lloyd George's maneuvers severely undermined the position of the Conservatives, who were already set to campaign by defending their unimpressive record. Conservatives generally responded to Lloyd George's unemployment plan by calling it empty rhetoric. But the plan put the Conservative Party on the defensive and shamed its proposals. By 22 March, the editor of *The Times* was warning of a "dangerous despondency" among Conservatives. They now faced serious tactical problems as the press concentrated its attention on Lloyd George and the Liberal Party. Like other Conservatives, the North Cornwall M.P., A. M. Williams, was forced to attack the plan as a stunt, but all he was offering voters was more years of apparently mediocre government. At Plymouth Lloyd George enjoyed himself at Conservative expense by ridiculing Baldwin's claims that increased broccoli exports from Cornwall indicated that the government was reviving the economy. (Baldwin's response was to wear broccoli on his lapel and display it at his rallies.) Central office responded to Lloyd George's plan with a detailed analysis of its shortcomings. Conservative Party magazines condemned the plan as a bureaucratic scam without long-term benefits and denounced "the Welsh Wizard" for financing a desperate "gambler's throw."[51]

The General Election of 1929

The government doggedly pursued its campaign plans even after they had been seriously undermined by the Liberals, kicking off with Churchill's budget, which abolished the tea duty. Baldwin quickly established the tone of the campaign in a speech at the Drury Lane Theatre on 18 April that was reprinted as a pamphlet and carried by the party magazines. In this age of democracy, he told his audience, people are apt to expect sensational promises, but voters should remember that they are shareholders in Britain and the Empire and, as such, should seek leaders capable of managing the enterprise efficiently and prosperously. The Conservative government had performed well, and it would continue to do so by encouraging emigration, training young people, and reducing the costs of manufacturing and agriculture through derating. These policies, Baldwin said, would lead to real economic improvement without borrowing and inflation. He also noted the need for colonial development and for social reforms, among them slum clearance, education, and health care for mothers and children. Baldwin ended by appealing to voters' sense of responsibility:

> There is a new spirit abroad in the land. People who think that pre-War electioneering is going to win a post-War election are making the mistake of their lives. The people think: they are thirsty for knowledge, they want to learn, and, above all, they want to do the right thing, and I cannot stand up, and I will not stand up, before a people like that and go one iota beyond what I know I can perform if I have the opportunity.
>
> The responsibility of our people is tremendous. For the first time . . . we are a complete democracy of men and women. There has never been anything in the world like a complete democracy responsible for what our people are responsible for. . . .
>
> We cannot live, if we would, for ourselves alone; and

> it is that deep sense of responsibility of our people, that
> will make them deaf to the appeals of cupidity that will
> reach them on the one hand or those of credulity which
> will be offered to them on the other.

In his Drury Lane speech, Baldwin set out the line he pursued throughout the election. He was offering more of the same: moderate and steady government.[52]

Among members of the Conservative Party, the response to Baldwin's speech varied. At the annual meeting of the Cornwall provincial division, the chairman, Lord Falmouth, expressed pleasure that the party was not bribing voters but offering "a great constructive policy . . . of enormous importance to every man and woman in the country." But many other Conservatives rejected this assessment. Baldwin's approach could backfire and give the opposition parties a chance to denigrate a less than stellar record. Amery thought that the speech conveyed the notion of "performance versus promise," but it was hardly inspiring that Baldwin seemed to be "reading out a certain amount of stuff from sundry dockets without much skill." The diehard Conservative and historian Sir Charles Petrie expressed disappointment, but added that "Bonar Law won without a policy in 1922, so perhaps history will repeat itself." The Conservative press was also uneasy. Lord Beaverbrook feared that Lloyd George was putting Baldwin to shame, although he admitted that the prime minister might get support for "cunningly posing as the typical John Bull." In *The Observer*, Garvin commented that the Conservatives had to offer more than "Safety First" to win the election.[53]

In the weeks following his Drury Lane speech, the prime minister expanded on the theme of performance, not promises. On 22 April a "horribly nervous" prime minister delivered the first of two BBC addresses. Beforehand Baldwin told his confidant Thomas Jones, deputy secretary to the Cabinet, that he was appealing to "the decency of the English people." With a measured and appealing delivery, Baldwin asked listeners to approach the election soberly and to ignore critics who expected the government to engage in "a kind of circus or auction." The welfare and peace of the whole Empire, Baldwin told listeners, "depend on the maintenance of stable government and wise statesmanship." To turn the government out now would undermine a decade of reconstruction. On 4 May, Baldwin issued a short "Message to Britain." Using an old rural saying, he emphasized that the Cabinet would always "Cut the cackle and get to the 'osses," in its search for prosperity. The statement claimed that the government had raised the standard of living, expanded social benefits, and revived the economy. Why then, Baldwin asked voters, would you gamble on "rash Socialist schemes" or impractical Liberal plans? Ignoring the differences between the previous and present elections, Baldwin said, "All that we ask is that you should give us an opportunity of carrying on and bringing to completion the great work which we have so successfully begun. . . . To build up on permanent and solid foundations the health of the individual, the health of industry, and the health of the nation is our aim and object, and we regard the fulfillment of our pledges in the past four years as a guarantee that once again we shall keep faith and shall not promise more than we can perform."[54]

In a long article entitled "Stable Government: How to Get It," the 8 May issue of *Daily Notes* repeated this argument, claiming that only a Conservative majority would give Britain stability and progress. Again alluding to Lloyd George's promises, Baldwin repeated his theme in a speech at the Albert Hall before setting off on his campaign tour: "While others talk and promise we are building roads, roads to prosperity. (Cheers.) If we can only all march together . . . and we pursue no devious routes down the red road or lose ourselves down the yellow by-pass (laughter), if we only go straight forward and united, we shall reach the goal of greater prosperity for our whole people."[55]

The references to moderation and achievement in both speeches and the "Message to Britain" also characterized Baldwin's election address, the party manifesto. Unlike earlier documents, the 1929 manifesto was a compilation of achievements and suggestions for future policy culled from various departmental papers, not a statement of aims and principles. A committee under Lord Chancellor Hailsham hastily assembled the manifesto, and central office wrote the introduction and the conclusion. The manifesto emphasized the Conservative record and promised to continue "the solid work of reconstruction." The Conservatives claimed to have revived the economy and lessened unemployment because, the coal industry aside, unemployment was less than in 1924. Unfortunately, however, coal miners made up 9 percent of all insured workers, and unemployment in their industry was 19 percent. The manifesto offered voters safeguarding and derating to spur economic growth, and a collection of practical but minor proposals for farmers and fishermen. Among these was a promise to use more domestic beef and flour to feed soldiers stationed in Britain, the result of discussions with farmers and the Conservative M.P.s agricultural committee.[56]

The manifesto presented a list, compiled by Neville Chamberlain, of the government's achievements and promises in social reform. Conservatives claimed credit for more housing, better pensions, and healthier children; they vaguely promised a more comprehensive and effective health-care system for children and pregnant women. The document also appealed to women by claiming that the government had improved living standards, lowered taxes, and protected mothers and children. Liberals and Labour, all voters were warned, intended to impose heavy taxes that would depress living standards and damage the economy. In conclusion the Conservatives asked if their record was better than the alternatives: "Socialism ... or a state of political chaos and uncertainty." In this there was little to inspire voters.[57]

At no time during the four weeks of campaigning was the 1929 election dominated by a single issue. Observers noted the campaign's relative calmness and the apparent lack of voter interest. Party organizers, however, pointed out that such impressions were in part due to the preference for house-to-house campaigning (especially for women voters) over rowdy public meetings. In addition, as the *Glasgow Herald* noted, this was the first election since 1906 not caused by a divisive policy or a crisis. As a consequence, small issues and incidents assumed greater importance, although unemployment and peace remained the most commonly discussed topics. On both these issues the government was forced onto the defensive, despite its intention of exploiting incumbency and offering voters safe, stable progress.[58]

During the campaign the government was assailed for failing to do anything to lessen unemployment. A Liberal campaign song seemed to characterize the government's outlook:

> Unemployment's so vast
> That for some years past
> For some cure we've been leisurely groping;
> But the thing's so involved
> That at last we're resolved
> Just to let the thing slide and keeping hoping.[59]

Some Conservatives responded by trying to downplay economics. Churchill claimed that unemployment was not a dangerous electoral issue since it was largely confined to Labour seats. The *Campaign Guide* minimized the issue by arguing that the unemployed were not "a standing army" but scattered individuals who were often unemployed only briefly.[60]

In general, however, Conservatives emphasized the economic progress achieved by the superior character and statesmanship of Baldwin's government and by safeguarding and derating. This type of argument dominated candidates' election addresses. Some of them used the national election address, the "Conservative Sun-Ray Treatment." The cover of this document showed the Houses of Parliament overlaid with a photograph of the candidate and a rising sun spreading its warm rays across Britain—a picture of the government's steady and practical work. Other Conservative candidates' addresses echoed Baldwin's emphasis on the government's achievements and denied charges that the party had no program for employment and peace. The Skipton candidate, Roy Bird, used phrases from Baldwin's speeches like "Performances Not Promises" and "Our First Duty Is to Run Straight." Candidates stressed derating and safeguarding as significant measures for economic revival, although even tariff reformers, like the Chichester candidate, Major Courtauld, downplayed protectionism. Local government reform was virtually ignored. Even Macmillan noted only that it would relieve Stockton's ratepayers, who were supporting unemployed shipyard workers. All candidates mentioned such government social policies as home construction and pension reform.[61]

The peace question was the second campaign issue that was troubling to the Conservatives. Because of rising antiwar sentiment, which the opposition parties mobilized, peace and disarmament figured prominently in the 1929 election. Central office advised Conservative candidates and workers to support pragmatic disarmament and pointed to the government's cutbacks in military spending and expected early withdrawal from the Rhineland. During the campaign Conservative candidates invariably noted the Baldwin government's successes, for example, the Locarno Treaties and the Kellogg Pact, and its support for reciprocal disarmament. Like most Conservative candidates, Sir Edmund Bushby supported disarmament and national security. Other Tory candidates showed their concern for peace by emphasizing their interest in cooperation and the League of Nations.[62]

Because the platform lacked a stirring issue, candidates generally based their campaigns on the prime minister's person and his government's record. The Conservative campaign exploited Baldwin's personal appeal in many ways. His speeches and radio addresses were heard by millions and sometimes distributed in printed form. Between 1926 and 1929, central office did a brisk trade in photographs, portraits, and Christmas cards that featured Baldwin. At the start of the campaign it released a biographical leaflet, "Stanley Baldwin: The Man," which claimed that the personality of its leader exemplified the party. The leaflet included extracts of Baldwin's better known, largely nonpartisan speeches, showing his esteem for "the spirit of our people, [and] the ideals that distinguish and unite English-speaking races." It was hoped that the leaflet would encourage nonaligned and new voters to put their trust in a leader who "speaks to them as man to man, revealing in homely, straightforward words his deeper feelings and his widest visions." The Conservatives also exploited its leader's appeal through songs and poems. The most famous of these, "Stanley Boy," was first sung to Baldwin by the audience at his Albert Hall meeting on 9 May 1929.[63] The words, written and first performed by the stockbroker and Conservative M.P. Waldron Smithers and set to the tune of "Sonny Boy," may have lacked artistic merit, but central office distributed ten million copies of the songsheet and ten thousand pressings of the record:

England for the Free;	Peace and Faith your Creed
Stanley Boy!	Stanley Boy!
You're the man for me	True in Word and Deed,
Stanley Boy!	Stanley Boy!
You've no way of knowing,	Socialists will hamper,
But I've a way of showing	Lloyd George prove a damper,
What you mean to me,	In our hours of need,
Stanley Boy!	Stanley Boy!

Chorus: When there are grey skies,
We don't mind the grey skies,
You make them Blue,
Stanley Boy!
Tho' foes may mistake thee,
We'll not forsake thee,
You'll pull us through.
Stanley Boy!
For country's sake you've striven,
As we know your worth.
Happiness you've given

To us right here on Earth.
Whatever you may say, Sir,
You will never stray, Sir,
For we love you so!
Stanley Boy!

An "anagram sonnet" in *The Times* conveyed the people's eternal trust and love for the prime minister, "custodian of your country's fate" and "the statesman that preserved the State." In his election address, A. M. Williams emphasized that Baldwin's "sound judgment and character" would provide stability.[64]

In conjunction with their Baldwin and "Safety First" campaign theme, Conservatives launched an attack on the opposition parties. Initially they concentrated on the failings of the Liberal Party and its leader. The first issue of *Daily Notes* developed what became a common line of attack. It quoted the Liberal M.P. Sir John Simon, who had warned his party in 1928 not to go into the election "like a cheap jack in a fair and announce we have got some patent remedy which will sweep unemployment away." Conservatives elaborated on this image to call Lloyd George a "cheap-jack." According to them, however, the government had enacted useful social reforms, lowered living costs and taxes, and had devised derating and safeguarding. Baldwin, "the steady Englishman," was compared to Lloyd George, the excitable Welshman, "flip-flopper," and dishonest "balloon man" (from a popular poster of Lloyd George as a seller of gas-filled balloons that burst), who was always ready to con voters. The anti-Liberal attack gained momentum after 12 May, when the government released a white paper detailing the shortcomings of the Liberal plan.[65]

Conservative campaigners were also not hesitant to attack the Labour Party. Months before the election, Churchill suggested to Baldwin that "everything should be done to confront the electors with the direct choice between Socialism and modern Conservatism." In a 12 February 1929 address to the Anti-Socialist and Anti-Communist Union, published as *Ringing the Bell*, Churchill launched an antisocialist offensive by speaking against the "sinister forces" of "a small secret international junta" within the Labour Party. In a speech on 8 May, he claimed that Labour supporters were working with Bolsheviks in India, Egypt, and China to destroy the Empire. *Daily Notes* soon began publishing information on the League against Imperialism, which, it alleged, channeled "Bolshevik propaganda" into the Empire. Because the league included Labour Party members and was headed by the ILP leader James Maxton, *Daily Notes* claimed that Labour was tied to the extremists. "Under MacDonald you find Maxton," *Daily Notes* stated, "and under Maxton you find Marx."[66]

Conservatives also tried to frighten voters with allegations about the Labour program. Both before and during the campaign, Conservatives claimed that a Labour victory would lead to the repeal of the 1927 trade union reforms and another general strike. They also attacked what Churchill termed Labour's "policy of plunder," or reckless taxation and spending, exemplified by Poplarism and the proposed 10 percent surtax on investments and property. Such policies, Conservatives claimed, would undermine British government and morality. In his Albert Hall speech on the third anniversary of the General Strike, Baldwin had already sounded the antisocialist theme. He reminded voters of Labour's support for the capital levy and for nationalization and warned of a possible increase in domestic violence if Labour won. He also claimed that Labour lacked the qualities of statesmanship and unity necessary for government. The argument was simple. Labour, according to this interpretation, never "hesitated to put Party interests before National interests," and its internal divisions were so great that "on many occasions ... control over Party policy ... passed into the hands of extremists."[67]

The fact that the Conservative campaign initially focused on Lloyd George and the Liberals may have reflected Conservative pique. After 1924 many Conservatives regarded the Liberal Party as an outdated organization that undermined antisocialist efforts. Yet despite their irritation, they appealed for Liberal support. During the Tavistock by-election in October 1928, Davidson arranged Liberal and non-party support for the Conservative fight against socialism and nationalization. Later attempts at this type of cooperation failed, however, when a number of Conservatives objected. In my constituency sample, only Conservatives in Bradford Central participated in an antisocialist pact, even though local election pacts already existed in Oswestry and Skipton. While some Conservatives attempted to appeal to Liberals by obtaining the support of local Liberals and espousing Liberal ideals, others bitterly rejected cooperation. Nationally there was little antisocialist cooperation. In fact, 1929 saw a record number of candidates. Only twenty-two divisions—mainly in Lancashire, the West Riding, and Bristol—lacked Conservative candidates, so it was impossible for Conservatives to support Liberals.[68]

Although the Conservative Party had difficulty appealing to Liberals in 1929, they were somewhat more successful with women. During the campaign there was a lot of discussion about the new woman voter; few observers could guess how women would vote. Despite the uncertainty, Conservatives tried a number of approaches. The April 1929 budget had removed the tea duty and lowered sugar duties. Macmillan flattered Churchill by calling this "a first class canvassing point," as WUO canvassers could mention the lower cost of living while casually drinking tea with women voters. But derating and the reassessments imbroglio made it appear to some women that the government was "giving with one hand and taking away with the other." The Conservative campaign also emphasized the government's passage of the equal suffrage act and its work on behalf of mothers and children. Concerned about the effect of the government's image as warmongering, campaigners printed a short message from Mrs. Baldwin emphasizing the Conservatives' desire for peace and security.[69]

In an election installment of "Mrs. Maggs and Betty," Mrs. Maggs explained that the choice was stability and progress under the Conservatives or "the country all turned topsy-turvy" under Labour. While the government had protected the nation's interests, she said, Labour would undermine the Constitution and leave "British people in China at the mercy of Chinese mobs." Furthermore, a Labour government would demand higher taxes from ordinary citizens in order to pay for handouts. In one of his speeches, Birkenhead showed his extemporaneous wit while presenting the chief Conservative appeals to women voters. Responding to a woman at a public meeting who complained that the government had done little, Birkenhead said, "My dear lady, the light in this hall is so dim as to prevent a clear sight of your undoubted charms, so that I am unable to say with certainty whether you are a virgin, a widow, or a matron, but in any case I will guarantee to prove that you are wrong. If you are a virgin flapper, we have given you the vote; if you are a wife, we have increased employment and reduced the cost of living; if you are a widow, we have given you a pension—and if you are none of these, but are foolish enough to be a tea drinker, we have reduced the tax on sugar." During the campaign Conservatives tried to convince women voters that the party cared about them, sending out 8.5 million copies of "The Woman To-day and To-morrow" at a cost of £17,984.[70]

In the second half of the campaign, Conservatives stepped up activity as they faced increasing resistance to derating, safeguarding, and several new issues. Under Churchill's derating plan, only a portion of the revenue lost by local government was made good by the exchequer, so that the policy was susceptible to claims that it was a dole for business paid for by the populace. This criticism was particularly effective in places like Bradford, where many voters thought that the government had not done enough to help unemployed workers. Liberals were quick to attack derating for subsidizing firms that were either already profitable or morally reprehensible (e.g., breweries). The issue became more difficult after a periodical reassessment that happened to occur during the campaign led to higher rates. Although the increases were primarily a result of higher property values, they were seen as part of derating. This cost the Conservatives support, especially among middle-class voters. Even in rural areas, where derating benefited farmers, the policy was vulnerable because it benefited large property owners more than tenant farmers. This was embarrassing for Conservative candidates like A. M. Williams and C. M. Barclay-Harvey, who were major landowners in their constituencies. Candidates in rural seats were already devoting a great deal of effort to defending the government record; derating hardly helped them.[71]

In the later stages of the campaign, protection became a significant issue despite Baldwin's earlier efforts to avoid it. Leaders of the National Farmers Union demanded agricultural safeguarding, but Conservative leaders firmly rejected it on the grounds that safeguarding would not lead to greater production at home and lower costs. The *1929 Campaign Guide* also made it clear that the party was committed to Baldwin's 1924 pledge not to adopt a system of import tariffs. Meanwhile, Conservatives were discussing the possibility of modifying the safeguarding procedure to facilitate wider application, and farmers, like the rest of the population, faced the possibility of higher prices if safeguarding was extended to a broad range of manufactured goods. The Liberals played upon fears that safeguarding was the beginning of protection and high prices.

> So long as a Tory is left to strive,
> Protection shall always be kept alive,
> For British traders we [Tories] fear the worst,
> If they are not coddled, and bribed, and nursed;
> But we won't tax foodstuffs—not just at first.[72]

Some Conservatives seemed to grasp safeguarding as, at the very least, a means of awakening the slumbering electorate. They tried to argue that safeguarding meant more jobs or, as an NUA Labour Committee leaflet stated, "safeguarding employment." When possible, campaigners used specific examples to prove the merits of safeguarding. In Stockton, the success-ful Teesside operation of Imperial Chemical Industries was credited to safeguarding, and Benjamin Talbot, head of Teesside iron and steel con-cerns and a Macmillan supporter, promised to open a plate mill if iron and steel was safeguarded. The West Riding appeared to have a great deal at stake in safeguarding. During the campaign, woollen workers staged walk-outs over proposed wage cuts, and it was widely rumored that the woollen trade's request for safeguarding had been approved by the board of trade. Yorkshire Conservatives believed that safeguarding woollens would win the West Riding for the party. Contrary to their hopes, however, Baldwin did not mention safeguarding when he visited Bradford on 22 May, and the board of trade report was not published until after the election.[73]

In working-class areas like Camlachie and Bradford, there were "storms" of questions and complaints against the "injustices" of the gov-ernment's social policies. Although half a million people benefited from the Pensions Act, central office believed that the exclusion of sixty thou-sand people from the plan for technical reasons hurt the party in some seats. Conservative candidates in the cities were also attacked for the gov-ernment's reduction of housing subsidies and milk grants. And Conserva-tives were unable to make use of the union issue until 17 May, when MacDonald vowed to repeal the "insulting and unjust" Trade Disputes and Trade Unions Act.[74]

Some issues were peculiar to certain constituencies. Conservatives had difficulties in areas like North Cornwall and Kincardine, where fishing was important. Fishermen had been promised assistance in 1924, but instead continued to suffer from foreign competition and high costs. Safeguarding and derating were unhelpful to them, although the provision of national insurance to fishermen was appreciated. In North Cornwall voters were concerned about whether Cornwall would benefit from Lloyd George's road construction plan. Toward the end of the campaign, Conservatives attacked the Liberals for neglecting Cornwall, and A. M. Williams re-printed the map from *We Can Conquer Unemployment*, which showed no road construction planned for Cornwall. Religious schools were an impor-tant issue in areas with large Catholic populations, such as Liverpool and Glasgow. The Conservative Party was committed to religious education, and some of its candidates explicitly supported religious schools. As a re-sult, some Catholic leaders advised their largely working-class flock to vote Conservative. Near the end of the campaign, Lewis Shedden, secretary of the SUA Western Division, quietly published and distributed a leaflet containing excerpts from a statement by Cardinal Bourne, the Archbishop of Westminster, that criticized Labour for promoting class antagonisms and denying the rights of private property.[75]

Conservatives became increasingly concerned that their platform was being labeled "standstillism." Before the election Lord Beaverbrook had warned of this possibility, especially since Baldwin "frittered away his heritage . . . and sits down in the garden with his arms folded and talks about the beauty of it while the weeds grow all about him." Some Conservatives tried to dispel the complacency implied by the "Safety First" theme. Speaking on behalf of Macmillan, Lord Percy tried to invoke a heroic spirit: "We are prepared to use every means; public credit, private enterprise, safeguarding, derating, and to get agreement between all sections of the country, and to base our policy on that agreement, representing all that is best in the policies of all the prewar Parties. That is our policy, that is our principle, and that is mainly why I ask you to back up a policy above all of national union." Baldwin himself tried to allay criticisms of "Safety First" during a 20 May speech at Blackpool. He explained that the campaign theme did not mean "smug self-satisfaction" but the opposite of "Rashness First." Conservative speakers and literature promulgated this "clarification," but with limited success. Lloyd George ended his campaign with a speech claiming, "Members of the Tory Party have been standing with their hands in their pockets, and in ours, looking on instead of trying their best to extricate the poor [unemployed] people."[76]

The Conservative campaign closed with a 27 May letter from the prime minister, sent to all voters, in which he appealed to their sense of national unity. Baldwin followed the letter with a tour of the Manchester area on 29 May. After speaking to more than a hundred thousand appreciative listeners at ten meetings, he delivered his second radio address from the BBC's Manchester studio. In his homely but effective manner he talked of his yearning for "peace and cooperation" after the turmoil of war, strikes, and economic disruption. He again spoke of each elector's duty to vote for the leader "you would prefer to see forming a Government . . . [and] hold[ing] the responsibility for your country and for the . . . Empire." He closed the address by saying, "You trusted me before; I ask you to trust me again." Once again the prime minister tried, as he had throughout the campaign, to exploit his reputation as "Straight, Steady & Sure."[77]

Voters went to the polls on 30 May with nearly all observers unable to predict the outcome. The great expansion in the electorate and the sedate pace of the campaign made it difficult to gauge opinion, particularly in the absence of any decisive issue. A correspondent from *The Times* concluded, "No party's campaign has furnished compelling progress measured against its rivals." Central office nevertheless estimated that the Conservatives would suffer a net loss of approximately sixty seats, while retaining a working majority of fifty to sixty. Baldwin was impressed by his favorable reception around the country and, confident of the outcome, he was already considering the composition of his next Cabinet. Those few, like Beatrice Webb and Lord Beaverbrook, who predicted a Conservative defeat, seemed unduly pessimistic. Several ministers and central office officials were confident enough to place substantial bets on a Conservative majority.[78]

It was thus with shock that Conservatives met the results on 31 May. Thomas Jones describes the rising disbelief in the small group that had gathered in the early morning at Downing Street. As the situation worsened, Churchill, never one to accept defeat easily, became quite angry and, according to Jones, "often [went] to glare at the [teletype] machine himself, hunching his shoulders, bowing his head like a bull about to charge." By 3:30 in the morning, Labour had amassed 117 victories to the Conservatives' 77, and already Steel-Maitland, the minister for labor, had been defeated. When the results were all in, the Labour Party lacked an overall majority, but it had won the election and become the largest party in the House of Commons. Labour built on its continued growth since 1918, winning 37 percent of the national popular vote and 287 seats. The Conservative Party's popular vote of 38 percent was slightly higher than Labour's, but, with only 260 seats, the Conservatives had a smaller parliamentary contingent. Despite winning more than 23 percent of the popular vote, the Liberals collected only 59 seats.[79]

Why Did the Conservatives Lose?

Several factors help to explain the Conservative Party's defeat in 1929. First, the Conservatives contested a record number of constituencies and faced a record number of opponents. Altogether there were 1,730 candidates in 1929 compared to 1400 plus in each of the three elections between 1922 and 1924. All but four of the 590 Conservative candidates who stood in 1929 were opposed; in most cases they faced two candidates. This explains in part why the average poll for opposed Conservative candidates was 39.4 percent, the lowest in a twentieth-century election, although slightly higher than the Labour candidates' average of 39.3 percent. Second, analysis shows that Conservative success varied greatly from region to region. In many cases these variations did not match those of the 1923 election, when Conservatives won 258 seats, almost the same number as in 1929. In 1923 the south, the core of Conservative support, was jeopardized by Liberal gains, but in 1929 Conservative losses were largely in urban and mining districts, particularly in the north of England, where Labour took more than seventy seats from the Conservatives. In every major city except Liverpool, the Conservatives failed to win a majority of constituencies. Nationally Labour's net gain over the Conservatives was about 120 seats; the Liberal Party's was only fourteen seats, mostly in rural and traditionally Liberal areas.[80]

While the decline in its representation was nearly 37 percent, and many candidates were defeated in some areas, the Conservative Party's results were fairly good in southeast England, and respectable in southwest England and the North Yorkshire and Cumbria regions. The Conservatives remained strong in the southeast, where they returned 100 M.P.s from 167 divisions. The worst results were in London, where the Conservative delegation was reduced from 39 to 24. This was the lowest number of Conservatives elected from London in the five interwar elections. For the first time Labour won a majority of the sixty-two London divisions, taking east London as well as seats in Islington, Wandsworth, and Hammersmith. In the rest of the southeast the Conservative Party won 76 of 105 seats, less than the 1924 record (97) but better than the 1923 results (68). The large middle-class and suburban vote in the southeast made the Liberal Party a more serious threat in this part of the country. In three-way contests at Wood Green and Clapham, Liberal candidates won approximately 28 percent of the vote. In both cases the incumbent Conservative retained his seat on a minority poll, with Labour and Liberal candidates splitting the opposition. Against a single Liberal opponent, the Conservative M.P. for Chichester, J. S. Courtauld, actually increased his poll slightly. Although the Conservatives kept many seats in the southeast, they may have lost voters through abstentions, since turnout in the three seats included in my sample declined more (from 72.7 percent in 1924 to 68.4 percent in 1929) than the national average (77.4 and 76.6 percent, respectively).[81]

In the southwest and North Yorkshire/Cumbria regions of England the Conservatives suffered a higher rate of loss than in the southeast, but still less than the national average. In southwest England the party retained a majority of the 43 seats, although dropping from 39 to 26 as a result of Labour's gains in Cardiff and Plymouth and of the Liberal sweep of Cornwall. A. M. Williams was unable to hold North Cornwall. (Here Liberal revival produced an 86 percent voter turnout, compared to 77 percent in 1924.) Conservative representation in the North Yorkshire and Cumbria region fell from 19 to 13 of the 21 divisions. The Liberals failed to score any wins, and Labour's victories were confined to mining seats and a few cities like York, whose M.P., Sir John Marriott, never again returned to Parliament. Skipton's energetic Liberals won more than 29 percent of the vote for Councillor Woffenden, but he placed third in a three-way contest.

In other regions of Britain, the Conservative Party suffered a major setback in 1929. Conservative representation in the West Midlands declined from 33 to 20, slightly more than the national average. The losses were particularly notable in the formerly Unionist seats of metropolitan Birmingham, which for the first time returned a large number of Labour M.P.s. Outside the metropolitan area, many Conservatives held their seats. In place of William Bridgeman, B. E. Parker Leighton, a local landowner, coal owner, and disabled war veteran, defeated two opponents to win Oswestry for the Conservatives with a respectable 47 percent of the vote. In the industrial regions of Lancastria and the Mid-North, Conservative representation declined by almost half, from 64 to 34. The Conservatives failed to win any seats in the borough of Bradford, where a record turnout benefited Labour. In Bradford Central the moderate Conservative M.P. Anthony Gadie was unable to prevent the former Labour M.P. William Leach from regaining his seat with 59 percent of the vote. The Liberal candidate in Wirral benefitted from his party's recovery, taking second with nearly 31 percent of the vote in a three-way contest. The Conservative M.P. John Grace retained Wirral, but with only about 48 percent of the vote. In nearby Birkenhead, the Conservative M.P. was defeated by a Liberal, but in heavily working-class Lancastria, the Conservative Party was decimated by Labour, which won its first regional majority with 43 of the 80 seats.

In East Anglia, the eastern Midlands, and northeast England the Conservatives did worse than the national average. They suffered many defeats in East Anglia, where their delegation in the nineteen divisions dropped from seventeen to nine. Most of the damage was caused by Liberals who revived the radical tradition and tapped farmers' resentments. Liberals took five Conservative seats and won a total of seven divisions in the region. In the eastern Midlands and northeast England, Conservative representation in the 66 seats (formerly 42) fell to a record low of 19. With the Liberal Party managing to elect only four M.P.s in the two regions, Labour took control of the East Midlands and Northeast England by winning 43 seats. In Stockton, Macmillan lost his seat. In the three-way contest he polled slightly more than 36 percent, but some Liberal voters apparently switched to the Labour candidate, who won with 41 percent. The result was symptomatic of an unexpectedly poor showing for Conservatives in the region.

In the 71 Scottish divisions, Unionist representation declined from 36 to 20. In Strathclyde's 36 seats there were few strong Liberal candidates, but they may have siphoned off enough votes to push the Unionists back to their pre-1924 position of holding only eight constituencies. Despite the larger electorate, the Unionist vote in half of Glasgow's divisions actually declined in 1929, and Labour was able to regain the two Glasgow constituencies it had lost in 1924.[82] In Camlachie the entry of a Scottish Nationalist candidate created excitement, but it did not enable James Stevenson to defeat the ILP M.P., the Rev. Campbell Stephen. In the rest of Scotland the Unionists fared somewhat better, although the Liberals defeated a few Unionists in northeast Scotland, including the M.P. for Kincardine and West Aberdeenshire, C. M. Barclay-Harvey. Like the rest of northeast Scotland, Kincardine was traditionally Liberal, but it had elected Barclay-Harvey in 1923 and 1924. In 1929, however, Barclay-Harvey lost by 668 votes to James Scott, a lawyer and champion of the crofters. Of the 39 Scottish divisions outside Strathclyde, Labour won seventeen (mainly in the industrial areas near Strathclyde), Unionists twelve, and Liberals ten.

The worst election results for the Conservative Party were in Wales, where the Conservative delegation fell from nine to one, leaving the Conservatives in control only of the Tory redoubt of Monmouth. This abysmal showing occurred despite the fact that the Conservatives contested every seat. The number of Conservative candidates increased from seventeen to thirty-five, but the party's share of the vote went from 28 to 22 percent. A third of the Conservative candidates forfeited their deposits after failing to poll the minimum 12.5 percent of the vote. The high unemployment in Wales created a great deal of voter interest, as demonstrated in a turnout in excess of 82 percent. Welsh voters did not want a Conservative government that seemed to offer very little, particularly since the Welsh identified Conservatism with English outsiders.[83] This was an important factor in Wrexham, where the Conservative candidate, the Englishman Sir Edmund Bushby, finished at the bottom of the poll, with 22.1 percent to the Liberal's 31.5 percent and the Labour candidate's 46.4 percent. The result was that the former Labour M.P. Robert Richards retook the seat from the Liberal incumbent, C. P. Williams.

Once it was clear that the government had been defeated, there was a flood of contradictory analyses and recriminations from Conservative newspapers, leaders and officials, and rank-and-file party members. Among the explanations offered for the defeat, the most common were the intervention of Liberal candidates, the unreasonable hostility of newspapers, and the flapper vote. The editor of *The Times* claimed that the election results were less a result of Labour popularity than of Liberal "maddogging." According to this interpretation, Liberal candidates' intervention in three-way contests gave Labour "at least 80" seats on minority polls. The Conservative principal agent, Robert Topping, agreed that Liberal intervention was responsible for some Conservative losses to Labour, but he put the number at about forty. Certainly Macmillan, among others, blamed his defeat on Liberals who abandoned him and allowed Labour to win a minority victory. Some critics of the party leaders agreed about the Liberals' role, but blamed "'stiff-necked, rubber-bottomed fools' in . . . Central Office" for alienating them in the first place.[84]

Although it is true that the Conservatives were not so successful in attracting Liberal voters as in 1924, the Liberal Party did not cause the Conservative defeat. In its survey of local Conservatives after the election, the NUCUA Executive found that Liberal intervention was considered secondary. A careful study of the Stockton results, for instance, shows that Liberal and Conservative candidates each increased their poll by about fourteen hundred votes—but the Labour candidate added seven thousand to his. Even if every Liberal vote had gone to Macmillan, he would still have been defeated by four thousand votes. In Bradford, where the same parties fought each of the four seats in 1924 and 1929, the pattern was similar. Between 1924 and 1929 the average poll of Conservative candidates in Bradford declined from 41 to 34 percent, but the Liberal vote also dropped from about 35 to 32 percent as Labour swept the city. Among the six divisions in my sample (Oswestry, Skipton, Stockton, Wood Green, Bradford Central, and Kincardine) in which the same parties ran candidates in 1924 and 1929, the Conservative vote fell from 51 to 42 percent. In those same seats, the Liberal vote rose from 28 to nearly 33 percent, and the Labour vote increased from 30 to 35 percent. This small sample suggests that the decline in Conservative support benefited both the Liberals and Labour. Butler found that, in seats with three-way contests in both 1924 and 1929, the average Conservative vote fell 9.1 percent, increasing the average poll for Labour and Liberal candidates to 3.5 percent and 5.6 percent, respectively. The struggle between Labour and the Liberal Party in 1929, did, however, give the Conservatives two or three dozen victories in rural, usually Liberal, seats. Triangular contests had a hand in Conservative losses, but the defeat was also due to Labour's popularity and to voter dissatisfaction with the government.[85]

One complaint raised by Conservatives after their defeat was that newspapers did not support the Conservative campaign. It was felt that editors of the major Conservative dailies, except the *Daily Telegraph,* had neglected their duty. The lack of support and even hostility of Conservative newspapers, compounded with the ceaseless attacks of opposition newspapers, it was claimed, pushed the public, especially new electors, into voting against the Conservatives. In the NUCUA questionnaire of Conservative associations, more than half the 315 respondents mentioned the hostility of the press as a major factor in the Conservative Party's defeat. In North Cornwall the association was so angered by press coverage that it later tried to buy a regional newspaper.[86] It is true that the Conservatives did not receive the ringing endorsements that they had in 1924, but then their campaign was not one to excite journalists, editors, or publishers.

The NUCUA Executive also found that many Conservatives blamed the new female voters, particularly young women. This was a popular explanation, since the stagnant Conservative poll allowed people to believe that the new electors had voted en masse for the opposition. A Stockton newspaper, for instance, surmised that the 7,013 additional votes polled by the local Labour candidate meant that 7,000 of the 10,000 new female electors had voted Labour. One of the most vehement attacks on "the flapper vote" was by Garvin, who now strongly criticized the Baldwin government for passing the reform act of 1928. In a 16 June editorial in *The Observer,* Garvin attacked the Conservative leaders who had "biassed the electoral and constitutional system of the country against Conservatism, not temporarily but permanently. That is why we say that 1929 marks a new epoch like 1832. Anyone tempted to doubt this conclusion has only got to look at the thing in another way. The older pre-war voters, full of traditional ideas and reserves, are dying off the electoral register every day. And every day more and more of the advanced younger people are coming on."[87] This sort of argument is easy to debunk. Many young men had always had the vote and millions of women were enfranchised in 1918—yet the Conservatives had not suffered.

The WUO Administrator, Marjorie Maxse, dismissed the attacks on women voters, and, at least in private, experienced Conservative officials agreed that women were not a decisive factor in the election outcome. In

Table 2
**1924 and 1929 Conservative Vote in Sample Constituencies with
Greater and Less than Average Increases in Women Voters after 1928**

	Conservative Vote (%)	
	1924	1929
Greater than average increase	53.5	44.6
Less than average increase	54.4	45.0

the estimation of P. J. Blair, political secretary to the Scottish whips' office, the new women's vote "accentuated the 'Labour' vote in strongly 'Labour' areas, although it is not apparent that a loss of any seats is due to the new women's franchise." Topping agreed after comparing the results in divisions with greater and less than average increases in electorates (on the assumption that this was a function of more or fewer numbers of new women voters). He concluded that Conservative candidates in seats with a greater than average increase in the electorate fared better than their colleagues, and Labour was more successful in those divisions where there were fewer new voters. If the eleven seats in my sample (no Tory contested Wrexham in 1924) are divided into those with higher and lower than average increases in female electorates, the fall in the Conservative vote is slightly less in seats with greater increases in women voters. This is not conclusive, but it tends to disprove claims that women were responsible for the Conservative defeat in 1929.[88]

The problem with explanations for the Conservative defeat is that losses are blamed on some outside force—the Liberals, the press, the "flappers"—rather than working through the reasons voters rejected the Conservative Party. Most Conservatives realized that the government's policies, its program, and its approach to the campaign undermined its chances in the 1929 election. After the election, the "wets" or so-called YMCA wing of the party argued that Baldwin and his government lost because they had not pursued a more progressive program. Other generally more influential Conservatives held that the party was defeated because it had not adhered to distinctively Conservative causes—low income taxes, Lords reform, and tariffs. In particular, although the demand for tariffs was in fact limited, proponents regarded tariffs as the Conservative Party's only "positive policy." In July a majority of the NUCUA council passed a resolution in favor of "Safeguarding of all the principal trades of the country, particularly of Iron and Steel." The economic depression that began in autumn 1929 further encouraged disaffected Conservatives to support the tariff campaign of Rothermere and Beaverbrook, which threatened to divide the party and destroy Baldwin. Tariff reformers' beliefs to the contrary, however, the Conservative Party's experiences in 1906 and 1923 showed that protectionism had disastrous electoral consequences.[89]

The Conservative Party was defeated in 1929 because it relied on what the *Glasgow Herald* called a "Ministerial" campaign, rather than presenting a substantial program. As Amery had predicted in late 1924, the government was so comfortably immersed in administrative matters that it was unable or unwilling to fight an election, and Baldwin was incapable of pushing the party toward it. The few policies presented to voters, especially derating, alienated more than they attracted. Derating and local government reform confused and sometimes irritated electors who associated them with higher assessments. Farm workers and most ratepayers saw farmers and businessmen receiving tax cuts, while they had to pay more, and the NUCUA questionnaire found that most supporters considered derating a major cause of defeat. The Conservatives simply did not present an attractive program as they had in 1924.[90]

Most of the government's other pledges were too vague to have much impact during the election, so candidates and voters focused on the government's record. Unfortunately, its achievements received as much criticism as praise. The public was as concerned about the lack of pensions for some people as it was pleased about the benefits for many more, as irritated with high income taxes as happy with the end of the tea duty. As Neville Chamberlain wrote, "Every grievance has been exploited to point to this moral—people who have not got pensions, people who have their assessments raised, people who could not get a municipal house, people whose wages were low or who were unemployed or were excluded from benefit, etc., etc.—all these were told this is what you must expect as long as you have a capitalist Government. And though they hardly expect the millennium, they have said well let us give these fellows a chance. Something is wrong, the present Govt haven't put it right, the other side say they would have righted it, let us see if they cant [*sic*] do something for us."[91] Voters, many of whom were suffering from the country's economic difficulties, thought that the Conservative Party had not done enough for them. In response the Conservatives tried to appeal for support based on its ability to provide stable government at home and peace abroad. Given, however, the government's failure to solve economic problems and secure international peace, and the quiescence of domestic threats, many voters were not attracted to promises of "Safety First" that really seemed to mean more suffering, insecurity, and uncertainty. The Conservative promise to continue to provide competent and experienced leadership failed to draw voters in 1929.

Because the Conservatives campaigned on the government's record more than on an attractive policy platform, they gave full rein to what contemporaries termed the "pendulum swing." A contributor to the October 1929 issue of the *Conservative Agents' Journal* presented a cogent explanation. The Conservative defeat, he argued, was a by-product of its 1924 victory. The government concentrated on fulfilling election pledges and providing stable government, and then asked voters in 1929 if they were happy with the results. Electors responded with a resounding negative, in the process demonstrating a key principle of modern elections:

> A democracy never *elects* a Government, it always *rejects* one. The verdict of the people [in 1924] was unquestionably against the Socialists, with a rider condemning the Liberals who had put them in office. It was pro-Conservative only in ... that the Conservatives were the trusted enemies of Socialism. ...
>
> The upshot was a Conservative triumph which surprised everybody. ... There was nothing for the Conservative Government to do but to go ahead ... with its programme, which was long enough and formidable enough to occupy every moment of its time. ... [Meanwhile] the country was asking, "Why doesn't the Government do something?" ...
>
> As early as 1927 one could perceive that, if things proceeded according to plan, the Conservatives would stagger to the polls under the load of their good deeds, while the Opposition would have the benefit of the accumulated discontent, resentment and boredom of the electorate.[92]

The claim that "a democracy always rejects" a government is untrue, but the author was right to regard an election as a referendum on a government's performance.

The only way the party might have escaped defeat was for its leaders to have devised a simple and far-reaching program. In his attack on the government, Garvin criticized Conservative leaders for failing to provide a good program until the last moment, when they

> adopted a meritorious and big policy of reforming local taxation and Local Government. They called it by the hopeless name of "Derating." Then they failed to realise that by itself it was not enough . . . for the social and economic requirements of the country.
>
> MR. LLOYD GEORGE forced Unemployment into the centre of politics—the question never really faced by Ministers, whether spending £50,000,000 for nothing [unemployment insurance] was the best thing we could do. They left a wide impression that it was the best thing *they* could do.
>
> They denied that Unemployment was very important at all. They said MR. LLOYD GEORGE'S proposals were a stunt. It was untrue. . . .
>
> MR. BALDWIN'S real programme was "moi." In the name of "performance against promise"—a threadbare tag in politics—he asked, in effect, for a blank cheque whereon he might write as much or as little as he pleased. It never is done that way.[93]

Given the worries about the economy and peace, "Safety First" meant more of the same, but voting Labour (or Liberal), no longer a risky experiment, at least gave some hope for change.

Five days after the government was replaced on 5 June, the defeated Wakefield M.P., Geoffrey Ellis, chairman of the Yorkshire provincial division and a key figure in the NUCUA Executive, wrote to Baldwin. He urged the party leader to recognize that the election verdict was not a consequence of flippancy or boredom. Unemployment, underemployment, and the threat of wage reductions, Ellis wrote, "left the people almost in despair. Without, as a rule, expressing any bitter feeling, they just turned quietly & voted for the only possible alternative Govt. Especially as the promises [by Labour] of high minimum wages & general employment were so profuse & general."[94] The public, bombarded with posters of Baldwin and a "Why Change?" slogan, voted in favor of change, any kind of change.

In the postelection rush to establish blame for the defeat, critics first attacked central office and its "Safety First" campaign, then implicated the Conservative leadership, and finally turned on Baldwin. Disgruntled Conservatives like Beaverbrook, who had long criticized Baldwin's failings as a leader, believed that the election confirmed their opinions. Baldwin's friend and former colleague, William Bridgeman, admitted to "a small criticism" of the former prime minister, who tended to be "too sanguine that things will come right without his having to take a strong line." Privately Neville Chamberlain also criticized Baldwin for having "no power of rapid decision and consequently no initiative." Some critics within the party, especially those who were never reconciled to Baldwin's leadership, began to attack the former prime minister. On 1 June 1929 Headlam, the defeated M.P. for Barnard Castle, was already condemning "Mr. B's stupidity." As a result of the election and of his shortcomings as an opposition leader, Baldwin faced a revolt that ended Davidson's tenure as party chairman and nearly brought down Baldwin himself before it collapsed in 1931.[95]

It is important, however, to remember the difficulties confronting Conservative leaders in the 1920s and the limited nature of the Conservative defeat in 1929. Although he overstates the case, Williamson is right to point out that contemporary critics were too harsh in their condemnation of Baldwin and his performance in the election.[96] In many cases they believed that he should have pursued such ultraconservative policies as income tax cuts and Lords reform. But these would have created greater difficulties, because they were never popular with the mass of electors. A Conservative Party that adopted such measures was liable to lose votes by becoming associated with the selfishly rich or privileged classes. Other critics, Beaverbrook, Garvin, and Amery among them, wanted what Garvin called an "Employment and Empire" program—duties and imperial preference. Tariff reform generated some popular support and had an idealistic element, but it alienated consumers, especially the middle-class and suburban voters on whom the Conservative Party depended. By avoiding tariffs, Baldwin retained many middle-class seats and avoided a repetition of the 1923 disaster.

In 1929 the Conservatives were not successful in appealing to voters who could choose between three viable parties, but conditions soon changed dramatically, as Labour's victory was tenuous. Labour's popular vote was less than the Conservatives', and more than two-fifths of Labour's 287 seats were minority victories in three-way contests. A small swing away from Labour could bring the Conservatives a working majority in the next election. This was especially true once the Liberal Party resumed its descent into obsolescence. After the burst of activity inspired by Lloyd George (and his money), the Liberals ceased to present a national challenge to the other parties in the 1930s. Conservative leaders were then able to present their party as the only effective antisocialist party. At the same time the growing influence of Neville Chamberlain and his newly created Conservative Research Department ensured that the Conservative Party benefited from the constant study and formulation of future policy. In his recent study of the 1931 election, Thorpe argues that by mid-1931 the Conservatives "were on course for a victory at least as conclusive as that of 1924." Conservative governments, however, particularly ones led by Baldwin, remained vulnerable to circumstances like those of 1929. That election demonstrated that the success of the innovative Conservative organization depended in part on the party's positioning itself as the safe yet progressive option.[97]

Conclusion

In May 1997, after a record eighteen years' continuous Conservative government, the Labour Party scored its greatest electoral triumph to date. This event has raised new questions about British politics, past and future. In part the questions have involved a revived interest in the fate of the Conservative Party. The Tories dominated politics for so long only to lose an election while the country experienced peace, stability, and economic growth, conditions that should have guaranteed a Conservative triumph. As one commentator wrote, "What, pray God, are the voters trying to tell their leaders?"[1]

These recent developments also compel the investigator to consider the party's history in the twentieth century. How does this history help us to interpret the significance of the recent turn of events? Some pundits see in the election only the regular swing of the political pendulum. Voters, tired of the government and, possibly, politics in general, reject incumbent M.P.s and parties. Other observers emphasize the resurgence of the Labour Party under Tony Blair. Undoubtedly both of these explanations help us to understand the last election, and similar interpretations can be applied to earlier episodes in Conservative history. In a new book, *A History of Conservative Politics, 1900–1996* (1996), John Charmley argues that the Conservatives have sought power and, as the party of the status quo, reaped the reward of their divided and at times incompetent opposition.[2] But is there more to the party's history of success punctuated by occasional failures? Moreover, how have Conservatives responded to social, cultural, political, and international changes in the twentieth century? What attitudes, principles, or policies have guided party members? Why, despite their recent defeat, have they usually managed to remain the strongest party in Britain? When they were unsuccessful, what were the reasons?

The Conservative Party established itself as the dominant twentieth-century party during the 1920s by adapting to the era of mass politics after the First World War. During the period between the two world wars, Britain changed, in the words of the historian and civil servant Max Beloff, "from a society based upon distinctions largely of property to a mass society in which privilege could fight at best only a rearguard action."[3] The years from 1918 to 1929 witnessed the final episodes of a century-long process of electoral reform that culminated in the Representation of the People Acts of 1918 and 1928, establishing universal adult suffrage in Britain. The Conservative Party played a largely reluctant role in the passage of the first measure, which transferred ultimate political power to the mass of citizens, and were also not eager to pass the second, which was more or less mandated by the remaining inequities against women. In the course of a decade, the two reform acts increased the number of voters from eight to twenty-nine million.

As they faced the expansion of the electorate and the introduction of women into the political arena, the Conservatives also confronted other associated developments. Among the most important were the growth of powerful trade unions, the increased interest in socialist thought, and the rise of the Labour Party. In addition, the aftermath of the Great War brought economic dislocation, long-term unemployment, and an uprooting of established politics and culture. These developments followed the dramatic constitutional crises of Edwardian Britain—Irish Home Rule and women's suffrage. Ultimately, however, all of these elements were linked to a central concern, the amorphous electorate that now controlled Britain's political system. This predicament led at least some Conservatives to think, as Headlam wrote in his diary, "Democracy is hurrying to its ruin."[4] Even Conservatives who were more optimistic about British politics had serious misgivings about the future of their country and their party. In a 1927 letter to Lord Irwin, Baldwin, who piloted the Conservative Party and the country through the tumultuous interwar decades, expressed his deep concern: "Democracy has arrived at a gallop in England, and I fear all the time that it is a race for life."[5]

With so much uncertainty in a political system that depended on a volatile mass electorate and three competing parties, how would the party survive? In 1924 the progressive Conservative M.P. Noel Skelton characterized the difference between prewar and interwar politics. Previously party battles were, he wrote, "fought on a narrow front and by small armies of professionals, whose passage through the life of the nation affected it hardly more than a charabanc disturbs the countryside to-day—some vapour and much noise, a rut left in the highway, a film of dust on the hedgerow. But [now] Socialism fights on the broadest of fronts, and this breadth of front must dominate the strategy and tactics of the new era; for envelopment and the crushing defeat . . . form the danger against which Conservatism must guard in the great battles ahead."[6] For interwar Conservatives there was no possibility of returning to a romanticized Edwardian period (during which, in any case, they had suffered some of their greatest failures). In an October 1918 letter to Balfour, Bonar Law, the leader of the Unionist Party, wrote, "I am perfectly certain, indeed I do not think any one can doubt this, that our Party on the old lines will never have any future again in this country."[7] Yet the Conservative Party not only survived after 1918; according to the most important indicator—elections—it prospered. Except for a two-year period from 1929 to 1931, the Conservatives were always the largest party, and they were the governing party for more than eighteen of the twenty-one years between the wars.

As I have shown, one of the most important reasons for the party's success was the innovative reorganization instituted by Conservative leaders. This involved both more intensive propaganda efforts to shape the voting decisions of tens of millions of voters and a new commitment to the education of the citizen voters who set the course of politics in Britain. Only then, Baldwin told the Cambridge University Conservative Association, would voters, particularly the new women voters, not "jump at any form of remedy that can be put before them by the smooth and clever tongues of those who propagate heresies in our country."[8]

At the very core of the Conservative Party's efforts was the development of mass organizations for women, young people, and wage earners. By combining a judicious mixture of political, social, and educational activities, these groups, particularly the Women's Unionist Organisation (WUO) and the Junior Imperial League (JIL), attracted hundreds of thousands of members. These two groups and, to a lesser extent, the Labour Committee, played a vital role by creating a base of electoral support for the Conservatives. Members of these organizations were, moreover, the key to the party's superior electioneering and organizational capabilities. Nearly all aspects of Conservative activity—from canvassing to propaganda—depended on thousands of volunteers. As the chairman of the JIL, Lord Stanley, noted in 1927, the party's efforts were based on these mass organizations, whose framework resembled, he said, "a stool with three legs to it—the men, women, and the juniors."[9]

Coupled with innovations in organization, Conservative leaders eventually developed political tactics and rhetoric that enabled them to establish their party as the only effective national and antisocialist party. Their first effort in the new political framework was to try to incorporate Lloyd George and his Liberal followers into the Conservative Party. The failure of Bonar Law and his successor, Austen Chamberlain, to achieve this goal led to the coalition's fall in October 1922. Once Bonar Law's Conservative government—the first since 1906—won a parliamentary majority in the succeeding election, the Conservatives abandoned fusion, but not their hope of drawing moderates. Unfortunately Conservative leaders had yet to settle on a distinctive response to democracy. Initially Baldwin pursued the old issue of tariff reform in the 1923 campaign, but the party's defeat confirmed for Conservative leaders the absolute necessity of attracting middle-class and moderate working-class voters and avoiding divisive rhetoric and policies.

The approach Conservative leaders successfully developed in the 1920s was based on mobilizing various segments of the electorate by presenting a national and antisocialist stance and by offering moderate government, safety, and a return to normality after years of upheaval. In concrete terms this meant a deflationary monetary policy, low taxation, trade union reform, moderate, largely consolidating, social reforms, the maintenance of order and stability at home, and the preservation of international peace. The Conservative defeats in 1923 and 1929 were the direct result of weakening the anti-Labour consensus and contravening its objectives. The tariff election of 1923 jeopardized the middle-class desire for prosperity and stability. The "Safety First" campaign of 1929 alienated a range of voters who were disappointed with the government's apparently lackluster record, particularly after mid-1927. Some voters felt that the second Baldwin government's inability to deal with the troubled economy—despite notable efforts in reforming local government, encouraging labor mobility, and pursuing business rationalization—was an indication of the Conservative leaders' poverty of ideas and lack of will.[10] Some voters preferred the alternatives offered by the other parties, neither of which seemed threatening in 1929.

The Conservatives' political strategy in the 1920s rested on two intertwined rhetorical tactics. First, the party dominated moderate opinion by conveying to the electorate the principles of Conservatism, its regard for what Skelton termed "the reality, the life, the organic, as opposed to the mechanical, quality of politics."[11] In a 1924 letter to *The Times*, a leading Conservative woman and future junior minister, the duchess of Atholl, provided a statement of her political faith, arguing that, most of all, Conservatism "stand[s] for national unity and good will—the promotion of a better understanding between all sections of our people." She argued that Conservatism offered a constructive approach to satisfy all segments of the nation. In her view, the Conservative Party stood "for the fullest development of individuality, desiring to see our country enriched not only by greater material prosperity . . . not only by opportunities for wider and more varied intellectual development for all, but by the encouragement and strengthening of those great qualities of rectitude and personal independence and habits of industry and thrift on which the greatness of our country has been built up."[12]

Baldwin played a crucial role in the party's rhetorical triumph. As Conservative leader, he reformulated the Disraelian concept of national unity by integrating it with liberal constitutionalism. Beginning with his leadership during the October 1922 party crisis, Baldwin consistently presented political choices in moral, ethical, and religious terms. In a typical statement, made during the General Strike, he articulated a heartfelt opposition to amoral Liberalism and socialism and advocated the ancient notion of the Englishman's birthright: the English traditions of individual liberty and the rule of law. As one historian notes, Baldwin "consciously attempted to build an organic and active relation between past and present, while at the same time suggesting that this relationship was already an integral, constitutive and permanent feature of English culture." In his most famous speech Baldwin evoked the sounds of rural England, which, he said, "strike down into the very depths of our nature, and touch chords that go back to the beginning of time and . . . are chords that with every year of our life sounds a deeper note in our innermost being." He adapted his party's message to universal suffrage in his actions and speeches so as to confront the dangerous and divisive present by evoking traditional, innately "English" values and a notion of Britain's historical evolution toward constitutional democracy. Baldwin argued that only the Conservative Party could be trusted as guardian of this delicate process. He created a Conservative (but antifascist) consensus that survived the tumultuous interwar years and, in somewhat different form, continued to dominate political discourse until the rise of Margaret Thatcher.[13]

Coupled with its conquest of the political middle ground was the

Conservative Party's attempt to push the opposition to the margins. Underlying Atholl's view of Conservatism was a critique of parties that allegedly attacked social classes, pursued destructive policies, and oppressed the individual. Members of the WUO often attached negative labels to Labour, claiming that it was antifamily and antiwoman. The Conservatives claimed to offer voters safety and nonintrusive government, which would protect them from organized labor and socialists while enabling them to pursue individual and family interests. Led by Stanley Baldwin, they dismissed the politics of the coalition era and of socialism as amoral, irreligious, overly intellectual, and subversive: in short, as an "un-English" disregard for duty to country and service to constitutional democracy.[14] This approach enabled the Conservatives to unify ideologically and socially diverse groups in British society.

In 1926 the prime minister and party leader, Baldwin, delivered one of his many successful expositions of interwar Conservatism. In his address to the party conference, he criticized opposition leaders and condemned "that spirit of faction . . . [whose] inevitable result is that public passions are excited for private ends, and popular improvement is lost sight of in particular aggrandisements."[15] After the Great War, he said, Britain was "giddy," and a majority of the electors, only recently enfranchised, were "without fixed principles . . . driven about this way and that, the prey of every specious speaker, of every quack." With three parties competing for votes and the party structure still in flux, Baldwin said, the Conservatives must act so that voters "believe that we are trying to the best of our ability to govern the country for the good of the whole country and not for a class. It is only by that support that any Government to-day can come in and can have the requisite power . . . to govern in this country at all." This was the image of itself that the interwar Conservative Party successfully projected as it struggled to deal with the aftermath of war, universal suffrage, and the rise of Labour. The 1920s inaugurated a political domination by the Conservative Party that lasted three-quarters of a century.

Appendix A

Conservative Election Results by Region, 1918–1929

Region and Number of Seats	1918	1922	1923	1924	1929
Southeast (71)	59	64	51	71	58
London (62)	44	43	29	39	24
London suburbs (34)	28	25	17	26	18
Southwest (43)	31	31	14	39	26
East Anglia (19)	8	13	7	17	9
East Midlands (36)	22	15	14	31	14
West Midlands (46)	32	36	30	33	20
Mid-North (43)	13	12	10	12	6
Lancastria (80)	51	48	28	52	28
N. Yorkshire (21) and Cumbria	16	13	15	19	13
Northeast (30)	11	7	6	11	5
Strathclyde (32)	17	8	8	16	8
Scotland outside Strathclyde (39)	13	5	6	20	12
Wales (35)	4	6	4	9	1
Universities (24) and Ulster	18*	18	19	20	18
Total (615)	367	344	258	415	260

*For comparison purposes the 1918 figure used for Ulster is an estimate based upon a proportional allocation of the actual results in the much smaller divisions that existed between 1918 and 1921.

Appendix B

Women Voters in the Sample Constituencies

Parliamentary Division	1921		1927		1928	
	No.	%	No.	%	No.	%
Bradford Central	19,335	43.8	18,825	44.4	28,826	54.7
Camlachie	14,436	40.5	15,385	43.6	22,592	52.6
Chichester	18,685	42.9	25,022	46.0	36,138	53.7
Clapham	16,069	45.3	17,345	46.8	26,482	55.1
Kincardine	9,386	41.0	9,483	42.6	15,066	53.0
North Cornwall	12,164	43.7	14,317	45.3	20,990	54.2
Oswestry	12,797	40.8	13,995	41.7	21,714	51.7
Skipton	15,535	42.2	17,266	43.3	26,953	53.5
Stockton-on-Tees	14,444	39.5	16,858	40.8	26,104	49.5
Wirral	12,929	40.0	20,361	43.0	33,496	53.2
Wood Green	20,826	44.8	25,454	45.9	39,435	55.2
Wrexham	15,157	38.7	16,715	39.3	25,378	48.5
National average (%)	—	42.6	—	42.8	—	52.7

Appendix C

Conservative Vote in Sample Constituencies

Constituency	Vote % and No. of Candidates				
	1918	1922	1923	1924	1929
Bradford Central	51.0 (3)	36.1 (3)	30.4 (3)	51.7 (2)	41.0 (2)
Camlachie	62.9 (3)	40.2 (3)	43.8 (2)	49.6 (2)	42.0 (3)
Chichester	68.4 (2)	74.3 (2)	47.9 (2)	59.3 (3)	60.2 (2)
Clapham	60.2 (4)	58.7 (3)	46.4 (3)	64.1 (2)	41.7 (3)
Kincardine	0.0* (1)	0.0 * (2)	51.0 (2)	54.5 (2)	48.2 (2)
North Cornwall	0.0* (1)	0.0* (1)	43.5 (2)	53.6 (2)	42.3 (3)
Oswestry	59.2 (2)	50.2 (3)	46.6 (3)	55.1 (3)	47.0 (3)
Skipton	55.0 (2)	41.7 (3)	39.9 (3)	46.0 (3)	39.5 (3)
Stockton-on-Tees	0.0 * (1)	0.0* (3)	34.3 (3)	42.0 (3)	36.1 (3)
Wirral	Unopposed Unionist (1)	51.0 (3)	46.4 (2)	60.2 (2)	47.5 (3)
Wood Green	71.9 (3)	70.0 (2)	46.5 (3)	57.9 (3)	47.6 (3)
Wrexham	0.0* (2)	31.6 (3)	27.6 (3)	0.0* (2)	22.1 (3)
Averages for sample	61.2 (2.1)	50.4 (2.6)	42.0 (2.6)	54.0 (2.4)	42.9 (2.8)
Averages for Britain	58.1 (2.3)	48.6 (2.3)	42.6 (2.4)	51.9 (2.3)	39.4 (2.8)

*No Conservative candidate.

Appendix D

Analysis of Constituency Sample

My work is largely based on twelve parliamentary divisions carefully chosen and researched in depth. These constituencies are broadly representative of the 591 non-university divisions in Britain between 1922 and 1945. The 89 Irish and twelve Ulster divisions have been excluded. The most important socioeconomic and cultural factors affecting modern political activity are regionalism, class composition, ruralism, and religion, although the importance of regionalism is a matter of some debate. William Miller considers geographical location to be relatively unimportant, but other historians note that the traditions of the different regions of Britain are not explicable solely in terms of social and economic determinants.[1] My twelve constituencies are a diverse group echoing the geographical, economic, social, religious, and political character of twentieth-century Britain.

The standard work on the geographical regions of Britain establishes a framework of fourteen provinces or regions. I have adapted this scheme by creating fewer, more politically homogenous regions.[2] First, I carved the region of London and its satellite suburbs out of rural Southeast England. Second, I incorporated Fawcett's Bristol, Wessex, and Central—each with eighteen or nineteen divisions—into the larger surrounding regions of the Southwest, Southeast, West Midlands, and East Midlands. Third, I created the industrial, mining, and anti-Conservative region of Mid-North from Peakdon, Derbyshire, and southern Yorkshire. I combined the rest of Yorkshire, which was rural and generally pro-Conservative, with the similar adjoining area of Cumbria. In Scotland I divided the industrial Strathclyde region surrounding Glasgow from the rest of Scotland, which was predominantly rural. The result is two Scottish regions, Wales, and ten English regions.

During the two decades after 1918, patterns of Conservative strength and weakness were fairly constant and followed earlier trends.[3] In the interwar period the Conservative Party had the strongest support in Southeast England and, until the 1930s, London, particularly the suburban and wealthy urban divisions. Another region that, despite Labour's gains, continued to incline toward Conservatism was the West Midlands. Southwest England also tended to favor the Conservatives, but Cornwall and parts of Devon were strongholds of English Liberalism. Labour's dominance of the Mid-North and Northeast regions meant that there were few opportunities for the Conservative Party, but the rural Yorkshire (similar to present-day North Yorkshire) and Cumbria regions produced a considerable number of Conservative M.P.s in the 1920s. The modern Conservative Party has always been weak in Wales and Scotland, making its only advance in "the Celtic fringe" in formerly Liberal, rural Scotland.

In choosing constituencies from each region for this study I considered four political factors: class, rusticity, religion, and party allegiance. There was a consistent correlation between the middle class and Conservative voting during the interwar years. Seats with a large trade-unionist population tended to support Labour, but as a group the rest of the working class and shopkeepers did not demonstrate a consistent party affiliation.[4] Although it is commonly claimed that rural Britain was Conservative, in the interwar period these areas were more anti-Labour than pro-Conservative. Furthermore, the Liberal Party depended more heavily on agricultural seats than the other two parties. There were, however, considerable differences in rural areas, especially between those with open and closed settlement patterns. Constituencies with nucleated villages and arable farming, like Chichester, tended to be Tory, while the others tended to be Liberal.[5]

The last determinant of political deviance was religion. Nonconformism was traditionally linked to Liberalism, but many middle-class Nonconformists, especially Wesleyans and residents of Southeast England, were voting Conservative by the end of the Edwardian period. In Wales and certain other areas, however, many Nonconformists shifted their allegiance to the Labour Party after the Great War. Nevertheless, after 1918, Nonconformists—and Catholics—were still more likely to vote Liberal or Labour than Conservative.[6]

In selecting twelve parliamentary seats for the sample, I made a careful attempt to include at least one constituency from every region and to reflect the religious, socioeconomic, and party characteristics of interwar Britain. One third of the seats studied had a significant Nonconformist population, compared to about 30 percent of the divisions nationally. Middle-class constituencies composed one third of the sample (the national figure is 32 percent). Safe Conservative seats were 43 percent of all seats, compared to one half of the sample. Another 35 percent of the nation's divisions were safe non-Conservative seats, compared to one third in the sample. The sample has a few shortcomings. First, there are no divisions from the East Midlands, which encompassed 8 percent of the constituencies in Britain, and there is also no East Anglian seat because no records from an association in a representative East Anglian constituency were located. (Fortunately, East Anglia accounts for only 3 percent of parliamentary divisions.) Second, only a quarter of Britain's seats were agricultural, compared to 42 percent in my sample (five seats).[7] Third, the Southeast and Lancastria regions represented 12 percent and 13 percent, respectively, of Britain's non-university seats, but only about 8 percent each of the sample. Nevertheless, the sample broadly reflects the factors relevant to political orientation in interwar Britain (see appendix E).

Notes

1. William L. Miller, *Electoral Dynamics in Britain since 1918* (New York: St. Martin's Press, 1977), 217; Henry Pelling, *The Social Geography of British Politics, 1885–1910* (New York: St. Martin's Press, 1967), 415; and J. P. D. Dunbabin, "British Elections in the Nineteenth and Twentieth Centuries: A Regional Approach," *English Historical Review* 95 (1980): 264–65.

2. C. B. Fawcett, *Provinces of England*, 2d ed. (London: Hutchinson, 1960), 162. In redrawing Fawcett's regional map, I relied heavily on Pelling, *Social Geography*.

3. See Miller, *Electoral Dynamics;* Dunbabin, "British Elections"; and Michael Kinnear, *The British Voter: An Atlas and Survey, 1885–1964* (New York: St. Martin's Press, 1968).

4. For discussion of class and party affiliations, see Pelling, *Social Geography*, 418; Miller, *Electoral Dynamics*, 137, 216–17; Kinnear, *British Voter*, 116, 124; and A. Lawrence Lowell, *The Government of England* (New York: Macmillan, 1908), 2:110.

5. Miller, *Electoral Dynamics*, 203; Kinnear, *British Voter*, 119–21; and Pelling, *Social Geography*, 426–28.

6. See Neal Blewett, *The Peers, the Parties and the People: The British General Elections of 1910* (Toronto: University of Toronto Press, 1972), 343; D. W. Bebbington, *The Nonconformist Conscience: Chapel and Politics, 1870–1914* (London: George Allen & Unwin, 1982), 92–93 and 153–60; Kinnear, *British Voter*, 129; and Miller, *Electoral Dynamics*, 230.

7. Agricultural seats are defined as those in which at least 20 percent of adult males worked in agriculture (Kinnear, *British Voter*, 119.)

Appendix E

List of Sample Constituencies

Parliamentary Division	Region	Social Geography			Dominant Political Party		
		Settlement Pattern	Dominant Social Class	Other Characteristics	pre-1914	1918–1939	post-1945
Bradford Central	Mid-North	urban	working class	Nonconformist	Liberal	marginally Labour	marginally Labour
Camlachie	Strathclyde	urban	working class	Catholic and Irish	marginally Liberal Unionist	Labour	Labour
Chichester	Southeast England	rural and suburban	middle class		Conservative	Conservative	Conservative
Clapham	London	suburban	middle class		Conservative	Conservative	Conservative
Kincardine	Northeast Scotland	rural	mixed		Liberal	marginally Conservative	marginally Conservative
North Cornwall	Southwest England	rural	mixed	Nonconformist	Liberal	marginally Liberal	marginally Liberal

continued

List of Sample Constituencies *continued*

Parliamentary Division	Region	Social Geography			Dominant Political Party		
		Settlement Pattern	Dominant Social Class	Other Characteristics	pre-1914	1918–1939	post-1945
Oswestry	West Midlands	rural	mixed	Nonconformist and Welsh	Conservative	Conservative	Conservative
Skipton	North England	rural	mixed	Nonconformist	marginally Liberal	marginally Conservative	Conservative
Stockton-on-Tees	Northeast England	urban	working class	Nonconformist	marginally Liberal	none	Labour
Wirral	Merseyside	suburban	middle class		Conservative	Conservative	Conservative
Wood Green	Southeast England	suburban	middle class		[new seat]	Conservative	Conservative
Wrexham	North Wales	mixed	working class	Nonconformist and Welsh	Liberal	marginally Labour	Labour

Notes

The following abbreviations have been used in the notes:

ACC	*Association of Conservative Clubs*
BLPES	*British Library of Political and Economic Science*
BWL	*British Workers League*
CAJ	*The Conservative Agents' Journal*
CPA	Conservative Party Archives
CUWFA	Conservative and Unionist Women's Reform Association
GUA	Glasgow Unionist Association
GLRO	Greater London Record Office
HLRO	House of Lords Record Office
ILP	Independent Labour Party
JIL	Junior Imperial League
JILG	*Junior Imperial League Gazette*
JIU	Junior Imperialist Union
NCL	National Conservative League
NDP	National Democratic and Labour Party
NUA	National Unionist Association
NUCUA	National Union of Conservative and Unionist Associations
SUA	Scottish Unionist Association
WUO	Women's Unionist Organisation
WUTRA	Women's Unionist and Tariff Reform Association

Introduction

1. Norman MacKenzie and Jeanne MacKenzie, eds., *The Diary of Beatrice Webb* (Cambridge, Mass.: Belknap Press, 1984), 3:315 (4 November 1918).

2. David Marquand, *The Progressive Dilemma* (London: William Heinemann, 1991), 10; Ross McKibbin, "Class and Conventional Wisdom: The Conservative Party and the 'Public' in Inter-War Britain," in *The Ideologies of Class*, edited by Ross McKibbin (Oxford: Clarendon Press, 1990), 259.

3. The number of parliamentary divisions from 1918 to 1921 was 707, but the

Sinn Fein M.P.s never came to Parliament, and after Irish independence in 1921 the number of M.P.s fell to 615.

4. See especially John Ramsden, *A History of the Conservative Party,* vol. 3, *The Age of Balfour and Baldwin, 1902–1940,* (London: Longman Group, 1978), 122–23.

5. On the prewar system, see Neal Blewett, *The Peers, the Parties, and the People: The British General Elections of 1910* (Toronto: University of Toronto Press, 1972), chap. 17.

6. John Graham Jones, "The General Election of 1929 in Wales," (M.A. thesis, University of Wales, 1980), xiv. See also Marquand, *Progressive Dilemma,* chaps. 1–5; and Tom Jeffery, "The Suburban Nation: Politics and Class in Lewisham," in *Metropolis—London: Histories and Representations since 1800,* edited by David Feldman and Gareth Stedman Jones (London: Routledge, 1989), 192–94.

7. Frans Coetzee, *For Party or Country: Nationalism and the Dilemma of Popular Conservatism in Edwardian England* (New York: Oxford University Press, 1990), 5.

8. See McKibbin, "Class and Conventional Wisdom," 260. Such a calculation is speculative rather than definitive.

9. Robert Blake, "The Historical Setting: Conservatism and Reform," in *Conservatism Today,* edited by Robert Blake (London: Conservative Political Centre, 1966), 14; David Jarvis, "The Road to 1931: The Conservative Party and Political Realignment in Early Twentieth-Century Britain," *Historical Journal* 36 (1993): 473.

10. Maurice Cowling, *The Impact of Labour, 1920–1924: The Beginning of Modern British Politics* (Cambridge: Cambridge University Press, 1971); Robert C. Self, *Tories and Tariffs: The Conservative Party and the Politics of Tariff Reform, 1922–1932* (New York: Garland, 1986), xxii.

11. Anthony Seldon and Stuart Ball, eds., *Conservative Century: The Conservative Party since 1900* (Oxford: Oxford University Press, 1994); Martin Pugh, "Popular Conservatism in Britain: Continuity and Change, 1880–1987," *Journal of British Studies* 27 (1988): 255.

12. Martin Pugh, *The Tories and the People, 1885–1935* (New York: Basil Blackwell, 1985); McKibbin, "Class and Conventional Wisdom."

13. David Jarvis, "British Conservatism and Class Politics in the 1920s," *English Historical Review* 211 (1996): 59–84; Philip Williamson, "The Doctrinal Politics of Stanley Baldwin," in *Public and Private Doctrine: Essays in British History Presented to Maurice Cowling,* edited by Michael Bentley (Cambridge: Cambridge University Press, 1993), 203. (For interpretations of interwar Conservatism similar to Williamson's, see Bill Schwarz, "The Language of Constitutionalism: Baldwinite Conservatism," in *Formations of Nation and People* [London: Routledge & Kegan Paul, 1984], 1–18; and Stuart Ball, "The Conservative Dominance, 1918–40," *Modern History Review* 3 [1991]: 25–28.)

14. Phrase from Pugh, *Tories and the People,* 2.

15. The personal papers of the M.P.s for North Cornwall, Oswestry, and Stockton were located, but the collection of the late Lord Stockton was still closed.

16. J. A. R. Marriott, *The Mechanism of the Modern State* (Oxford: Clarendon Press, 1927), 2:453.

Chapter 1

1. John Stubbs, "The Impact of the Great War on the Conservative Party," in *The Politics of Reappraisal, 1918–1939,* edited by Gillian Peele and Chris Cook (London: Macmillan, 1975), 21–24; D. H. Close, "The Growth of Backbench Organisation in the Conservative Party," *Parliamentary Affairs* 27 (1974): 375; JIL Executive Committee, 10 February 1915, CPA; JIL Executive Committee, Circular to JIL Branches, 27 February 1918.

2. Skipton Conservative Association, Executive Committee, 26 September 1914, 22 January 1916, and 2 February 1918; GUA Annual Reports, Camlachie Unionist Association, Annual Report 1918, SCCO; SUA Eastern Division, Executive Committee, 8 October 1914, SCCO.

3. *CAJ,* October 1916, 228; April 1916, 127; October 1916, 230–36; Homer Lawrence Morris, "Parliamentary Franchise Reform in England from 1885 to 1918," (Ph.D. diss., Columbia University, 1921), 124–26; John Turner, *British Politics and the Great War: Coalition and Conflict, 1915–1918* (New Haven: Yale University Press, 1992), 117–20.

4. W. H. Dickinson, "An Account of the Speaker's Conference," in J. Renwick Seager, *The Reform Act of 1918* (London: Liberal Publication Department, 1918), 9; Lord Selborne to Lord Salisbury, 25 August 1916, in *The Crisis of British Unionism: Lord Selborne's Domestic Political Papers, 1885–1922,* edited by George Boyce (London: Historians' Press, 1987), 194–95.

5. Walter [Long] to Dick [Richard Long], 29 March 1917, Walter Long of Wraxall Papers 947/675, Wiltshire Record Office; Pat Jalland, *Women, Marriage and Politics, 1860–1914* (Oxford: Clarendon Press, 1986), 239–40; Martin Pugh, *Electoral Reform in War and Peace, 1916–18* (Boston: Routledge & Kegan Paul, 1978), 25–26.

The last issue of *The Conservative and Unionist Women's Franchise Review* was in early 1916, and some time shortly after 1917 the CUWFA became the Conservative Women's Reform Association. I was unable to locate any CUWFA records.

Sandra Stanley Holton, *Feminism and Democracy: Women's Suffrage and Reform Politics in Britain, 1900–1918* (Cambridge: Cambridge University Press, 1986), 123.

6. David Close, "The Collapse of Resistance to Democracy: Conservatives, Adult Suffrage, and Second Chamber Reform, 1911–1928," *Historical Journal* 20 (1977): 894–95; Pugh, *Electoral Reform,* 26–43; Katherine, duchess of Atholl, *Working Partnership* (London: Arthur Barker, 1958), 73.

Brian Harrison's remark that the duchess was politicized by her opposition to women's politicization is inaccurate. She was president of the West Perthshire Women's Unionist Association and active in local politics before 1918 (Atholl, *Working Partnership*, 55–57; Harrison, *Separate Spheres: The Opposition to Women's Suffrage in Britain* [London: Croom Helm, 1978], 113, 73–79).

7. Alfred, Lord Tennyson, *The Princess* (1847), part 5, lines 437–41, quoted in Lisa Tickner, *The Spectacle of Women: Imagery of the Suffrage Campaign, 1907–14* (Chicago: University of Chicago Press, 1988), 154.

8. Quoted in Harrison, *Separate Spheres*, 57.

9. "Memorandum for the [NUA] Executive Committee," Sir Arthur Steel-Maitland Papers, GD193/202, Scottish Record Office. See also Steel-Maitland to Long, 3 February 1917, Steel-Maitland Papers, GD193/202. On Steel-Maitland's unhappiness with his position, see Steel-Maitland to Bonar Law, 19 July 1917, Andrew Bonar Law Papers, 82/2/10, HLRO.

10. Draft Report of the Subcommittee to the NUA Executive Committee, 13 March 1917, Steel-Maitland Papers, GD193/202. Except as noted, the remainder of the paragraph is based on this document, which does not survive in the NUA records, but matches excerpts in the subcommittee's June report. On the creation of the subcommittee, see NUA Labour Committee Minute book, Subcommittee of the NUA Executive Committee, 28 February 1917, NUA 6/1/1, CPA. Beginning in 1919 the minute book was used by the NUA Labour Committee.

11. Excerpt of the 13 March 1917 subcommittee report contained in Report of the Subcommittee, NUA Executive Committee, 7 June 1917.

12. John D. Fair, *British Interparty Conferences: A Study of the Procedure of Conciliation in British Politics, 1867–1921* (Oxford: Clarendon Press, 1980), 177.

13. *CAJ*, April 1917, 59–61, 54; July 1917, 92–97.

14. Yorkshire Provincial Division Council, 29 June 1917; J. E. Fawcett to Boraston, 18 June 1917, Long Papers 947/675.

NUA Executive Committee, 8 May 1917. The summary gives only the total number of responses for and against reform, against reform during wartime, against proportional representation, and for or against the enfranchisement of women. Because the categories were not mutually exclusive, the totals do not tally, and we do not know how many constituencies responded. Therefore it is difficult to know the exact meaning of the large number of responses categorized as opposed to the Speaker's Report.

15. Cornwall Provincial Division, Annual Meetings, 1 March 1917 and 24 April 1918, CPA; Skipton Conservative Association, Executive Committee, 14 July 1917.

16. Long to George [Younger], 29 March 1917, Long Papers, 947/675; Christopher Addison, *Four and a Half Years* (London: Hutchinson, 1934), 348; NUA Council, 17 April 1917. For more information about second chamber reform, see Neal R. McCrillis, "Taming Democracy? The Conservative Party and House of Lords' Reform, 1916–1929," *Parliamentary History* 12 (1993): 259–80.

17. NUA Labour Committee Minute Book, Subcommittee of the NUA Executive Committee, 24 May 1917, NUA 6/1/1; NUA Executive Committee, 7 June 1917; NUA Council, 8 June 1917; NUA Executive Committee, Report of the Subcommittee, 7 June 1917. With alternative voting if no candidate won a majority, votes would be redistributed from the last candidate according to preferences on the ballots. If necessary the process would continue. Unionists feared that the procedure would strengthen the old Liberal-Labour alliance.

18. Yorkshire Provincial Division Council, 8 November 1917.

19. *CAJ*, July 1917, 89; Earl Russell, 17 December 1917, quoted in Harrison, *Separate Spheres*, 220 (see also Pugh, *Electoral Reform*, chap. 5); John Vincent, ed., *The Crawford Papers: The Journals of David Lindsay, Twenty-Seventh Earl of Crawford and Tenth Earl of Balcarres, 1871–1940, during the Years 1892 to 1940* (Manchester: Manchester University Press), 382 (entry for 11 December 1917).

20. *Gleanings and Memoranda,* March 1917-November 1918, 228; report of the NUA Executive Committee to the Council, 9 April 1918 (summary of changes in the reform bill); Morris, "Parliamentary Franchise Reform," 177–87; Michael Kinnear, *The British Voter* (New York: St. Martin's Press, 1968), 70–72 (on the 1918 redistribution).

21. Pugh, *Electoral Reform*, 196; and D. E. Butler, *The Electoral System in Britain since 1918* (Oxford: Clarendon Press, 1963), 146–48; H. C. G. Matthew, R. I. McKibbin, and J. A. Kay, "The Franchise Factor in the Rise of the Labour Party," *English Historical Review* 91 (1976): 727–35 (residential franchise debate); Duncan Tanner, "The Parliamentary Electoral System, the 'Fourth' Reform Act and the Rise of Labour in England and Wales," *Bulletin of the Institute of Historical Research* 56 (1983): 206–17.

22. Both quotations are from *CAJ*, January 1918, 6–7.

23. Long to Cave, 7 February 1918, Viscount Cave Papers, 62497; J. A. R. Marriott, *The Mechanism of the Modern State* (Oxford: Clarendon Press, 1927), 2:20.

24. Norman MacKenzie and Jeanne MacKenzie, eds., *The Diary of Beatrice Webb* (Cambridge, Mass.: Belknap Press, 1984), 3:308–9 (16 June 1918).

25. For views of the new method of registration, see G. H. Edwards [Metropolitan Conservative Agents Association] to Younger, 17 July 1919 (copy), Clapham Conservative Association, miscellaneous items; and J. M. Lee, *Social Leaders and Public Persons: A Study of County Government in Cheshire since 1888* (Oxford: Clarendon Press, 1963), 53.

Shortly after the reform act was passed, the speaker of the house received a drawing from his son-in-law, Sir Mark Sykes, a Hull M.P. and amateur cartoonist, that depicted Hull's future M.P.s as stereotypical radicals, anarchists, and socialists (James William Lowther, *A Speaker's Commentaries* [London: Edward Arnold, 1925], between 226 and 227).

26. D. L. LeMahieu, *A Culture for Democracy* (Oxford: Clarendon Press, 1988); Owen Paul Lippert, "The British General Election of 1918: Class Conflict, War and

Politics" (Ph.D. diss., University of Notre Dame, 1983), 95–96; and Christine Collette, *For Labour and for Women: The Women's Labour League, 1906–1918* (New York: Manchester University Press, 1989), 175–78.

27. Special NUA Conference, 30 November 1917.

28. "The Representation of the People Bill (1917), Report of the Secretary," Bonar Law Papers, 82/4/7.

29. Yorkshire Provincial Division Council, 8 November 1917.

30. Special NUA Conference, 30 November 1917.

31. Open letter from Marjorie Maxse, chairman of the Women's Unionist and Tariff Reform Association, June 1917, Viscountess Bridgeman Papers, 4629/1917/3; Talbot to Caroline Bridgeman, 3 May 1917, and William Bridgeman to Caroline Bridgeman, 18 January 1918, Bridgeman Papers, 4629/1918/4, 17.

32. See Primrose League Grand Council, "Report of the Joint Conference of 12 December 1917," 7 February 1918; and Martin Pugh, *The Tories and the People, 1880–1935* (New York: Basil Blackwell, 1985). The Grand Master of the League, Lord Home of the Hirsel, commemorated the centenary of Disraeli's death with a ceremony at St. Margaret's Church (*The Times*, 10 April 1981).

33. NUA Executive Committee, "Notes on Women's Organisation under the Representation of the People Bill," 21 January 1918, "Notes on a Women's Central Organisation," 16 January 1918, and report of the NUA Executive Committee to the Council, 9 April 1918.

34. See, for instance, Metropolitan Conservative Agents' Association, General Meeting, 26 March 1918.

35. William Bridgeman to Caroline Bridgeman, 16, 17, and 20 January 1918, Bridgeman Papers, 4629/1918/13, 14, and 18; memorandum by Caroline Bridgeman, undated, Viscountess Bridgeman Papers, SRO/CCB.

36. When the WUO began operations is unknown, but its rules were approved by the NUA council on 9 April 1918. The WUTRA held its last annual meeting in May, and by July Younger had ceased dealing with the WUTRA (*The Times*, 15 May 1918; NUA Executive Committee, 9 July 1918). The WUO organization was probably in place by late spring.

37. Oswestry Women's Constitutional Association, Annual Report, 1913–14; and Oswestry Unionist Association, Special Council, 31 August 1928. The other four women's branches were in Chichester, Skipton, Wirral, and Camlachie.

38. Oswestry Women's Constitutional Association, General Meeting [of reformed branch], 29 March 1919; Bradford Central Women's Conservative and Unionist Association, General Meeting, 8 March 1919; Wood Green Women's Constitutional Association, General Meeting, 19 April 1919; and Clapham Conservative Association Council, 15 December 1919.

39. North Cornwall Unionist Association, "Report of Secretary W. J. Hendy on Reorganisation," 25 February 1919; and Wirral Conservative Association, Special Executive Committee Meeting, 8 April 1918.

40. Yorkshire Provincial Division, Women's Conservative Federation, Secretaries' Conference, 28 February 1918; idem, Half Yearly Report, June 1918; idem, Women's Federation, 5 November 1918; Cornwall Provincial Division, Provisional Committee of Cornish Women Unionists, 26 June 1918.

41. SUA Executive Committee, 7 November 1917; SUA Council, 15 February 1918; GUA Annual Reports, Camlachie Unionist Association, Annual Reports, 1919 and 1923.

42. SUA Council, 15 February 1918.

43. Stockton Constitutional Organisation, Executive Committee, 23 July 1918, and Annual Meeting, 26 February 1919; Wirral Conservative Association, Executive Committee, 8 April 1918; Chichester Unionist Association, Women's Council, Executive Committee, 29 May 1918; Palmers Green Constitutional Association, General Meeting, 8 January 1919.

44. SUA Council, "Representation of the People Act, Memorandum by Central Council," 15 February 1918.

45. John Ramsden, ed., *Real Old Tory Politics: The Political Diaries of Sir Robert Sanders, Lord Bayford, 1910–35* (London: Historians' Press, 1984), 100 (10 February 1918).

46. William Bridgeman to Caroline Bridgeman, 1 and 5 August 1918, Bridgeman Papers, 4629/1918/45, 48; Oswestry Unionist Association, Council, Rules and Regulations, 31 August 1918, and Report of the Executive Committee to the Council, 12 April 1919; William Bridgeman to Caroline Bridgeman, 15 November 1918, Bridgeman Papers, 4629/1918/89.

47. NUA Executive Committee, 9 April 1918, "Report of the Subcommittee Appointed to Re-Draft the Rules"; NUA Conference, 10 June 1920, "Constitution and Rules of the National Unionist Association"; NUA Executive Committee, 14 May and 9 July 1918, 11 March 1919.

48. NUA Executive Committee, 17 June and 15 July 1924; *CAJ*, August 1924, 185–89; and NUA Conference, 2 October 1924. The organization's name was also changed to the National Union of Conservative and Unionist Associations (NUCUA) in recognition of Ireland's diminished importance.

49. Yorkshire Provincial Division Council, 8 November 1917; Special NUA Conference, 30 November 1917; Long to Younger, 12 and 15 September 1918, and Younger to Long, 14 September 1918, Long Papers, 947/682.
On the BWL see John O. Stubbs, "Lord Milner and Patriotic Labour," *English Historical Review* 87 (1972): 717–42; and Roy Douglas, "The National Democratic Party and the British Workers' League," *Historical Journal* 15 (1972): 533–52.

50. Bentley B. Gilbert, *British Social Policy, 1914–1939* (London: B. T. Batsford, 1970), 5–6; Yorkshire Provincial Division, Council, 8 November 1917.

51. Yorkshire Provincial Division, Council, 1 February 1918.

52. Stanley Salvidge, *Salvidge of Liverpool: Behind the Political Scene, 1890–1928* (London: Hodder & Stoughton, 1934), 162.

53. See, for instance, *The Archives of the British Conservative and Unionist Party,* series 1, *Pamphlets and Leaflets* (Hassocks, W. Sussex: Harvester Press, 1978), 1918/5, microfiche.

54. "Fundamental Points of Policy of the National Party," October 1918, Bonar Law Papers, 84/2/15; and *CAJ,* October 1917, 119. The only account of the National Party is William D. Rubinstein, "Henry Page Croft and the National Party, 1917–22," *Journal of Contemporary History* 9 (1974).

55. Oliver to Lord Selborne, 5 September 1917, 2d Earl of Selborne Papers, 87/16–18.

56. See Ramsden, *Sanders' Diaries,* 89–90 (3 October 1917); and Morrison to Reginald Bennett, 12 August 1918, Primrose League Grand Council Minute Book.

57. Bonar Law to Sir Thomas Wrightson [former chairman of the NUA council], 15 September 1917, and Bonar Law to [Lord] Edmund [Talbot], 11 September 1917, Bonar Law Papers, 84/6/124, 123; *CAJ,* October 1917, 151; Yorkshire Provincial Division, Executive Committee, 26 October 1917.

58. NUA Executive Committee, 27 July 1917 and 12 February 1918; Talbot to [Sir] George [Younger], 16 September 1917, Bonar Law Papers, 82/4/22; Cheshire Provincial Division, Annual Meeting, 15 January 1918 (*Crewe Guardian,* undated cutting); Bonar Law Papers, 83/6/10 and 83/3/11; Ramsden, *Sanders' Diaries,* 104 (5 May 1918); [Lord] Henry Cavendish-Bentinck, *Tory Democracy* (London: Methuen, [1918]), 8–9.

59. Panikos Panayi, "The British Empire Union in the First World War," in *The Politics of Marginality: Race, the Radical Right and Minorities in Twentieth Century Britain,* edited by Tony Kushner and Kenneth Lunn (London: Frank Cass, 1990), 118, 125; NUA Executive Committee, 9 July 1918; J. A. Turner, "The British Commonwealth Union and the General Election of 1918," *English Historical Review* 93 (1978): 536–39. See also Lawrence to Bonar Law, 17 July 1918, Bonar Law Papers, 83/5/15.

60. NUA Executive Committee, 13 November 1917; Special NUA Conference, 30 November 1917.

61. Younger to J. C. C. Davidson, 17 April 1918, Bonar Law Papers, 83/2/18; Bradford Central Conservative Association, Council, 14 January 1916, and Annual Meeting, 6 April 1916.

62. Yorkshire Provincial Division, Executive Committee, 5 April 1918.

63. Memorandum on colonial office meeting, [early March 1917], Long Papers, 947/167; Younger to Bonar Law, 16 March 1918, Bonar Law Papers, 83/1/19.

64. J. M. McEwen, ed., *The Riddell Diaries, 1908–1923* (London: Athlone Press, 1986), 230, 234 (30 June, August 1918); William Bridgeman to Caroline Bridgeman, 1 August 1918, Bridgeman Papers, 4629/1918/45; NUA Executive Committee, Report of the Publications Subcommittee, 9 July 1918.

65. On developments among coalition Liberals, see Lippert, "General Elec-

tion of 1918," 135–45; McEwen, *Riddell Diaries*, 4–6 (30 June 1918), 230–37 (August 1918, 22 September 1918); and Addison, *Four and a Half Years*, 588.

66. Younger to Bonar Law, 10 August 1918, and copy of Lloyd George's proposals, both Bonar Law Papers, 83/6/19 (the statements appear in Addison, *Four and a Half Years*, 553–56); paper analyzing the differences between the Lloyd George and Conservative policy statements, undated, Bonar Law Papers, 95/1; Younger to Long, 31 August 1918, Long Papers, 947/682; Bonar Law to Long, 31 August 1918, Bonar Law Papers, 84/7/75.

67. New draft of government platform, 3 September 1918, David Lloyd George Papers, F/236; William Bridgeman to Caroline Bridgeman, 6 September 1918, Bridgeman Papers, 4629/1918/64; Long to Younger, 12 September 1918, Long Papers, 947/682; Yorkshire Provincial Division Council, 10 September 1918; McEwen, *Riddell Diaries*, 238 (27 and 28 September 1918).

68. NUA Executive Committee, 8 October 1918; Younger, memorandum to Bonar Law, 10 October 1918, Bonar Law Papers, 95/1.

69. Long to Bonar Law, 1 September 1918, Bonar Law Papers, 84/1/1; Ramsden, *Sanders' Diaries*, 109 (13 October 1918); for a similar remark by a prominent journalist, see William Robertson Nicoll to John Buchan, 29 November 1918, quoted in T. H. Darlow, *William Robertson Nicoll: Life and Letters* (London: Hodder & Stoughton, 1925), 281.

70. Lippert, "General Election of 1918," 181; Lloyd George to Bonar Law, 2 November 1918 (copy), Bonar Law Papers, and opinions on Lloyd George's letter, both Bonar Law Papers, 95/1; McEwen, *Riddell Diaries*, 244, 251 (30 October, 9 December 1918); Riddell to Lloyd George, 31 October 1918, McEwen, *Riddell Diaries*, 421; Turner, *British Politics and the Great War*, 301–11.

71. Report of the proceedings of Connaught Meeting, 12 November 1918, Bonar Law Papers, 95/3; diary of Walter Long, 12 November 1918, Long Papers.

72. Long diary, 14 November 1918; John Ramsden, *A History of the Conservative Party*, vol. 3, *The Age of Balfour and Baldwin, 1902–1940* (London: Longman Group, 1978), 140; Report of the Coalition Party Meeting, 16 November 1918, Bonar Law Papers, 95/3.

73. Turner, *British Politics and the Great War*, 308; Guest to Lloyd George, 29 October and 15 November 1918, Lloyd George Papers, F/21/2/46, 47 (for the coupon episode, see Roy Douglas, "The Background to the 'Coupon' Election Arrangements," *English Historical Review* 86 [1971]: 318–36); Skipton Conservative Association, Executive Committee, 26 October 1918; Younger to Long, 31 August 1918, Long Papers; and Ramsden, *Sanders' Diaries*, 117 (27 November 1918); Younger to Bonar Law, 20 November 1918, Bonar Law Papers, 95/4.

74. Ramsden, *Sanders' Diaries*, 101 (3 March 1918); Robert Sanders, memorandum on BWL, Bonar Law Papers, 83/5/14; Sanders to Bonar Law, 18 March 1918, Bonar Law Papers, 83/1/15; Talbot to Sanders, 25 March 1918, and Sanders to Bonar

Law, 26 March 1918, Bonar Law Papers, 83/1/21; Yorkshire Provincial Division, Executive Committee, 5 April 1918 (examples of tensions); Ramsden, *Sanders' Diaries*, 105–7 (6 June, 14 July 1918); Fisher to Bonar Law, 5 July 1918, Bonar Law Papers, 83/5/5; Stubbs, "Patriotic Labour," 733–46.

75. Stockton Constitutional Organisation, Special Committee, 16 September 1918; North Cornwall Unionist Association, Executive Committee, 27 November 1918; *Launceston Weekly News*, 30 November 1918; copies of telegram from Murray of Elibank to Colonel Murray and reply, 18 November 1918, Lloyd George Papers, F/41/5/28; Kincardine and West Aberdeenshire Unionist Association, Executive Committee, 28 November 1918; Wrexham and East Denbighshire Constitutional Association, Special General Meeting, 15 November 1918; *North Wales Guardian*, 22 and 29 November 1918.

76. William Bridgeman to Caroline Bridgeman, 27 November, 4 and 6 December 1918, Bridgeman Papers, 4629/1918/95, 100, 103; *Birkenhead Advertiser*, 30 November 1918 (Stewart's case).

77. Kenneth O. Morgan, *Consensus and Disunity: The Lloyd George Coalition Government, 1918–1922* (Oxford: Clarendon Press, 1979), 42. For the traditional interpretation, see Robert Graves and Alan Hodge, *The Long Weekend* (New York: W. W. Norton, 1963), 19.

78. *Craven Herald*, 22 November 1918; *Glasgow Herald*, 18 November 1918; William Bridgeman to Caroline Bridgeman, 27 November 1918, Bridgeman Papers, 4629/1918/95.

79. *Clapham Observer*, 15 November 1918; John Barnes and David Nicholson, eds., *The Leo Amery Diaries* (London: Hutchinson, 1980), 1:246–47; *Pamphlets and Leaflets*, 1918/34 (*Election Notes* were central office leaflets issued each day during a general election); C. F. G. Masterman, *Contemporary Review*, February 1919, quoted in Lucy Masterman, *C. F. G. Masterman* (London: Frank Cass, 1968), 308; Bonar Law Papers, 104/3/51; *Clapham Observer*, 13 December 1918; *Bradford Daily Argus*, 6 December 1918; *Craven Herald*, 29 November 1918; *North Middlesex Chronicle*, 7 December 1918.

80. *Pamphlets and Leaflets*, 1918/29–31, 34.

81. Ibid., 1918/41; William Bridgeman to Caroline Bridgeman, 26 November 1918, Bridgeman Papers, 4629/1918/94; *Clapham Observer*, 29 November 1918 (Beamish's later work is covered in Gisela Lebzelter, *Political Anti-Semitism in England, 1918–1939* [New York: Holmes & Meier, 1978], 49–51); *Bradford Daily Argus*, 30 November 1918 (Ratcliffe quotation).

82. *Pamphlets and Leaflets*, 1918/34; *Chichester Observer*, 11 December 1918; *Bradford Daily Argus*, 28 November 1918; *North Middlesex Chronicle*, 30 November 1918; *Craven Herald*, 6 December 1918; *Glasgow Herald*, 12 December 1918.

83. *Clapham Observer*, 15 and 22 November 1918.

84. Ramsden, *Sanders' Diaries*, 122 (5 January 1919); *Chichester Observer*, 4

December 1918; election address of Halford Mackinder, 1918; *Clapham Observer,* 15 November 1918.

85. Close, "Backbench Organization," 377 (I want to thank Bentley B. Gilbert for suggesting this line of investigation); *The Times,* 16 and 20 November 1918.

86. Lippert, "Election of 1918," 224–28; *The Times,* 30 November 1918; *Glasgow Herald,* 30 November 1918.

87. *Clapham Observer,* 29 November 1918; William Bridgeman to Caroline Bridgeman, 26 and 28 November 1918, Bridgeman Papers, 4629/1918/94, 96; *Craven Herald,* 6 and 13 December 1918; *Muswell Hill Record,* 29 November 1918; *North Middlesex Chronicle,* 30 November 1918; *Bradford Daily Argus,* 30 November 1918.

88. Reports from central office agents, 3–6 December 1918, Bonar Law Papers, 95/2; Peter Bull, *Bulls in the Meadows* (London: Peter Davies, 1957), 150.

89. *Muswell Hill Record,* 6 December 1918.

90. See Lippert, "Election of 1918," 226–28, and *North Wales Guardian,* 6 December 1918 (both on virulently anti-German speeches by coalition Liberal and Labour leaders); *Muswell Hill Record,* 6 December 1918; *Craven Herald,* 6 December 1918; *Bradford Daily Argus,* 11 and 13 December 1918.

91. William Bridgeman to Caroline Bridgeman, 12 December 1918, Bridgeman Papers, 4629/1918/112; *Chichester Observer,* 4 December 1918; *Craven Herald,* 6 December 1918. (For more information on the conscription issue, see Lippert, "Election of 1918," 249–51.)

92. *The Times,* 10 December 1918; Mackinder, election address; *Pamphlets and Leaflets,* 1918/4, 13, 48; "A Word to the Ladies!" Neville Chamberlain Papers, NC 5/12/8.

93. "General Election, December 1918: Forecast of Result," 12 December 1918, Bonar Law Papers, 95/2.

94. Long to Lord Derby, 31 December 1918, Long Papers 947/548; Kinnear, *British Voter,* 38; Turner, *British Politics and the Great War,* 432.

95. My calculations are based on F. W. S. Craig, *British Parliamentary Election Results, 1918–1949* (Glasgow: Political Reference Publications, 1969). I excluded double-member seats and counted only candidates adopted by party associations.

96. Morgan, *Consensus and Disunity;* Michael Kinnear, *The Fall of Lloyd George: The Political Crisis of 1922* (Toronto: University of Toronto Press, 1973).

Chapter 2

1. Lord Dartmouth to Caroline Bridgeman, 2 October 1923, Viscountess Bridgeman Papers, SRO/CCB.

2. Asquith to Mrs. Harrison, 30 January 1920, in H. H. A[squith], *Letters of*

the Earl of Oxford and Asquith to a Friend (London: Geoffrey Bles, 1933–34), 1:124–25.

3. Beatrix Campbell, *The Iron Ladies: Why Do Women Vote Tory?* (London: Virago Press, 1987), 1.

4. *Gleanings and Memoranda,* June 1921, 542, and every June issue of *Home and Politics;* Southeastern Area Women's Parliamentary Committee, Annual Meeting, 30 June 1926; Principal Agent's Report on the Central Office, 1927–28, Stanley Baldwin Papers, 53/101–7; Chris Cook, *The Age of Alignment: Electoral Politics in Britain, 1922–1929* (Toronto: University of Toronto Press, 1975), 37–38; Pamela M. Graves, *Labour Women: Women in British Working-Class Politics, 1918–1939* (Cambridge: Cambridge University Press, 1994), 231. It is not clear whether Graves's figures include members both of the Women's Co-operative Guild and of the Labour Party. According to one author, there were only about 150,000 members in the 1,332 women's sections of the Labour Party (G. D. H. Cole, *A History of the Labour Party from 1914* [London: Routledge & Kegan Paul, 1948], 141).

5. "Report of the Committee Appointed by the Chairman of the Party to Enquire into the Working of the Central Office and to Make Recommendations for Reorganisation," 9 March 1931, CCO500/1/5, CPA.

6. Caroline Bridgeman to J. C. C. Davidson, 1 December 1929, J. C. C. Davidson Papers; *The Times,* 17 February 1966. Unfortunately, the published diary of Henry Channon does not contain information on the WUO or Lady Iveagh's work for the group.

7. *The Times,* 6 May 1975; *Home and Politics,* August 1923; Report of the Conservative Central Office Reorganisation Committee, 20 December 1927, CCO500/1/4; *Gleanings and Memoranda,* May 1928, 364; Sir Geoffrey Shakespeare, *Let Candles Be Brought In* (London: Macdonald, 1949), chap. 13.

8. Conservative and Unionist Central Office list of staff, [c. February 1928], Davidson Papers; Mrs. Costello to Miss Mackenzie, 24 August 1923, Mackenzie to Vice Admiral Sir Reginald Hall, 27 August 1923, and Pembroke Wicks to Costello, 27 January 1928, CCO 4/1/40; Central Office income and expenditure accounts, 1928, Davidson Papers; "The Women's Unionist Organisation of the National Unionist Association," *Archives of the British Conservative and Unionist Party,* series 1, *Pamphlets and Leaflets* (Hassocks, W. Sussex: Harvester Press, 1978), 1921/8, microfiche; memorandum from Miss Johnson [central office agent for Lancashire and Cheshire] to Lady Falmouth, 15 November 1930, CCO 500/1/5.

9. *Home and Politics,* August 1927; reports of the NUA/NUCUA Executive Committee to the Council, 29 June 1923, 28 February and 26 June 1928, and 26 February 1929, CPA. (Una Norris, a propagandist and the only female, nonclerical member of the Central Office Periodicals Section, was probably the editor of *Home and Politics.*) Wirral Conservative Association, Annual Meeting, 3 May 1926.

10. *Home and Politics,* June 1923 and August 1927.

11. NUA Executive Committee, 24 June 1919, CPA; *Pamphlets and Leaflets,* 1921/8; *Home and Politics,* June 1921.

12. Report of the NUA Council to the Conference, 1923; Stockton Women's Constitutional Organisation, Secretary's Reports, 1926 and 1928, and Annual Meetings, 17 February 1925 and 11 February 1926; Oswestry Women's Constitutional Association, Executive Committee, 9 July 1924, and Annual Report, 1928–29.

13. Bradford (City) Conservative Association, Annual Report, *Bradford Daily Argus,* 4 April 1921; Oswestry Women's Constitutional Association, Annual Report, 1920–21; Wirral Conservative Association, Women's Central Committee, 30 October 1923, and Annual Report, 1930; Launceston and District Women's Unionist Association, Annual Meeting, 17 January 1927; *Craven Herald,* 28 January 1927.

14. Stockton Women's Constitutional Organisation, Annual Meeting, 17 February 1925; Chichester Unionist Association, Organisation Subcommittee, 11 January 1928.

15. North Cornwall Conservative and Unionist Association, Executive Committee, 17 December 1925, 9 March and 12 July 1926, and 28 June 1927; SUA Eastern Division, Treasurer's Committee, 28 May and 18 July 1919; Council, 25 June 1919 and 27 July 1923; Executive Committee, 10 November 1924; and Special Committee, 9 December 1924.

16. Kincardine and West Aberdeenshire (hereafter Kincardine) Unionist Association, General Meeting, 28 September 1923, and Executive Committee, 13 June 1924; Camlachie Unionist Association, Annual Report, GUA Annual Report, 1926; SUA Eastern Division, Organisation and Propaganda Subcommittee, 12 June 1929.

17. Wrexham Women's Constitutional Association, Executive Committee, 10 March 1925; SUA Eastern Division, Annual Report, 1928.

18. NUA Conference, 18 November 1921; and *Home and Politics,* June 1923.

19. J. F. S. Ross, "Women and Parliamentary Elections," *British Journal of Sociology* 4 (1953): 23; Conservative Women's National Committee, *Fair Comment* (London: Conservative Central Office, [c. 1986], 48, for persistence of problem); Molly Izzard, *A Heroine in Her Time: A Life of Dame Helen Gwynne-Vaughan, 1879–1967* (London: Macmillan, 1969), 225–26.

20. NUA Conference, 25 October 1923; Jill Hills, "Britain," in *The Politics of the Second Electorate: Women and Public Participation,* edited by Joni Lovenduski and Jill Hills (London: Routledge & Kegan Paul, 1981), 20.

21. *CAJ,* April 1923, 68; *Primrose League Gazette,* June 1924; GUA Annual Report, 1928; *Launceston Weekly News,* 1 March 1924.

22. Oswestry Women's Constitutional Association, General Meeting, 20 November 1923, and Executive Committee, 5 January 1924; Harold Macmillan, *Winds of Change, 1914–1939* (London: Macmillan, 1966), 144.

23. Southgate Conservative and Unionist Association, Special Meeting, 18

April 1921, GLRO; *Pamphlets and Leaflets*, 1919/17–20 (includes "Who Are Ministers?" and "How Laws are Made").

24. GUA Executive Committee, 31 May 1920, 3 and 29 March 1926; Kincardine Unionist Association, Women's Committee, 20 February 1925; Launceston and District Women's Unionist Association, Executive Committee, 4 November and 10 December 1925, 4 April 1927.

25. According to the lists provided in the reports of the NUA/NUCUA Conferences, during 1920–29, 128 of 271 of the delegates from the ten English and Welsh divisions in my sample were women. These figures exclude agents, who were not counted as delegates.

26. The quotation is from the Stockton Women's Constitutional Organisation, General Meeting, 28 May 1925.

27. SUA Eastern Division, Training Subcommittee of the Women's Committee, 9 October 1923, and Annual Reports, 1924 and 1926; SUA Western Division, Annual Report, 1925; report of the NUCUA Council to the Conference, 1928.

28. *Home and Politics*, September 1923; Bradford Central Women's Conservative Association, 29 January 1929.

29. Wood Green Women's Constitutional Association, Annual Meeting, 22 February 1927.

30. *Bradford Daily Argus*, 5 November 1925; Wood Green Women's Constitutional Association, Executive Committee, 14 May 1919; *CAJ*, February 1925, 38; Palmers Green Constitutional Association, 19 March 1920.

31. *CAJ*, April 1922, 7–12.

32. *Home and Politics*, August 1927; *Launceston Weekly News*, 4 February 1928. See also Wood Green Women's Constitutional Association, Annual Meeting, 15 March 1922; *North Middlesex Chronicle*, 16 February 1929.

33. *Home and Politics*, August 1926, October 1923; SUA Eastern Division, Executive Committee, 23 January and 26 June 1929; report of the NUCUA Council to the Conference, 1926; Wrexham Women's Constitutional Association, Annual Meeting, 25 March 1924; idem, Executive Committee, 11 February 1925; and idem, Meeting of Branch Presidents and Secretaries, 16 February 1925; NUA Conference, 9 October 1925; *CAJ*, February 1926, 50.

34. *CAJ*, September 1923, 188–190; October 1923, 221; November 1923, 244, 251–52.

35. *CAJ*, August 1926, 261; December 1926, 375; April 1927, 108; June 1927, 154; Brian Harrison, *Separate Spheres: The Opposition to Women's Suffrage in Britain* (London: Croom Helm, 1978), 105; *Home and Politics*, March 1928; Conservative Women's National Committee, *Fair Comment*, 7.

36. *CAJ*, September 1919, 8.

37. Ibid., June 1920, 6–8.

38. Ibid., August 1920, 7–10.

39. Ibid., September 1920, 6–8; February 1921, 16–17.

40. Ibid., October 1920, 2–3.

41. Ibid., May 1924, 108; June 1924, 139.

42. Ibid., June 1924, 123; July 1924, 157–58; Metropolitan Conservative Agents' Association, Council, 16 May and 2 June 1924 (Maxse's speeches to London agents); *CAJ*, November 1927, 343, 303.

43. *CAJ*, January 1923, 36; J. C. C. Davidson, memorandum on "M" [Leigh Maclachlan], [c. 1927], Davidson Papers; Southeastern Area Women's Parliamentary Committee, 14 April 1921, and Annual Meeting, 27 June 1923.

44. Stockton Constitutional Organisation, Executive Committee, 18 September 1923; idem, Annual Meeting, 17 February 1925; and idem, Executive Committee, 20 February 1929; Chichester Women's Unionist Association, Annual Meeting, 7 February 1922, and Rules Subcommittee, 25 November 1925; *Chichester Observer*, 31 March 1926.

45. Clapham Conservative Association, Annual Meeting, 1 February 1926; Kincardine Unionist Association, Executive Committee, 4 January 1924; Yorkshire Provincial Division, Finance and General Purposes Committee, 28 May 1925; Wrexham Constitutional Association, Annual Meeting, 2 August 1919; Skipton Conservative Association, Executive Committee, 5 March 1921, 8 March 1924, and 31 January 1925.

46. Penycae Conservative Association, Annual Meeting, 11 June 1933. On the prewar era, see Patricia Hollis, *Ladies Elect: Women in Local Government, 1865–1914* (Oxford: Clarendon Press, 1987), 15.

47. For a recent balanced assessment of the impact of suffrage, see Martin Pugh, "The Impact of Women's Enfranchisement in Britain," in *Suffrage and Beyond: International Feminist Perspectives*, edited by Caroline Daley and Melanie Nolan (New York: New York University Press, 1994).

48. F. W. S. Craig, *British General Election Manifestos, 1918–1966* (Chichester, W. Sussex: Parliamentary Research Services, 1981), 10; *Home and Politics*, November 1922. For examples of the party's appeals to women, see W. A. S. Hewins Papers, 82; *Bradford Daily Argus*, 14 November 1922; and *Chichester Observer*, 15 November 1922.

49. *Pamphlets and Leaflets*, 1922/42, 51, 60; election address of Sir Henry S. Keith, 1923, SCCO; *Daily Notes*, 13 October 1924; election address of Alfred M. Williams, 1924, CPA.

50. *Pamphlets and Leaflets*, 1923/146–57; election address of Sir John Leigh, 1923, CPA; *Pamphlets and Leaflets*, 1923/171. (For an example of the use of this pamphlet in a newspaper, see *Launceston Weekly News*, 24 November 1923.)

51. The constituencies with a larger than average female electorate were Clapham, Wood Green, North Cornwall, Bradford Central, Chichester, and Skipton. Those with a smaller than average one included Kincardine, Oswestry, Wirral, Camlachie, Stockton, and Wrexham (see appendixes B and C).

John Turner, *British Politics and the Great War: Coalition and Conflict, 1915–1918* (New Haven: Yale University Press, 1992), 413–15.

52. Austen Chamberlain to Neville Chamberlain, 15 October 1923, quoted in Sir Charles Petrie, *The Life and Letters of the Right Hon. Sir Austen Chamberlain* (London: Cassell, 1940), 229; cutting from *Evening News*, 8 December 1923, David Lloyd George Papers, H/387; Cornwall Provincial Division, Annual Report, 1923; Sir William Bull to Hillary Bull, 11 February 1924, Sir William Bull Papers, 5/11, Churchill College Records Office, Cambridge University; *Home and Politics*, January 1924; *CAJ*, February 1924, 16; Lady Astor to [Sir John] Baird, 14 December 1923 (copy), Baldwin Papers, 35/129.

53. *Mearns Leader*, 31 October 1924; *Launceston Weekly News*, 8 November 1924; Stockton Constitutional Organisation, Women's Branch, Annual Meeting, 17 February 1925; *CAJ*, July 1926, 217. On the Empire products campaign, see also *Pamphlets and Leaflets*, 1925/12–14, 25.

54. Sir Samuel Hoare to Andrew Bonar Law, 31 October 1922, Bonar Law Papers, 109/2/22b; NUA, *The 1922 Campaign Guide* (Hassocks, W. Sussex: Harvester Press, 1976), 807–35 and 898–914, microfiche; *Glasgow Herald*, 14 November 1922.

55. *Bradford Daily Argus*, 22 and 25 October 1924; *Pamphlets and Leaflets*, 1924/208; *North Middlesex Chronicle*, 18 October 1924; Craig, *Election Manifestos*, 33–34.

56. *CAJ*, November 1927, 301; *Glasgow Herald*, 23 October 1926; Arthur Henderson, foreword to *Women and the Labour Party*, edited by Marion Phillips (New York: B. W. Huebsch, 1918), 5; Brian Harrison, *Prudent Revolutionaries: Portraits of British Feminists between the Wars* (Oxford: Clarendon Press, 1987), 307; Dorothy Howell-Thompson, *Socialism in West Sussex* (n.p., [c. 1983]), 22; Eleanor Gordon, *Women and the Labour Movement in Scotland, 1850–1914* (Oxford: Clarendon Press, 1991), chap. 7. See also Graves, *Labour Women*.

57. Frances Power Cobbe, *The Duties of Women* (1881), quoted in Pat Jalland, *Women, Marriage and Politics, 1860–1914* (Oxford: Clarendon Press, 1986), 7; *Primrose League Gazette*, 24 May 1890, quoted in Linda Walker, "Party Political Women: A Comparative Study of Liberal Women and the Primrose League, 1890–1914," in *Equal or Different: Women's Politics, 1800–1914*, edited by Jane Rendall (Oxford: Basil Blackwell, 1987), 173.

58. The Rev. Whitwell Elwin to Emily Lutton, 17 October 1893, quoted in Lady Emily Lutyens, *A Blessed Girl* (New York: J. B. Lippincott, 1954), 246; Lisa Tickner, *The Spectacle of Women: Imagery of the Suffrage Campaign, 1907–14* (Chicago: University of Chicago Press, 1988), 199; Harrison, *Separate Spheres*, 148; Sir Almroth Wright, *The Unexpurgated Case against Women's Suffrage* (1913), quoted in Tickner, *Spectacle of Women*, 156.

59. Mrs. Pankhurst quoted in Sandra Stanley Holton, *Feminism and Democracy: Women's Suffrage and Reform Politics in Britain, 1900–1918* (Cambridge: Cam-

bridge University Press, 1986), 14; Brian Harrison, "For Church, Queen and Family: The Girls' Friendly Society, 1874–1920," *Past & Present* 61 (1973): 107–38.

60. *Aberdeen Journal,* 29 September 1923; *Home and Politics,* June 1922, April 1924. There are essays by members of other WUO branches in the April through November 1924 issues.

61. *Home and Politics,* January and August 1921; Christopher Sykes, *Nancy: The Life of Nancy Astor* (New York: Harper & Row, 1972; reprint, Chicago: Academy Chicago Publishers, 1984), 219.

62. *1922 Campaign Guide,* 981, microfiche.

63. NUA Conference, 11 June 1920.

64. Ibid., 26 October 1923; Stockton Women's Constitutional Organisation, Executive Committee, 26 July 1928, and Annual Meeting, 17 February 1925.

65. NUA Conference, 26 October 1923; *The Times,* 27 October 1923, 11 May 1928; *Glasgow Herald,* 14 November 1925; *Home and Politics,* June 1928; Southeast Area Women's Parliamentary Committee, Executive Committee, 16 December 1925.

66. *Chichester Observer,* 28 February 1923; Hollis, *Ladies Elect,* 52; Sir Reginald Mitchell Banks, *The Conservative Outlook* (London: Chapman & Hall, 1929), 214.

67. Sykes, *Nancy,* 299–309; *Home and Politics,* June 1924 and May 1925 (discussions at the 1924 and 1925 WUO conferences about prohibiting alcohol); NUCUA Conference, 8 October 1926; *Home and Politics,* August 1923; SUA Eastern Division, Executive Committee, 28 March and 27 April 1923.

68. William Bridgeman to Caroline Bridgeman, 8 October 1921, Bridgeman Papers, 4629/1921/22; memoranda from the Records Branch [of the National Liberal Organisation], February 1920, Lloyd George Papers, G/119; NUA Executive Committee, 11 July 1922; Launceston and District Women's Unionist Association, Executive Committee, 11 July 1928; SUA Conference, 13 November 1924; address by WUO Organising Secretary Miss Goring-Thomas, Wood Green Women's Constitutional Association, Executive Committee, 7 April 1920; NUCUA, *The 1929 Campaign Guide* (Hassocks, W. Sussex: Harvester Press, 1976), 49, microfiche.

In disputing the argument that the 1920s was a wasted decade for the women's movement, Martin Pugh lists several major reforms for women, but fails to mention that the legislation was the work of the Conservatives (Pugh, "Impact," 321).

69. Duchess of Atholl, *Women and Politics* (London: Philip Allan, 1931), 118, 123; Sykes, *Nancy,* 251.

70. Campbell, *Iron Ladies,* 63; *Gleanings and Memoranda,* December 1918– April 1919, 67, 68; *Pamphlets and Leaflets,* 1920/3.

71. Nesta H. Webster, *World Revolution: The Plot against Civilization* (Boston: Small, Maynard, 1921), 324; *Pamphlets and Leaflets,* 1920/40; *Home and Politics,* July 1925.

72. *Primrose League Gazette,* September 1924; *Pamphlets and Leaflets,* 1924/22; "To Women," CCO 4/1/20; *North Middlesex Chronicle,* 10 May 1924.

73. Tickner, *Spectacle of Women,* 164 (quotation from *Punch,* 3 May 1871), and 210–11 (reproductions of relevant posters).

74. F. J. C. Hearnshaw, *Democracy and Labour* (London: Macmillan, 1924), 199.

75. *Home and Politics,* May 1922; *Pamphlets and Leaflets,* 1922/95.

76. *Pamphlets and Leaflets,* 1924/23, 1925/72, 1926/72. Jarvis claims that Lady Monica was modeled on Cynthia Mosley but offers no evidence (David Jarvis, "British Conservatism and Class Politics in the 1920s," *English Historical Review* 211 [1996]: 73).

77. *North Middlesex Chronicle,* 6 September 1919 (mothers of the Empire theme; cf. Anna Davin, "Imperialism and Motherhood," *History Workshop* 5 [1978]: 9–65); *Home and Politics,* April 1924 (women's censorship activities; cf. also SUA Conference, 13 November 1924, and SUA Eastern Division, Executive Committee, 23 June 1926); *Home and Politics,* June 1924; Southeast Area Women's Parliamentary Committee, Executive Committee, 16 December 1925; Lancashire and Cheshire Provincial Division, Annual Report, 1925–26.

78. Asquith to Mrs. Harrison, 4 January 1920, Asquith, *Letters of the Earl of Oxford,* 2:120–21; Hugh Dalton, *The Political Diaries of Hugh Dalton, 1918–40, 1945–60,* edited by Ben Pimlott (London: Jonathan Cape, 1986), 18 (3 May 1919); Lord Esher to Sir Philip Sassoon, 19 November 1922, quoted in Gilbert Martin, *Winston S. Churchill,* vol. 4, *1916–1922: The Stricken World* (Boston: Houghton Mifflin, 1975), 890.

79. Harrison, *Prudent Revolutionaries,* 75–77; Nancy Astor to Sir John Baird, 14 December 1923 (copy), Baldwin Papers 35/129; Sykes, *Nancy,* 354; John Barnes and David Nicholson, eds., *The Leo Amery Diaries* (London: Hutchinson, 1980), 1:569 (2 November 1928, discussing Lady Stanley); Robert Rhodes James, ed., *Chips: The Diaries of Sir Henry Channon* (London: Weidenfeld & Nicolson, 1967), 36 (16 June 1935).

80. Jix [Joynson-Hicks] to the prime minister [Baldwin], 2 April 1929, Baldwin Papers, 48/142–43; minutes of the Cabinet Policy Committee, Sir Laming Worthington-Evans Papers, 895/123–26; diary of Neville Chamberlain, 20 December 1926, Chamberlain Papers (reference to Birkenhead); John Grace to Egerton Macdona, (copy), 16 July 1931, Wirral Conservative Association Minute Book; Stanley Baldwin, *Our Inheritance* (Garden City, N.J.: Doubleday, Doran, 1928 [Baldwin's speech to the Union of Girls' Schools]); Miss Muriel Beckwith to J. C. C. Davidson, 7 November 1948, Davidson Papers; Thomas Jones, *Whitehall Diary,* edited by Keith Middlemas (London: Oxford University Press, 1969), 2:179 (13 April 1929).

81. S. J. Hetherington, *Katherine Atholl, 1874–1960: Against the Tide* (Aberdeen: Aberdeen University Press, 1989), chap. 11.

82. Atholl, *Women and Politics*, 168, 118; Lord Riddell, *Lord Riddell's Intimate Diary of the Peace Conference and After, 1918–1923* (New York: Reynal & Hitchcock, 1934), 316 (29 August 1921).

83. *The Times*, 15 May 1931; Graves, *Labour Women*, 85–98; and Sam Davies, "Class, Religion and Gender: Liverpool Labour Party and Women, 1918–1939," in *Popular Politics, Riot and Labour: Essays in Liverpool History, 1790–1940*, edited by John Belcham (Liverpool: Liverpool University Press, 1992), 217.

84. Tickner, *Spectacle of Women*, 213.

85. *Home and Politics*, May 1923; Campbell, *Iron Ladies*, 3.

86. On recent antifeminist thought, see Judith Stacy, "The New Conservative Feminism," *Feminist Studies* 9 (1983): 559–83; and Caroline Quest, ed., *Liberating Women . . . From Modern Feminism* (London: IEA Health and Welfare Unit, 1994). Kay Ebeling, "The Failure of Feminism" (*Newsweek*, 19 November 1990, 9) is one woman's challenge to feminism.

See also Hills, "Britain," 17; Joni Lovenduski, Pippa Norris, and Catriona Burness, "The Party and Women," in *Conservative Century: The Conservative Party since 1900*, edited by Anthony Seldon and Stuart Ball (Oxford: Oxford University Press, 1994), 615–16; *The Economist*, 13 January 1996, 54.

Chapter 3

1. John Springhall, *Youth, Empire and Society: British Youth Movements, 1883–1940* (London: Croom Helm, 1977), 134; Allen Warren, "'Mothers for the Empire'? The Girl Guides Association in Britain, 1909–1939," in *Making Imperial Mentalities: Socialisation and British Imperialism*, edited by J. A. Mangan (Manchester: Manchester University Press, 1990), 100; G. D. H. Cole, *A History of the Labour Party from 1914* (1948; reprint, London: Routledge & Kegan Paul, 1978), 143.

2. SUA Eastern Division, Annual Report, 1929.

3. *Launceston Weekly News*, 27 February 1926.

4. Announcement of inaugural meeting of the Junior Imperial and Constitutional League, 3 July 1906, CCO 506/1/1; *The Times* (London), 20 December 1906; *Junior Imperial and Constitutional League Handbook*, [c. 1905] CCO 506/1/7; and JIL Minute book, 1 November 1905–14 July 1909. (Note that honorary members dominated the JIL central body by virtue of their hefty subscriptions and regardless of their age, especially since there were few local branches to send representatives.) JIL Executive Committee, 15 October 1908, 13 September 1911, and 8 May 1912; Junior Imperial and Constitutional League Rules, 10 January 1912, CCO 506/1/1; Sir Herbert Williams, *Politics—Grave and Gay* (London: Hutchinson, [c. 1948]), 38; JIL Annual Report, 1911; Gerald Warner, *The Scottish Tory Party: A History* (London: Weidenfeld & Nicolson, 1988), 179.

5. Sheila Fitzpatrick, *The Russian Revolution, 1917–1932* (Oxford: Oxford University Press, 1982), 22; JIL Council, 20 February 1923; SUA Conference, 13 November 1924.

6. *Home and Politics*, June 1924; NUCUA Conference, 8 October 1926; NUCUA Council, 1 March 1927.

7. *Socialist and Other Sunday Schools*, April 1925, *Archives of the British Conservative and Unionist Party*, series 1, *Pamphlets and Leaflets* (Hassocks, W. Sussex: Harvester Press, 1978), 1925/7, microfiche. As examples of the concern about the Socialist Sunday Schools, see *Craven Herald*, 6 February 1925; cutting about 11 October 1922 social, North Ribblesdale Habitation of the Primrose League, Skipton and Ripon Conservative Central Office; Manningham Ward Conservative Association [in Bradford Central], 17 March 1922; Stockton JIL, 26 February 1924; *Aberdeen Press and Journal*, 1 October 1926; Washaway and District Unionist Association [in North Cornwall], 6 October 1926; Yorkshire Provincial Division Council, 19 November 1926; *The Times*, 16 May 1927; *Primrose League Gazette*, January 1921; *Home and Politics*, October 1927; *Popular View*, November 1921.

8. *Popular View*, April 1924; Lancashire and Cheshire Provincial Division, Council, 20 November 1926; *CAJ*, March 1927, 73–74; *Launceston Weekly News*, 17 October 1925; Launceston and District Women's Unionist Association, Executive Committee, 7 February 1927.

Southeastern Area Women's Parliamentary Committee, 16 December 1925. Bills similar to the Sedition and Blasphemous Teaching to Children bill also did not have party leaders' support (NUCUA Council, 28 June 1927; Primrose League Grand Council, 13 October 1927).

9. *CAJ*, September 1925, 212; *The Young Spirit in an Old Party*, February 1925, 75–76, *Pamphlets and Leaflets*, 1925/1; *Man in the Street*, August 1926.

10. Circular letter from the JIL Executive to the branches, October 1919, CCO 506/1/2; JIL Executive Committee, Publications Committee List of Pamphlets, 18 December 1919; JIL Council, 11 February 1920.

11. JIL Council, 10 December 1919, 12 May 1920; JIL Executive Committee, 15 June 1921; JIL Annual Report, 1921.

12. JIL Executive Committee, 28 May 1919; circular letter to the branches, October 1919. (*Young Spirit*, 77, claimed that 10 percent of JIL branches were segregated, but I found no good statistical information on this issue.) Tracy H. Koon, *Believe, Obey, Fight: Political Socialization of Youth in Fascist Italy, 1922–1943* (Chapel Hill: University of North Carolina Press, 1985); *JILG*, October 1921, March 1924; *Imp*, August 1925, March 1928.

13. *JILG*, August 1921; *Imp*, January 1927, May 1925.

14. Oswestry Women's Constitutional Association, Executive Committee, 9 July 1924; *Home and Politics*, October 1924; Oswestry Unionist Association, Annual Report, 1925; Stockton JIL, 26 September, 4 October 1923; Lancashire and Cheshire

Federation of Junior Conservative and Unionist Associations, Annual Meetings, 1 March 1924, 10 September 1921, 31 March 1928, and Special General Meeting, 12 November 1927; *Young Spirit*, 39–40.

15. Sir Malcolm Fraser to Lt. Col. R. D. Waterhouse [Andrew Bonar Law's secretary], 18 February 1921, Andrew Bonar Law Papers, 96/7; Sir H. M. Imbert-Terry to Fraser, 8 and 10 February 1921, CCO 4/1/28; Fraser to H. H. Cannell, 10 February 1921, CCO 4/1/28; JIL Council, 9 February 1921; JIL Executive Committee, Publications Subcommittee, 13 January–12 May 1920, 11 May 1921; JIL Executive Committee, 12 October, 14 December 1921; *The Times*, 10 April 1922.

16. NUA Conference, 15 December 1922; JIL Council, 13 June 1923.

17. NUA Executive Committee, 13 March and 12 June 1923, 15 July and 9 September 1924; JIL Finance Committee, 14 March 1923; JIL Annual Report, 1924; *JILG*, April 1924; JIL Council, 12 November 1924.

18. JIL Council, 13 October 1926; JIL Executive Committee, 27 October 1926, 12 November 1924; Bonar Law to Imbert-Terry, 15 April 1918, Bonar Law Papers 84/7/21; diary of Sir Cuthbert Morley Headlam, 3 October 1924; JIL Executive Committee, 13 April and 4 May 1927.

19. *Imp*, April 1928, June 1927.

20. JIL Executive Committee, 12 February and 13 July 1927; JIL Finance Committee, 23 May 1928; Leigh Maclachlan, Central Office Report for 1927, 1st Earl Baldwin of Bewdley Papers, 53/103–6; report from the general director of central office to the chairman of the Cuts and Reorganisation Committee, 30 July 1931, 3, Central Office Reorganisation Committee, CCO 500/1/5; JIL Executive Committee, 8 October 1924; JIL Annual Report, 1925; reports of the NUA Executive to the Council, 1 July 1924, 22 June 1926, 28 February 1928, and 26 February 1929; and JIL Annual Reports, 1926 and 1927.

21. *The Junior Imperial and Constitutional League Handbook for Organisers and Workers*, [c. 1925], 12–13, CCO 506/5/2 (lowering the affiliation fee from 10s plus 5s for each group of five branches beyond the first ten, to a straight fee of 2s 6d for every five branches in the federation); Yorkshire Provincial Division Council, 18 December 1924; JIL Annual Reports, 1925 and 1929; JIL Council, 10 November 1928.

22. The Stockton branch was an exception, but it had to be re-formed in 1923 (Stockton Constitutional Organisation, Annual Meeting, 26 February 1919).

23. *Imp*, July 1926; JIL Executive Committee, 10 October 1928; JIL Council, 23 February 1929; JIL Annual Report, 1929; North Cornwall JIL Minute Book, 1928–1929; North Cornwall Conservative and Unionist Association, Annual Meeting, 14 March 1927.

24. JIL Executive, 9 February 1921; *JILG*, September and October 1921; Stockton JIL, 4–16 October 1923; Bradford (City) Conservative Association, Executive Committee, 25 February 1924. (The minute book of the Bradford Central JIL dates from 1929, but internal evidence and the *JILG* [April 1924] suggest that it was

formed in 1924 and re-formed in 1928 ["Alterations to Branch Rules," 10 November 1928, Bradford Central Junior Imperial League Minute Book].) The quotation is from Headlam diary, 4 September 1924.

25. SUA Western Division, Annual Reports, 1925–29; GUA Annual Reports, 1914 and 1921–23; *Glasgow Herald,* 7 April 1922, 24 January 1929, 23 November 1928; SUA Eastern Division, Executive Committee, 22 June 1927 and 3 October 1929; idem, Literature Committee, 5 March 1928; idem, Annual Report, 1929; Kincardine and West Aberdeenshire (hereafter Kincardine) Unionist Association, Organisation Committee, 24 April and 18 December 1925; *Mearns Leader,* 26 August 1927; Kincardine Unionist Association, Executive Committee, 13 December 1929; Col. P. J. Blair [political secretary to the Scottish whip], "Impressions of the General Election," 12 July 1929, Sir John Gilmour Papers, GD 383/29/34x.

26. JIL Council, 11 February 1914; Imbert-Terry to Chamberlain, 31 January 1922, Sir Austen Chamberlain Papers, AC 32/3/5; Sir Alan J. Sykes to Sir William Bull, 12 January 1922, Sir William Bull Papers, 5/5, Churchill College Record Office; JIL Executive Committee, 12 November 1919.

27. Oswestry Women's Constitutional Association, Executive Committee, 9 July 1924 and 17 January 1925, and Annual Meeting, 9 May 1925.

28. JIL Executive Committee, 14 April 1920; *Imp,* September 1925; *CAJ,* December 1927, 347; J. C. C. Davidson, notes of a meeting with Lord Stanley and H. Robert Topping, 12 March 1928, J. C. C. Davidson Papers; Lord Stanley to Lord Beaverbrook and reply, 12 and 13 November 1928, Lord Beaverbrook Papers, B/32.

29. Launceston and District Women's Unionist Association, Executive Committee, 29 May 1925; *Launceston Weekly News,* 17 October 1925; *Imp,* April 1927; Oswestry Unionist Association, Executive Committee, 9 May 1925; Chichester Unionist Association, Financial and General Purposes Committee, 29 October 1928, 26 August 1929; Wrexham and East Denbighshire Constitutional Association, Executive Committee, 7 April; Bradford Central Junior Conservative and Unionist Association, January–December 1929.

30. *JILG,* March 1924; Wood Green Constitutional Association, receipts and expenditures, 1928–29; JIL Conference, 2 November 1929 (*The Times,* 4 November 1929). The membership figure is a rough estimate. Before the war there were about 285 members per branch. If this ratio is used for 1929, when there were 1,690 active branches, JIL membership was almost half a million. Rural Cornwall, however, had an average of 123 members in 35 branches but 300 Imps in Launceston (Cornwall Provincial Division, 1928 Annual Report; and *Launceston Weekly News,* 29 January 1927). A 1934 document claimed that there were six million youths in the organization, but this probably indicated participants rather than members ("The Junior Imperial and Constitutional League," October 1934, CCO 506/5/7).

31. *JILG,* November 1923; *JIL Handbook* (1925), 22. In practice subscriptions were often lower (*Home and Politics,* October 1924).

32. *Imp*, October 1925; JIL Annual Report, 1926.

33. *JILG*, September 1923.

34. Williams, *Politics*, 220; NUA Executive Committee, Report of the Speakers' Subcommittee, 10 February 1920; GUA Annual Report, 1922; *JILG*, August 1921, January 1922, October 1923; Leigh Maclachlan, Central Office Report for 1927, Baldwin Papers, 53/105–6; Bradford Central Junior Conservative and Unionist Association, 14 February 1929; Stockton JIL, 26 February 1924–17 March 1925.

35. Stockton JIL, 19 December 1923–15 April 1924; Bradford Central Junior Conservative and Unionist Association, Executive Committee, 11 November 1929 and 13 January 1930; Stockton JIL, 13 January and 17 February 1925; *Imp*, August 1925 (list of seventy-one different topics).

36. *Launceston Weekly News*, 6 March 1926; Stockton JIL, 3 March 1925.

37. JIL Annual Reports, 1924 and 1925; *Young Spirit*, 55–56; *JILG*, July 1923; *Imp*, August 1928.

38. *Imp*, April 1927; Southeastern Area Women's Advisory Council, Executive Committee, 30 January 1929 (and cf. Patrick Hannon diary, 16 April 1921, Sir Patrick Hannon Papers); *JILG*, September 1923.

39. Stanley Baldwin, "Democracy and the Spirit of Service," "Rhetoric," in idem, *On England* (London: Philip Allan, 1926), 91, 96; *Imp*, July 1926; Lucy Masterman, *C. F. G. Masterman* (London: Frank Cass, 1968), 337 (Masterman quotation).

40. *Imp*, April 1928 (Baldwin's speech). The "Whisper" was an innovation of the interwar JIL and an early sign of Britain's burgeoning youth culture. Sir Archibald Salvidge to Lord Derby, 12 March 1928, 17th Earl of Derby Papers, 920 DER (17)/8/7; JIL Executive Committee, 28 March 1928. The speech appeared as the leaflet "Democracy, Youth and Patriotism" (*Pamphlets and Leaflets*, 1928/6) and later as "Be Ready!" in Stanley Baldwin, *This Torch of Freedom* (London: Hodder & Stoughton, 1935), 308–15.

41. JIL Executive Committee, 23 June 1920; JIL Annual Report, 1921; JIL Executive Committee, 15 March 1922, 11 November 1925; "Hints on Canvassing," *Pamphlets and Leaflets*, 1924/69; Bradford Central Junior Conservative and Unionist Association, Executive Committee, 8 April 1929; GUA Executive Committee, 25 April 1921; *JIL Handbook* (1925), 30–31.

42. *JILG*, December 1923.

43. Ibid., February 1924.

44. North Cornwall Conservative and Unionist Association, Executive Committee, 4 November 1929, and Finance Committee, 25 January 1930; Stockton Women's Constitutional Organisation, Annual Meeting, 11 February 1926.

45. *Imp*, January 1927; *The Times*, 4 July 1929.

46. *Imp*, March 1927, November 1926, August 1925; *The Times*, 4 November 1929, 9 May 1938 (attempts to alter the name).

47. *JIL Handbook* (1925), 26; *Imp*, January 1927; JIL Annual Reports, 1921 and

1925. Supporters established the prizes just before the war (JIL Council, 11 November 1913; JIL Executive Committee, 14 January 1914).

48. Caption to photograph of the Greenwich Branch Fete, JIL Scrapbook, CCO 506/3/1; JIL Annual Report, 1921; *JILG*, July and October 1923; Bradford Central Junior Conservative and Unionist Association, Executive Committee, 18 March–30 May 1929; Stockton JIL, 29 January 1924; Wrexham Women's Constitutional Association, Annual Meeting, 25 March 1924; GUA Executive Committee, 29 May 1922; SUA Eastern Division, Executive Committee, 23 May and 26 June 1928; JIL Executive Committee, 2 November 1927 and 11 January 1928 (summer camp); *Imp* December 1927 (summer camp); *Primrose League Gazette*, September 1924.

On the origins of the national sports day, see JIL Sports Subcommittee, 28 March–14 May 1930; and "The Junior Imperial and Constitutional League," 1934. On sports and Conservatism, see John M. MacKenzie, *Propaganda and Empire: The Manipulation of British Public Opinion, 1880–1960* (Dover, N.H.: Manchester University Press, 1984), 228–29.

49. *JILG*, August 1923, January 1922; *Imp*, January 1927; Sir Colin Norman Thornton-Kelmsley, *Through Winds and Tides* (Montrose, Scotland: Standard Press, 1974), 34; *News Chronicle*, cutting, 23 January 1960, JIL Press-Cuttings File, CCO 506/3/3; NUCUA Conference, 6 October 1927.

50. *Young Spirit*, 42, 9–11; *Imp*, October 1925.

51. Martin Pugh, *The Tories and the People* (New York: Basil Blackwell, 1985), 163–83; Primrose League Grand Council, 4 February 1926.

52. *Primrose League Gazette*, [Autumn 1922]. Because members had to pay a five-shilling entry charge and a two-and-a-half-shilling subscription, few working-class children could have afforded to join the Buds. See also Primrose League Grand Council, 7 June 1923, and Juniors Report, 1 November 1923.

53. NUA Executive Committee, 9 June 1925; JIL Council, 12 November 1924 and 11 February 1925. Unfortunately none of the minute books of the Young Britons has survived. See also NUCUA, *Handbook on the Young Britons* (1931) 4, CCO 506/7/1.

54. *Home and Politics*, August 1925; reports of the NUCUA Executive Committee to the Council, 1 March 1927, 28 February 1928, and 26 February 1929; *CAJ*, July 1927, 203–4.

55. *Handbook on Young Britons*, 5; *The Times*, 5 January 1926; Launceston and District Women's Unionist Association, 1 February, 1 March, and 12 April 1926, and the association's cutting of the *Launceston Weekly News*, 8 January 1926; Stockton Women's Constitutional Organisation, 11 November 1927; Kincardine Unionist Association, Women's Committee, 2 October 1925 and 23 April 1926, and Organisation Committee, 18 December 1925.

56. Young Britons Annual Meeting, 28 May 1927 (*Home and Politics*, July 1927); JIL Executive Committee, 11 January and 18 February 1928, 10 April and 9 October 1929, and 21 July 1926.

57. SUA Eastern Division, Executive Committee, 23 February and 23 March 1921; *Glasgow Herald*, 1 March and 14 November 1924, 26 January 1925; SUA Western Division, Annual Reports, 1925, 1927, 1928; GUA Annual Reports, 1927, 1929.

58. *Pamphlets and Leaflets*, 1927/42.

59. *Home and Politics*, May 1925.

60. *Young Briton*, February 1926. The elements described are repeated endlessly and can be found in any issue of the magazine.

61. *Pamphlets and Leaflets*, 1925/58, 1926/23–27.

62. *Handbook on Young Britons*, 13, 19; *Launceston Weekly News*, 8 January and 4 February 1926 (see also 4 September 1926).

63. *Handbook on Young Britons*, 20, 25; "Empire Day," *Pamphlets and Leaflets*, 1925/55; Anne Bloomfield, "Drill and Dance as Symbols of Imperialism," in Mangan, ed., *Imperial Mentalities*, 81; *Launceston Weekly News*, 30 October 1926.

64. Una Norris, *The Flag of the Free* (*Pamphlets and Leaflets*, 1928/85).

65. *Mearns Leader*, 28 May 1926.

66. *Home and Politics*, July 1928.

67. Report of the Committee Appointed by the Chairman of the Party to Enquire into the Working of the Central Office and to Make Recommendations for Re-Organisation, 9 March 1931, Central Office Re-Organisation Committee, CCO 500/1/5.

68. *Home and Politics*, October 1927.

69. JIL Scrapbook, CCO 506/3/1.

Chapter 4

1. See Eric Nordlinger, *The Working-Class Tories: Authority, Deference and Stable Democracy* (Los Angeles: University of California Press, 1967); and Robert McKenzie and Alan Silver, *Angels in Marble: Working Class Conservatives in Urban England* (Chicago: University of Chicago Press, 1968). For a recent critique of the traditional, teleological interpretation, see John Turner, *British Politics and the Great War: Coalition and Conflict, 1915–1918* (New Haven: Yale University Press, 1992), 435–36.

2. For an example of the traditional interpretation in one of the few scholarly studies of the 1927 legislation, see Melvin C. Shefftz, "The Trade Disputes and Trade Unions Act of 1927: The Aftermath of the General Strike," *The Review of Politics* 29 (1967): 387–406.

3. A. Lawrence Lowell, *The Government of England* (New York: Macmillan, 1908), 2:7; Cornwall Provincial Division, Annual Meeting, 9 December 1920; Wrexham and East Denbighshire (hereafter Wrexham) Constitutional Association, Executive Committee, 31 March 1924, and Organisation Committee, 19 August 1924; Lancashire and Cheshire Provincial Division Council, 17 November 1928; Stanley

Salvidge, *Salvidge of Liverpool: Behind the Political Scene, 1890–1928* (London: Hodder & Stoughton, 1934), 15–17; final report of the Unionist Reorganisation Committee, June 1911, CCO 500/1/2; report from the general director of publicity to the chairman of the Cuts and Reorganisation Committee, 30 July 1931, Central Office Reorganisation Committee, CCO 500/1/5.

4. *CAJ*, May 1925, 92–93; diary of Sir Cuthbert Morley Headlam, 25 and 29 September 1924. On the pre-1914 history of Conservative efforts, see letters to the editor, *CAJ*, May-July 1925; John Richard Greenwood, "Central Control and Constituency Autonomy in the Conservative Party: The Organisation of 'Labour' and Trade Unionist Support, 1918–1970" (Ph.D. diss., University of Reading, 1981), 54–57; NUA Labour Committee, 8 December 1924 and 12 January 1925, NUA 6/1/2; *The Young Spirit in an Old Party*, February 1925, *The Archives of the British Conservative and Unionist Party*, series 1, *Pamphlets and Leaflets* (Hassocks, W. Sussex: Harvester Press, 1978), 1925/1, microfiche, 20–27.

5. *CAJ*, May 1920, 4; Lancashire Provincial Division Account Book, Labour Committee Accounts, September 1918–December 1919; letters between Long and Younger, 12–15 September 1918, Walter Long Papers, 947/682, Wiltshire Record Office.

6. NUA Labour Committee, 2 July, 22 July, and 5 August 1919, NUA 6/1/3, 6/1/1; NUA Executive Committee, 15 July and 14 October 1919; *CAJ*, May 1924, 110–11; and *The Times*, 20 March 1930.

7. NUA Council, 18 November 1919, CPA; *Gleanings and Memoranda*, April 1920, 262; report of the NUA Executive Committee to the Council, 14 October 1919; NUA Labour Committee, Report of the Southport Conference, 16 March 1920, NUA 6/1/3; *Pamphlets and Leaflets*, 1920/36; *Home and Politics*, November 1920.

8. *CAJ*, May 1920, 8; Greenwood, "Organisation of 'Labour,'" 92–93; *CAJ*, November 1923, 256.

9. NUA Conference, 15–16 December 1922; Younger to Bonar Law, 30 December 1922, Andrew Bonar Law Papers, 111/34/162; Yorkshire Provincial Division Council, 9 March 1923; Wirral Conservative Association, Annual Meeting, 11 May 1923 (*Birkenhead Advertiser*, 12 May 1923); NUA Executive Committee, 12 June 1923.

10. NUA Conference, 25 October 1923; *Home and Politics*, February 1924.

11. *CAJ*, October 1923, 217; NUA Conference, 2 October 1924; NUA Executive Committee, 9 December 1924. NUA Labour Committee, 7 March 1921, 10 September and 9 October 1922, NUA 6/1/1; report of the NUA Executive Committee to the Council, 5 February 1923. W. A. Appleton discusses the work and attitudes of a GFTU leader in *Trade Unions: Their Past, Present, and Future* (London: Philip Allan, 1925).

12. Report of the Principal Agent to the [NUA] Executive Committee, 22 July 1924, NUA Labour Committee, NUA 6/1/3.

13. NUA Executive Committee, 15 July 1924; NUA Conference, 2 October 1924; *Home and Politics*, November 1924; NUCUA Executive Committee, 10 Febru-

ary and 10 March 1925; NUCUA Labour Committee, 7 November 1927, NUA 6/1/ 4; Greenwood, "Organisation of 'Labour,'" 111–13.

14. Lancashire and Cheshire Provincial Division Council, Labour Advisory Committee Report, 3 November and 5 December 1925; Yorkshire Provincial Division, Executive Committee, 2 May 1924; report of the NUCUA Council to the Conference, 1929; Cornwall Provincial Division, Executive Committee, 29 April 1920, and Annual Meeting, 9 December 1920.

15. J. T. Ward, *The First Century: A History of Scottish Tory Organisation, 1882–1982* (Edinburgh: Scottish Unionist and Conservative Association, 1982), 22; *Man in the Street,* January 1925; SUA Eastern Division, Treasurers' Committee, 8 May 1919; idem, Executive Committee, 26 January 1921; and idem, Council, 26 October [1923]; Special Meeting of Unionist Workers' League and SUA Eastern Division, 29 September 1924; SUA Eastern Division, Executive Committee, 10 November 1924, and Treasurers' Committee, 29 April 1925; SUA Annual Report, 1928.

16. NUA Labour Committee, 15 November and 13 December 1920, NUA 6/1/ 3; Clapham Conservative Association, Rules, [c. 1920]; Clapham Conservative Association, 14 May 1923; North Cornwall Conservative and Unionist Association, Executive Committee, 9 March 1925, 9 March and 12 July 1926.

17. Greenwood, "Organisation of 'Labour,'" 88; Wrexham Constitutional Association, Annual Meeting, 18 April 1921, and Finance Committee, 25 May 1922; *North Wales Guardian,* 12 May 1922; Bradford Central Conservative Association, Annual Meeting, 17 March 1921 (*Bradford Daily Argus,* 18 March 1921); Bradford (City) Conservative Association, Annual Meeting, 5 April 1921, (*Bradford Daily Argus,* 6 April 1921); Stockton-on-Tees (hereafter Stockton) Constitutional Organisation, Executive Committee, 25 September 1925; Stockton Unionist Labour Advisory Committee, 7 October 1925–28 January 1926, membership lists, [1925?], 1927, 1930, and 1931, and membership lists for Norton and Thornaby NCL lodges, undated.

18. North Cornwall Unionist Association, Rules, 25 February 1919; Chichester Unionist Association, Finance and General Purposes Committee, 16 September 1924; Skipton Conservative Association, Executive Committee, 15 January 1921; Oswestry Women's Constitutional Association, Executive Committee, 27 March 1920; and Oswestry Unionist Association, Executive Committee, 3 February 1925.

19. Oswestry Unionist Association, Executive Committee, 12 April 1924, 22 August 1925, and 8 December 1928; Oswestry Women's Constitutional Association, Executive Committee, 18 December 1925; Chichester Unionist Association, Finance and General Purposes Committee, 17 December 1924; North Cornwall Unionist Association, Finance Committee, 26 February 1924; Yorkshire Provincial Division Council, 2 May 1924. See also Skipton Conservative Association, Executive Committee, 30 September 1922.

20. Yorkshire Provincial Division Council, 25 March 1927; Chichester Unionist Association, Finance and General Purposes Committee, 9 February and 28 October 1925; NUCUA Executive Committee, 9 December 1924.

21. Report of the NUCUA Executive to the Council, 2 July 1929.

22. *CAJ*, March 1920, 2; Stockton Unionist Labour Advisory Committee, 5 November 1925 and 11 February 1926; Stockton Constitutional Organisation, Education and Entertainment Committee, 11 November 1926 and 11 January 1927.

23. NUA Executive Committee, Report of the Labour Committee, 16 November 1920; Bradford (City) Conservative Association, Annual Report, 1922 (*Bradford Daily Argus*, 22 March 1922); Wrexham Constitutional Association, Finance Committee, 25 May 1922; NUA Labour Committee, 6 February 1922, NUA 6/1/1; Greenwood, "Organisation of 'Labour,'" 146–47; NUCUA Council, 24 February 1925.

24. NUCUA Conference, 27 September 1928.

25. NUA Executive Committee, 7 June 1921; Greenwood, "Organisation of 'Labour,'" 152, 151; Michael Shanks, *Political Quarterly* (1959), quoted in Greenwood, "Organisation of 'Labour,'" 384.

26. NUA Executive, 16 November 1920; Stockton Unionist Labour Advisory Committee, 23 November 1927, 13 February 1929. See also Frank Solbe [secretary of the Association of Conservative Clubs] to Bonar Law, 9 November 1922, Bonar Law Papers, 114/5/1.

27. Yorkshire Provincial Division, Executive Committee, 17 July 1925; *CAJ*, November 1926, 344; Stockton Unionist Labour Advisory Committee, 28 January 1926–19 January 1927, 2 November 1927–18 January 1928.

28. For the trade union–Labour perspective, see D. F. MacDonald, *The State and the Trade Unions* (London: Macmillan, 1976); for the traditional interpretation, see Shefftz, "Trade Disputes Act," 396.

29. R. C. K. Ensor, *England, 1870–1914* (Oxford: Clarendon Press, 1936), 438.

30. Michael Pinto-Duschinsky, *British Political Finances, 1830–1980* (Washington, D.C.: American Enterprise Institute for Public Policy Research, 1981), 67–72; *Annual Abstract of Statistics for the United Kingdom*, vol. 75, 1913 and 1917–1930 (reprint, Nendeln, Liechtenstein: Kraus, 1966), 109–13 (figures refer only to the official political funds of registered unions); Stockton Unionist Labour Advisory Committee, 14 October 1925.

31. Lancashire and Cheshire Federation of Junior Conservative and Unionist Associations, Annual Meeting, 11 September 1920; SUA Eastern Division Council, 22 June 1921; NUA Council, 22 February and 21 June 1921; SUA Conference, 31 January 1923; Lady Glenarthur to Bonar Law, 16 February 1923, Bonar Law Papers, 112/20/1; WUO Conference, 8 May 1924 (*Home and Politics*, June 1924); Eden Philpotts, letter to the editor of *The Times*, 13 April 1921; Patrick Ford, letter to the editor of *The Times*, 13 October 1925; Austen Chamberlain to Sir John Gilmour, 7 July 1921, Chamberlain Papers, AC 24/3/45 (copy); *CAJ*, October 1923, 216.

32. L. S. Amery to Stanley Baldwin, 3 August 1927, 1st Earl Baldwin of Bewdley Papers, 59/154–61; *Gleanings and Memoranda*, April 1925, 451; George N. Barnes, *From Workshop to War Cabinet* (New York: D. Appleton, 1924), 50–51, 59.

33. NUA Conference, 10 June 1920; NUA Labour Committee, 8 November 1920, NUA 6/1/1; *CAJ*, March 1920, 5; WUO Conference, 20 October 1920 (*Home and Politics*, November 1920); Greenwood, "Organisation of 'Labour,'" 129; F. J. C. Hearnshaw, *Democracy and Labour* (London: Macmillan, 1924), 99–100.

34. Tribute for Henry Wilson-Fox, *The Times*, 25 November 1921; *House of Commons Debates* (hereafter *H.C. Debates*), 5th ser., 140, col. 1889 (20 April 1921); NUA Executive Committee, Labour Committee Reports, 8 March and 10 May 1921; SUA Conference, 19 January 1922; NUA Conference, 18 November 1922; *H.C. Debates*, 154, cols. 692–93, 727, 741 (19 May 1922).

35. NUA Council, 27 June 1922; *CAJ*, July 1922, 21; Skipton Conservative Association, Executive Committee, 26 June 1922; Bradford (City) Conservative Association, Executive Committee, 16 May 1922; North Cornwall Unionist Association, Executive Committee, 16 June 1922; Cheshire Provincial Division, Annual Meeting, 22 July 1922; JIL Executive Committee, 14 June 1922; SUA Eastern Division Council, 23 June 1922; NUA Executive Committee, 13 June 1922; *Home and Politics*, July 1922; *Gleanings and Memoranda*, June 1922, 518.

36. Cornwall Provincial Division, Annual Report, 1922; *Popular View*, August 1922; *CAJ*, October 1922, 8–9; untitled newspaper cutting of Durham Provincial Division, Annual Meeting, 2 September 1922 (Stockton Constitutional Organisation Minute Book); Derby to Austen Chamberlain, 11 September 1922, Chamberlain Papers, AC 33/2/15; Wilson to Chamberlain, September 1922, Chamberlain Papers, AC 33/2/26; NUA Executive Committee, 10 October 1922.

37. Sir George Younger to Andrew Bonar Law, 30 December 1922, Bonar Law Papers, 111/34/162; Younger to Ronald Waterhouse, 21 March [1923], Bonar Law Papers, 114/9; NUA Council, 29 June 1923; Hall to [J. C. C.] David[son], 23 July 1923, J. C. C. Davidson Papers; *The Times*, 26 October 1923; NUA Labour Committee, 12 November 1923, NUA 6/1/1.

38. *H.C. Debates*, 5th ser., 170, cols. 2778–79 (14 March 1924); NUA Labour Committee, 10 March 1924, NUA 6/1/1; NUA Executive Committee, 8 April 1924; memorandum from the Labour Committee, undated, Unionist Leaders' Conference, Viscount Cave Papers, 62489 35(4); *Gleanings and Memoranda*, April 1924, 451–52; memoranda on the earlier history of the Trade Unions Act of 1913 Amendment Bill, 3 and 12 March 1924, Cave Papers, 62489 35(4); NUA Labour Committee, 12 May 1924, NUA 6/1/1; NUA Executive Committee, 13 and 17 May 1924; Unionist Leaders' Conference, 14 and 28 May 1924, Cave Papers, 62489 35(4); *Looking Ahead* (London: National Unionist Association, [1924]), 7.

39. NUCUA Executive Committee, 13 January and 10 February 1925; NUCUA Labour Committee, 8 December 1924, NUA 6/1/2; *Gleanings and Memoranda*, April 1925, 448; NUCUA Council, 24 February 1925; Philip Goodhart with Ursula Branston, *The 1922: The Story of the Conservative Backbenchers Parliamentary Committee* (London: Macmillan, 1973), 28. See also Skipton Conservative Association,

21 February 1925; *Craven Herald*, 6 March 1925; Wrexham Constitutional Association, Executive Committee, 3 March 1925; and GUA, Executive Committee, 23 February 1925.

40. Kincardine and West Aberdeenshire Unionist Association, Executive Committee, 27 February 1925, photocopy of Minute Book; Alfred Duff Cooper, *Old Men Forget* (New York: Carroll & Graf, 1988), 143; John Campbell, *F. E. Smith: First Earl of Birkenhead* (London: Jonathan Cape, 1983), 764; John Evelyn Wrench, *Geoffrey Dawson and Our Times* (London: Hutchinson, 1955), 237; Webb to Professor William Robson, 18 February 1925, in *The Letters of Sidney and Beatrice Webb*, edited by Norman MacKenzie (Cambridge: Cambridge University Press, 1978), 224.

41. Excerpts of letter from Macquisten to Baldwin, 23 October 1925 (*The Times*, 29 October 1925); Stanley Baldwin, "Peace in Industry I," in Stanley Baldwin, *On England* (London: Philip Allan, 1926), 33.

42. *H.C. Debates*, 5th ser., 181, cols. 822, 838–40 (6 March 1925); *The Times*, 7 March 1925. For examples of the bemused reaction, see *H.C. Debates*, 181, col. 882; and Cooper, *Old Men Forget*, 143. Baldwin's speech was widely distributed by central office (report of the NUCUA Executive Committee to the Council, 30 June 1925).

43. *H.C. Debates*, 5th ser., 181, cols. 850–53, 870–71, 875 (6 March 1925); and *The Times*, 7 March 1925.

44. NUCUA Executive Committee, 10 March 1925; F. Stanley Jackson to Lord Derby, 24 March 1925, 17th Earl of Derby Papers, 920 DER (17)/31/4; NUCUA Labour Committee, 6 April 1925, NUA 6/1/2; *Man in the Street*, September 1925; *Trade Unionism at the Cross-Roads: Soviets or Sanity*, (*Pamphlets and Leaflets*, 1925/67).

45. NUCUA Conference, 8–9 October 1925.

46. Excerpts of letter from Macquisten to Baldwin, [23 October 1925] (*The Times*, 29 October 1925); NUCUA Council, 23 February 1926; Patrick Renshaw, "Anti-Labour Politics in Britain, 1918–27," *Journal of Contemporary History* 12 (1977): 700–701; Birkenhead to Lord Reading, 8 October 1925 (quoted in Campbell, *F. E. Smith*, 768); *Gleanings and Memoranda*, December 1925, 658.

47. Barnes, *War Cabinet*, 102; report of the NUCUA Executive Committee to the Council, 22 June 1926; *Pamphlets and Leaflets*, 1926/45 and 1926/50; Baldwin quoted in Adam Gowans Whyte, *Stanley Baldwin* (London: Chapman & Hall, 1926), 159–60; Bradford (City) Conservative Association, Executive Committee, copy of resolution of support, [6 May 1926]; resolution from the Stockton-on-Tees Lodge of the National Conservative League, 15 May 1926, Baldwin Papers, 138/220. (In the Baldwin papers are two files containing nearly three hundred letters of support from Conservative organizations [Baldwin Papers, 137–38]).

48. *H.C. Debates*, 5th ser., 196, cols. 1966–67 (14 June 1926); 198, cols. 2618–19 (2 August 1926); Lord Swinton, *I Remember* (London: Hutchinson, [1948]), 48; diary of Neville Chamberlain, 10 and 16 March 1927, Chamberlain Papers, NC 2/22; Keith Feiling, *The Life of Neville Chamberlain* (1946; reprint, Hamden, Conn.:

Archon Books, 1970), 159; Goodhart, *1922 Committee*, 34; NUCUA Conference, 7 October 1926; Cornwall Provincial Division, Annual Report, 1926; *The Times*, 14 May–26 June 1926; *Birkenhead Advertiser*, 26 June 1926; *North Middlesex Chronicle*, 26 June 1926; *Darlington and Stockton Times*, 24 July 1926; Wirral Conservative Association, Annual Meeting, 17 June 1927; Skipton Conservative Association, Executive Committee, 22 June 1926.

49. NUCUA Council, 22 June 1926; John Barnes and David Nicholson, eds., *The Leo Amery Diaries* (London: Hutchinson, 1980), 1:458 (22 June 1926); NUCUA Labour Committee, 12 July 1926, NUA 6/1/2; NUCUA Executive Committee, 13 July and 7 September 1926; *House of Lords Debates* (hereafter *H.L. Debates*), 5th ser., 59, cols. 77–79 (20 July 1926).

50. NUCUA Conference, 7 October 1926; Barnes and Nicholson, eds., *Amery Diaries*, 1:460 (7 October 1926); Pembroke Wicks, notes on the Scarborough Conference, 7 October 1926, Baldwin Papers, 48/46–49; SUA Conference, 12 November 1926; Primrose League Grand Council, 4 November 1926; *H.C. Debates*, 5th ser., 200, col. 1873 (7 December 1926); NUCUA Labour Committee, 15 November 1926, NUA 6/1/2.

51. *The Times*, 2 and 9 February, 24 March 1927; J. C. C. Davidson to Sir Arthur S[teel]-M[aitland], 29 December 1926, (copy), Baldwin Papers, 53/34–39.

52. *The Times*, 5 April 1927.

53. *H.C. Debates*, 5th ser., 205, col. 1327 (2 May 1927); cols. 1657–69 (4 May 1927); cols. 1340, 1410–11 (2 May 1927); col. 1527 (3 May 1927); cols. 1417–25 (2 May 1927); cols. 1467–76 (3 May 1927); col. 2364 (27 May 1927).

54. *The Times*, 6 and 7 April, 4 May 1927; NUCUA Labour Committee, 11 April 1927, NUA 6/1/4; *Imp*, May 1927; *The Times*, 4 May 1927; *H.L. Debates*, 5th ser., 68, cols. 161–62, 135 (5 July 1927).

55. *Man in the Street*, February 1927; *H.C. Debates*, 5th ser., 205, col. 1803 (5 May 1927); *H.L. Debates*, 5th ser., 68, col. 819 (25 July 1927); and Thomas Jones, *Whitehall Diary* (London: Oxford University Press, 1969), 2:100 (11 May 1927).

56. *The Times*, 6 April 1927; NUCUA Labour Committee, 9 May 1927, NUA 6/1/4; *Man in the Street*, March 1927; *Glasgow Herald*, 26 April 1927; *H.C. Debates*, 5th ser., 205, col. 1536 (3 May 1927); *CAJ*, May 1927, 120–21.

57. *Gleanings and Memoranda*, June 1927, 730–84; reports of the NUCUA Executive to the Council, 28 June 1927 and 28 February 1928; *Home and Politics*, September 1927; Joseph Ball, Director of Publicity, Report for 1927, Baldwin Papers, 53/108–17; Sir Leigh Maclachlan, Principal Agent's Report for 1927, Baldwin Papers, 53/104; *The Times*, 9 May 1927; Central Office summary of area agents' reports for 1927, Baldwin Papers, 53/118–49; SUA Western Division, Annual Report, 1927.

58. Pinto-Duschinsky, *Political Finance*, 75–77; Macdonald, *Trade Unions*, 110; *The Times*, 31 January 1927 (letter of the Welsh miner James Meadow).

59. *The Times*, 4 May 1927; *Bradford Trades and Labour Council Yearbook*, 1928, quoted in Fenner Brockway, *Socialism over Sixty Years: The Life of Jowett of Bradford*

(1864–1944) (London: George Allen & Unwin, 1946), 245; Alan Bullock, *The Life and Times of Ernest Bevin* (London: William Heinemann, 1960), 378–79 (cf. also Shefftz, "Trades Disputes," 403–6); Julian Symons, *The General Strike* (London: Century Hutchinson, 1987), 226; Renshaw, "Anti-Labour Politics," 703–4; John Graham Jones, "The General Election of 1929 in Wales" (M.A. thesis, University of Wales, 1980), 45–49; Davidson to Lord Irwin, 17 August 1927, Davidson Papers; Robert Rhodes James, *Memoirs of a Conservative: J. C. C. Davidson's Memoirs and Papers, 1910–37* (London: Macmillan, 1970), 297–98.

60. Lancashire and Cheshire Provincial Division, Annual Report, 1927–28; *The Co-operative Movement (Pamphlets and Leaflets*, 1927/56); NUCUA Labour Committee, 7 December 1925, 12 April and 13 December 1926, 14 February 1927, NUA 6/1/2, 6/1/4.

61. *Annual Abstract of Statistics*, 109; and John Stevenson, *British Society, 1914–1945* (Harmondsworth, Middlesex: Penguin Books, 1984), 187.

62. David Marquand, *The Progressive Dilemma* (London: William Heinemann, 1991), 59.

63. Appleton, *Trade Unions*, 121, 119, 173; Barnes, *War Cabinet*, 8; Richard N. Kelly, *Conservative Party Conferences: The Hidden System* (Manchester: Manchester University Press, 1989), 174–75 (on recent Conservative trade unionism).

64. David Jarvis, "British Conservatism and Class Politics in the 1920s," *English Historical Review* 211 (1996): 74–75; Philip Williamson, "The Doctrinal Politics of Stanley Baldwin," in *Public and Private Doctrine: Essays in British History Presented to Maurice Cowling*, edited by Michael Bentley (Cambridge: Cambridge University Press, 1993), 194.

65. Nordlinger, *Working-Class Tories*, 66–73, 100, 108–9; McKenzie and Silver, *Angels in Marble*, 134–37, 196–97; Duff Cooper, *Old Men Forget*, 125.

66. F. E. Smith, *Unionist Policy and Other Essays*, 31, quoted in McKenzie and Silver, *Angels in Marble*, 23; *Pamphlets and Leaflets*, 1920/42; Baldwin, speech for the National Trust, quoted in Williamson, "Stanley Baldwin," 193.

67. *Home and Politics*, November 1924; Nordlinger, *Working-Class Tories*, 150–51; Nigel Birch, *The Conservative Party* (London: Collins, 1949), 36; *Pamphlets and Leaflets*, 1923/7, 163.

68. *Bradford Daily Argus*, 14 November 1922; *Glasgow Herald*, 4 November 1922; Younger, quoted in the *Evening News*, 13 November 1923, cutting, David Lloyd George Papers, H/387; Harold Cox, *The Capital Levy: Its Real Purpose* (London: National Unionist Association, [1923]), 12–38 and 67–70; report of the NUA Executive Committee to the Council, 20 February 1923 (on the role of the NUA); election address of Godfrey Locker-Lampson, 1923, CPA.

69. NUA, *The 1922 Campaign Guide* (Hassocks, W. Sussex: Harvester Press, 1976), 43–48, 149–54, 232–33, 282–93, and 438–43, microfiche; Stockton JIL, 31 March 1925; *Primrose League Gazette*, February 1926; *Pamphlets and Leaflets*, 1924/246; Barnes, *War Cabinet*, 42.

70. *1922 Campaign Guide*, 317–18; Stockton Constitutional Organisation, Annual Meeting, 28 February 1923; A[lfred] Duff Cooper, *The Conservative Point of View*, 38 (*Pamphlets and Leaflets*, 1925/41); *Pamphlets and Leaflets*, 1927/7–10; *Gleanings and Memoranda*, April 1927, 403.

71. John Buchan, *Memory Hold-the-Door* (London: Hodder & Stoughton, 1940), 125; *Home and Empire*, May 1927. See also W. A. S. Hewins, *The Apologia of an Imperialist* (London: Constable, 1929), 326; Sir William Joynson-Hicks, "The Future of India," *Home and Politics*, April 1921.

72. Camlachie Unionist Association, Annual Meeting, 21 January 1925 (*Glasgow Herald*, 22 January 1922); John M. Mackenzie, *Propaganda and Empire: The Manipulation of British Public Opinion, 1880–1960* (Manchester: Manchester University Press, 1984), 150.

73. See "Suggestions for an Eve-of-Poll Speech," *Pamphlets and Leaflets*, 1923/269; *Yorkshire Evening Argus*, 30 November 1923; *Pamphlets and Leaflets*, 1923/8; *Birkenhead Advertiser*, 1 December 1923; *Shrewsbury Chronicle*, 23 November 1923; *Pamphlets and Leaflets* 1923/146; *Bradford Daily Argus*, 29 November 1923; *North Wales Guardian*, 7 December 1923. (See also *Launceston Weekly News*, 24 November 1923; and *Birkenhead Advertiser*, 24 November 1923, for Wirral and North Cornwall, respectively).

74. Election address of Sir John Leigh, 1923, CPA.

75. *Pamphlets and Leaflets*, 1923/245, 270; *Yorkshire Evening Argus*, 30 November 1923; *Daily Notes*, 23 November (*Pamphlets and Leaflets*, 1923/270); *Craven Herald*, 23 November 1923; election address of Sir John Leigh, 1923, CPA.

76. Macmillan, *Winds of Change*, 145.

77. Greenwood, "Organisation of 'Labour,'" 87; NUCUA Labour Committee, 11 February and 13 January 1929, NUA 6/1/4; Report of the Committee Appointed by the Chairman of the Party to Enquire into the Working of the Central Office and to Make Recommendations for Re-Organisation, 9 March 1931, Central Office Re-Organisation Committee, CCO 500/1/5.

78. *Gleanings and Memoranda*, April 1920, 262.

79. Kenneth O. Morgan, *The People's Peace: British History, 1945–1990* (Oxford: Oxford University Press, 1992), 475.

For post–World War II developments, see Andrew Rowe, "Conservatives and Trade Unionists," in *Conservative Party Politics*, edited by Zig Layton-Henry (London: Macmillan, 1980), 210–30.

Chapter 5

1. John A. Ramsden, "The Organisation of the Conservative and Unionist Party in Britain, 1910 to 1930" (Ph.D. diss., Oxford University, 1974), 215; reports of the NUCUA Executive Committee to the Council, 28 June 1927 and 28 February

1928; Yorkshire Provincial Division, Annual Report, 1927; North Cornwall Conservative and Unionist Association, Finance and General Purposes Committee, 14 January 1928.

2. The only contemporary scholarly assessment of Conservative educational activities is Joseph R. Starr, "The Summer Schools and Other Educational Activities of the British Conservative Party," *American Political Science Review* 33 (1939): 656–72. Important works on British propaganda include Mariel Grant, *Propaganda and the Role of the State in Inter-War Britain* (Oxford: Oxford University Press, 1995); Nicholas Pronay, ed., *Propaganda, Politics and Film, 1918–45* (London: Macmillan, 1982); Philip M. Taylor and M. L. Sanders, *British Propaganda during the First World War, 1914–18* (London: Macmillan, 1982); Timothy John Hollins, "The Presentation of Politics: The Place of Party Publicity, Broadcasting and Film in British Politics, 1918–1939" (Ph.D. diss., University of Leeds, 1981); and idem, "The Conservative Party and Film Propaganda between the Wars," *English Historical Review* 96 (1981): 359–69.

3. J. R. MacDonald, *A Policy for the Labour Party* (1920), 53, quoted in Hollins, "Presentation of Politics," 126–27.

4. Reynell J. R. G. Wreford, "The Lure of the Stunt," *Nineteenth Century and After* 93 (1923): 148–50; Philip G. Cambray, *The Game of Politics: A Study of Principles of British Political Strategy* (London: John Murray, [1932]), 1–10.

5. Reynell J. R. G. Wreford, "Propaganda, Evil and Good," *Nineteenth Century and After* 93 (1923): 524; Harold F. Wyatt, "Peace or Truce? After the Signature," *Nineteenth Century and After* 86 (1919): 29.

6. See Hollins, "Presentation of Politics," chap. 2; Noel Skelton, *Constructive Conservatism* (London: Blackwood & Sons, 1924), 13; Sir Charles Higham, *Advertising: Its Use and Abuse* (London: Williams & Norgate, 1925), 238.

7. Sir Charles Higham, *Looking Forward: Mass Education through Publicity* (New York: Alfred A. Knopf, 1920), 35–36; *Morning Post*, 16 November 1932, quoted in G. C. Webber, *The Ideology of the British Right, 1918–1939* (London: Croom Helm, 1986), 53; Pronay, ed., *Propaganda, Politics and Film*, 17.

8. D. M. Sutherland, Scheme for Conservative Propaganda, [c. winter 1922–23], 1st Earl Baldwin of Bewdley Papers, 48/2–9.

9. Ramsden, "Organisation of the Conservative Party," 297; Report of Conservative Central Office Re-Organisation Committee, 20 December 1927, CCO 500/1/4 (same as Baldwin Papers, 53/43–49); Conservative and Unionist Central Office list of staff, [February 1928], J. C. C. Davidson Papers; Robert Rhodes James, ed., *Memoirs of a Conservative: J. C. C. Davidson's Memoirs and Papers, 1920–37* (n.p.: Macmillan, 1970), 271–72; *CAJ*, April 1928, 97–98; Davidson to Gilbert, 29 February 1928, note on 21 February 1928 meeting with [Patrick] Gower, and "M[aclachlan]'s Attitude," [1927], all three in Davidson Papers.

10. [Sir] G[eorge] J[oseph] B[all], "The Present Situation," [spring 1927], Davidson Papers.

11. SUA, Annual Reports, 1923–29; SUA Eastern Division, Annual Report, 1925, and Executive Committee, 23 February 1927.

12. *CAJ*, February 1926, 40; Ramsden, "Organisation of the Conservative Party," 244–46; Central Office list of staff. According to Ramsden there were 53 speakers in 1928, but the list shows only 39.

13. Hollins, "Presentation of Politics," 43, 154, 46–47; report of the NUCUA Executive Committee to the Council, 28 February 1928; SUA Western Division, Annual Report, 1929. The SUA Western Division produced five million leaflets, but no figures are available for the smaller, less populous Eastern Division.

14. Reports of the NUA/NUCUA Executive Committee to the Council, 19 October 1920, 23 February 1926, 28 February 1928, and 26 February 1929; Cambray, *Game of Politics*, 177.

15. Reports of the NUCUA Executive Committee to the Council, 30 June 1925 and 26 February 1929; Cambray, *Game of Politics*, 178.

16. *CAJ*, January 1926, 3–4; December 1927, 333; April 1925, 83, 84–85. The names of the earlier, largely unsuccessful popular magazines were *The Conservative and Unionist* (1905–12) and *Our Flag* (1912–14).

17. SUA Eastern Division, Council, Treasurer's Committee, 8 May, 28 May, and 25 June 1919, and 5 April 1921.

18. "The Publicity and Propaganda Department," [1927 or early 1928], CCO 4/1/27; SUA Council, 12 January 1923; SUA Eastern Division Council, Literature Committee, 18 May 1925; SUA Western Division, Annual Report, 1925; reports of the NUA/NUCUA Executive Committee to the Council, 1922–29.

19. Wirral Conservative Association, Annual Meeting, 3 May 1926; Oswestry Women's Constitutional Association, Executive Committee, 2 February and 23 March 1929; JIL, Executive Committee, 25 April 1928; reports of the NUCUA Executive Committee to the Council, 22 June 1926 and 26 February 1929; Chichester Unionist Association, Finance and General Purposes Committee, 14 February–20 May 1925, 25 October 1926, and 19 December 1927; Kincardine and West Aberdeenshire (hereafter Kincardine) Unionist Association, Propaganda Committee, 19 September 1924, 10 September 1926, and 28 October 1927; report of the NUCUA Executive Committee to the Council, 26 February 1929; Conservative Women's National Committee, *Fair Comment* (London: Conservative Central Office, [c. 1985]), 31.

20. Frederick Guest to David Lloyd George, 30 December 1919, David Lloyd George Papers, F/21/4/34; and David Butler and Jennie Freeman, *British Political Facts, 1900–1960* (New York: St. Martin's Press, 1963), 205–14.

21. Skipton Conservative Association, Executive Committee, 4 June 1928; Chichester Conservative Association, Finance and General Purposes Committee, 25 April and 23 May 1927; Palmers Green Constitutional Association [in Wood Green], 27 September 1927 and 6 December 1929; Kincardine Unionist Association, Finance Committee, 13 June 1924; idem, Special Subcommittee, 19 September and 14 November 1924.

22. Unionist Organisation Committee [Final] Report, June 1911, CCO 500/1/2; Mr. [G.] Burchett [head of the Lobby Press Service], memorandum on the Lobby Press Service, [mid-1927], CCO 4/1/82; Philip Cambray, memorandum to Herbert Blain, 26 November 1925, CCO 4/1/52. (Examples of local newspapers carrying Conservative material include *Birkenhead Advertiser*, 24 November 1923; *Craven Herald*, 26 October 1923; and numerous cartoons and columns in the *Launceston Weekly News* during 1927.)

Report of the General Director of Publicity to the Chairman of the Cuts and Re-Organisation Committee, 30 July 1931, CCO 500/1/5; E. J. Moyle, memorandum on press publicity to Chief Whip Eyres Monsell, [late 1924], Papers of the Conservative Whips' Office, WHP 1, CPA; Thomas Jones, *Whitehall Diaries*, edited by Keith Middlemas (London: Oxford University Press, 1969), 1:139 (7 April 1921).

23. Baldwin, quoted in Asa Briggs, *The History of Broadcasting in the United Kingdom* (London: Oxford University Press, 1961), 1:271; J. C. W. Reith, *Into the Wind* (London: Hodder & Stoughton, 1949), 136.

24. *CAJ*, June 1927, 157–60; Hollins, "Presentation of Politics," 51; Mr. G. Absolom [phonofilm operator] to Mr. Wilson, 15 May 1929, CCO 4/1/1.

25. Oswestry Women's Constitutional Association, Annual Report, 1925–26; *Home and Politics*, September 1927.

26. *Home and Politics*, January, June, and August 1927; *Imp*, February 1928; report of the NUCUA Executive Committee to the Council, 28 February 1928; *CAJ*, May 1927, 135; Oswestry Unionist Association, Executive Committee, 10 December 1927, and Annual Meeting, 21 April 1928; Oswestry Women's Constitutional Association, Executive Committee, 14 January 1928.

27. NUA Executive Committee, report of the Publications Subcommittee, 18 November 1919, and report of the Speakers' Subcommittee, 10 February 1920; Primrose League Grand Council, Junior Branch Reports, 4 November 1920, 11 October 1926; report of the NUA Executive Committee to the Council, 20 February 1923; *Home and Politics*, March 1924.

28. *CAJ*, June 1926, 171; JIL Executive Committee, 9 December 1925; *Home and Politics*, March 1924; North Cornwall Conservative and Unionist Association, Executive Committee, 2 July 1925; cf. Cornwall Provincial Division, Executive Committee, 23 November 1927; and Launceston and District Women's Unionist Association, 18 December 1924.

29. Higham, *Looking Forward*, 155; Nicholas Pronay, "The Political Censorship of Films in Britain between the Wars," in Pronay, ed., *Propaganda, Politics and Film*, 111; J. A. Ramsden, "Baldwin and Film," in Pronay, ed., *Propaganda, Politics and Film*, 136; Nicholas Pronay, "The Newsreels: The Illusion of Actuality," in *The Historian and Film*, edited by Paul Smith (Cambridge: Cambridge University Press, 1976), 118; and Hollins, "The Conservative Party and Film Propaganda," 364 and 367.

30. JIL Executive Committee, report of the Publicity Committee, 13 Septem-

ber 1928; *The Times* (London), 17 May 1918; Nicholas Reeves, *Official British Film Propaganda during the First World War* (London: Croom Helm, 1986), 226.

31. *CAJ*, February 1926, 42; *Man in the Street*, August 1926; *The Times*, 8 April 1926. Hollins ("Presentation of Politics," 55) dates the first van to 1925, but an agent who was familiar with the van trials noted in *CAJ* that a van was used in 1924. Cf. *CAJ*, September 1925, 215, on film subjects.

32. Oswestry Unionist Association, Special Committee, 15 January 1927, Executive Committee, 2 April 1927, and Annual Report, 1927; Report of Outdoor Cinema Van Tour, April–November 1926, Baldwin Papers, 48/74–79; Draft Instructions to Cinema Van Staff, [1928], CCO 4/1/34. For local responses, see Chichester Unionist Association, Finance and General Purposes Committee, 26 November 1928; Wadebridge Area [North Cornwall] Conservative and Unionist Association, 10 November 1930.

33. Primrose League Grand Council, General Purposes Committee, 2 October 1919; Sir Maurice Hankey to Cabinet Ministers, 22 July 1926, Baldwin Papers, 161/46; Austen Chamberlain to Baldwin, 23 July 1926, Baldwin Papers, 161/45; *The Times*, 8 April 1926; *Man in the Street*, August 1926; Joseph Ball, Publicity Report for 1927, Baldwin Papers, 53/108–17; Hollins, "The Presentation of Politics," 113–16. Hollins incorrectly states that the 1927 film describing the government's work was made in 1926, and he does not mention the phonofilms of Cabinet ministers that were made in 1928.

34. Rachael Low, *The History of the British Film, 1918–1929* (London: George Allen & Unwin, 1971), 202–3; Ball, Publicity Report for 1927; John Barnes and David Nicholson, eds., *The Leo Amery Diaries* (London: Hutchinson, 1980), 1:552–53 (28 June 1928).

35. Davidson to Austen Chamberlain, 5 April 1928, Davidson Papers; Ball, memorandum to Robert Topping, 22 October 1928, CCO 4/1/34; Hollins, "Presentation of Politics," 59; reports of G. A. Absolom, 12–29 May 1929, CCO 4/1/1; Lord Butler, *The Art of the Possible* (London: Hamish Hamilton, 1971), 22.

36. Central Office list of staff; Whyte, memorandum, 26 September 1927, CCO 4/1/82; Report of Chief Publicity Officer to the General Director of Publicity on Cuts, [early 1931], Central Office Reorganisation Committee, CCO 500/1/5; Hollins, "Presentation of Politics," 63.

37. Sir Alan Sykes, memorandum, 4 March 1919, Primrose League Grand Council Minute Book; *Imp*, October 1927.

38. *Home and Politics*, March 1923; Joseph R. Starr, "The Summer Schools and Other Educational Activities of British Socialist Groups," *American Political Science Review* 30 (1936): 957–66 (survey of Labour Party activities); SUA, Annual Report, 1926.

39. GUA, Executive Committee, 24 February 1919 and 22 February 1926; *Glasgow Herald*, 8 September 1924; Primrose League Grand Council, General Purposes Committee Report, 4 December 1919; *Home and Politics*, September 1921.

40. *Aberdeen Press and Journal,* 23 February 1926; Stockton-on-Tees (hereafter Stockton) Constitutional Organisation, Education and Literature Committee, 19 March 1924; GUA Annual Reports, Camlachie Unionist Association, Annual Report, 1921; Clapham Conservative Association, Annual Report, 17 October 1921; Chichester (City) Unionist Association, Executive Committee, 4 February–6 December 1920, 5 March–3 October 1923, 24 March 1924, and 25 May 1925; Bradford Central Women's Conservative and Unionist Association, Executive Committee, 21 July 1924; Skipton Conservative Association, Executive Committee, 17 February 1923.

41. SUA Eastern Division, Executive Committee, 24 November 1920, and Council, 20 December 1920.

42. Report of the NUA Executive Committee to the Council, 29 June 1923; NUA Conference, 25 October 1923; *Home and Politics,* July 1923.

43. Yorkshire Provincial Division, Finance and General Purposes Committee, Receipts and Payments, 1923 and 1924; NUA Executive Committee, 13 November 1923; *The Archives of the British Conservative and Unionist Party,* series 1, *Pamphlets and Leaflets* (Hassocks, Sussex: Harvester Press, 1978), 1924/18, microfiche.

44. Reports of the NUA/NUCUA Executive Committee to the Council, 1 July 1924, 23 February 1926, 1 March 1927, and 26 February 1929.

45. Wood Green Women's Constitutional Association, 4 and 17 June 1924; Oswestry Unionist Association, Annual Report, 1925; North Cornwall Conservative and Unionist Association, Executive Committee, 14 December 1926, and Wrexham Constitutional Association, Special Meeting of Branch Chairmen and Secretaries, 9 November 1927 [1926] and 9 December 1926 (both on the inadequate response); *CAJ,* January 1927, 29, 8.

46. *CAJ,* February 1926, 42; June 1926, 173–74; December 1926, 386–87; January 1927, 9; *The Times,* 10 March 1927; Ball, Publicity Report for 1927; SUA Eastern Division, Annual Report, 1927.

47. NUA Executive Committee, report of the Speakers' Subcommittee, 10 February 1920; Starr, "Conservative Educational Activities," 668; Primrose League Grand Council, General Purposes Committee Report, 4 December 1919; *Primrose League Gazette,* September 1920; GUA Executive Committee, 9 January 1922 and 1 October 1923.

48. SUA Eastern Division, Council, 21 January and 28 April 1920, and Executive Committee, 24 January and 25 February 1920; Sir John Marriott, *Memories of Four Score Years* (London: Blackie & Sons, 1946), 176–77; NUA Labour Committee, 10 May–12 October 1920, NUA 6/1/1.

49. *CAJ,* September 1920, 11–12; NUA Labour Committee, 8 November 1920–7 February 1921, NUA 6/1/1; SUA Eastern Division, Executive Committee, 24 November 1920, and Council, 23 March 1921; *CAJ,* June 1921, 2.

50. *CAJ,* October 1921, 15; *Glasgow Herald,* 23 July 1921.

51. *Glasgow Herald,* 23 February 1924; and SUA Western Division, Annual Report, 1925.

52. *Glasgow Herald,* 2 June 1925, 18–20 May 1927; SUA Eastern Division, Annual Report, 1925 (there is no record of the number of schools in the Western Division), and Organisation Committee, 12 December 1927; Kincardine Unionist Association, Women's Committee, 16 April 1926; *Aberdeen Press and Journal,* 1–2 October 1926.

53. *CAJ,* April 1928, 108–9; Launceston and District Women's Unionist Association, 5 September 1928; Starr, "Conservative Educational Activities," 670; JIL Council, 9 June 1928; *Imp,* July 1928; Primrose League Grand Council, 2 July 1925; *Primrose League Gazette,* August 1925 and July 1926; Primrose League Grand Council, General Purposes Committee Report, 7 April 1927, and Executive Committee, 7 July 1927.

54. *CAJ,* September 1920, 12; SUA Executive Committee, 4 November 1921; NUA Labour Committee, 8 May–10 July 1922, NUA 6/1/1; SUA Council, 26 April 1922; Marriott, *Memories,* 177.

55. NUA Labour Committee, 5 February and 16 April 1923, NUA 6/1/2; report of the NUA Executive Committee to the Council, 20 February 1923.

56. *The Times,* 29 March and 26 September 1923; Bradford (City) Conservative Association, Executive Committee, 20 April 1923; *CAJ,* July 1923, 151; *JILG,* July 1923; JIL Council, 13 June 1923; Metropolitan Conservative Agents' Association, Council, 6 April 1923.

57. NUA Labour Committee, 16 April and 11 June 1923, NUA 6/1/2; *Primrose League Gazette,* July 1924; *JILG,* November 1923 (Baldwin's speech; it reappeared as "Political Education," in Stanley Baldwin, *On England* [London: Philip Allan, 1926], 147–59).

58. *JILG,* April 1924; NUA Labour Committee, Education Subcommittee, 16 June 1924, 8 June 1925, and 13 December 1926, NUA 6/1/2; [Principal Agent Admiral Sir] R[eginald] Hall to Marriott, 8 January 1924, Sir J. A. R. Marriott Papers; fragment of letter from Jackson to Marriott, [c. 1924], Marriott Papers; report of the NUCUA Executive Committee to the Council, 22 June 1926.

59. Report of the NUCUA Executive Committee to the Council, 24 February 1925; *The Times,* 28 July 1925 and 3 April 1926; JIL Executive Committee, 9 June 1926; JIL Annual Reports, 1925–27, CPA; *The Times,* 26 September 1923; *Home and Politics,* April 1924; report of the NUCUA Executive Committee to the Council, 24 February 1925; report of Principal Agent Maclachlan for 1927, Baldwin Papers, 53/101–7.

60. *JILG,* August 1923; *The Times,* 5 August 1924, and cf. F. J. C. Hearnshaw, *Conservatism in England* (1933; reprint, New York: Howard Fertig, 1967), 9–10; *Imp,* August 1927; John Buchan, foreword to Arthur Bryant, *The Spirit of Conservatism* (London: Methuen, 1929), vii.

61. Barnes and Nicholson, eds., *Amery Diaries,* 1:347n; *The Times,* 27 September 1923 (cf. the 23 June 1924 issue); *Imp,* August 1927; W. A. S. Hewins, *The Apologia of an Imperialist* (London: Constable, 1929), 2:297–99; Lord Templemore to Marriott, 18 December 1926, Marriott Papers; *Imp,* August 1928.

62. Marriott, *Memories,* 175; *The Times,* 3 April 1926. On religion at Stott, see also Lord Selborne to Marriott, December 1925, Marriott Papers; report of the NUCUA Executive Committee to the Council, 22 June 1926; and *The Times,* 3 April 1926.

63. *Imp,* July 1925; *Man in the Street,* November 1925.

64. *Man in the Street,* August 1926; report of the NUCUA Executive Committee to the Council, 23 February 1926; letters regarding invitations to visit Stott in 1926, Marriott Papers; *JILG,* October 1923; NUA Labour Committee, Education Subcommittee, 16 June 1924, NUA 6/1/2; *CAJ,* July 1925; Lancashire and Cheshire Provincial Division, Council, Annual Report, 1925–26, CPA.

65. Yorkshire Provincial Division, Council, 9 March 1923; SUA Eastern Division, Council, 17 July 1925; Davidson to Sir Reginald Hall, 19 December 1923, Davidson Papers; NUCUA Conference, 22 November 1929; Ball, Publicity Report for 1927.

66. *The Times,* 3 April 1926, 14 April 1927; report of the NUCUA Executive Committee to the Council, 22 June 1926; letters to the editor, *CAJ,* November and December 1926; *CAJ,* May 1927, 122; NUCUA Labour Committee, 11 April 1927, NUA 6/1/4; *Imp,* April 1927, August and September 1928; *Man in the Street,* July 1927; JIL Executive Committee, 9 June 1928. On derating see chapter 6 below.

67. Report of the NUCUA Executive Committee to the Council, 1 March 1927; *Man in the Street,* March 1928; *Gleanings and Memoranda,* March 1928, 181.

68. John Buchan, "Political Research and Adult Education," Baldwin Papers, 53/79–90; Ball to Col. Sir Ronald Waterhouse, 10 January 1928, Baldwin Papers, 53/97.

69. *CAJ,* April 1928, 89–90; *The Times,* 21, 22, and 24 May 1928.

70. Davidson to Lord Beaverbrook, 25 May 1928, Lord Beaverbrook Papers, BBK C/111; *The Times,* 14 May 1928; Arthur Bryant, "The Story of Ashridge," *Nineteenth Century and After* 106 (1929): 107–17; Claude Davis, private secretary to Sir Patrick Gower, to John Russell, 14 May 1929, Davidson Papers; record of interview between J. C. C. Davidson and Edward Brotherton, 9 May 1929, Davidson Papers; Starr, "Conservative Educational Activities," 664–66; Davidson to Geoffrey Lloyd, 15 March 1932, Davidson Papers.

71. Oswestry Women's Constitutional Association, Special Meeting of Local Branch Officers, 28 April 1923, and Annual Report, 1923–24; Cornwall Provincial Division, Annual Report, 1924; Wadebridge Area [North Cornwall] Conservative and Unionist Association, Executive Committee, 9 November 1925; Chichester Unionist Association Women's Council, Executive Committee, 29 October 1923 and

26 March 1928, and Finance and General Purposes Committee, 20 January 1926; Stockton Constitutional Organisation, Executive Committee, 25 September 1925, and Education and Entertainment Committee, 5 October 1925; Wrexham Constitutional Association, Executive Committee, 7 April 1925; *CAJ*, December 1925, 275–76.

72. Stockton Unionist Labour Advisory Committee, 12 November 1925 and 25 August 1926; Skipton Conservative Association, Annual Meeting, 30 January 1926 (*Craven Herald*, 5 February 1926); Bradford (City) Conservative Association, Executive Committee, 20 April 1923; Oswestry Unionist Association, Annual Reports, 1923–25; Wrexham Women's Constitutional Association, Executive Committee, 1 June 1928; Kincardine Unionist Association, Propaganda Committee, 16 March 1928; Manningham Ward [Bradford Central] Conservative Association, Special Meeting, 2 May 1923; Bradford Central Junior and Conservative Association, Executive Committee, 30 September 1929; Bradford Central Women's Conservative and Unionist Association, Executive Committee, 21 May and 21 July 1924, 27 May 1925, and 11 May 1926.

For examples of local divisions' paying for students to attend Stott, see North Cornwall Conservative and Unionist Association, Executive Committee, 7 April and 7 June 1924, 21 July 1925, and 26 May 1928; and Cornwall Provincial Division, Finance and Emergency Committee, 2 April and 23 July 1924, and 25 April 1928.

Cornwall Provincial Division, Finance and Emergency Committee, 25 April 1928; Oswestry Unionist Association, Annual Reports, 1923–25; Oswestry Women's Constitutional Association, Executive Committee, 9 May 1925 and 13 August 1927, and Annual Report, 1927–28; Stockton Women's Constitutional Organisation, Executive Committee, 9 December 1926 and 5 August 1927; idem, Secretary's Report for 1926; and idem, General Meeting, 25 November 1926.

73. After the war Ashridge continued as a school for citizenship and then as a business consultancy center (*The Times*, 27 September 1947 and 27 March 1948; Guy Hunter, *Residential Colleges: Some New Developments in British Education* [Pasadena, Calif.: Fund for Adult Education, (c.1952)]; *The Economist*, 12 April 1997, 9); diary of Sir Cuthbert Morley Headlam, 5 March 1924; John Green, *Mr. Baldwin: A Study in Post-War Conservatism* (London: Sampson Low, Marston, [c. 1933]), 179.

74. R. S. Milne and H. C. MacKenzie, *Straight Fight: A Study of Voting Behaviour in the Constituency of Bristol North-East at the General Election of 1951* (London: Hansard Society, 1954), 118.

75. *CAJ*, April 1923, 68; Col. P. J. Blair [political secretary of the Scottish Unionist whips' office], memorandum, 12 July 1929, Sir John Gilmour Papers, GD 383/29/33x-35x; Milne and MacKenzie, *Straight Fight*, 98–99; Higham, *Looking Forward*, 58.

76. Headlam diary, 19 April 1924; Bill Schwarz, "The Language of Constitu-

tionalism: Baldwinite Conservatism," in *Formations of Nation and People* (London: Routledge & Kegan Paul, 1984), 1; D. L. LeMahieu, *A Culture for Democracy* (Oxford: Clarendon Press, 1988), 256.

77. Barnes and Nicholson, eds., *Amery Diaries,* 1:570 (7 November 1928); J. Gammie, "Women *Are* Interested in Newsreels," *Film Weekly,* 18 November 1932, quoted in Hollins, "Presentation of Politics," 626; Bechhofer Roberts, *Stanley Baldwin: Man or Miracle?* (New York: Greenberg, 1937), 110, 157–58. (For a more appreciative account of a Baldwin "performance," see A. W. Baldwin, *My Father: The True Story* [London: George Allen & Unwin, 1955], 138–39.) Adam Gowans Whyte, *Stanley Baldwin* (London: Chapman & Hall, 1926), 127; Stanley Baldwin, *Our Inheritance* (Garden City, N.J.: Doubleday, Doran, 1928), 35.

78. SUA Eastern Division, Executive Committee, 24 June 1923.

79. *CAJ,* January 1927, 12–13; Milne and MacKenzie, *Straight Fight,* 122.

Chapter 6

1. John Ramsden, *A History of the Conservative Party,* vol. 3, *The Age of Balfour and Baldwin, 1902–1940* (London: Longman Group, 1978), 290. A more recent work does not list the 1928 act in its index, although the legislation is discussed very briefly in one essay (Joni Lovenduski, Pippa Norris, and Catriona Burness, "The Party and Women," in *Conservative Century: The Conservative Party since 1900,* edited by Anthony Seldon and Stuart Ball [Oxford: Oxford University Press, 1994], 614–15). The only comprehensive account of the 1928 act is in D. E. Butler, *The Electoral System in Britain since 1918* (Oxford: Clarendon Press, 1963).

2. David Close, "The Collapse of Resistance to Democracy: Conservatives, Adult Suffrage, and Second Chamber Reform, 1911–1928," *Historical Journal* 20 (1977): 909.

3. Butler, *Electoral System,* 17–21; NUA Executive Committee, 11 March 1924; *CAJ,* April 1924, 85–86.

4. Close, "Collapse of Resistance," 914; Butler, *Electoral System,* 21–22; Lady Maude Selborne to Sir William Bull, 12 May 1922, Sir William Bull Papers, 5/5 (on Conservative cautiousness); F. J. C. Hearnshaw, *Democracy and Labour* (London: Macmillan, 1924), 58.

5. *Gleanings and Memoranda,* April 1926, 340; Thomas Jones, *Whitehall Diary* (London: Oxford University Press, 1969), 2:98 (12 April 1927); *Home and Politics,* May 1926; Lady Maude Selborne to Sir William Bull, 12 May 1922, Bull Papers, 5/5; Yorkshire Provincial Division, Executive Committee, 25 January 1923; William Bridgeman to Stanley Baldwin, 16 December 1926, 1st Earl Baldwin of Bewdley Papers, 175/29; Skipton Women's Conservative Association, Annual Meeting, 22 January 1927 (*Craven Herald,* 28 January 1927).

6. *Home and Politics,* June 1924; John Ramsden, ed., *Real Old Tory Politics:*

The Political Diaries of Sir Robert Sanders, Lord Bayford, 1910–35 (London: Historians' Press, 1984), 215 (24 June 1924); John Buchan, draft speech on women's suffrage, 29 October 1910, John Buchan Papers, ACC 9058, 4/1; *Mearns Leader*, 25 April 1924.

7. Report of the NUCUA Council to the Conference, 1925 (see also *Gleanings and Memoranda*, April 1925, 388–90); Launceston and District Women's Unionist Association, Annual Meeting, 5 March 1925; *CAJ*, February 1927, 50–51.

8. See *House of Commons Debates* (hereafter *H.C. Debates*), 5th ser., 180, cols. 1518–19, 1539–40, 1495 (20 February 1925).

9. Ibid., cols. 1543–45; *CAJ*, February 1927, 50–51; NUCUA Council, 1 March 1927; Butler, *Electoral System*, 27; Bradford (City) Conservative Association, Council, 30 March 1927.

10. Jones, *Whitehall Diary*, 2:98–99 (12 April 1927); John Barnes and David Nicholson, eds., *The Leo Amery Diaries* (London: Hutchinson, 1980), 1:504 (12 April 1927); diary of Neville Chamberlain, 12 April 1927, Chamberlain Papers, NC 2/22; Ramsden, *Sanders' Diaries*, 232 (25 and 27 April 1927); Davidson to Stanley Baldwin, 6 April 1927, with summary of agents' views, Baldwin Papers, 52/136–42; Butler, *Electoral System*, 28.

11. Duchess of Atholl to Stanley Baldwin, 13 April 1927, Baldwin Papers, 162/7–9; Billie Melman, *Women and the Popular Imagination of the Twenties* (New York: St. Martin's Press, 1988), chap. 1.

12. *Gleanings and Memoranda*, July 1927, 36; *CAJ*, June 1927, 164 and 152.

13. NUCUA Executive Committee, 14 June 1927; Chichester Unionist Association, Finance and General Purposes Committee, 27 June 1927; Skipton Conservative Association, Executive Committee, 7 May 1927; GUA Executive Committee, 25 April 1927; *Glasgow Herald*, 20 October 1927; Davidson to Stanley Baldwin, 20 June 1927, Baldwin Papers, 52/185–86; Lancashire and Cheshire Federation of Junior Conservative and Unionist Associations, Annual Meeting, 30 April 1927; *Imp*, May and June 1927; Oswestry Women's Constitutional Association, Executive Committee, 13 August 1927; Oswestry Unionist Association, Executive Committee, 19 August 1927; *Launceston Weekly News*, 23 April 1927; *Birkenhead Advertiser*, 22 June 1927.

14. *CAJ*, October 1927, 267–68; NUCUA Conference, 6 October 1927 (unless noted, this is the source for information on the conference); *The Times*, 7 October 1927.

15. *The Times*, 7 October 1927.

16. SUA Conference, 3 November 1927; *Glasgow Herald*, 4 November 1927.

17. *Man in the Street*, January 1928; Stockton-on-Tees (hereafter Stockton) Women's Constitutional Organisation, General Meeting, 20 October 1927; *Darlington and Stockton Times*, 15 October 1927; Skipton Women's Conservative Association, Annual Meeting, 21 January 1928 (*Craven Herald*, 27 January 1928); Skipton Conservative Association, Annual Meeting, 28 January 1928 (*Craven Herald*, 3

February 1928); cuttings of the *Glasgow Herald*, 10 October 1927, and *Daily Mail*, 21 November 1927, David Lloyd George Papers, H/287; Philip Goodhart with Ursula Branston, *The 1922: The Story of the Conservative Backbenchers Parliamentary Committee* (London: Macmillan, 1973), 34–36; Yorkshire Provincial Division, Half-Yearly General Meeting, 10 December 1927.

18. *The Times*, 14 March 1928; *H.C. Debates*, 5th ser., 215, cols. 1379, 1431 (29 March 1928).

19. *H.C. Debates*, 215, cols. 1412–14, 1451–52 and 1393–94, 1476–77, 1429–30.

20. Ibid., 216, cols. 221–64 (18 April 1928); 215, col. 1415 (29 March 1928); 216, cols. 653–704 (23 April 1928); *The Times*, 15 and 31 March 1928, and 19 April 1928.

21. *House of Lords Debates*, 5th ser., 71, cols. 169–82, 195–96 (21 May 1928), 221–22, 254 (22 May 1928).

The suffrage debate after 1924 raised two related issues: disfranchisement of paupers and House of Lords reform. Because of an anticipated local government bill and worries about voter backlash, the government rejected pauper disfranchisement (see Lord Jessel, Report of the London Department to the Chairman of the Party, January–June 1926, Baldwin Papers, 52/114; *Gleanings and Memoranda*, March 1926, 283–84; and Davidson to Baldwin, 14 February 1928, Baldwin Papers, 52/198–201). On second chamber reform, see Neal R. McCrillis, "Taming Democracy? The Conservative Party and House of Lords' Reform, 1916–1929," *Parliamentary History* 12 (1993): 259–80.

22. *Gleanings and Memoranda*, May 1928, 377–78; and *British General Election Campaign Guides, 1885–1950. Election Notes for Conservative Speakers and Workers: General Election, 1929* (hereafter *1929 Campaign Guide*) (Hassocks, W. Sussex: Harvester Press, 1976), 255–56, microfiche.

23. *Man in the Street*, July 1928; NUCUA Conference, 27 September 1928.

24. Sir Gervais Rentoul, *This Is My Case: An Autobiography* (London: Hutchinson, [n.d.]), 80; Launceston and District Women's Unionist Association, General Meeting, 11 February 1928; *Gleanings and Memoranda*, April 1928, 302.

25. Lord Irwin to Davidson, 24 September 1927, J. C. C. Davidson Papers; report of the NUCUA Council to the Conference, 1929 (cf. Report from the General Director of Publicity to the Chairman of [the] Cuts and Reorganisation [Committee], 30 July 1931, Central Office Reorganisation Committee, CCO 500/1/5.

26. *Archives of the British Conservative and Unionist Party*, series 1, *Pamphlets and Leaflets* (Hassocks, W. Sussex: Harvester Press, 1978), 1928/32, microfiche.

27. Report of the NUCUA Council to the Conference, 1929; publicity department's costs for the 1929 election, Conservative Party revenue and expenditure accounts, Davidson Papers; *Home and Politics*, January 1929.

28. NUCUA Executive Committee, 10 July 1928; NUCUA Conference, 27 September 1928; and Robert Topping, memorandum from the Principal Agent to Party Chairman Neville Chamberlain on Re-Organisation, 23 October 1930, Central

Office Reorganisation Committee, CCO 500/1/5. The NUCUA rules went into effect after the 1928 conference.

29. Southeastern Area Women's Parliamentary Committee, 13 May, 17 June, and 31 July 1920, 28 April 1925, and 3 February and 16 March 1926; idem, Annual Meeting, 30 June 1926. See also Cornwall Provincial Division, 19 January 1927; Miss Johnson [a women's area agent], memorandum to Lady Falmouth, 18 November 1930, Central Office Reorganisation Committee, CCO 500/1/5.

30. North Cornwall Conservative and Unionist Association, Executive Committee, 17 December 1925–12 July 1926; Wrexham Women's Constitutional Association, Special Meeting of Branch Chairwomen and Secretaries, 9 November 1927 [1926], and Executive Committee, 9 December 1926–23 March 1928; Kincardine and West Aberdeenshire (hereafter Kincardine) Unionist Association, Report of the Special Committee to [the] Executive Committee, 30 October 1930.

31. *Imp,* April and May 1928, January 1929; JIL Executive Committee, 28 March 1928, 12 February and 13 July 1927, 23 May–10 October 1928; *Pamphlets and Leaflets* 1928/6; Leigh Maclachlan, Central Office Report for 1927, Baldwin Papers, 53/103–6; JIL Annual Report, 1928; *Imp,* September 1928.

32. *Home and Politics,* July 1928; Wrexham Women's Constitutional Association, Executive Committee, 16 October 1928, and Finance Committee, 9 November 1928; North Cornwall Conservative and Unionist Association, Finance and General Purposes Committee, 26 May and 8 September 1928; JIL Annual Report, 1928; JIL Executive Committee, 17 January, 10 April, and 26 June 1929.

33. *Home and Politics,* February 1929; report of the NUCUA Executive Committee to the Council, 26 February 1929; SUA Eastern Division, Annual Report, 1929; SUA Western Division, Annual Report, 1929.

34. Kincardine Unionist Association, Organisation Committee, 28 September 1928, and Conference of Office Bearers, 11 October 1928; *Home and Politics,* April 1928, March and April 1929; Wrexham Women's Constitutional Association, Executive Committee, 22 January 1929; *Launceston Weekly News,* 23 February 1929; North Cornwall Conservative and Unionist Association, Finance Committee, 25 March 1929; Stockton Women's Constitutional Organisation, Executive Committee, 20 February 1929; Wadebridge Area Conservative and Unionist Association, 12 November 1928; Wrexham Women's Constitutional Association, Finance Committee, 24 April 1929.

35. NUCUA Council, 28 February 1928 and 26 February 1929; J. C. C. Davidson to the home secretary [Sir William Joynson-Hicks], 25 January and 11 February 1928, and Joynson-Hicks to Stanley Baldwin, 2 April 1929, Baldwin Papers, 48/133–43. See also Wirral Conservative Association, Annual Meeting, 17 June 1927 (*Birkenhead Advertiser,* 22 June 1927); Bradford (City) Conservative Association, Council, 30 March 1927; Oswestry Unionist Association, Annual Meeting, 9 April 1927; Davidson to Baldwin, 13 September 1928, Davidson Papers.

36. Area Agents' Report for 1927, Baldwin Papers, 53/118–49, and report of the NUCUA Executive Committee to the Council, 28 June 1927 (contrasting assessments); *Man in the Street,* August 1928; GUA Executive Committee, 25 February 1929; Wirral Conservative Association, Annual Meeting, 17 June 1927, (*Birkenhead Advertiser,* 22 June 1927); Southgate Conservative and Unionist Association, 1926–30, GLRO.

37. Eustace Percy, *Some Memories* (London: Eyre & Spottiswoode, 1958), 138–39; Sir Reginald Mitchell Banks, *The Conservative Outlook* (London: Chapman & Hall, 1929), 155.

38. *Annual Abstract of Statistics of the United Kingdom,* vol. 75, 1913 and 1917–1930 (1932; reprint, Nendeln, Liechtenstein: Kraus, 1966), 97, 102–5, 238–41, and 248–49 (unemployment statistics); Bentley B. Gilbert, *British Social Policy, 1914–1939* (London: B. T. Batsford, 1970), 312; J. A. Jowett and K. Laybourn, "The Wool Textile Dispute of 1925," *The Journal of Local Studies* 2 (1982): 10–23; David Marquand, *Ramsay MacDonald* (London: Jonathan Cape, 1977), 479; John Graham Jones, "The General Election of 1929 in Wales," (M.A. thesis, University of Wales, 1980), 266.

39. Davidson to Baldwin, 13 June 1927, Baldwin Papers, 36/67–68; *CAJ,* April 1927, 92–93, and August 1927, 211; H. A. Gwynne to Stanley Baldwin, 3 April 1929, Baldwin Papers, 36/111–15; Conservative MPs Agricultural Committee, Baldwin Papers, 25/266–90; Thomas Jones, *Lloyd George* (Cambridge: Harvard University Press, 1951), 216; Ramsden, *Sanders' Diaries,* 234 (10 November 1927); J. C. C. Davidson, interview with Sir William Berry, Bt., 5 May 1928, Davidson Papers; *Launceston Weekly News,* 14 February and 25 July 1925; audiotape of interview between A. M. Williams and Hugh Williams, c. 1974, Alfred M. Williams Papers; *Western Morning News,* cutting, 26 October 1925, Lloyd George Papers, H/270.

40. 2d Earl of Birkenhead, *Halifax: The Life of Lord Halifax* (Boston: Houghton Mifflin, 1966), 162; *Gleanings and Memoranda,* May 1926, 518; NUCUA Council, 28 June 1927 and 28 February 1928; Ramsden, *Sanders' Diaries,* 234 (10 November 1927); Draft Conclusions of Cabinet Policy Committee, 16 July 1928, Sir Laming Worthington-Evans Papers, W-E 896/28–29; *Bradford Daily Telegraph and Argus,* 1 December 1927; *Pamphlets and Leaflets,* 1928/7; Sir John Green, "Mr. Lloyd George's Land Policy," *CAJ,* October 1925, 223–27, and *Political Pills for Farming Ills* (Peterborough: n. p., 1926), v-vi; *Man in the Street,* November 1925; "The Land," *Pamphlets and Leaflets,* 1926/18–22; *Gleanings and Memoranda,* April 1929, 424–26; Robert C. Self, *Tories and Tariffs: The Conservative Party and the Politics of Tariff Reform, 1922–1932* (New York: Garland, 1986), 417.

41. L. S. Amery, memorandum on Central Office Policy Secretariat, 18 November 1924, Baldwin Papers, 48/24–27 (early failed attempt to develop a program); Davidson to Baldwin, 13 June 1927, Baldwin Papers, 36/66–70; Baldwin, notes on Cabinet Policy Committee, Baldwin Papers, 36/72–75; Cabinet Policy

Committee, Worthington-Evans Papers, 895; Draft Conclusions of Policy Committee, 16 July 1928, Worthington-Evans Papers, 896/28–29.

42. Leather and fabric gloves, commercial vehicles, gas mantles, wrapping paper, china tableware, automobile tires, and rayon were safeguarded. For an account of safeguarding developments, see Viscount Swinton, *I Remember* (London: Hutchinson, [1948]), 31–38.

43. NUCUA Conference, 8 October 1926; J. A. Corcoran, director of the National Union of Manufacturers, letter to the editor, *The Times,* 8 February 1927; Amery to Baldwin, April 1927, quoted in L. S. Amery, *My Political Life* (London: Hutchinson, 1953), 2:488.

44. Barnes and Nicholson, eds., *Amery Diaries,* August and September 1928, 1:560–64; *The Times,* 29 July and 3 August 1928; *The Observer,* 29 July and 5 August 1928.

45. Bridgeman to Baldwin, 28 August 1928, Baldwin Papers, 175/42–44; NUCUA Conference, 27 September 1928; *The Times,* 28 September 1928; *Gleanings and Memoranda,* January 1929, 72–75, and February 1929, 181–83; *The Times,* 26 March 1929; NUCUA Council, 26 February 1929; Barnes and Nicholson, eds., *Amery Diaries,* 1:595 (1 May 1929).

46. Martin Gilbert, *Winston S. Churchill,* vol. 5, *1922–1939: The Prophet of Truth* (Boston: Houghton Mifflin, 1977), 293; Robert Boothby et al., *Industry and the State: A Conservative View* (London: Macmillan, 1927), 82–87; Churchill to Baldwin, 6 June 1927, and Macmillan to Churchill, 14 March 1928, quoted in Gilbert, *Churchill,* 5:273.

47. Stockton Constitutional Organisation, Annual Meeting, 22 May 1928; *Man in the Street,* June 1928 (cf. Sir Reginald Mitchell Banks, *Conservative Outlook,* 177); NUCUA Council, 26 June 1928; P. D. Ridge-Beedle, quoted in the *Glasgow Herald,* 23 November 1928; *Home and Politics,* December 1928; *Man in the Street,* March 1929; diary of Percy Cohen [head of the library and information department]. (The "diary," which starts in 1928, lists all written queries and includes requests from all of my sample constituencies except Stockton. The seven popular topics I list accounted for 57 percent of all queries.)

48. NUCUA Conference, 28 September 1928.

49. Jones, *Whitehall Diary,* 2:143 (1 October 1928); memorandum from Topping to Davidson, forwarded to the prime minister, 12 October 1928, Baldwin Papers, 36/79–81.

50. *The Times,* 2, 13, and 27 March 1929.

51. Ibid., 22 March 1929; *Launceston Weekly News,* 13 April 1929; A. H. Booth, *British Hustings, 1924–1950* (London: Frederick Muller, 1956), 78; *The Times,* 14 and 31 May 1929; *Man in the Street,* April 1929; *Home and Politics,* April 1929. For the Conservative critique of Lloyd George, see *Gleanings and Memoranda,* April–June 1929.

52. *The Times*, 2 May 1929; Baldwin, quoted in *Imp*, May 1929.

53. Cornwall Provincial Division, Annual Meeting, 25 April 1929; Barnes and Nicholson, eds., *Amery Diaries*, 1:594 (18 April 1929); Petrie to Lord Beaverbrook, 18 April 1929, Baron Beaverbrook Papers, C/270; Lord Beaverbrook to Sir Robert Borden [former Canadian prime minister], 30 April 1929, quoted in A. J. P. Taylor, *Beaverbrook* (London: Hamish Hamilton, 1972), 260; *The Observer*, 21 April and 19 May 1929 (cf. also *The Times*, 1 May 1929).

54. Charles Stuart, ed., *The Reith Diaries* (London: William Collins Sons, 1975), 102 (22 April 1929); Jones, *Whitehall Diary*, 2:182 (22 April 1929); *The Times*, 23 April 1929 (source for the 22 April address), 6 May 1929 ("Message to Britain").

55. *Daily Notes*, 8 May 1929 (*Pamphlets and Leaflets*, 1929/201); *The Times*, 10 May 1929.

56. *The Times*, 13 May 1929; Barnes and Nicholson, eds., *Amery Diaries*, 1:595 (2 and 3 May 1929); Jones, *Whitehall Diary*, 2:183 (2 May 1929); F. W. S. Craig, *British General Election Manifestos, 1918–1966* (Chichester, W. Sussex: Political Reference Publications, 1969), 44; *Craven Herald*, 2 November 1928; Conservative MPs Agricultural Committee, Baldwin Papers, 25/266–90; Thomas Davies to Stanley Baldwin, 27 March 1929, Baldwin Papers, 25/300.

57. Craig, *Manifestos*, 54.

58. *The Times*, 30 May 1929; *Glasgow Herald*, 27 May 1929.

59. Quoted in Jones, "Election of 1929 in Wales," 791.

60. Gilbert, *Churchill*, 5:306; *1929 Campaign Guide*, 140–42.

61. Election address of Roy Bird, 1929, CPA; election addresses of Major J. S. Courtauld and Harold Macmillan, 1929.

62. *1929 Campaign Guide*, 294–306; Central Office Circular on Disarmament Arbitration, Conservative Research Department—General and By-Elections File, CRD 1/7/5. (This was the work of Lord Hailsham's Cabinet Emergency Business Committee, which served as a clearinghouse for questions forwarded to the Cabinet, government departments, or central office [Conservative Research Department—General Elections and By-Elections File, CRD 1/7/1].) *Birkenhead Advertiser*, 11 May 1929; *North Wales Chronicle*, 29 May 1929; election addresses of Harold Macmillan and Roy Bird, 1929; *North Middlesex Chronicle*, 10 March 1928.

63. Reports of the NUCUA Executive Committee to the Council, 28 June 1927 and 26 February 1929; Wood Green Women's Constitutional Association, 11 December 1928; *Pamphlets and Leaflets*, 1929/197; central office press department release for "Stanley Boy," 9 May 1929, Baldwin Papers, 55/100–102; Booth, *British Hustings*, 79–80.

64. *The Times*, 29 May 1929; election address of A. M. Williams, 1929.

65. *Daily Notes*, 7, 8, and 14 May 1929; *The Elector*, May 1929 (*Pamphlets and Leaflets*, 1929/179); *Craven Herald*, 17 May 1929; election addresses of John Grace and Sir Edmund Bushby, 1929; *The Times*, 13 May 1929.

66. Churchill to Baldwin, 7 January 1929, quoted in Gilbert, *Churchill*, 5:310; *Glasgow Herald*, 9 May 1929; *Daily Notes*, 10, 13, 20, 23, 25, and 27 May.

67. Wood Green Constitutional Association, Annual Meeting, 25 March 1929, *North Middlesex Chronicle*, 6 April 1929; *Glasgow Herald*, 9 May 1929; *1929 Campaign Guide*, 376–404; *North Middlesex Chronicle*, 16 February 1929; *Daily Notes*, 10 May 1929.

68. Notes for a speech at Boness, Linlithgow, 21 February 1928, John Buchan Papers, 4/2, ACC 9058; Davidson to Sir Alfred Goodson, 13 and 18 September 1928, and copy of public letter concerning the Tavistock by-election, Davidson Papers. (Of the nine individuals who signed the letter, five indicated a Liberal affiliation in *Who's Who*. The other four did not state a party affiliation.)

Sir Alfred Goodson to Davidson, 4 May 1929, and Davidson to Goodson, 7 and 13 May 1929, Davidson Papers; letters to the editor, *The Times*, 3 April 1929; *Bradford Daily Telegraph and Argus*, 20 May 1929, and Stockton Constitutional Organisation, General and Adoption Meeting, 13 May 1929 (both appeals to Liberals); *North Wales Guardian*, 8 May 1929 (bitter relations with Liberals); *The Times*, 2 May 1929.

69. *The Times*, 30 May 1929; Macmillan to Churchill, 27 March 1929, quoted in Gilbert, *Churchill*, 5:320; Craig, *Manifestos*, 51–53; *The Times*, 15 May 1929. See also public letter by Norah Leigh, election address of Sir John Leigh, 1929.

70. *Home and Politics*, May 1929; Birkenhead, quoted in Winston S. Churchill, *Great Contemporaries* (1937; reprint, Chicago: University of Chicago Press, 1973), 177; report of the NUCUA Council to the Conference, 1929; publicity department costs for 1929 election, Davidson Papers.

71. Fenner Brockway, *Socialism over Sixty Years: The Life of Jowett of Bradford (1864–1944)* (London: George Allen & Unwin, 1946), 248; *Bradford Daily Telegraph and Argus*, 16–18 May 1929; *North Middlesex Chronicle*, 18 May 1929; *The Times*, 15 and 22 May 1929; Harold Macmillan, *Winds of Change, 1914–1939* (London: Macmillan, 1966), 244; C. S. Ainslie to Wilfrid William Ashley [minister of transport], undated, Baron Mount Temple Papers, BR 73/14; *Aberdeen Press and Journal*, 11 May 1929; *Western Morning News*, cutting, 15 May 1929, Lloyd George Papers, H/270; *Glasgow Herald*, 24 May 1929; *Launceston Weekly News*, 25 May 1929; *Craven Herald*, 31 May 1929.

72. Cabinet Emergency Business Committee, 13 May 1929, CRD 1/7/1; *Daily Notes*, 17 May 1929; *1929 Campaign Guide*, 115–18. See also *Aberdeen Press and Journal*, 23 and 27–28 May 1929.

73. "What's in a name?" quoted in Jones, "Election of 1929 in Wales," 792; *Pamphlets and Leaflets*, 1929/21; *Darlington and Stockton Times*, 25 May and 1 June 1929; *The Times*, 16, 17, 21, and 25 May 1929; *Craven Herald*, 24 May 1929.

74. *Glasgow Herald*, 3 and 24 May 1929; *Bradford Daily Telegraph and Argus*, 29 May 1929; Cabinet Emergency Business Committee, 13 May 1929, CRD 1/7/3; *Daily Notes*, 11 May 1929; *The Times*, 18 May 1929.

75. *1929 Campaign Guide,* 123–24; *Pamphlets and Leaflets,* 1929/161 and 201; *Daily Notes,* 20 May 1929; *Western Morning News,* cutting, 22 May 1929, Lloyd George Papers, H/270; *Launceston Weekly News,* 25 May 1929; *The Times,* 30 May 1929; *Craven Herald,* 31 May 1929, and *Darlington and Stockton Times,* 18 May 1929 (both on Conservative support for religious schools); *Glasgow Herald,* 25 May 1929.

76. Lord Beaverbrook to J. M. Patterson, 24 March 1929, quoted in Taylor, *Beaverbrook,* 259; *Darlington and Stockton Times,* 18 May 1929; *Daily Notes,* 22 May 1929; *The Times,* 30 May 1929; Jones, *Whitehall Diary,* 2:186 (1 June 1929).

77. Jones, "Election of 1929 in Wales," 359 (on Baldwin's letter); *The Times,* 30 May 1929 (source for Baldwin's address); Stuart, *Reith Diaries,* 103 (29 May 1929); *The Elector,* May 1929.

78. *The Times,* 30 May 1929 (see also *Glasgow Herald,* 30 May 1929); Ramsden, *Sanders' Diaries,* 242 (29 April 1929); Jones, *Whitehall Diary,* 2:185–86 (1 June 1929); material concerning wagers on 1929 election, 27–28 May 1929, Davidson Papers; William Harrison to Worthington-Evans, 8 February 1929, Worthington-Evans Papers, WE/896/57.

79. Jones, *Whitehall Diary,* 2:186 (1 June 1929); *The Times,* 31 May 1929.

80. *The Times,* 1 June 1929; [H. Robert Topping], report on the 1929 election, 4, Percy Cohen Papers. These sources show that for many Conservatives the election results were unexpectedly poor.

81. *The Times,* 3 June 1929.

82. *Glasgow Herald,* 1 June 1929.

83. See Jones, "Election of 1929 in Wales," 463.

84. *The Times,* 1 and 3 June 1929. On 3 June the paper reduced its estimate of losses from Liberal intervention to "at least" 40.

Report from Robert Topping to the NUCUA Executive on the 1929 general election, Cohen Papers; Macmillan, *Winds of Change,* 247; *The Observer,* 2 June 1929. See also Brendon Bracken to J. L. Garvin, 2 June 1929, quoted in David Ayerst, *Garvin of the Observer* (London: Croom Helm, 1985), 218; Sir Cuthbert Morley Headlam diary, 31 May 1929; Wadebridge Area Unionist Association, 14 March 1930.

85. Summary of Responses to NUCUA Questionnaire, in Stuart Ball, *Baldwin and the Conservative Party: The Crisis of 1929–1931* (New Haven: Yale University Press, 1988), 221. There are some problems with this material because M.P.s, candidates, agents, and association officers sometimes influenced the results or even answered the questionnaire themselves (see NUCUA Conference, 21 November 1929; Wrexham Women's Constitutional Association, Executive Committee, 25 November 1929 and 23 January 1930). Butler, *Electoral System,* 180; *The Observer,* 16 June 1929. The totals are over 100 percent because in 2 seats, the contests were between Conservatives and only one other party, thus pushing up the average.

86. North Cornwall Conservative and Unionist Association, Executive Committee, 29 June 1929–25 January 1930.

87. *Darlington and Stockton Times*, 1 June 1929 (cf. *Glasgow Herald*, 1 June 1929; Headlam Diary, 1 June 1929; and Bradford [City] Conservative Association, Executive Committee, 22 July 1929); *The Observer*, 16 June 1929.

88. *Home and Politics*, June 1929; P. J. Blair, "Impressions of the General Election," 12 July 1929, GD 383/29/32x, Sir John Gilmour Papers; Topping, report to the NUCUA Executive.

89. J. L. Garvin, "The Foozled Election," *The Observer*, 2 June 1929; Wickham Steed, *The Real Stanley Baldwin* (London: Nisbet, 1930), 96–98; Macmillan, *Winds of Change*, 222; NUCUA Council, 2 July 1929 (cf. also Barnes and Nicholson, eds., *Amery Diaries*, 1:597 [3 June 1929]; Amery, *My Political Life*, 2:498–501).

90. *Glasgow Herald*, 12 July 1929; L. S. Amery, memorandum to Stanley Baldwin, November 1924, quoted in John Ramsden, *The Making of Conservative Party Policy: The Conservative Research Department since 1929* (New York: Longman, 1980), 25; Philip Williamson, ed., *The Modernisation of Conservative Politics: The Diaries and Letters of William Bridgeman, 1904–1935* (London: Historians' Press, 1988), 224–25 (July 1929); Blair, "General Election," 12 July 1929; Ramsden, *Sanders' Diaries*, 244 (7 February 1930), and Ball, *Baldwin and the Conservative Party*, 221 (both on derating as a cause of defeat).

91. Chamberlain diary, 8 June 1929.

92. *CAJ*, October 1929, 177–78.

93. *The Observer*, 2 June 1929.

94. Ellis to Baldwin, 10 June 1929, Baldwin Papers, 36/256–59.

95. NUCUA Executive Committee, 18 June 1929; Thomas Jones to A. B. Houghton [former American ambassador], 19 June 1929, quoted in Jones, *Whitehall Diary*, 2:189; Beaverbrook to R. B. Bennett, 14 November 1927, quoted in Taylor, *Beaverbrook*, 253; Beaverbrook to Lord Derby, 6 June 1929, Beaverbrook Papers, BBK C/113; Williamson, *Bridgeman Diaries*, 225 (July 1929); Chamberlain diary, 8 June 1929; Headlam diary, 1 June 1929.

96. Philip Williamson, "'Safety First': Baldwin, the Conservative Party, and the 1929 General Election," *Historical Journal* 25 (1982): 387.

97. See Andrew Thorpe, *The British General Election of 1931* (Oxford: Clarendon Press, 1991), 31, 46.

Conclusion

1. Bagehot [pseud.], "The Flock Instinct," *The Economist*, 29 March 1997, 65.

2. See Neal R. McCrillis, review of *A History of Conservative Politics, 1900–1996*, by John Charmley, and of *Contemporary British Conservatism*, by Steve Ludlam and Martin J. Smith (*British Politics Group Newsletter*, Winter 1997, 27).

3. Max Beloff, introduction to *The Politics of Reappraisal, 1918–1939*, edited by Chris Cook and Gillian Peele (London: Macmillan, 1975), 3.

4. Diary of Sir Cuthbert Morley Headlam, 13 April 1924, Sir Cuthbert Morley Headlam Papers.

5. Baldwin to Irwin, 26 June 1927, quoted in Philip Williamson, "The Doctrinal Politics of Stanley Baldwin," in *Public and Private Doctrine: Essays in British History Presented to Maurice Cowling*, edited by Michael Bentley (Cambridge: Cambridge University Press, 1993), 190.

6. Noel Skelton, *Constructive Conservatism* (London: Blackwood & Sons, 1924), 14.

7. Bonar Law, quoted in John Ramsden, *A History of the Conservative Party*, vol. 3, *The Age of Balfour and Baldwin, 1902–1940* (London: Longman Group, 1978), 109.

8. Stanley Baldwin, *Our Inheritance* (Garden City, N.J.: Doubleday, Doran, 1928), 36.

9. *Imp*, June 1927.

10. For a favorable assessment of the second Baldwin government, see Anthony Seldon, "Conservative Century," in *Conservative Century: The Conservative Party since 1900*, edited by Anthony Seldon and Stuart Ball (Oxford: Oxford University Press, 1994), 34.

11. Skelton, *Constructive Conservatism*, 16.

12. Katherine Atholl, letter to the editor, *The Times*, 10 March 1924.

13. Bill Schwarz, "The Language of Constitutionalism: Baldwinite Conservatism," in *Formations of Nation and People* (London: Routledge & Kegan Paul, 1984), 7–10, 13, 17; Stanley Baldwin, *On England*, (London: Philip Allan, 1926), 17.

14. For examples of this argument, see Baldwin, *On England*, 219–26; and idem, *This Torch of Freedom* (London: Hodder & Stoughton, 1935), 308–39. Cf. Williamson, "Doctrinal Politics of Stanley Baldwin," 195–96; Ross McKibbin, "Class and Conventional Wisdom: The Conservative Party and the 'Public' in Inter-War Britain," in *The Ideologies of Class* (Oxford: Clarendon Press, 1990), 281; and see James J. Sack, *From Jacobite to Conservative: Reaction and Orthodoxy in Britain, c. 1760–1832* (Cambridge: Cambridge University Press, 1993), 38–45, on a similar Tory response to 1789.

15. NUCUA Conference, 7 October 1926, CPA.

Bibliography

Primary Sources

Manuscript Collections

1st Earl Baldwin of Bewdley Papers, Cambridge University Library, Cambridge.
Baron Beaverbrook Papers, HLRO.
Viscount and Viscountess Bridgeman Papers, Shropshire Record Office, Shrews-
  bury, Shropshire.
John Buchan Papers, National Library of Scotland, Edinburgh.
Sir William Bull Papers, HLRO; and Churchill College Record Office, Cambridge
  University, Cambridge.
Viscount Cave Papers, British Library, London.
Sir Austen Chamberlain Papers, University of Birmingham Library, Birmingham.
Neville Chamberlain Papers, University of Birmingham Library, Birmingham.
Percy Cohen Papers, CPA.
J. C. C. Davidson Papers, HLRO.
17th Earl of Derby Papers, Liverpool City Library, Liverpool.
Viscount Elibank Papers, National Library of Scotland, Edinburgh.
Sir John Gilmour Papers, Scottish Record Office, Edinburgh.
Sir Arthur Griffith-Boscawen Papers, Bodleian Library, Oxford University, Oxford.
Sir Reginald Hall Papers, Churchill College Record Office, Cambridge University,
  Cambridge.
Sir Patrick Hannon Papers, HLRO.
Sir Cuthbert Morley Headlam Papers, Durham Record Office, Durham.
W. A. S. Hewins Papers, Sheffield University Library, Sheffield.
Andrew Bonar Law Papers, HLRO.
David Lloyd George Papers, HLRO; and National Library of Wales, Aberystwyth.

Walter Long Papers, Wiltshire Record Office, Trowbridge; and British Library, London.
Sir J. A. R. Marriott Papers, City of York Archives, York.
Baron Mount Temple Papers, Southampton University Archives and Special Collections, Southampton.
Sir J. C. W. Reith Papers, BBC Written Archives Center, Reading.
2d Earl of Selborne Papers, Bodleian Library, Oxford University.
Sir Arthur Steel-Maitland Papers, Scottish Record Office, Edinburgh.
Joe St. Loe Strachey Papers, HLRO.
Alfred M. Williams Papers, Hugh Williams, Peter Tavy, Devon.
Sir Laming Worthington-Evans Papers, Bodleian Library, Oxford University.

National Conservative Party Records

Conservative Central Office Records, CPA.
Conservative Research Department Records, CPA.
Conservative Whips' Office. Electoral Reform and Miscellaneous Memoranda, CPA.
General Election and By-Election Addresses, 1922–1929, CPA.
Junior Imperial League, CPA.
    Annual Reports, 1913 and 1921–1930.
    Council and Committee Minute Books, 1905–1944.
    Press cuttings.
    Scrapbook.
Labour Committee of the National Unionist Association Executive Committee. Minute Books, 1909–1935, CPA.
National Unionist Association. Annual Conference Reports, 1916–1929, CPA.
———. Annual Reports of the Executive Committee to the Central Council, 1918–1929, CPA.
———. *The Campaign Guide,* 1922 and 1929. Hassocks, Sussex: Harvester Press, 1976. Microfiche.
———. Central Council Minute Books, 1918–1929, CPA.
———. *The Constitutional Year Book,* 1916–1930.
———. Executive Committee Minute Books, 1917–1930, CPA.
———. *The Archives of the British Conservative and Unionist Party.* Series I. *Pamphlets and Leaflets.* Hassocks, W. Sussex: Harvester Press, 1978. Microfiche.
Primrose League Grand Council Minute Books, 1914–1932, Bodleian Library.

Regional Conservative Party Records

Cheshire Provincial Division Minute Book, 1918–1925, CPA.
Cornwall Provincial Division Minute Books, 1908–1936, CPA.

Lancashire Provincial Division, CPA.
    Account Book, 1907–1922.
    Cashbook, 1918–1924.
Lancashire and Cheshire Federation of Junior Conservative and Unionist Associations, CPA.
    Annual General Meetings Minute Book, 1920–1935.
    Executive Committee Minute Book, 1926–1939.
Lancashire and Cheshire Provincial Division, CPA.
    Account Books, 1925–1934.
    Council Minute Book, 1925–1932.
Metropolitan Conservative Agents' Association Minute Books, 1918–1924, BLPES, London.
Scottish Unionist Association, Scottish Conservative Central Office, Edinburgh.
    Annual Reports, 1924–1929.
    Council Minute Book, 1913–1930.
    Eastern Division Committee Minute Books, 1913–1930.
    Eastern Division Council Minute Book, 1913–1934.
    Election Addresses of Scottish Divisions, 1918–1929.
Southeastern Area Women's Parliamentary Committee Minute Books, 1920–1933, CPA.
Yorkshire Provincial Division, Yorkshire Area Central Office, Leeds.
    Council Minute Books, 1909–1967.
    Executive Committee Minute Book, 1916–1953.
    Finance and General Purposes Committee Minute Book, 1912–1933.
    Women's Federation Minute Book, 1917–1920.
    Women's Federation Executive Committee Minute Book, 1921–1924

Local Conservative Party Records

Bradford Central Conservative Association, West Yorkshire Archive Service, Bradford.
    Council and Executive Committee Minute Books, 1906–1949.
    Junior Conservative and Unionist Association Minute Book, 1929–1942.
    Manningham Ward Minute Book, 1899–1923.
    Women's Conservative and Unionist Association Minute Book, 1919–1930.
Bradford (City) Conservative Association General Council Minute Book, 1902–1934, West Yorkshire Archive Service, Bradford.
Chichester Unionist Association, West Sussex Record Office, Chichester.
    Chichester (City) Executive Committee Minute Book, 1914–1949.
    Committees Minute Book, 1923–1931.
    Lodsworth Branch Women's Association Minute Book, 1924–1949.
    Women's Council Minute Book, 1918–1949.

Clapham Conservative Association, BLPES, London.
  Clapham Park South Branch Minute Book, 1907–1936.
  Council Minute Book, 1918–1925.
Glasgow Unionist Association, Scottish Conservative Central Office, Edinburgh.
  Annual Reports, 1914–1930.
  Committees Minute Books, 1918–1941.
Kincardine and West Aberdeenshire Unionist Association, photocopy of Minute
  Books, 1909–1930, Aberdeen University Library, King's College, Aberdeen.
North Cornwall Unionist Association, Cornwall Record Office, Truro.
  Committees Minute Books, 1919–1931.
  Junior Imperial League Minute Book, 1928–1939.
  Launceston and District Women's Unionist Association Minute Book,
    1924–1928.
  Wadebridge Area Association Minute Book, 1924–1937.
  Washaway and District Association Minute Book, 1926–1937.
Oswestry Unionist Association, North Shropshire Conservative Central Office,
  Oswestry.
  Central Council & Committees Minute Books, 1918–1938.
  Hadnall Polling District Minute Book, 1923–1964.
  Women's Constitutional Association Minute Books, 1908–1936.
Skipton Conservative Association, Skipton and Ripon Conservative Central
  Office, Skipton.
  Annual and Half-Yearly Reports and Meetings Minute Book, 1885–1945.
  Executive Committee Minute Book, 1911–1946.
  North Ribblesdale Habitation of the Primrose League Minute Book,
    1906–1928.
  Women's Association General Meetings Minute Book, 1910–1982.
Skipton Public Library Local History Notes and Cuttings, Skipton.
Stockton-on-Tees Constitutional Organisation, Durham County Record Office,
  Durham.
  Minute Books, 1900–1931.
  Junior Imperial League Minute Books, 1923–1925 and 1937.
  Unionist Labour Advisory Committee Minute Book, 1925–1934.
  Women's Constitutional Organisation Minute Books, 1923–1934.
Wirral Conservative Association Minute Book, 1911–1951, Wirral West Conservative
  Central Office, Hoylake, Merseyside.
Wood Green Constitutional Association, GLRO.
  Palmers Green Constitutional Association Minute Book, 1916–1929.
  Palmers Green Unionist Association Entertainment Committee Minute
    Book, 1916–1928.
  Receipt and Expenditure Accounts, 1918–1933.
  Southgate Conservative and Unionist Association Minute Book, 1906–1931.

Women's Constitutional Association Minute Book, 1919–1930.
Wrexham Conservative Club Minute Book, 1913–1927, National Library of Wales, Aberystwyth.
Wrexham and East Denbighshire Constitutional Association, National Library of Wales, Aberystwyth.
    Minute Book, 1918–1926.
    Penycae Conservative Association Minute Book, 1929–1946.
    Women's Constitutional Association Minute Book, 1923–1934.

Newspapers and Periodicals

Aberdeen Daily Journal
Aberdeen Press and Journal
Birkenhead and Cheshire Advertiser and Wallasey Guardian
Bradford Daily Argus
Bradford Daily Telegraph and Argus
Chichester Observer and West Sussex Recorder
Clapham Observer
The Conservative Agents' Journal
Craven Herald
Darlington and Stockton Times
Edinburgh Review
Fortnightly Review
Glasgow Herald
Gleanings and Memoranda
Home and Politics
Imp
Junior Imperial League Gazette
Launceston Weekly News
Man in the Street
Mearns Leader
Nineteenth Century and After
North Middlesex Chronicle
North Wales Guardian
The Observer (London)
Popular View
Primrose League Gazette
Shrewsbury Chronicle
The Times (London)
Yorkshire Evening Argus
Young Briton

Interviews

Robert M. Balfour, Director of Organisation, Scottish Conservative Central Office. Interviewed May 26, 1989, in Edinburgh.

Peter Robinson, Agent and Secretary, Wirral West Conservative Association. Interviewed June 26, 1989, in Hoylake.

Alec Thomas, retired staff member of *Oswestry Advertiser.* Interviewed September 19, 1989, in Oswestry.

Secondary Sources

Addison, Christopher. *Four and a Half Years.* London: Hutchinson, 1934.

Amery, L. S. *My Political Life.* 3 vols. London: Hutchinson, 1953.

Annual Abstract of Statistics for the United Kingdom. No. 75. 1913 and 1917–30. Reprint. Nendeln, Liechtenstein: Kraus, 1966.

Appleton, W. A. *Trade Unions: Their Past, Present, and Future.* London: Philip Allan, 1925.

Asquith, Henry Herbert. *Letters of the Earl of Oxford and Asquith to a Friend, 1915–1927.* 2 vols. London: Geoffrey Bles, 1933–1934.

Atholl, Katherine Marjory Stewart-Murray, Duchess of. *Women and Politics.* London: Philip Allan, 1931.

———. *Working Partnership.* London: Arthur Barker, 1958.

Ayerst, David. *Garvin of the* Observer. London: Croom Helm, 1985.

Baldwin, A. W. *My Father: The True Story.* London: George Allen & Unwin, 1955.

Baldwin, Stanley. *On England.* London: Philip Allan, 1926.

———. *Our Inheritance.* Garden City, N.J.: Doubleday, Doran, 1928.

———. *This Torch of Freedom.* London: Hodder & Stoughton, 1935.

Ball, Stuart. *Baldwin and the Conservative Party: The Crisis of 1929–1931.* New Haven: Yale University Press, 1988.

———. "The Conservative Dominance, 1918–40." *Modern History Review* 3 (1991): 25–28.

Banks, Sir Reginald Mitchell. *The Conservative Outlook.* London: Chapman & Hall, 1929.

Barnes, George N. *From Workshop to War Cabinet.* New York: D. Appleton, 1924.

Barnes, John, and David Nicholson, eds. *The Leo Amery Diaries.* 2 vols. London: Hutchinson, 1980.

Beaverbrook, William Maxwell, Lord of. *The Decline and Fall of Lloyd George.* New York: Duell, Sloan & Pearse, 1963.

———. *Politicians and the Press.* London: Hutchinson, [1925].

Bebbington, D. W. *The Nonconformist Conscience: Chapel and Politics, 1870–1914.* London: George Allen & Unwin, 1982.

Bentinck, Lord Henry. *Tory Democracy.* London: Methuen, [1918].

Birkenhead, Frederick Edwin Smith, Earl of. *Contemporary Personalities*. London: Cassell, 1924.

Birkenhead, Frederick Winston Furneaux Smith, Second Earl of. *F. E., The Life of F. E. Smith*. London: Eyre & Spottiswoode, 1959.

———. *Halifax*. Boston: Houghton Mifflin, 1966.

Blake, Robert. *The Conservative Party from Peel to Thatcher*. London: Methuen, 1985.

———. *The Unknown Prime Minister: The Life and Times of Andrew Bonar Law, 1858–1923*. London: Eyre & Spottiswoode, 1955.

Block, Geoffrey D. M. *A Source Book of Conservatism*. London: Conservative Political Centre, 1964.

Blouet, Brian W. *Halford Mackinder*. College Station: Texas A.& M. University Press, 1987.

Booth, A. H. *British Hustings, 1924–1950*. London: Frederick Muller, 1956.

Boothby, Robert, Loder, John de V., Macmillan, Harold, and Stanley, Oliver. *Industry and the State: A Conservative View*. London: Macmillan, 1927.

Boyce, D. George. *The Crisis of British Unionism: The Domestic Political Papers of the Second Earl of Selborne, 1885–1922*. London: Historians' Press, 1987.

Briggs, Asa. *The History of Broadcasting in the United Kingdom*. Vol. 1. *The Birth of Broadcasting*. London: Oxford University Press, 1961.

Brockway, Fenner. *Socialism over Sixty Years: The Life of Jowett of Bradford (1864–1944)*. London: George Allen & Unwin, 1946.

Brown, Kenneth, ed. *Essays in Anti-Labour History*. Hamden, Conn.: Archon Books, 1974.

Bryant, Arthur. *The Spirit of Conservatism*. London: Methuen, 1929.

Buchan, John. *Memory Hold-the-Door*. London: Hodder & Stoughton, 1940.

Bull, Peter. *Bulls in the Meadow*. London: Peter Davies, 1957.

Bullock, Alan. *The Life and Times of Ernest Bevin*. 2 vols. London: William Heinemann, 1960.

Butler, D[avid] E. *The Electoral System in Britain since 1918*. Oxford: Clarendon Press, 1963.

Butler, Lord R[obert] A[usten]. *The Art of the Possible*. London: Hamish Hamilton, 1971.

———, ed. *The Conservatives: A History from their Origins to 1965*. London: George Allen & Unwin, 1977.

Butt, John. "Working-Class Housing in Glasgow, 1900–39." In *Essays in Scottish Labour History*, edited by Ian MacDougall. Edinburgh: John Donald Publishers, [c. 1978].

Cambray, Philip G. *The Game of Politics: A Study of the Principles of British Political Strategy*. London: John Murray, 1932.

Campbell, Beatrix. *The Iron Ladies: Why Do Women Vote Tory?* London: Virago Press, 1987.

Campbell, John. *F. E. Smith: First Earl of Birkenhead.* London: Jonathan Cape, 1983.
———. *Lloyd George: The Goat in the Wilderness, 1922–1931.* London: Jonathan Cape, 1977.
Camrose, William Berry, Viscount. *British Newspapers and Their Controllers.* London: Cassell, [1947].
Cecil of Chelwood, Robert Cecil, Viscount. *All the Way.* London: Hodder & Stoughton, 1949.
Cecil, Lord Hugh. *Conservatism.* London: Williams and Norgate, [1912].
Cesarani, David. "The Anti-Jewish Career of Sir William Joynson-Hicks, Cabinet Minister." *Journal of Contemporary History* 24 (1989): 461–82.
Chamberlain, Sir Austen. *Down the Years.* London: Cassell, 1935.
———. *Politics from Inside.* New Haven, Conn.: Yale University Press, 1937.
Chester, Lewis, Fay, Stephen, and Young, Hugo. *The Zinoviev Letter.* London: William Heinemann, 1967.
Churchill, Randolph S. *Lord Derby: "King of Lancashire".* London: Heinemann, 1959.
Clarke, P. F. "Liberals, Labour and the Franchise." *English Historical Review* 92 (1977): 582–90.
Close, David H. "The Collapse of Resistance to Democracy: Conservatives, Adult Suffrage, and Second Chamber Reform, 1911–1928." *Historical Journal* 20 (1977): 893–918.
———. "Conservatives and Coalition after the First World War." *Journal of Modern History* 45 (1973): 240–60.
———. "The Growth of Backbench Organisation in the Conservative Party." *Parliamentary Affairs* 27 (1974): 371–83.
Coetzee, Frans. *For Party or Country: Nationalism and the Dilemmas of Popular Conservatism in Edwardian England.* New York: Oxford University Press, 1990.
Cole, G. D. H. *A History of the Labour Party from 1914.* 1948. Reprint, Boston: Routledge & Kegan Paul, 1978.
Collette, Christine. *For Labour and for Women: The Women's Labour League, 1906–1918.* New York: Manchester University Press, 1989.
Conservative Women's National Committee. *Fair Comment.* London: Conservative Central Office, [1985?].
Cook, Chris. *The Age of Alignment: Electoral Politics in Britain, 1922–1929.* Toronto: University of Toronto Press, 1975.
———. "Wales and the General Election of 1923." *Welsh History Review* 4 (1969): 387–95.
Cook, Chris, and Gillian Peele, eds. *The Politics of Reappraisal, 1918–1939.* London: Macmillan, 1975.
Cooper, Duff Cooper. *Old Men Forget.* New York: Carroll & Graf, 1988.
Coote, Colin. *A Companion of Honour.* London: Collins, 1965.

Cowling, Maurice. *The Impact of Labour, 1920–1924: The Beginning of Modern British Politics.* Cambridge: Cambridge University Press, 1971.

Cox, Harold. *The Capital Levy: Its Real Purpose.* London: National Unionist Association, [1923].

Craig, F. W. S. *Boundaries of Parliamentary Constituencies, 1885–1972.* Chichester: Political Reference Publications, 1972.

———. *British Electoral Facts, 1832–1980.* 4th ed. Chichester: Parliamentary Research Services, 1981.

———. *British General Election Manifestos, 1918–1966.* Chichester: Political Reference Publications, 1969.

———. *British Parliamentary Election Results, 1918–1949.* Glasgow: Political Reference Publications, 1970.

Croft, Lord Henry Page. *My Life of Strife.* London: Hutchinson, n.d.

Cross, J. A. *Sir Samuel Hoare.* London: Jonathan Cape, 1977.

Cunningham, Hugh. "The Conservative Party and Patriotism." In *Englishness: Politics and Culture, 1880–1920,* edited by Robert Colls and Philip Dodd, 283–307. London: Croom Helm, 1986.

Cuthbert, D. D. "Lloyd George and the Conservative Central Office, 1918–22." In *Lloyd George: Twelve Essays,* edited by A. J. P. Taylor, 167–87. New York: Atheneum, 1971.

Dalton, Hugh. *Call Back Yesterday: Memories, 1887–1931.* London: Frederick Miller, 1953.

———. *The Capital Levy Explained.* New York: Alfred Knopf, 1923.

Damer, Sean. "State, Local State and Local Struggle: The Clydebank Rent Strike of the 1920's." Center for Urban and Regional Research Discussion Paper No. 22, December 1985.

Darlow, T. H. *William Robertson Nicholl: Life and Letters.* London: Hodder & Stoughton, 1925.

Davies, Sam. "Class, Religion and Gender: Liverpool Labour Party and Women, 1918–1939." In *Popular Politics, Riot and Labour: Essays in Liverpool History, 1790–1940,* edited by John Belcham, 217–46. Liverpool: Liverpool University Press, 1992.

Davin, Anna. "Imperialism and Motherhood." *History Workshop* 5 (1978): 9–65.

Dawson, Geoffrey. *Walter Morrison.* London: National Review Office, [1922].

Douglas, Roy. "The Background to the 'Coupon' Election Arrangements." *English Historical Review* 86 (1971): 318–36.

———. "The National Democratic Party and the British Workers' League." *Historical Journal* 15 (1972): 533–52.

Du Cross, Sir Arthur. *Wheels of Fortune.* London: Chapman & Hall, 1938.

Dugdale, Blanche E. C. *Arthur James Balfour.* 2 vols. London: Hutchinson, 1936.

Dunbabin, J. P. D. "British Elections in the Nineteenth and Twentieth Centuries, a Regional Approach." *English Historical Review* 95 (1980): 241–67.

Dutton, David. *Austen Chamberlain: Gentleman in Politics.* Bolton: Ross Anderson, 1985.

Egremont, Max. *Balfour: A Life of Arthur James Balfour.* London: William Collins Sons, 1980.

Fair, John D. *British Interparty Conferences: A Study of the Procedures of Conciliation in British Politics, 1867–1921.* Oxford: Clarendon Press, 1980.

Fair, John D., and John A. Hutcheson, Jr. "British Conservatism in the Twentieth Century: An Emerging Ideological Tradition." *Albion* 19 (1987): 549–78.

Fawcett, Arthur William Potter. *Conservative Agent.* n.p.: National Society of Conservative and Unionist Agents, 1967.

Fawcett, C. B. *Provinces of England.* 2d rev. ed. London: Hutchinson, 1960.

Feiling, Keith. *The Life of Neville Chamberlain.* 2d ed. Hamden, Conn.: Archon Books, 1970.

Fisher, H. A. L. *An Unfinished Autobiography.* London: Oxford University Press, 1940.

———. *James Bryce.* 2 vols. London: Macmillan, 1927.

Gilbert, Martin. *Winston S. Churchill.* Vols. 4 & 5. Boston: Houghton Mifflin, 1975, 1977.

Glickman, Harvey. "The Toryness of English Conservatism." *Journal of British Studies* 1 (1961): 111–43.

Goodhart, Philip. *The 1922: The Story of the Conservative Backbenchers Parliamentary Committee.* London: Macmillan, 1973.

Graves, Pamela M. *Labour Women: Women in British Working-Class Politics.* Cambridge: Cambridge University Press, 1994.

Green, E. H. H. "Radical Conservatism: The Electoral Genesis of Tariff Reform." *Historical Journal* 28 (1985): 667–92.

———. "The Strange Death of Tory England." *Twentieth Century British History* 2 (1991): 67–88.

Green, John. *Mr. Baldwin: A Study in Post-War Conservatism.* London: Sampson Low, Marston, [1933].

Green, Sir John Little. *Political Pills for Farming Ills.* Peterborough, Cambridgeshire: n. p., 1926.

Greenleaf, W. "The Character of Modern British Conservatism." In *Knowledge and Belief in Politics,* edited by Robert Benewick, R. N. Berki, and Bhikhu Parekh, 177–212. London: George Allen & Unwin, 1973.

Greenwood, John Richard. "Central Control and Constituency Autonomy in the Conservative Party: The Organisation of 'Labour' and Trade Unionist Support, 1918–1970." Ph.D. diss., University of Reading, 1981.

Griffith-Boscawen, Sir Arthur. *Memories.* London: John Murray, 1925.

Halifax, Edward Wood, Lord. *Fullness of Days.* New York: Dodd, Mead, 1957.

Hambro, C. J. *Newspaper Lords in British Politics.* London: MacDonald, 1958.

Harrison, Brian. "For Church, Queen and Family: The Girls' Friendly Society, 1874–1920." *Past & Present* 61 (1973): 107–38.

———. *Prudent Revolutionaries: Portraits of British Feminists between the Wars.* Oxford: Clarendon Press, 1987.

———. *Separate Spheres: The Opposition to Women's Suffrage in Britain.* London: Croom Helm, 1978.

Hearnshaw, F. J. C. *Conservatism in England.* 1933. Reprint, New York: Howard Fertig, 1967.

———. *Democracy and Labour.* London: Macmillan, 1924.

Hemingford, Dennis Henry Herbert, Lord. *Backbencher and Chairman.* London: John Murray, 1946.

Herbert, Trevor, and Elwyn Jones. *Wales between the Wars.* Cardiff: University of Wales Press, 1988.

Hetherington, S. J. *Katherine Atholl, 1874–1960: Against the Tide.* Aberdeen: Aberdeen University Press, 1989.

Hewins, W. A. S. *The Apologia of an Imperialist.* 2 vols. London: Constable, 1929.

———. *Trade in the Balance.* London: Philip Allan, 1924.

Higham, Sir Charles. *Advertising: Its Use and Abuse.* London: Williams & Norgate, 1925.

———. *Looking Forward: Mass Education through Publicity.* New York: Alfred A. Knopf, 1920.

Hills, Jill. "Britain." In *The Politics of the Second Electorate: Women and Public Participation,* edited by Joni Lovenduski and Jill Hills, 8–32. London: Routledge & Kegan Paul, 1981.

The History of "The Times". Vol. 4. *The 150th Anniversary and Beyond, 1912–1948.* New York: Macmillan, 1952.

Hoggart, Richard. *The Uses of Literacy: Changing Patterns in English Mass Culture.* Fair Lawn, N.J.: Essential Books, 1957.

Hollins, T[imothy] J. "The Conservative Party and Film Propaganda between the Wars." *English Historical Review* 96 (1981): 359–69.

———. "The Presentation of Politics: The Place of Party Publicity Broadcasting and Film in British Politics, 1918–1939." Ph.D. diss., University of Leeds, 1981.

Hollis, Patricia. *Ladies Elect: Women in Local Government, 1865–1914.* Oxford: Clarendon Press, 1987.

Holloway, Francis Walter. "The Interwar Depression in the Wrexham Coalfield." *Denbighshire Historical Society Transactions* 27 (1970): 49–88.

Holmes, Colin. *Anti-Semitism in British Society, 1876–1939.* New York: Holmes & Meier, 1979.

Holton, Sandra Stanley. *Feminism and Democracy: Women's Suffrage and Reform Politics in Britain, 1900–1918.* Cambridge: Cambridge University Press, 1986.

Horne, Alistair. *Macmillan, 1894–1956.* 2 vols. London: Macmillan, 1988.

Hyde, H. Montgomery. *Baldwin: The Unexpected Prime Minister.* London: Hart-Davis, MacGibbon, 1973.

———. *Carson.* 1953. Reprint. New York: Octagon Books, 1974.

Izzard, Molly. *A Heroine in Her Time: A Life of Dame Helen Gwynne-Vaughan, 1879–1967.* London: Macmillan, 1969.

Jalland, Pat. *Women, Marriage and Politics, 1860–1914.* Oxford: Clarendon Press, 1986.

James, Sir William. *The Eyes of the Navy: A Biographical Study of Admiral Sir Reginald Hall.* London: Methuen, 1955.

James, Robert Rhodes. *Anthony Eden.* London: Weidenfeld & Nicolson, 1986.

———, ed. *Memoirs of a Conservative: J. C. C. Davidson's Memoirs and Papers.* n.p.: Macmillan, 1969.

Jarvis, David. "British Conservatism and Class Politics in the 1920s." *English Historical Review* 211 (1995): 59–84.

———. "The Road to 1931: The Conservative Party and Political Realignment in Early Twentieth-Century Britain." *Historical Journal* 36 (1993): 469–75.

Jeffery, Tom. "The Suburban Nation: Politics and Class in Lewisham." In *Metropolis—London: Histories and Representations since 1800,* edited by David Feldman and Gareth Stedman Jones, 189–216. London: Routledge, 1989.

Jones, John Graham. "The General Election of 1929 in Wales." Master's thesis, University of Wales, 1980.

Jones, R. B. "Balfour's Reform of Party Organization." *Bulletin of the Institute of Historical Research* 38 (1965): 94–101.

Jones, Thomas. *Whitehall Diary.* 2 vols. Edited by Keith Middlemas. London: Oxford University Press, 1969.

Jowett, J. A., and K. Laybourn. "The Wool Textile Dispute of 1925." *Journal of Local Studies* 2 (1982): 10–27.

Joynson-Hicks, W. "The Land Question." In *After-War Problems,* edited by William Harbutt Dawson, 185–90. New York: Macmillan, [1917?].

Kelly, Richard N. *Conservative Party Conferences: The Hidden System.* Manchester: Manchester University Press, 1989.

Kenney, Annie. *Memories of a Militant.* London: Edward Arnold, 1924.

Kinnear, Michael. *The British Voter: An Atlas and Survey, 1885–1964.* New York: St. Martin's Press, 1968.

———. *The Fall of Lloyd George: The Political Crisis of 1922.* Toronto: University of Toronto Press, 1973.

Koon, Tracy H. *Believe, Obey, Fight: Political Socialization of Youth in Fascist Italy, 1922–1943.* Chapel Hill: University of North Carolina Press, 1985.

Koss, Stephen. *Asquith.* New York: St. Martin's Press, 1976.

Krehbiel, Edward. "Geographic Influences in British Elections." Pamphlet reprint from *Geographic Review* 3 (1916).

The Labour Who's Who. London: Labour Publishing, 1924.

Law, Andrew Bonar. [*Ambition*] "Address delivered to University of Glasgow by the Lord Rector of the University in Saint Andrew's Hall, Glasgow on March 10th 1921." Glasgow: MacLehose, Jackson, 1921.

Layton-Henry, Z[ig]. "The Young Conservatives, 1945–70." *Journal of Contemporary History* 8 (1973): 143–56.

Lebzelter, Gisela C. *Political Anti-Semitism in England, 1918–1939.* New York: Holmes & Meier, 1978.

Lee, J. M. *Social Leaders and Public Persons: A Study of County Government in Cheshire since 1888.* Oxford: Clarendon Press, 1963.

LeMahieu, D. L. *A Culture for Democracy: Mass Communication and the Cultivated Mind in Britain between the Wars.* Oxford: Clarendon Press, 1988.

Lewis, Jane. *The Politics of Motherhood: Child and Maternal Welfare in England, 1900–1939.* London: Croom Helm, 1980.

Lindsay, T. F., and Michael Harrington. *The Conservative Party, 1918–1970.* New York: St. Martin's Press, 1974.

Lippert, Owen Paul. "The British General Election of 1918: Class Conflict, War and Politics." Ph.D. diss., University of Notre Dame, 1983.

Long of Wraxall, Walter Long, Viscount. *Memories.* London: Hutchinson, 1923.

Lowell, A. Lawrence. *The Government of England.* 2 vols. New York: Macmillan, 1908.

Lowther, James William. *A Speaker's Commentaries.* 2 vols. London: Edward Arnold, 1925.

Lutyens, Lady Emily. *A Blessed Girl: Memories of a Victorian Girlhood Chronicled in an Exchange of Letter, 1887–1896.* New York: J. B. Lippincott, 1954.

Lyman, Richard. *The First Labour Government, 1924.* London: Chapman & Hall, [c. 1957].

Mackenzie, John M. *Propaganda and Empire: The Manipulation of British Public Opinion, 1880–1960.* Manchester: Manchester University Press, 1984.

MacKenzie, Norman, ed. *The Letters of Sidney and Beatrice Webb.* 4 vols. Cambridge: Cambridge University Press, 1978.

MacKenzie, Norman, and Jeanne MacKenzie, eds. *The Diaries of Beatrice Webb.* 4 vols. Cambridge, Mass.: Belknap Press, 1984, 1985.

Macmillan, Harold. *Winds of Change, 1914–1939.* London: Macmillan, 1966.

Mallet, Sir Charles. *Lord Cave: A Memoir.* London: John Murray, 1931.

Mangan, J. A. *Making Imperial Mentalities: Socialisation and British Imperialism.* Manchester: Manchester University Press, 1990.

Marquand, David. *The Progressive Dilemma.* London: William Heinemann, 1991.

———. *Ramsay MacDonald.* London: Jonathan Cape, 1977.

Marriott, Sir John Arthur Ransome. *The Constitution in Transition, 1910–1924.* Oxford: Clarendon Press, 1924.

———. *Economics and Ethics.* London: Methuen, 1923.

———. *The Mechanism of the Modern State.* 2 vols. Oxford: Clarendon Press, 1927.

———. *Memories of Four Score Years*. London: Blackie & Sons, 1946.

Martelli, George. *The Elveden Enterprise: A Story of the Second Agricultural Revolution*. London: Faber & Faber, 1952.

Masterman, Charles F. G. *England after War*. New York: Harcourt, Brace, 1923.

Masterman, Lucy. *C. F. G. Masterman*. London: Frank Cass, 1968.

Matthew, H. C. G., McKibbin, R. I., and Kay, J. A. "The Franchise Factor in the Rise of the Labour Party." *English Historical Review* 91 (1976): 723–52.

McCrillis, Neal R. "Taming Democracy?: The Conservative Party and House of Lords' Reform." *Parliamentary History* 12 (1993): 259–80.

McDowell, R. B. *British Conservatism, 1832–1914*. London: Faber & Faber, 1959. Reprint, Westport, Conn.: Greenwood Press, 1974.

McEwen, J. M. "The Coupon Election of 1918 and Unionist Members of Parliament." *Journal of Modern History* 34 (1962): 294–306.

———, ed. *The Riddell Diaries, 1908–1923*. London: Athlone Press, 1986.

McKay, Ruddock F. *Balfour: Intellectual Statesman*. Oxford: Oxford University Press, 1985.

McKenzie, R. T. *British Political Parties: The Distribution of Power within the Conservative and Labour Parties*. New York: Frederick A. Praeger, 1963.

McKenzie, Robert, and Allan Silver. *Angels in Marble: Working Class Conservatives in Urban England*. Chicago: University of Chicago Press, 1968.

McKibbin, Ross. *The Evolution of the Labour Party, 1920–1924*. London: Oxford University Press, 1974.

Melman, Billie. *Women and the Popular Imagination of the Twenties*. New York: St. Martin's Press, 1988.

Middlemas, Keith, and John Barnes. *Baldwin: A Biography*. n.p.: Macmillan, 1970.

Middlemas, Robert Keith. *The Clydesiders*. London: Hutchinson, 1965.

Miller, William. "Cross-Voting and the Dimensionality of Party Conflict in Britain during the Period of Realignment: 1918–31." *Political Studies* 19 (1983): 455–61.

———. *Electoral Dynamics in Britain since 1918*. New York: St. Martin's Press, 1977.

———. "The Interdependence of Candidacy Voting and Victory during the Liberal Decline, 1918–1945." Paper read at the Mathematics Social Science Board Conference on Quantitative Studies in Popular Voting Behavior, June 11–13, 1973, at Cornell University.

Milne, R. S., and H. C. MacKenzie. *Straight Fight: A Study of Voting Behaviour in the Constituency of Bristol North-East at the General Election of 1951*. London: Hansard Society, 1954.

Moore, Simon. "The Agrarian Conservative Party in Parliament, 1920–1929." *Parliamentary History* 10 (1991): 342–62.

Morgan, Kenneth O. *Consensus and Disunity: The Lloyd George Coalition Government, 1918–1922*. Oxford: Clarendon Press, 1979.

Morris, Homer Lawrence. "Parliamentary Franchise Reform in England from 1885 to 1918." Ph.D. diss., Columbia University, 1921.

Murray, Arthur C., 3d Viscount Elibank. *Master and Brother: Murrays of Elibank.* London: John Murray, 1945.

Murray, Gideon, 2d Viscount Elibank. *A Man's Life.* London: Hutchinson, [1934].

National Unionist Association. *Looking Ahead.* London: National Unionist Association, [1924].

Nicholas, Katherine. *The Social Effects of Unemployment in Teesside.* Manchester: Manchester University Press, 1986.

Nordlinger, Eric A. *The Working-Class Tories: Authority, Deference and Stable Democracy.* Los Angeles: University of California Press, 1967.

Norton, Philip, and Arthur Aughey. *Conservatives and Conservatism.* London: Maurice Temple Smith, 1981.

Ostrogorski, M. *Democracy and the Organization of Political Parties.* Vol. 1. *England.* 1902. Reprint, Chicago: Quadrangle Books, 1964.

Panayi, Panikos. "The British Empire Union in the First World War." In *The Politics of Marginality: Race, the Radical Right and Minorities in Twentieth Century Britain,* edited by Tony Kushner and Kenneth Lunn, 113–28. London: Frank Cass, 1990.

Pelling, Henry. *Social Geography of British Politics, 1885–1910.* New York: St. Martin's Press, 1967.

Percy, Eustace. *Some Memories.* London: Eyre & Spottiswoode, 1958.

Petrie, Sir Charles. *A Historian Looks at His World.* London: Sidgwick & Jackson, 1972.

———. *The Life and Letters of the Right Hon. Sir Austen Chamberlain.* London: Cassell, 1940.

———. *Walter Long and His Times.* London: Hutchinson, [1936].

Phillips, Marion, ed. *Women and the Labour Party.* New York: B. W. Huebsch, 1918.

Pimlott, Ben. *Hugh Dalton.* London: Jonathan Cape, 1985.

———, ed. *The Political Diaries of Hugh Dalton, 1918–40 and 1945–60.* London: Jonathan Cape, 1986.

Pinto-Duschinsky, Michael. *British Political Finance, 1830–1980.* Washington, D.C.: American Enterprise Institute for Public Policy Research, 1981.

———. "Central Office and 'Power' in the Conservative Party." *Political Studies* 20 (1972): 1–16.

Pollock, James K. "British Party Organization." *Political Science Quarterly* 45 (1930):161–80.

Pronay, Nicholas. "The Newsreels: The Illusion of Actuality." In *The Historian and Film,* edited by Paul Smith, 95–119. Cambridge: Cambridge University Press, 1976.

Pronay, Nicholas, and D. W. Spring. *Propaganda, Politics and Film, 1918–45.* London: Macmillan, 1982.

Pugh, Martin. *Electoral Reform in War and Peace, 1906–18.* Boston: Routledge & Kegan Paul, 1978.

———. "The Impact of Women's Enfranchisement in Britain." In *Suffrage and Beyond: International Feminist Perspectives,* edited by Caroline Daley and Melanie Nolan, 313–28. New York: New York University Press, 1994.

———. "Politicians and the Woman's Vote, 1914–1918." *History* 59 (1974): 358–74.

———. "Popular Conservatism in Britain: Continuity and Change, 1880–1987." *Journal of British Studies* 27 (1988): 254–82.

———. *The Tories and the People, 1880–1935.* New York: Basil Blackwell, 1985.

Ramsden, John. *A History of the Conservative Party.* Vol 3. *The Age of Balfour and Baldwin, 1902–1940.* New York: Longman Group, 1978.

———. *The Making of Conservative Party Policy: The Conservative Research Department since 1929.* New York: Longman, 1980.

———. "The Organisation of the Conservative and Unionist Party in Britain, 1910 to 1930." Ph.D. diss., Oxford University, 1974.

———, ed. *Real Old Tory Politics: The Political Diaries of Sir Robert Sanders, Lord Bayford, 1910–35.* London: Historians' Press, 1984.

Reeves, Nicholas. *Official British Film Propaganda during the First World War.* London: Croom Helm, 1986.

Reith, Sir J. C. W. *Into the Wind.* London: Hodder & Stoughton, 1949.

Rentoul, Sir Gervais. *Sometimes I Think.* London: Hodder & Stoughton, 1940.

———. *This Is My Case: An Autobiography.* London: Hutchinson, n.d.

Report of the Boundary Commission (England & Wales) & Schedule Parts I & II; 1917–18. Cd. 8756, 8757 & 8758, XIII.

Report of the Boundary Commission (Scotland) Schedule Parts I & II; 1917–18. Cd. 8759, XIV.

Reynolds, Jack, and Keith Laybourn. *Labour Heartland: A History of the Labour Party in West Yorkshire during the Inter War Years, 1918–1939.* n.p.: University of Bradford, 1987.

Riddell, Lord George. *Lord Riddell's Intimate Diary of the Peace Conference and After, 1918–1923.* New York: Reynal & Hitchcock, 1934.

Roberts, Bechhofer. *Stanley Baldwin: Man or Miracle?* New York: Greenberg, 1937.

Ronaldshay, Lawrence Dundas, Earl of. *The Life of Lord Curzon.* 3 vols. London: Ernest Benn, [1928?].

Ross, J. F. S. "Women and Parliamentary Elections." *British Journal of Sociology* 4 (1953): 14–24.

Rowe, Arthur. "Conservatives and Trade Unionists." In *Conservative Party Politics,* edited by Zig Layton-Henry, 210–30. London: Macmillan, 1980.

Rubinstein, William D. "Henry Page Croft and the National Party 1917–22." *Journal of Contemporary History* 9 (1974): 129–48.

Salvidge, Stanley. *Salvidge of Liverpool: Behind the Political Scene, 1890–1928.* London: Hodder & Stoughton, 1934.

Sanders, M. L., and Philip M. Taylor. *British Propaganda during the First World War, 1914–18.* London: Macmillan, 1982.

Schwarz, Bill. "The Language of Constitutionalism: Baldwinite Conservatism." In *Formations of Nation and People*, 1–18. London: Routledge & Kegan Paul, 1984.

Seager, J. Renwick. *The Reform Act of 1918*. London: Liberal Publications Department, 1918.

Seldon, Anthony and Stuart Ball. *Conservative Century: The Conservative Party since 1900*. Oxford: Oxford University Press, 1994.

Self, Robert C. *Tories and Tariffs: The Conservative Party and the Politics of Tariff Reform, 1922–1932*. New York: Garland, 1986.

Shadwell, Arthur. *The Socialist Movement, 1824–1924: Its Origins and Meaning, Progress and Prospects*. 2 vols. London: Philip Allan, 1925.

Shefftz, Melvin C. "The Trade Disputes and Trade Unions Act of 1927: The Aftermath of the General Strike." *The Review of Politics* 29 (1967): 387–406.

Skelley, Jeffrey, ed. *The General Strike, 1926*. London: Lawrence & Wishart, 1976.

Skelton, Noel. *Constructive Conservatism*. London: Blackwood & Sons, 1924.

Smith, Janet Adam. *John Buchan*. Boston: Little, Brown, 1965.

Spender, J. A. *Life, Journalism and Politics*. 2 vols. New York: Frederick A. Stokes, [1927].

———. *A Short History of Our Times*. New York: Frederick A. Stokes, [1934].

———. *Sir Robert Hudson*. London: Cassell, 1930.

Stacy, Judith. "The New Conservative Feminism." *Feminist Studies* 9 (1983): 559–83.

Steed, Wickham. *The Real Stanley Baldwin*. London: Nisbet, 1930.

———. *Through Thirty Years, 1892–1922*. 2 vols. Garden City, N.Y.: Doubleday, Page, 1924.

Stuart, Charles, ed. *The Reith Diaries*. London: William Collins Sons, 1975.

Stubbs, John O. "Lord Milner and Patriotic Labour, 1914–1918." *English Historical Review* 87 (1972): 717–54.

Swinton, Philip Lloyd-Greame, Lord. *I Remember*. London: Hutchinson, [1948].

Sykes, Christopher. *Nancy: The Life of Nancy Astor*. Reprint, Chicago: Academy Chicago, 1984.

Tanner, Duncan. "The Parliamentary Electoral System, the 'Fourth' Reform Act and the Rise of Labour in England and Wales." *Bulletin of the Institute of Historical Research* 56 (1983): 205–19.

Taylor, A. J. P. *Beaverbrook*. London: Hamish Hamilton, 1972.

———, ed. *Lloyd George: A Diary by Francis Stevenson*. New York: Harper & Row, 1971.

———, ed. *My Darling Pussy: The Letters of Lloyd George and Francis Stevenson, 1913–41*. London: Weidenfeld & Nicolson, 1975.

Taylor, H. A. *The Strange Case of Andrew Bonar Law*. London: Stanley Paul, n.d.

Thomson, Basil. *My Experiences at Scotland Yard*. Garden City, N.Y.: Doubleday, Page, 1923.

Thornton, Percy Melville. *Some Things We Have Remembered*. London: Longmans, Green, 1912.

Thornton-Kelmsley, Sir Colin Norman. *Through Winds & Tides*. Montrose, Scotland: Standard Press, 1974.

Thorpe, Andrew. *The British General Election of 1931*. Oxford: Clarendon Press, 1991.

Tickner, Lisa. *The Spectacle of Women: The Imagery of the Suffrage Campaign, 1907–14*. Chicago: University of Chicago Press, 1988.

Turner, J[ohn] A. "The British Commonwealth Union and the General Election of 1918." *English Historical Review* 93 (1978): 528–59.

———. *British Politics and the Great War: Coalition and Conflict, 1915–1918*. New Haven: Yale University Press, 1992.

Urwin, Derek W. "The Development of the Conservative Party Organisation in Scotland until 1912." *Scottish Historical Review* 44 (1965): 89–111.

Vincent, John. *The Crawford Papers: The Journals of David Lindsay, Twenty-Seventh Earl of Crawford and Tenth Earl of Balcarres, 1871–1940, during the Years 1892 to 1940*. Manchester: Manchester University Press, 1984.

Walker, Linda. "Party Political Women: A Comparative Study of Liberal Women and the Primrose League, 1890–1914." In *Equal or Different: Women's Politics, 1800–1914*, edited by Jane Rendall, 165–91. Oxford: Basil Blackwell, 1987.

Waller, Robert. *The Almanac of British Politics*. London: Croom Helm, 1983.

Wallis, Peter Vaughan. "Political Change and Development in London, 1918–1935." Ph.D. diss., Cambridge University, 1973.

Ward, J. T. *The First Century: A History of Scottish Tory Organisation, 1882–1982*. Edinburgh: Scottish Conservative & Unionist Association, 1982.

Warner, Gerald. *The Scottish Tory Party: A History*. London: Weidenfeld & Nicolson, 1988.

Waterhouse, Nourah. *Private and Official*. London: Jonathan Cape, 1942.

Webber, G. C. *The Ideology of the British Right, 1918–1939*. London: Croom Helm, 1986.

Webster, Nesta H. *World Revolution: The Plot against Civilization*. Boston: Small, Maynard, 1921.

West, Gordon. *Lloyd George's Last Fight*. London: Alston Rivers, 1930.

West, Nigel. *MI5: British Security Service Operations, 1909–1945*. London: Bodley Head, 1982.

Who's Who in Wales, 1921 & 1933.

Whyte, Adam Gowans. *Stanley Baldwin*. London: Chapman & Hall, 1926.

Wilkinson, Paul. "English Youth Movements, 1908–30." *Journal of Contemporary History* 4 (1969): 3–23.

Williams, Herbert G. *Politics and Economics*. London: John Murray, 1926.

———. *Politics—Grave and Gay*. London: Hutchinson, [c. 1948].

———. *Through Tariffs to Prosperity*. n.p.: Philip Allan, 1931.

Williamson, Philip. "The Doctrinal Politics of Stanley Baldwin." In *Public and Pri-*

vate Doctrine: Essays in British History presented to Maurice Cowling, edited by Michael Bentley, 181–208. Cambridge: Cambridge University Press, 1993.

———, ed. *The Modernisation of Conservative Politics: The Diaries and Letters of William Bridgeman, 1904–1935*. London: Historians' Press, 1988.

———. "'Safety First': Baldwin, the Conservative Party, and the 1929 General Election." *Historical Journal* 25 (1982): 385–409.

Wilson, Trevor. *The Downfall of the Liberal Party, 1914–1935*. Ithaca: Cornell University Press, 1966.

———, ed. *The Political Diaries of C. P. Scott, 1911–1928*. Ithaca: Cornell University Press, 1970.

Winterton, Earl Edward Turnour. *Orders of the Day*. London: Cassell, 1953.

Withers, Hartley. *The Case for Capitalism*. New York: E. P. Dutton, 1920.

Wrench, John Evelyn. *Geoffrey Dawson and Our Times*. London: Hutchinson, 1955.

Wrigley, Chris. *Lloyd George and the Challenge of Labour: The Post-War Coalition, 1918–1922*. Hemel Hempstead, Herts.: Harvester Wheatsheaf, 1990.

Young, Kenneth. *Stanley Baldwin*. London: Weidenfeld & Nicolson, 1976.

Zebel, Sydney H. *Balfour: A Political Biography*. Cambridge: Cambridge University Press, 1973.

Index

Agricultural and rural constituencies, 16, 42, 51, 233; in election of 1929, 193–94, 201–2, 208, 214, 216–17

Amery, Leopold, 140, 167, 168–69, 175, 182, 200

Asquith, Herbert Henry, 28, 46, 70, 78–79

Association of Conservative Clubs, 74–75, 111

Astor, Nancy, Viscountess, 53, 71, 74, 79, 180, 181

Atholl, Katherine Marjory Stewart-Murray, Duchess of, 68, 73, 75, 79, 80, 165, 194, 227

Baldwin, Stanley, 141; education, concern for, 97–98, 167, 224, 225; election of 1929, 195–96, 198–201, 206, 209, 210, 220–22; Representation of the People Act of 1928, views on, 182–83, 184, 186, 188; on trade union reform and the General Strike, 126, 127, 130, 133, 134. *See also* Conservatism: Baldwin redefining

Ball, Sir Joseph, 149, 171

Beaverbrook, Sir William Maxwell Aitken, 1st Baronet, 200, 210

Birkenhead, Frederick Edwin Smith, 1st Earl of, 79, 85–86, 127, 129–30, 131, 138; election of 1929, 207; Representa-tion of the People Act of 1928, response to, 182, 186

Blain, Sir Herbert, 26, 115–16

Bonar Law, Andrew, 19, 30–32, 34–35, 172, 225

Bradford Central, 15, 30, 57, 181; election of 1929, 206, 209; Labour Commit-tee, 118, 120, 141, 166

Bridgeman, Caroline, 55, 114, 195; as Os-westry Women's Constitutional Asso-ciation chairwoman, 22; as WUO chairwoman, 48

British Workers League, 35; as the National Democratic and Labour Party, 23, 36

Buchan, Sir John, 140, 162, 168, 171–72, 180

Cambray, Philip, 146, 149, 151, 162

Camlachie, Glasgow, 11, 24, 92, 140; elec-tion of 1929, 210, 214

Cannell, H. H., 84, 89, 90

Cave, Sir George, 17, 131

Chamberlain, Austen, 126

Chamberlain, Neville, 127, 130, 182; elec-tion of 1929, 202, 218, 221, 222

Chichester, 10, 118, 119, 160, 172; Wom-en's Unionist Organisation, 48, 63–64

Chinese Crisis (Cantonese riots) of 1927, 192, 205, 207

Churchill, Winston, 29, 182; election of 1929, 196, 199, 205, 211

Clapham, 92, 117, 160; Women's Unionist Organisation, 38, 39

Conservatism
anti-alienism, 29–30, 35, 139–40, 141–42
anticommunism and antisocialism, 1, 31–32, 39, 76–78, 85–87, 96, 108, 138–39, 149, 159, 160, 165, 205–6, 228
Baldwin redefining, 97–98, 128, 137, 167, 175, 227–28
constitutionalism, 130, 168
electoral pacts in constituencies, 30
Lloyd George Coalition, 28–31, 89, 93
nationalism, patriotism, and unity, 37, 105–6, 138–39, 155, 166, 169–70
postwar questions, 5–9
postwar transformation, 226–28
relations with other parties: cooperation with and appeals to Liberals, 194, 206, 226
women's impact on, 65–66, 72, 76–77
working-class deference to, 138. *See also* Imperialism

Conservative and Unionist Films Association, 158

Conservative and Unionist Women's Franchise Association, 12

Davidson, J. C. C., 135, 148–49, 157, 170; election of 1929, 194, 221; personal papers as source, 10; Representation of the People Act of 1928, 182, 184, 189

Derating, 203, 207, 208, 218; as 1928 campaign issue, 196–97; teaching Junior Imperial League about, 170–71

Education: Conservative and Unionist Educational Institute, 162, 165, 168; Conservative Party college, 97, 163, 165–73; constituencies, 172–73; debate as a teaching tool, 160; early Conservative attempts at, 158–60, 163; education department in central office, 161–62; information and research department in central office, 162, 171; Junior Imperial League, 95–98, 165, 166, 167–68, 169, 170–71; significance of, 145–46, 173–74; study circles, 160–62; summer and weekend schools, 163–65; training party volunteers, 159, 162–63, 170–71; Westminster Library book series, 161; Women's Unionist Organisation, 55–56, 159–61, 165, 168

Election of 1918: analysis, 43–45; anti-alienism, 29–30, 35, 38–39, 41; "coupons," 35, 38; electoral cooperation and tensions, 34–36; jingoism, increase of, 39–42; Labour Party, attacks on, 39; Lloyd George, focus on, 37–38; national unity theme, 37–39, 44–45; program for, 31–34; results, 43

Election of 1922: education, increased interest in, 160–61; Labour Committee, 139–40; women, 62, 65–66

Election of 1923: education, increased interest in, 161; Junior Imperial League, 99; Labour Committee, 139, 140; women, 65–67

Election of 1924: women's role in, 65, 68

Election of 1929: analysis of defeat, 215–22; Baldwin, blamed for defeat, 220–22; —, campaign focus on, 203–5; BBC, 210; candidates' addresses, 150, 203; defeat and contemporary explanations, 211–15; defensiveness of Conservatives on peace and economic questions, 202–3, 210, 214, 220; discussion of election program, 195–96; economic depression, 193–94; international disappointments, 192, 203, 207; Liberals, attacks on, 205–6; —, cooperation with, 206, 212; Lloyd George, attacks on, 201, 205; malaise among Conservatives, 191–92; manifesto, 201–2; "performance not promises" and "safety first" theme, 176, 198, 200–1, 210, 218–20; preparation, 197–99; program for, 194–200; tariffs

and safeguarding, 203, 208–9;
women, appeals to, 206–7. *See also*
Derating
Elveden, Gwendolen Florence Mary Guinness, Viscountess of, 48, 185, 191

Films, and the Conservative Party: censorship and restrictions, 78, 85, 156; cinema vans, 156–58; Conservative and Unionist Films Association, 158; use of films, 134, 156–58. *See also*
Propaganda
Fraser, Sir Malcolm, 145, 153

Gower, Sir Patrick, 149, 158

Hall, Admiral Sir Reginald, 59, 126
Higham, Sir Charles, views on propaganda, 147–48

Imbert-Terry, Sir Henry, 84, 93
Imperialism, 155, 156, 205; Conservative Party college, 168–69; Junior Imperial League and Young Britons, 104–7; Labour Committee, 140–41; Women's Unionist Organisation, 67, 78. *See also* Chinese Crisis (Cantonese riots) of 1927
International affairs: disarmament and peace efforts, 192, 203; Soviet Union, 85–86. *See also* Imperialism
Iveagh, Gwendolen Florence Mary Guinness, Countess of. *See* Elveden.

Jackson, Sir F. Stanley, 167
Junior Imperial League: activities, 95–102; affiliated federations of, 91; Albert Hall Rally, 90, 98, 190; anthem, 108–9; branches, 87–88, 91–92, 93, 100–101, 190; Conservative Party, relationship to, 88–94, 92–94, 99–100, 190; education, 165, 166, 167–68, 169, 170–71; growth, post-1918, 85–87; history, pre-1918, 84–85; *Junior Imperial League Gazette* and *Imp*, 89, 91, 151, 152; membership, characteristics of,

87–88, 94–95; Representation of the People Act of 1928, 90–91, 190–91; Scottish counterparts, 85, 92; significance, 83–84, 95, 109; social aspects, 101–2
Joynson-Hicks, Sir William, 195; Representation of the People Act of 1928, 181, 182, 185

Kincardine and West Aberdeenshire, 92, 127, 153, 165; election of 1929, 191, 214

Labour Committee: activities, 113–14, 119–22; branches and membership, 115–19; Conservative Party and organizations, relations with, 114–19, 143; cooperatives, views of, 136; educational work, 119–20, 163, 166, 171, 172; history, 27, 111–13; leadership, 115; National Conservative League, relationship to, 112, 118; periodical, lack of, 115; reforms in 1924, 115–17; Scottish counterpart, 117; significance, 110, 143–44. *See also* Working class; Trade union reform; Trade unions
Labour Party: Conservative fears of, 1–2, 4–5, 19, 147, 149, 159, 171–72, 205–6; trade union reform, response to, 132–35
Liberal Party. *See* Lloyd George, David
Lloyd George, David: Conservative attacks on during election of 1929, 157, 194, 197, 198–99; Conservative attitudes toward, 28, 33; election of 1918, 32, 37, 40, 42; and Liberal Party during election of 1929, 193, 198, 212–13, 214, 215–16, 221
Local Conservative Party associations: constituency agents, 18, 170; Labour Committee, relations with, 114; Representation of the People Act of 1918, 24–26; Women's Unionist Organisation, relations with, 59, 60, 62–63. *See also* Conservatives: relations with other parties.
Long, Walter, 11–12, 16, 27

MacDonald, James Ramsay, 39, 138–39
Maclachlan, Leigh, 149; and Women's
   Unionist Organisation, 60–61, 63
Macmillan, Harold, 184, 196, 213–14. *See
   also* Stockton-on-Tees
Marriott, Sir John A. R., 213; Conservative
   Party education, 163, 166, 167, 169,
   171; Representation of the People Act
   of 1918, view of, 7
Mathams, R. M., 115, 126–27, 163, 167
Maxse, Marjorie, 48–49, 62, 68, 190, 216
Middle class: importance in the Conserva-
   tive Party, 73, 94–95, 115, 119, 136; elec-
   tion of 1923, 142–43; election of 1929,
   208, 212, 221; electorate, 17, 233
Mitchell, A. G., 90
Municipal elections, 150, 154

National Citizens Union, 132
National Party, 29, 38
National Unionist Association/National
   Union of Conservatives and Unionists: election of 1918, 31–33; Representation of the People Act of 1918,
   14–18; Representation of the People
   Act of 1928, 183, 191; structure and
   rules, 26–27, 189; trade union reform,
   131; women's advisory committee, 50,
   189; working-class participation in
   the council, lack of, 114–16
1922 Committee, 128, 185, 187
North Cornwall, 36, 193, 209; education,
   172, 173; Junior Imperial League and
   Young Britons, 84, 92, 94, 106; Representation of the People Act of 1928,
   183, 191; Women's Unionist Organisation, 52, 55, 56, 58

Oswestry: cinema vans, 157; education,
   172, 173; election of 1929, 213; Labour
   Committee, lack of, 118; Representation of the People Act of 1918, 22, 25,
   36, 44

Page-Croft, Sir Henry, 29, 195. *See also*
   National Party

Primrose League, 131; Buds, 102; education, 158, 159, 163, 165; history, 5, 21;
   propaganda, 77–78, 155; Young Conservatives Union, 168, 170
Propaganda: audio systems, 154; BBC, 154,
   210; Conservative Musical Union,
   154–55, 188; continuous distribution
   of, 149, 150–51; early development,
   145, 146–51; lantern lectures, 155;
   leaflets, pamphlets, and posters, 145,
   148, 150, 151; magazines, 151–52; performance propaganda, 154; press, use
   of, 152–42, 216; Publicity Department, creation of, 149; significance,
   145–46, 174–77; speakers, 150, 163;
   spending, 145, 148–49; volunteers,
   dependence on, 149, 150. *See also*
   Films, and the Conservative Party

Reform acts. *See* Representation of the
   People Act of 1918; Representation of
   the People Act of 1928
Religion: Anglican Church in Wales, 32,
   34; in Conservatism, 75–76, 78, 86,
   169, 227; Nonconformists, voting of,
   214; Roman Catholic Church in election of 1929, 209–10
Representation of the People Act of 1918,
   17; Conservative response, 2–6,
   19–28; impact, 2–3, 17–19, 225; origins, 11–12; Scottish Unionist Association response, 23–25; Speaker's
   Conference of 1917 and Conservative
   response, 12–16; women, Conservative views of, 12–15
Representation of the People Act of 1928,
   90, 185–87; Cabinet committee, 182;
   Conservative conflicts about, 179–83;
   origins and early bills, 178, 179; Rothermere, Lord, and the "flapper folly"
   agitation, 182; significance of, 187
Rowlands, Gwilym, 116, 120

Safeguarding, 38, 141, 194–95, 283 n. 42
Salvidge, Sir Archibald, 19–20, 28
Sanders, Sir Robert, 30, 35, 134, 185

Scottish 1924 Club, 149–50, 162
Skipton, 10, 31, 153; election of 1918, 41, 42; Representation of the People of Act of 1918, 15, 23; Representation of the People Act of 1928, 184
Social issues and legislation: election of 1929, 202, 209; housing, 42, 43, 67–68, 73, 157, 159; moral concerns, 74–75; pensions, 68, 73; women and children, 74–75, 80–81; Women's Unionist Organisation, 67–68, 73–78
Stanley, Lord Edward Montagu Cavendish, 90, 93
Steel-Maitland, Sir Arthur, 12, 14, 41–42, 126
Stewart-Murray, Katherine Marjory. *See* Atholl, Katherine Margory Stewart-Murray, Duchess of
Stockton-on-Tees: 36, 100, 173, 100; election of 1929, 208–9, 213–14, 215; Labour Committee, 118, 121–22, 131, 139, 173; Women's Unionist Organisation, 51, 63. *See also* Macmillan, Harold
Stott, Sir Philip, 129, 163, 165–66
Suffrage. *See* Representation of the People Act of 1918; Representation of the People Act of 1928

Tariffs, 5–6, 33, 34, 38, 165; election of 1923, 65–67, 141–42; election of 1929, 195, 203, 208–9, 217–18, 221. *See also* Safeguarding
Topping, H. Robert, 61, 149, 215, 217
Trade union reform: Conservative demand for, 122–27; election of 1929, 206, 209; General Strike and increased Conservative demands for, 129–31; Lloyd George Coalition and Conservative pressure, 123–26, 164; Macquisten bill of 1925, 127–28; Trade Disputes and Trade Unions Act of 1927, 132–33; —, responses to, 134–35. *See also* Working class; Labour Committee
Trade unions, Conservative fear of social-ist domination, 112–13, 122–23, 129, 131. *See also* Trade union reform

Walker, G. E. M., 115, 134
Whittaker, John, 113, 116
Wirral, 14, 36, 131, 213
Women, and the Conservative Party: anti-communism and antisocialism, 76–78; anti-feminism, 77–78, 81; civic morality, 79–80; Conservatism, 1, 50, 55, 60, 61, 63, 64–81; role in, 19–20, 50, 51, 58–65; election of 1918, 42, 43; election of 1923, 142; election of 1929, blamed for defeat in, 216–17; home-centeredness and religious beliefs, 71–75, 80–81, 187; Junior Imperial League, 87–88; separate spheres ideology, 13, 69–71; voting, 65–68, 185
Women's Department, 49, 59
Women's Unionist and Tariff Reform Association, 20–21
Women's Unionist Organisation: branches, 50–53, 60–64; candidates, lack of, 53–54; education, 55–56, 159–61, 165, 168; electioneering, 54; election of 1929, 189–91; finance, 57–58; *Home and Politics*, 49–50, 151; legislative views and agenda, 54, 71–75; organizers, 59–60, 190; origins, 21–22; regional organizations, 23, 189–90; Representation of the People Act of 1928, 180, 184, 187; significance of, 46–47, 81–82; social activities, 57; women's advisory committee of the National Unionist Association, 50, 189; working men's clubs and Labour Committee, relations with, 48–49, 74–75, 79, 111–12
Wood Green, 11; Women's Unionist Organisation, 41–42
Working class: Conservative candidates, lack of, 113, 115, 120–21; Conservative Party supporters, ethos of, 124–25, 136–42; role in Conservative Party, 27. *See also* Labour Committee; Trade union reform

World War I: effect on party organization, 10–11; impact on political system, 1–2, 101, 122, 146–47, 156, 228; as impetus for Representation of People Act of 1918, 11–16

Worthington-Evans, Sir Laming, 31, 194

Wrexham: 36, 118, 214; Women's Unionist Organisation, 53, 64, 190

Young Britons: Conservative Party, dependence on, 104, 107; contradictory aims of, 107–8; membership, 107; origins, 102–3; Scottish counterparts, 104–5; *Young Briton,* 105

Younger, Sir George: election of 1918, preparations for, 32–33; Labour Committee, support of, 120, 126; Representation of the People Act of 1918, 20–22, 27; Representation of the People Act of 1928, opposition to, 185

Young people and children. *See* Junior Imperial League; Primrose League: Buds, Young Conservatives Union; Young Britons; Women, and the Conservative Party: home-centeredness and religious beliefs